THE TASTE OF
BRITAIN

THE TASTE OF BRITAIN

Marc and Kim Millon

Grange
BOOKS

To the Kenyon College/University of Exeter program,
which brought me to Britain, and us together.

Published by Grange Books
An imprint of Grange Books Limited
The Grange
Grange Yard
London SE1 3AG

ISBN 1 85627 325 3

Reprinted 1993

First published by Webb & Bower
(Publishers) Limited 1985

Printed and bound in Singapore.

CONTENTS

INTRODUCTION

From the street stalls of London across the Irish Sea to the steamy pubs of Dublin; from the strawberries-and-cream beauty of Devon, up through the Lake District and the North of England to the rugged Scottish Highlands where men in tartan gather to recite the poetry of Robbie Burns while downing drams of whisky; from the daily indoor market at Swansea where the lovely singsong of Welsh is heard, where laver, a type of edible seaweed gathered from the Pembrokeshire coast, is sold, across the hearty Midlands to the hop fields of Kent, the wide broads and flat fens of East Anglia: England, Ireland, Scotland and Wales are a vast panoramic culinary patchwork.

Virtually every corner of these islands yields superb products and produce, fine things to eat and drink: Scotch beef; English and Welsh spring lamb; Irish and Scotch salmon; a colourful and varied catch of fish and shellfish landed at virtually every nook and cranny in these islands' considerable miles of coastline; freshwater fish from Welsh streams, Ulster lakes and Scottish lochs; game from forests in Hampshire and Highland moors; vegetables and fruits from Evesham and Kent; regionally cured hams from

Fruits and vegetables, freshly-picked, for sale at a roadside stand near Evesham.

Cumberland, Suffolk, York, Cookstown; smoked fish from Arbroath, Craster, the Isle of Man, Great Yarmouth; local cheeses still produced in their regions of origin: Stilton, Cheshire, Lancashire, Wensleydale, Cotherstone, Orkney; local cakes, biscuits and breads; traditional cask-conditioned beers; stout from Ireland; whisky from Scotland; gin from London; cider from the West Country; and much else.

Food and drink in Great Britain and Ireland varies considerably from region to region and county to county. North of Hadrian's Wall, it is a reflection of a hardy and resilient land and people: thick oatmeal porridges, rib-sticking stews and barley broths, game such as pheasant or partridge stuffed with oatmeal, and the beloved haggis (in truth, just an overgrown, glorified sausage) are accompanied by straight nips of peaty malt whisky, or, on Hogmanay, by the warming het pint. Ireland likewise retains its

own solitary culinary traditions, which have re-emerged proud and intact after centuries of English provincial domination. The Irishman's beloved 'murphy', the potato, naturally remains the national staple, but the Emerald Isle boasts more elegant specialities, too, such as fine Shannon salmon, Dublin Bay prawns, and exciting new farmhouse cheeses. In Wales, traditional foods, like the Welsh language itself, have been jealously safeguarded and passed down by word of mouth from mother to daughter and son. Thus each home has its own recipe for *cawl* (a classic one-pot meal), *teisen lap* (a moist cake) and *bara brith* (a currant bread).

In the Shires, pork pies and other portable fare became popular as a sustaining food while hunting, and in Cornwall, the humble pasty, a pastry filled with a highly seasoned mixture of potatoes and meat, was the workers' lunch, easily carried down into the damp tin mines of Zennor, St Just

Leadenhall Market, a Victorian covered shopping arcade in London.

Tea rooms throughout Great Britain and Ireland offer travellers refreshment and hospitality.

and Penzance. The verdant pastures and lush meadows of glorious Devon result in gallons of rich, creamy milk to create such unique specialities as Devonshire clotted cream, fresh farmhouse butter and real farmhouse Cheddar, one of the world's greatest cheeses. East Anglia supports enviable supplies of game, and samphire, a vegetable from the salt marshes of The Wash eaten like asparagus, remains a seasonal delicacy only encountered here. Yorkshiremen, Lancastrians and Cumbrians are notable trenchermen – no surprise, then, that the famous Yorkshire pudding is little more than an egg, flour and milk batter baked in beef dripping and served before the meal, dredged with hot onion gravy or raspberry vinegar, to fill up cavernous empty stomachs, that substantial 'hot dinners' such as Lancashire hot pot, cottage or fish pie are served at midday together with ample portions of potatoes and bread, or that hearty pork products such as Cumberland sausage and black pudding remain firm favourites.

Certain localities, it will be seen, are inextricably linked with certain foods; some have been adopted nationally (such as Yorkshire pudding), but others remain very much tied to a single area, indeed even to a single village. Bloaters are mainly to be had only in the east coast area around Great Yarmouth; tomato sausage is a speciality of Lincolnshire; Banbury cakes remain much in evidence in this small market town, but are not widely available outside it.

Drink in Great Britain and Ireland is also very much a matter of local taste. Most Irish men and women, for example, believe that no nectar on earth or in heaven is finer than a creamy pint of Guinness (though many might say that Black Bush whiskey comes a close second). In the West Country, on the other hand, ciders from bittersweet and bittersharp cider apples are produced on farms and available in country pubs. Such 'scrumpy' is virtually unobtainable anywhere else in the country. English wines – and there are hundreds of them – are often available only from the vineyard itself.

British beers, too, are unique regional products, for most cask-conditioned traditional draught ales from independent breweries are available only within a short radius of the brewery. It would be difficult to purchase a pint of Timothy Taylor's (a much-loved creamy Yorkshire beer) in Suffolk, while it would be an equal feat to find a pub serving Adnams (a well-hopped brew from that latter county) in, say, Devon or Cornwall. Many brewers of such traditional ales restrict their distribution to a relatively confined area on purpose, for it is essential, with this delicate, living product, that a strict control on quality can be maintained. Thus they only deliver to places that their draymen can reach in a single day, a circumstance which makes matters considerably more enjoyable for beer-loving travellers, for they can mark their progress by the local beers available in each area.

We have spent the better part of a year travelling throughout Great Britain and Ireland, marking *our* progress not only by the contrasts between the foods and drinks, produce and products of each area, but by the contrasts between the regions themselves. Overall, what has been most impressive is the sincere and quiet dedication that we have encountered throughout: butchers whose families have been traditionally curing hams for six generations; earnest (almost evangelical) vine growers and wine makers in Sussex, Kent, Somerset and elsewhere; traditional village grocers offering a personal service that must be nearly extinct anywhere else in the world; women in Devon, Ross & Cromarty and Co. Derry beavering away baking breads and cakes, making jars of jams, marmalades and chutneys; cheese makers; experienced brewers of ales and stout; and all the many others who are devoted unselfconsciously to carrying on the best British and Irish food and drink traditions.

A positive national pride is evident, too, in a new breed of talented chefs who are developing repertoires of exciting English, Scottish, Welsh and Irish dishes. Based on both traditional foods and cooking methods as well as innovative trends, they hunt out and make use of the very finest local produce; moreover such chefs eschew a past habit of giving their new creations French names (why, after all, should a Cornish fish stew be called *bouillabaisse*?); there is a certain grandeur – a magic, even – in simply and proudly naming such foods by what they actually are: roast leg of Exmoor lamb, fried Ballycotton plaice, Topsham smoked mackerel paste, potted Morecambe Bay shrimps, Shetland lamb, Aberdeen-Angus beef, Hampshire watercress soup, poached Teifi *sewin* (sea trout), and so on.

We have not attempted in this book to include every recipe with regional associations, a task well beyond us. Rather, our aim is to give a taste of each region or country, and not just of its foods and drinks. It has been extremely pleasurable gathering the information and pictures for this book, and we look forward to meeting again those new friends who made our task so enjoyable.

A NOTE ON MEASUREMENTS: It is difficult if not impossible to convert measures from one system into convenient measures in another. In those recipes where precision is important, we have tried to be as exact as possible, but elsewhere, we have rounded the metric and US conversions up or down to the nearest round number.

Real Cask-conditioned Ales

British and Irish beers are unique, different to those brewed and drunk in most of the rest of the world. Whereas light-coloured lagers produced with bottom-fermenting yeasts are favoured elsewhere, here traditional top-fermenting beers ranging in colour from light amber to black are by far the favourite national type. Such beers (bitters, milds and stouts) generally have more robust flavours and a fuller body than lager, and most are drunk at cellar temperature, not chilled. In Britain and Ireland, the favourite way to enjoy such drinks is by the pint, in public houses, hotel bars and working men's and other clubs.

One of the most interesting and unique features of the best British beers is that they reach the drinker in an unpasteurized, unpressurized form in wooden or aluminium casks, so allowing them to continue to mature and condition through a natural secondary fermentation in the cask. Such traditional beer is known as cask-conditioned, naturally-conditioned or real ale. It is often drawn from the cellar by tall ceramic hand-pumps on the bar top, by electric pumps without the addition of any extraneous carbon dioxide, or, in Scotland, by a unique system of air pressure. Cask-conditioned ale is also served straight from the cask, by gravity. Brewery-conditioned keg, tank, or bright beer, on the other hand, is matured in the brewery, then usually filtered, pasteurized and served under pressure. Cask-conditioned ales have a maturity and complexity of flavour and aroma lacking in most brewery-conditioned products. Moreover, while brewery-conditioned beers, due to their stability, may be available nationally, the delicate nature of the cask-conditioned product generally means that it is available within a limited area only.

Cask-conditioned real ales are therefore more interesting for the beer lover with catholic tastes travelling throughout Britain. It is for this reason (as much as for lack of space) that we have mainly listed cask-conditioned ales in our compilation of breweries in Great Britain (cask-conditioned ales, though available in limited amounts in Ireland, are not as important to drinkers there; however, in its own country Guinness is not pasteurized – one reason, perhaps, why it tastes so fine in its native land).

While we have tried to gather a comprehensive listing of breweries and cask-conditioned beers, our task has been a frustrating one; new mini-breweries have been opening (and sometimes closing) virtually by the week. However, the rise of such small companies serving local areas is a most welcome development for the beer drinker.

ORIGINAL GRAVITY: A MEASURE OF POTENTIAL STRENGTH

Beer is an alcoholic beverage fermented from a sweet, malty liquid known as wort. The potential alcoholic strength of the subsequent finished beer is indicated by the amount of fermentable material present in the wort, measured with an instrument called a hydrometer. In our listing of beers, therefore, we have given original gravity ratings (o.g.) where possible. Generally speaking, milds and light 'session' bitters (for a long evening's drinking) might have original gravities of around 1030–34; ordinary bitter probably ranges from o.g. 1035 to 1038, while best, or premium, bitters can vary between o.g. 1038 and 1046; old ales or winter warmers are strong draught beers with original gravities of 1050 and higher.

THE NORTH

Harry Ramsden's, a remarkable emporium in Guiseley, Yorkshire, located in a pre-war brick building that looks more like a cinema or a fire station than a world famous restaurant, epitomizes a certain attitude to food and drink in the North of England. The car park beside this unique establishment has up to sixteen coaches dozing in it at any time; numerous cars, too, of every size, type and age are also parked here, while a noisy amusement arcade has grown up on the periphery of the site. Outside the building a queue of thirty or forty people stretches around the side. Those waiting to be seated appear somewhat anxious, like the children queuing to ride the Big Dipper. There is a sense of excitement. Harry Ramsden's is not merely a restaurant: it is an event.

Inside the vast carpeted dining-room, elegant cut-glass chandeliers dangle down to illuminate tables laid with homely blue-checked table-cloths, ordinary practical plates, cups and saucers, bottles of malt vinegar, tomato ketchup and HP sauce. For everyone is here merely to enjoy the simplest, favourite food of the land, fish and chips, cooked to perfection, in a unique environment. Harry Ramsden's menu is straightforward: fried haddock, halibut or plaice, served with thick-cut chips, 'mushy' peas, sliced white bread and butter, and pots of strong tea served with milk and sugar. Yet everything is done so exceedingly well. The fish (mainly haddock, the most popular in the North) is skinned and dipped in a simple, secret batter made with no salt, no milk and no egg, then fried, not in vegetable oil, not in lard, but in pure beef dripping ('we're a funny lot here: we like our fish to taste like meat'). The light batter lifts from the fish, which, sealed within this crispy packet, steams to a perfect, moist flakiness. The chips, made from Maris Piper, Crown, King Edward and Scotch new potatoes (depending on the season) are equally superb, while the 'mushy' peas – dried marrowfat peas soaked overnight then boiled – are a favourite staple of the North. This simple feast has been served to film stars and prime ministers, colliers and mill-workers, management and shop stewards alike. Harry Ramsden's is an English celebration of simple, unpretentious value-for-money food, served stylishly, and enjoyed by all.

The North is profoundly different from the South, politically, economically, geographically and socially; all of these factors affect attitudes to eating and drinking. The region as a whole is hard-working, encompassing such major industrial centres as Liverpool, Manchester, Bradford, Leeds, Sheffield, and Newcastle-upon-Tyne. Lancashire and Yorkshire are both major textile-manufacturing areas. Grimsby and Hull are centres of the fishing industry and Tyneside is famous for its shipbuilding. Outside the cities, the North boasts some of England's most magnificent country: Cumbria's Lake District, the Yorkshire Dales and moors, the Cheviots stretching up to the Scottish border, areas that remain both scenically beautiful as well as centres of rural country life, with strong dairy, sheep and other farming traditions.

Food in these regions is necessarily both hearty and economical, the sort to satisfy these miners, fishermen, farmers and fell runners. The North's best-known contribution to British food, Yorkshire pudding, reflects this, for originally the famous puffy batter, dredged with hot onion gravy or raspberry vinegar, was eaten first, to stave off hunger before the meat course. Lancashire hot pot is a frugal stew made from scrag- or best-end-of-neck lamb topped simply with layers of sliced potatoes and onions. Liverpool lobscouse is an equally substantial and economical dish, a sort of soupy stew made from beef or

Fish and chips and 'mushy' peas: an honest value-for-money food enjoyed by all.

10

mutton, vegetables and barley. Tripe and onions is a favourite of Manchester, while all manner of sausages, black puddings, potted and pressed meats, even cow heel (sold already boiled, and added to stews and rabbit pie to give them a chewy thickness), elder (cow's udder served cold in slices), sweetbreads and lamb's fry are all popular foods in the industrial North-West.

To those gazing up-country from comfortable armchairs in Surrey or Sussex, the North (which to many southerners proverbially begins at Watford Gap) may well seem a single amorphous mass; up here, however, the perspective is rather sharper (one has only to recall the intense rivalry between the Houses of York and Lancaster which resulted in the intermittent Wars of the Roses, a rivalry that remains, to a certain extent, even today between the counties of Yorkshire and Lancashire). The North-West, the Lake District of Cumbria, Yorkshire and Humberside, Northumbria: all are distinct regions with their own proud heritage of food and drink traditions.

Cumbria's Lakeland is rich in regional foods and specialities. Perhaps, with its high fells and remote valleys which separate the region from the rest of the North, the Lake District has been able to resist change better than elsewhere. This, for example, is one of the few remaining areas in Britain where mutton (once a common staple) is still eaten regularly. Herdwick mutton comes from an old breed of sheep unique to this area, and is most highly prized for its strong, sweet flavour, served in such regional favourites as Westmorland tatie pot, simply roasted, or made into excellent mutton hams. Deep lakes such as Windermere, Derwentwater and Bassenthwaite, their names as lovely as their aspects, provide a rare fish little known elsewhere, the char, caught with unique handmade gold and silver spinners, dangled a hundred feet down and more. Potted char is a distinctive Lakeland favourite, while small shrimps from Morecambe Bay are also packed into pots and sealed with butter. Cumberland sausage is, to our way of thinking, the very best in the country, made with pure, coarsely-ground pork – no rusk or other cereals – seasoned with salt and plenty of black pepper, and sold in long, linkless coils. Dry-cured Cumberland hams are still made by butchers here, excellent served

Ullswater.

hot with fruity Cumberland sauce. In the eighteenth century, the region's hard-working seaside ports such as Maryport, Workington and Whitehaven carried on a lively trade with the West Indies, and thus much rum and brown sugar, lemons and spices found their way into the local kitchens, resulting in specialities such as Cumberland rum nicky (a sweet date and rum tart) and Cumberland rum butter.

Cumbria's Lakeland remains today remarkably remote and unspoiled, a factor that has attracted walkers and nature-lovers for centuries. Today, as in the past, people come to conquer surprisingly bleak, rugged peaks such as Scafell, Skiddaw, Helvellyn, Coniston Old Man, Harrison Stickle and many others. (Kendal mint cake, a hard, minty, sugary slab of instant energy, has helped spur on many a flagging hiker and climber – four firms still make this local speciality which has been taken on expeditions to Everest and elsewhere.) Such strenuous activity seems to work up appetites to the extreme. Indeed, to

Kendal mint cake, taken on expeditions to Everest, Annapurna, Kilimanjaro and (on this occasion) Skiddaw.

many the whole object of the exercise (even of the gentlest ramble around Buttermere or Grasmere) is simply to work up an appetite for enormous four- and five-course dinners served in some of the country's finest restaurants, including Sharrow Bay, Tullythwaite House, the Rothay Manor and Miller Howe. These restaurants prepare the region's excellent produce – venison, wild duck from Derwentwater, lamb, mutton, trout, char and salmon – in traditional and imaginative ways.

A tradition of serious eating and appreciation of food – both elaborate and simple – is apparent throughout the North. Yorkshire is an area particularly known for its hungry trenchermen. At Betty's, an establishment – indeed a veritable institution – in York and Harrogate, one can observe the prodigious Yorkshire appetite at first-hand: come here early for hearty cooked Yorkshire breakfasts; mid-morning for coffee and cream and other cakes, fruit loaf, parkin and Yorkshire curd slice; midday for 'dinner'; mid-afternoon for tea, consisting of tea, rich fruit cakes, scones, tarts and sandwiches; early even-

ing for high tea, a substantial meal of eggs, sausage and bacon, fried fish and chips or oak-smoked York ham cut from the bone, followed by bread, butter and tea. A hungry Yorkshireman might conceivably eat all – or most – of the above meals, and follow them in the evening with a man-sized Barnsley chop (a double lamb chop) or a pint or two of creamy Tetley's 'down at pub'.

Within an area as distinct as Yorkshire, there are a considerable number of specialities unique to certain localities. Each village or town, it seems, has its own rich fruit cake which it claims to have invented: Ilkley cake, Ripon cake, Batley cake, Brontë liqueur cake, climb-a-mountain cake – all are variations on a theme. Ask any number of Yorkshirewomen the correct method of making curd tart or parkin and each will tell you a different way, and insist that all the others are wrong or not authentic. Havvercake, similarly, was the Dales staple for centuries, but this basic oatcake differed considerably in com-

Two great cheeses of the North: *(above)* Blue Cheshire, made on one farm only, and *(opposite)*, almost as rare, Farmhouse Lancashire.

position and manner of making between the West and North Ridings. And even today, a cheese maker tells us that it is impossible to sell red Cheshire cheese in the West Riding, but equally impossible to sell white Cheshire elsewhere in the county. Yorkshire folk are nothing if not opinionated. Other specialities associated with this large county include brandy snaps, fat rascals, Pontefract cakes, Harrogate toffee, and much else.

The North-West, encompassing Greater Manchester, Merseyside, Cheshire and Lancashire, has a strong industrial heritage that has influenced eating habits, as already mentioned. The region, though, contrasts its intensive urban areas with unspoiled agricultural countryside.

Cheshire, for example, is a beautiful county of rich dairy land. The traditional breeds of cattle such as the Dairy Shorthorn graze on the salty, mineral-rich pastures, and yield a milk with small, hard fat globules ideal for cheese making. Farmhouse Cheshire is one of England's great traditional cheeses, but even today it is still eaten mostly in this area. To the north, similarly, the rich pasturelands of Lancashire contrast with industrial centres such as Preston and Blackburn; today, sadly, only four farms remain producing traditional farmhouse Lancashire cheese, also one of England's greatest.

The north-west coast, with its popular holiday resorts like Blackpool and Morecambe, is also a provider of a good selection of excellent fish and shellfish: hake, cod, plaice, shrimp and herring are all eaten as staples here. Half-way across to Ireland, herring landed on the Isle of Man is kippered – that is, split and brined – then smoked

for several hours. Manx kippers, together with those from Craster, on the north-east coast, are considered the finest in the country. The kippering process was actually developed in Northumberland in the last century; at that time there were hundreds of smokehouses up and down the east coast, around towns such as Craster, Seahouses and Boulmer.

Inland, Northumbria's border country provides plentiful beef, lamb from the Cheviot hills, venison and other game, and trout and salmon from the Tweed. This is rich, unspoiled land, as remote as any part of England, with vast stretches of open moorland and heather-clad hills. Yet the ruins of many castles testify to an era when numerous battles were waged for these strategic, rich border lands. South of Northumberland, Tyne & Wear is another intensive north-eastern industrial concentration made up of such important cities as Newcastle-upon-Tyne and

Sunderland. Here numerous Geordie specialities accompany the beloved pint-bottle of 'broon ale': simple, tasty foods such as pan haggerty, pease pudding, leek and lamb pasties, and singin' hinnies.

The North, from the west coast to the east, from Cheshire and Humberside to the Scottish border, has not forgotten its hard-working roots. Foods with origins in a harsher past – industrial and agricultural – remain favourites today, for a practical nature at once thrifty and ingenious has devised a range of simple, economical foods utilizing the best from each locality, born from necessity but which continue to satisfy. Such undue hardship may be mainly a thing of the past for most, yet one senses that an innate Northern pride remains, coupled with an ingrained scorn of wastefulness, a straightforward appreciation of the simple, the unpretentious, the honest.

Kippers

Visit any fishmonger in the land and you'll see these small, split, orange smoked fish laid out on marble slabs. Though kippers today are available nationally, the actual process of kippering herring first began in Northumberland. Here in the North-East, in the little town of Craster, some of the very best kippers in the country are still cured traditionally (two other areas noted for fine kippers are the Isle of Man and the west coast of Scotland around Loch Fyne). Though herring is no longer landed in great quantity in the North-East (the kipper industry originally prospered here when the fishermen began to cure their own catch), the methods – indeed the very smokerooms themselves – have remained unchanged for well over a hundred years.

Fat herring with a high oil content make the best kippers. Catch of this quality is generally landed from June to September. The fish are brought to Craster where they are first split, then lightly brined for about twenty minutes. Deft, well-experienced hands position the splayed, silvery fish on to tenterhooks, some sixteen herring to each tenterstick. These tentersticks are then threaded into the oily, jet-black smokerooms, thickly encrusted with over a hundred years of oozing wood resins and fish oil. The fires are carefully laid the length of the smokeroom, a most skilful and intuitive task, for it is essential that they smoulder at just the right, slow speed, but do not expire prematurely. White wood shavings and oak sawdust (in the past it came from the great shipyards of the North-East) give the best flavour to the fish. The slow-smouldering fires only last a few hours, and since a full ten hours of smoking are required for Craster kippers, men have to come back to the smokehouse even in the dead of night to rekindle the fires. A traditionally-cured, oak-smoked Craster kipper is undyed; it gains its rich colour and assertive flavour from this lengthy period of smoking (dyed kippers are smoked for considerably shorter periods, resulting in a softer texture and milder flavour).

For breakfast, dinner or high tea, nothing can beat a pair of kippers, sandwiched together with a dab of butter and grilled, fried or jugged in boiling hot water.

Recipes from the North

Potted Morecambe Bay Shrimps

Morecambe Bay, off the north-west coast, is renowned for its finely-flavoured, succulent little shrimps, delicious when potted then spread on toast for tea. Many who come to this popular holiday area take home tubs as souvenirs; but potted shrimps are very easy to make, so long as the shellfish that you use are very fresh.

225 g/8 oz/2 sticks unsalted butter	Pinch of cayenne pepper
450 g/1 lb fresh shrimps, peeled	Pinch of freshly-grated nutmeg
1 tsp ground mace	Salt

To clarify the butter, place in a saucepan over a low heat. Melt, remove from the heat, and allow to stand while the sediment sinks to the bottom. Strain the butter through fine cotton into a jug. Re-heat about three-quarters of the clarified butter in a saucepan. Add the shrimps, mace, cayenne pepper and nutmeg. Stir over a very low heat until the shrimps have absorbed the butter (do not overcook, or they will toughen). Season with salt to taste. Pour into small pots and allow to set. Melt the remaining clarified butter and pour over the surface to seal. Chill and serve with hot toast.

Potted Char or Trout   (Serves 4)

Char is a rare fish caught only in the deepest waters of the Lake District, using handmade gold and silver char spinners dangled from rods with several lines each. Related to the salmon, char has a lovely pink flesh and a distinctive flavour. Potted char has been a Lakeland delicacy for hundreds of years; the fish used to be packed into beautiful hand-decorated char pots which

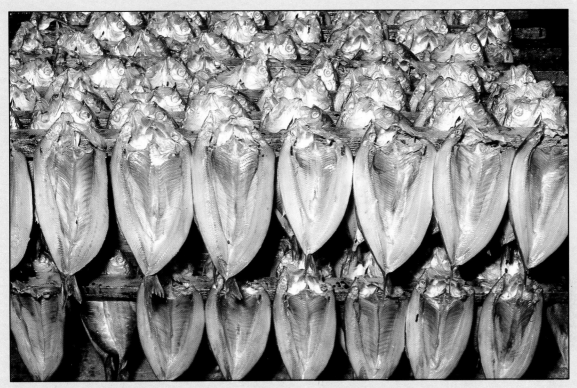

Craster kippers gain their colour from a lengthy process of oak-smoking.

are now collectors' items. Char are scarce, even in the Lake District, so trout can be substituted instead.

4 medium-sized char or trout	Pinch of freshly-grated nutmeg
Salt	Pinch of ground cloves
Freshly-ground black pepper	100 g/4 oz/1 stick melted clarified butter (see shrimp recipe above)
Pinch of ground mace	

Clean and wash the char or trout and pat dry. Season inside and out with salt, pepper, mace, nutmeg and cloves. Place in a covered dish and gently poach the fish until tender and cooked through, about 30–45 minutes. Skin and flake the fish, removing all the bones. Adjust seasoning and mash well. Pack into pots and cover with melted clarified butter to seal. Chill and serve with brown bread and butter.

Cumberland sausage, always sold by the length, should be made from pure meat and seasoning only.

The Great English Breakfast

In the South, those living in Surrey, Berkshire and Buckinghamshire may well start the day with *café au lait* and *croissants*, muesli, bran flakes and freshly-squeezed paw-paw juice: here in the North, though (where folk know a thing or two about what's what), there's still nothing to beat the Great English Breakfast. What could be a better start to the day than bowls of steaming porridge, half a grapefruit, or a bowl of stewed prunes, followed by hot plates of thick, meaty bacon rashers, juicy pork sausages, black pudding, fried bread, grilled tomatoes and mushrooms, and perfectly cooked free-range eggs, the yellow yolks just set, the whites made firm with a spoonful of sizzling bacon fat dribbled over them? In the Lake District, walkers in knee-breeches pore over maps and Wainwright guides while tucking into fried trout or grilled lamb chops. Kippers and poached egg are another favourite start to the day, while smoked haddock is served both on its own, or in a curry-flavoured rice dish brought back from India, kedgeree. Racks of hot buttered toast and teapots kept warm with hand-knitted cosys are both constantly replenished. Such substantial feasts are common everyday fare in farmhouses and homes throughout the region, as well as in guesthouses and 'bed & breakfasts': hearty man-sized breakfasts for hard-working and -playing people.

Yorkshire Pudding (Serves 4)

Yorkshire pudding is traditionally served with gravy before the main course to take the edge off North Country appetites. Originally it was cooked underneath the joint of beef roasting on a spit in front of a roaring farmhouse fire (though we wonder how it puffed up with this open method of cooking?). As it cooked under the meat the pudding caught the dripping juices which gave it a delicious flavour. Today 'Yorkshires' are cooked in a very hot oven causing them to swell to the light, crisp, puffy consistency so loved by all. Here in Yorkshire, this favourite is still served before the meat with plenty of gravy, as well as with the main course, and even afterwards, as a sweet pudding with jam and cream.

75 g/3 oz/$\frac{3}{5}$ cup plain flour	1 egg
1 tsp salt	300 ml/$\frac{1}{2}$ pt/$1\frac{1}{4}$ cups milk

Sieve the flour and salt into a large mixing bowl. Make a well in the centre and break the egg into it. Gradually stir the flour into the egg and slowly add the milk. Beat until the batter is smooth. Cover and set aside in a cool place for 1 hour. Pour a little dripping from the roast beef into a large tin and place in the hot oven for 5 minutes until sizzling hot. Remove and pour in the batter. Bake in a hot oven (220°C/425°F/Gas Mark 7) without opening the door for 35–40 minutes or until well-risen and golden brown. Serve first with the gravy, or as an accompaniment to the roast.

Tripe and Onions (Serves 4–6)

Tripe and onions is an example of the way in which North Country folk make a lot out of a little, using thrifty ingenuity rather than money to make satisfying meals. Tripe, incidentally, is a favourite throughout the year in the Manchester area. In summer it is very popular purchased already cooked, and served cold with vinegar and salad.

900 g/2 lb dressed tripe	Salt
3 large onions, finely sliced	Freshly-ground black
600 ml/1 pt/$2\frac{1}{2}$ cups milk	pepper
300 ml/$\frac{1}{2}$ pt/$1\frac{1}{4}$ cups water	1 tbsp butter
1 bay leaf	1 tbsp flour
Pinch of mace	
Pinch of freshly-grated	
nutmeg	

Wash the tripe and soak if necessary. Cut into 5 cm/2 in squares and place in a large saucepan. Cover with cold water, bring to the boil and cook for 10–15 minutes. Drain and discard the water. Add the sliced onions to the tripe, together with the milk, water, bay leaf, mace, nutmeg, salt and pepper. Simmer for 2 hours, or until tender. Melt the butter in a separate saucepan. Stir in the flour and cook for about 3 minutes. Spoon in a ladleful of hot liquid from the tripe and stir well to make a smooth sauce. Add another ladleful and stir. When smooth and runny, add to the tripe and onions mixture, stir to mix well, and cook for a further 15 minutes until thickened. Adjust seasoning and serve hot.

Fish and Chips   (Serves 4)

Fish and chips is a favourite throughout the land. Though there is considerable debate as to the origins of this famous English fast food, most agree that the finest fish and chips in the land are to be had in the North. Here the most popular fish to be fried is haddock (landed at Grimsby and delivered fresh, not frozen, to fryers throughout the area) and beef dripping is the favoured cooking medium. While most of us indulge in fish and chips purchased from the corner shop, eaten out of vinegar-stained paper with the fingers, it is a meal that can easily be made at home.

175 g/6 oz/1 cup plain flour	Vegetable oil, lard or beef
1 tsp bicarbonate of soda	dripping for deep frying
Pinch of salt	4 haddock fillets,
300 ml/$\frac{1}{2}$ pt/1$\frac{1}{4}$ cups water	unskinned
900 g/2 lb potatoes, peeled	Malt vinegar

Sieve the flour, bicarbonate of soda and salt into a large mixing bowl. Make a well in the centre and gradually add the water. Stir in the flour from around the edges and beat until a smooth pouring batter is obtained. Set aside to stand for about 1 hour.

Cut the potatoes lengthways into thick chips 1.3 cm/$\frac{1}{2}$ in wide. Pat them dry with a paper towel. Heat the oil, lard or dripping in a deep pan until a small stale bread cube will brown in a minute or so (it is essential to have the oil sufficiently hot for frying). Fry the chips in small batches until they are crisp and golden. Drain and transfer them to a dish, and keep warm in a pre-heated moderate oven (180°C/350°F/Gas Mark 4).

Pat the pieces of fish dry and lightly dust with flour. Dip them into the batter one at a time and gently shake to remove any excess. Drop into the hot oil, two at a time and fry until golden all over. Transfer to a hot plate and serve with chips and mushy peas. Add salt and malt vinegar to taste.

Pan Haggerty   (Serves 4)

A hearty Northumberland dish, delicious with plainly boiled gammon or roast meats.

50 g/2 oz/$\frac{1}{4}$ cup bacon fat or	100 g/4 oz/1$\frac{1}{3}$ cups grated
lard	Cheddar
450 g/1 lb potatoes, peeled	Salt
and thinly sliced	Freshly-ground black
2 onions, finely chopped	pepper

Heat the bacon fat or lard in a large heavy-based frying pan. Add a layer of potatoes, the chopped onions, grated cheese, and finally another layer of potatoes. Season each layer well with salt and pepper. Cook over a fairly gentle heat for about 30 minutes. Invert onto a plate and slide back into the pan to brown the other side (or, if preferred, brown under the grill). Slide on to a warm plate and serve at once.

Liverpool Lobscouse   (Serves 6)

Lobscouse has been eaten in Liverpool for centuries: a warming one-pot medley of cheap meat such as mutton, beef or lamb, potatoes, carrots, dried peas and a handful of barley, all simmered together for hours over an open fire. 'Scouse' has since come to mean anything Liverpudlian.

50 g/2 oz/$\frac{1}{4}$ cup beef	225 g/$\frac{1}{2}$ lb dried peas,
dripping	soaked overnight
675 g/1$\frac{1}{2}$ lb stewing beef or	Bouquet of fresh thyme
lamb, cut into cubes	Salt
1 large onion, quartered	Freshly-ground black
3 carrots, sliced	pepper
675 g/1$\frac{1}{2}$ lb potatoes, peeled	4 tbsp pearl barley
and quartered	Stock or water to cover

Melt the dripping in a large casserole. Toss in the meat and brown quickly on all sides. Add the onion, carrots and potatoes and stir to coat with fat. Drain the peas and add them to the pot together with the thyme, salt and pepper, and pearl barley. Add enough stock or water to cover. Bring to the boil, skim, cover and simmer for about 2$\frac{1}{2}$ hours. Serve hot from the pot.

Pease Pudding   (Serves 4–6)

Pease pudding is an old favourite of the North-East. Left-over pease pudding can be fried or eaten cold, as in the children's rhyme:

> Pease pudding hot! Pease pudding cold!
> Pease pudding in the pot
> Nine days old.

450 g/1 lb dried yellow split	Salt
peas, soaked overnight	Freshly-ground black
50 g/2 oz/$\frac{1}{2}$ stick butter	pepper
1 egg, beaten	

Drain the soaked peas and place in a saucepan. Cover with water, bring to the boil and simmer for an hour or until tender. Drain, then liquidize. Turn into a bowl and mix in the butter, egg, salt and pepper. Butter a pudding basin and spoon in the mixture. Cover with foil and steam for 1 hour or until the pudding is firm. Turn it out and serve with boiled beef or gammon.

Lancashire Hot Pot   (Serves 6)

Lancashire hot pot.

Lancashire hot pot was originally made with mutton and often the addition of a dozen or so oysters (when they were plentiful and cheap). It is traditionally cooked in and served from a deep brown earthenware pot with a lid.

1.35 kg/3 lb best-end-of-
  neck lamb chops
Salt
Freshly-ground black
  pepper
450 g/1 lb onions, sliced
900 g/2 lb potatoes, peeled
  and thickly sliced
600 ml/1 pt/2½ cups stock
25 g/1 oz/¼ stick butter

Trim the chops if necessary and place a layer in a large earthenware pot or casserole. Cover with a layer of onions then a layer of potatoes, seasoning each layer well with salt and plenty of black pepper. Repeat with the rest of the lamb, onions and potatoes (ending with a layer of potatoes). Pour on the stock, and dot the top layer with butter. Cover and cook in a moderate oven (160°C/325°F/Gas Mark 3) for about 2 hours. Remove the lid and cook for a further 30 minutes to brown the potatoes. Serve from the casserole.

Cumberland Hams

As recently as the early part of this century, nearly every village in the land had at least one or two ham curers; most farms, too, slaughtered their own pigs to home cure ham and bacon. Preserving with salt is one of the most ancient methods of keeping meat or fish, and in the past, all stock was killed off before the winter, then salted down to be eaten throughout the cold months. Recipes for curing hams varied from region to region, indeed from farm to farm, and thus there was once a profusion of traditional cures. Some remain, such as the sweet-pickled hams of Suffolk, the shiny black Bradenhams, the sweet-tasting, oak-smoked hams of York, and the meaty, firm hams of Cumberland. In most parts of the country, though, hams are now cured by the Wiltshire method of brining; such brine curing takes far less time than the older methods, for it is no longer necessary to cure hams to preserve them. Nevertheless, the traditional cures, with their lengthier processes, result in hams with finer, unique flavours that cannot be achieved by other methods. Those that still remain need to be treasured.

Cumberland hams, for example, are still produced in exactly the same manner as they have been for generations. One ham specialist in Waberthwaite explained the process to us. Pigs are specially reared and selected on the family's own farm. The hams are trimmed and shaped, for Cumberland hams are customarily large, pear-shaped hams with a rounded end and a high fat content. They are then rubbed and laid on a bed of salt, and completely covered with a mixture of salt, brown sugar and saltpetre. The hams are left in this simple dry cure for one month, during which time the juices are drawn out from the meat, form a brine, and then, by capillary action, are drawn back into the ham, thus curing it completely through to the bone. Afterwards, the hams are put in a drying shed, then hung from rafters in a ham loft to mature, ideally for at least three months. Some people prefer hams which have matured for as long as twelve months (the meat becomes drier and more strongly flavoured).

Traditional Cumberland hams may be boiled or baked. First soak the ham in cold water, for 24–48 hours, depending on its age. The purpose is not to de-salt the ham but to improve its texture. While a mature ham of six months or older is best boiled, a three- to six-month-old ham is delicious roasted. Either wrap it in foil or encase it in a bread dough, then roast in a moderate oven (180° C/350° F/Gas Mark 4) for about 15 minutes to the pound. To test whether it is done, push a skewer into the ham about 15 minutes before you think it should be ready. If it goes in nice and easily then the ham is done. If it needs to be pushed in, then it is not quite fully cooked. When the cooking time is up, let the ham cool, remove the skin, score the fat in a diamond pattern and cover it with demerara sugar. Place the ham in a very hot oven for a few minutes until the sugar has glazed, then garnish with cherries. Serve hot with Cumberland sauce, or cold.

Cumberland hams, one of few remaining regional cures, are matured for several months in ham lofts.

Shepherd's Pie   (Serves 6)

Shepherd's pie, like the proverbial ploughman and his lunch, has little to do with shepherds or sheep these days. Rather, it is the name under which any number of meat and mashed potato dishes masquerade, served in public houses up and down the country. However, just as Devon farmers really do tuck into platters of real Cheddar, crusty bread, pickled onions and chutney after a morning's work in the fields, so is it probable that shepherds in the Dales or in Cumbria devised the original version of shepherd's pie using left-over meat and potatoes.

Melt the butter in a saucepan, and fry the onions until golden. Add the minced lamb and season well with salt and plenty of freshly-ground pepper. Fry until the meat is nicely browned. Add a dash of Worcestershire sauce to taste. Stir in the flour, then add the stock to moisten and form a gravy. Remove from the heat. Transfer this meat mixture to a well-greased ovenproof dish. Top with mashed potatoes, and make peaks with a fork. Dot with butter, and place in a moderate oven (160°C/325°F/Gas Mark 3) for about 30–45 minutes or until the top is well browned.

1 tbsp butter
1 medium onion, finely chopped
900 g/2 lb minced lamb (raw or left-over cooked meat)
Salt
Freshly-ground black pepper
Dash of Worcestershire sauce
1 tsp flour
Stock to moisten (about 300 ml/$\frac{1}{2}$ pt/$1\frac{1}{4}$ cups)
450 g/1 lb left-over mashed potatoes
Butter

Black Pudding

The Wars of the Roses may have ended centuries ago, but nothing separates folk up here into red and white camps more quickly than a discussion of the relative merits of Lancashire- and Yorkshire-made black puddings. It seems surprising, perhaps, that such a humble food should arouse passions so greatly; yet without a doubt black puddings, like county cricket, strike a particular cord in the northern character.

Though the actual process of making black puddings may seem gruesome, it is a perfectly natural and ancient one. When pigs were slaughtered for the winter nothing was wasted whatsoever ('except the squeak'); thus even blood was collected, and mixed with boiled barley, diced suet or back fat and seasonings, then stuffed back into natural casings. Black puddings remain basically no more than this, yet what variety exists within this simple equation! The seasoning, for example, is very individual; Yorkshire-made puddings would not sell well in Lancashire or Staffordshire. The shapes of puddings also differ between various regions. Bury-type puddings (from the Lancashire town whose market is famous for its stalls selling hot boiled black puddings) are small, individual puddings formed into tight rings. In the South, puddings are often made into large hoops, while elsewhere they are formed into straight stick shapes. In Cumbria, on the other hand, the pudding mixture is sometimes spread on to baking trays and cooked without a casing.

An international black pudding contest takes place each year in France, and Lancashire and Yorkshire pudding makers alike have carried off gold medals. The rivalry continues at home, too; 'The Best Black Pudding in Great Britain Competition' now takes place each year in Bolton, Lancashire, and attracts over a hundred entries.

Black puddings are best eaten straight from the saucepan, at a factory or at a stall in the Bury market. A gold-medal winner told us that, 'to me, the only way to eat a black pudding is to boil it, split it from end to end, and eat it with the fingers, with hot English mustard or piccalilli relish. It is definitely not a knife and fork food'. Many prefer black puddings grilled or fried; others like to dip them in batter and deep-fry them. Black puddings are already cooked, so they can also be simply sliced and served cold, with a pint of Sam Smith's or Boddingtons', depending upon your allegiance.

Cumberland Sauce

Cumberland sauce is traditionally served with the region's excellent dry-cured ham, but is also delicious with boiled bacon or roast venison.

Juice and rind of 2 oranges
Juice and rind of 1 lemon
4 tbsp redcurrant jelly
4 tbsp port or elderberry wine

In a small saucepan heat the juices and rind, and simmer gently. Add the redcurrant jelly and stir until it has dissolved. Add the port or elderberry wine and heat through. Serve warm with hot boiled or roasted Cumberland ham.

Witherslack Damson Cobbler (Serves 6)

The Lakeland is not generally renowned for its fruit, but in the Lyth Valley, south of Windermere, damsons grow in abundance, and thus a number of Cumberland recipes make use of this richly-coloured, tart fruit, known locally as the Witherslack damson.

900 g/2 lb damsons
225 g/½ lb/1 cup sugar
225 g/½ lb/1 ⅗ cup plain flour
1 tsp baking powder
50 g/2 oz/½ stick butter
1 egg
Milk to mix

Clean the damsons and place in a saucepan with about three-quarters of the sugar. Add a little water, cover, and stew until tender. Meanwhile sieve the flour and baking powder together and mix in the sugar. Rub in the butter and add the egg and enough milk to make a soft dough. Roll out on to a floured board and cut into small round scones. Remove the stones from the damsons and transfer to a pie dish. Place the scones in overlapping circles on top of the damsons, brush with milk, and cook in a hot oven (220°C/425°F/Gas Mark 7) for about 15 minutes or until the scones are browned and well risen. Serve with rich double cream, such as that from the Jersey herd at the Calthwaite Dairy, between Penrith and Carlisle.

Gold medal black puddings from Farnworth, Lancashire.

Cumberland rum butter.

Cumberland Rum Butter

Cumberland ports such as Workington and White-haven once carried on a considerable trade with the West Indies, and it was after one particularly rough passage (so the story goes) that rum butter was invented. For the barrels containing Barbados sugar, dark rum, spices and butter had broken up in the hold, and the ingredients all sloshed together, creating this much-loved speciality. Unlikely? Perhaps, but however it came about, rum butter remains a firm favourite here, made at Christmas, christenings and other special occasions to very personal family recipes. It is usually served with scones for tea, or with plum and other puddings.

225 g/8 oz/2 sticks unsalted   Pinch of freshly-grated
   butter   nutmeg
450 g/1 lb soft brown sugar   Pinch of cinnamon
150 ml/¼ pt/⅔ cup dark rum

Soften the butter and beat in the sugar. Gradually blend in the rum and flavour with the spices to taste. Pack into a bowl and set aside to harden.

Brandy Snaps   (Makes about 12)

Yorkshire's East Riding (now part of Humberside) lays claim to these popular biscuits, best served filled with whipped cream.

50 g/2 oz/½ stick butter   50 g/2 oz/⅖ cup plain flour,
50 g/2 oz golden syrup   sieved
50 g/2 oz/¼ cup castor sugar   1 tsp ground ginger
1 tbsp brandy   1 tsp lemon juice
Pinch of salt   Whipped cream to fill

Melt the butter, golden syrup and sugar over a gentle heat and stir in the brandy. Remove from the heat and stir in the salt, sieved flour, ginger and lemon juice. Grease three baking sheets and drop teaspoons of the mixture at wide intervals. Bake in a pre-heated slow oven (150°C/300°F/Gas Mark 2) for 8–10 minutes until lightly golden. Remove and allow to stand for 1 minute, then roll each one up around the handle of a wooden spoon. If they harden before curling, return to the oven for a few minutes to soften. Cool on a wire rack, then fill with whipped cream.

A selection of Yorkshire baked goods at Betty's Tea Rooms, Harrogate.

Yorkshire Curd Tarts

(Makes 1 large tart or 24 small ones)

This speciality of the Dales was in the past made with the fresh curds left over from cheese making. The cheesecake, filled with currants and baked to a rich brown on top, has a drier, more crumbly texture than most other types. It can be made as a single large tart or as individually-sized ones. When it is made into a rectangular shape, it becomes Yorkshire curd slice.

225 g/8 oz shortcrust pastry (see following recipe)
75 g/3 oz/¾ stick butter
50 g/2 oz/⅓ cup castor sugar
225 g/8 oz fresh curds or curd cheese
100 g/4 oz/⅔ cup currants
2 eggs, beaten
Pinch of freshly-grated nutmeg

Roll out the pastry and line a 22 cm/9 in flan tin or 24 patty tins. Cream the butter and sugar together and mix in the curd cheese, currants, eggs and nutmeg to taste. Pour into the pastry case or cases and bake in a moderate oven (180°C/350°F/Gas Mark 4) for 30–40 minutes until the filling is firm and golden on top.

Shortcrust Pastry

(Makes 225 g/8 oz pastry)

225 g/8 oz/1⅘ cups plain flour
Pinch of salt
75 g/3 oz/¾ stick butter
2 tbsp lard
4–6 tbsp cold water

Sieve the flour and salt into a large mixing bowl. Add the butter and lard cut into small pieces and rub into the flour until mixture resembles fine breadcrumbs. Make a well in the centre and gradually add the cold water, stirring it in with a knife. Add just enough to make a soft but not sticky dough. Form into a ball, put in a plastic bag, and refrigerate for at least an hour before using.

Cheeses of the North

Cheshire Cheshire is the oldest named cheese in Britain, mentioned in the Domesday Book, popular in Elizabethan times, and favourite of, among others, Dr Johnson, who enjoyed it at the pub of the same name off Fleet Street. Though its name is not legally protected, the finest Cheshire cheese cannot be made outside the Cheshire/Shropshire region, for its character, like all great cheese, is dependent upon local factors, including the rich grazing lands which are the basis of local farming. The rolling fields of Cheshire consist of heavy clay on a substantial bed of rock salt, and this gives the milk a characteristic taste which is further emphasized by the liberal use of Cheshire rock salt in the cheese-making process.

Farmhouse Cheshire is still produced on a small scale, with methods not far different from those which applied when nearly every Cheshire farmwife made at least a few cheeses each day in the dairy beside her farmhouse. Both white and red Cheshire are produced, the latter coloured with annatto dye. Though identical in every way except appearance, in some areas it is impossible to sell a white cheese, while in others the reverse is the case. Traditional farmhouse cheese is clothbound, and sometimes waxed.

Blue Cheshire Though Stilton is considered by many the supreme British blue cheese, other connoisseurs seek and prefer the much rarer Blue Cheshire, made on one farm only, Hinton Bank Farm, Whitchurch, near the Shropshire–Cheshire border. In the past some Cheshires used to blue naturally (many were discarded as useless when this happened), but this virtually ceased when the cheese makers began to wax the cheese rather than simply wrap it in cloth. Since 1968, however, Blue Cheshire has been made consistently by traditional methods at Hinton Bank Farm, using unpasteurized milk from the farm's own herd of Dairy Shorthorns. Blue Cheshire follows a similar method of manufacture to normal Cheshire, resulting in an open-textured, high acid, hard-pressed cheese (indeed, it is the only hard-pressed blue cheese in the world). The young cheeses are stored and turned regularly while they mature, a process lasting just two months. After four or five weeks, the cheeses are pierced with stainless steel needles to encourage

Breaking up the curds by hand, a delicate operation which ensures that farmhouse Lancashire has a creamy, open texture.

the development of blue veins. When ready to eat, Blue Cheshire has a firm, creamy texture and a mild but full-bodied blue flavour, not a pungent, aggressive one.

Lancashire True traditional farmhouse Lancashire, produced on only four farms in Lancashire, is one of the rarest regional English cheeses, and one of the very finest. Unlike most other hard English cheeses, farmhouse Lancashire is a semi-hard cheese with a spreadable texture and a rich, mellow, full-bodied flavour. Making farmhouse Lancashire is an extremely delicate operation to ensure that the resulting cheeses have both the distinctive flavour and the much-loved 'buttery crumble'.

Farmhouse Lancashire should ideally be stored for at least three to four months; mature cheeses six months and older are superb, with a deep, rich flavour that is strong but not at all sharp, and with an exquisite creamy, almost runny texture. Small quantities of Sage Lancashire are made on some of the farms, with sage grown in the farmhouse gardens. It is a traditional Christmas favourite.

Wensleydale Cistercian monks were the first to make Dales cheese on any large scale when they came to Jervaulx Abbey in the twelfth century. Today this magnificent ruin nestles in the lap of the rolling hills, topped by groves of oak trees, the green limestone pastures dotted with herds of Friesians and Northern Dairy Shorthorns, and with fat, curly-wooled Wensleydale sheep. Originally, the Dales cheese made at Jervaulx was supposedly similar to Roquefort cheese, the famous blue ewes' milk cheese produced then ripened in moist caves in that part of southern France, for the Cistercians had brought that cheese recipe over with them.

When the monasteries were dissolved, cheese making was continued on Dales farms by farmers' wives, daughters and dairy maids. Cheese making then was primarily a summer occupation, for after the cows had calved there was a flush of rich surplus milk.

Today, there is no production of farmhouse Wensleydale; however, clothbound or waxed traditional cheeses are still produced in the area in creameries such as that at Kirby Malzeard, a Milk Marketing Board creamery which specializes in the production of a range of excellent traditional cheeses. Both traditional Wensleydale and Blue Wensleydale are produced here (though the blue cheeses are sent elsewhere to mature). Traditional Wensleydale is a fairly acid cheese with a meaty, firm texture and a mellow, nutty character. It remains the favourite in this part of the country, where folk say fondly, 'apple pie without cheese is like a kiss without a squeeze'.

Cotherstone If Wensleydale cheese is no longer made on farms in the Dales, small amounts of other handmade cheeses are still being produced elsewhere in the area. Cotherstone is one such, a rare English cheese with a semi-soft texture and a rich complex flavour. It is well worth seeking.

Botton This traditionally-made cheese from the village of the same name is a hard-pressed Cheddar type, available in the area and sometimes further afield.

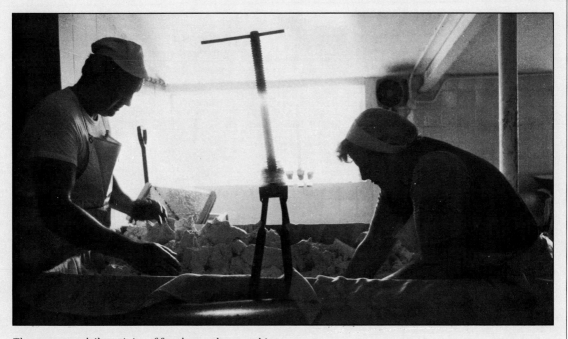

The strenuous daily activity of farmhouse cheese making.

Cumberland rum nicky.

Parkin

Folk in the North are extremely partial to sweets, especially those made with treacle and ginger. There are many variations of parkin, such as Yorkshire sticky parkin loaf (almost black and very chewy), and moggy (from the old Norse name for parkin, this variety is made with pinhead oatmeal). This recipe, though, comes from Lancashire.

100 g/4 oz/$\frac{4}{5}$ cup plain flour	225 g/$\frac{1}{2}$ lb golden syrup
Pinch of salt	100 g/$\frac{1}{4}$ lb treacle
1 tbsp ground ginger	75 g/3 oz/$\frac{3}{4}$ stick butter
1 tsp bicarbonate of soda	75 g/3 oz/$\frac{1}{2}$ cup castor sugar
350 g/12 oz/3 cups medium oatmeal	1 egg, beaten

Sieve the flour, salt, ginger and bicarbonate of soda into a large mixing bowl. Stir in the oatmeal. Warm the syrup, treacle, butter and sugar in a saucepan over a low heat and beat until creamy. Stir this into the flour mixture, add the beaten egg, and mix well.

Line a rectangular baking tin with greaseproof paper and pour in the mixture. Bake in a slow oven (150°C/300°F/Gas Mark 2) for about 40 minutes or until a skewer comes out clean. Leave for a week before eating, to allow the flavour to develop.

Cumberland Rum Nicky

(Makes 1 large tart)

This rich, sticky regional favourite reflects Cumberland's former trade with the West Indies, and the North's love, in general, of all things sweet and beautiful.

350 g/12 oz shortcrust pastry (see p. 25)	50 g/2 oz/$\frac{1}{3}$ cup soft brown sugar
350 g/12 oz dates, stoned and roughly chopped	2 pieces of crystallized ginger, roughly chopped
50 g/2 oz/$\frac{1}{2}$ stick butter	3 tbsp dark rum

Roll out the pastry and line a large flan case, setting aside enough to make a lattice top. Soak the chopped dates in boiling water for about half an hour. Meanwhile cream the butter and sugar together. Drain the dates and mix with the chopped ginger. Spoon into the pastry case and dot with the creamed butter and sugar. Decorate with a pastry lattice, and bake in a moderately hot oven (190°C/375°F/Gas Mark 5) for about 40–45 minutes. When cool, pour the rum over the nicky and serve with whipped cream.

Apple pie and Wensleydale cheese, on the steps of Jervaulx Abbey. They say up here that 'apple pie without cheese is like a kiss without a squeeze'.

Eccles Cakes   (Makes about 10)

Eccles cakes were always popular at the Eccles Wake in Lancashire and are still consumed today in great quantities throughout England, especially those from the Cake Shop in (where else?) Eccles, Lancashire.

225 g/8 oz rough puff pastry (see p. 66)
100 g/4 oz/$\frac{2}{3}$ cup currants
2 tbsp candied lemon peel, finely chopped
$\frac{1}{2}$ tsp allspice
$\frac{1}{2}$ tsp freshly-grated nutmeg
1 tbsp soft brown sugar
25 g/1 oz/$\frac{1}{4}$ stick butter
1 egg white
Castor sugar to sprinkle

Roll out the pastry and cut into 10 cm/4 in rounds. Mix the currants, lemon peel and spices together. Melt the butter and sugar in a small pan and pour into the currants. Stir in well. When cool, put a heaped teaspoonful in the middle of each pastry round. Moisten the edges with water and gather up to enclose the currant mixture. Pinch firmly together to seal, turn over, and flatten a little with a rolling pin. Place on a greased baking tray, make 3 slits in the top of each, brush with egg white and sprinkle with castor sugar. Bake in a hot oven (220°C/425°F/Gas Mark 7) for 15 minutes or until golden. Eat as soon as possible, for they are best while still warm.

Apple Pie   (Serves 6)

175 g/6 oz/1$\frac{1}{4}$ cups plain flour
75 g/3 oz/$\frac{3}{4}$ stick cold unsalted butter
2 tbsp lard
3–4 tbsp water
675 g/1$\frac{1}{2}$ lb cooking apples, peeled, cored and sliced
1 tsp cinnamon
4 tbsp sugar
Knob of butter
Egg for glazing
Wensleydale cheese

Sieve the flour into a large cold mixing bowl. Cut the butter and lard into small pieces and rub into the flour with cool fingertips. Stir in the water and form into a ball. Set aside in refrigerator, preferably overnight. Divide the pastry into two, and roll out on a floured board. Line a buttered pie plate about 25 cm/10 in across with the rolled pastry, and pile in the apple. Sprinkle with cinnamon and sugar and dot with butter. Roll out the remaining pastry. Dampen the edges of the filled pie, and place the top circle of pastry over this. Press the edges together to seal, and trim. Brush the top with beaten egg and bake in a moderately hot oven (200°C/400°F/Gas Mark 6) for 35–45 minutes. Serve hot, with cheese.

Drink in the North

The North of England is a great region for the beer drinker, offering possibly the largest choice and variety of styles of beers anywhere in the country. In addition to beer, tea is the most important drink here, brewed strongly, drunk with milk and plenty of sugar at all meals – especially the favourite high tea. Less well-known drinks are also produced in the North, such as Lindisfarne mead, made on the Holy Island of Lindisfarne, and the honey-flavoured Brontë liqueur.

Hours: In general, public houses are open in England on weekdays 11.00–15.00 and 17.30–23.00. Sunday hours are 12.00–14.00 and 19.00–22.30. Weekday hours, generally totalling nine hours, may be varied from district to district, but must not begin before 10.00 or terminate after 23.00. There must be a two-hour afternoon break, though local extensions do apply in some areas. In particular, local markets are still an important focus of life in many rural towns and villages in the North and elsewhere, and consequently there are weekly licence extensions on market days where in many cases the pubs stay open for most or all of an afternoon. The Isle of Man is governed by seasonal summer and winter hours, though throughout the year there is no required afternoon break on Saturdays.

Traditional Beer

There are great variations in taste and style of beers from local breweries, as well as from breweries within the different regions of the North, but beer drinkers throughout this vast section of the country almost unanimously agree on one feature essential to a decent pint: a tight, creamy head that clings to the glass all the way down. In the South, pints of real ale drawn direct from the cask are often served with little or no head whatsoever. Here in the North, however, straight 'jars' are presented with foamy heads so large that they appear (almost) like ice-cream cones. The use of a 'sparkler' on hand pumps forces the beer through a tiny aperture

Assorted mats and labels of the region.

which aerates it and helps achieve the required foaming head. Beer drinkers here, who naturally wish to see their pint and drink it, too, have campaigned for the use of over-sized marked glasses which allow a full pint of liquid plus space for the beloved foam.

There is no shortage of choice when it comes to beer in the North. The North-West area alone, around Manchester and the surrounding area, has an unusually large concentration of independent breweries all offering beer drinkers a variety of traditional bitters and dark and light milds with individual character and taste: beers from Boddingtons, Holt, Matthew Brown, Greenall Whitley, Robinson, Hydes, Lees, Wilson, Thwaites, Yates & Jackson and others. Yorkshire ales are traditionally brewed by the Yorkshire square system, a unique method of two-tiered fermentation in slate or stainless steel squares which allows excess yeast to be separated and drawn away without disturbing the beer below. This method results in rich, full-bodied beers such as Tetley's and Sam Smith's. Timothy Taylor's and Theakston's are two other highly-regarded Yorkshire breweries producing excellent traditional ales. The latter, incidentally, brews both in Masham in North Yorkshire as well as in Carlisle, Cumbria, where two other breweries also supply thirsty Lake District walkers with traditional ales: Hartleys' of Ulverston and Jennings Brothers of Cockermouth.

In the North-East (and to a considerable but lesser extent throughout other parts of the North, especially Merseyside, Greater Manchester and South Yorkshire) the main outlets for drinking beer are not public houses but working men's social clubs. Entry to such establishments is limited to members or to members of affiliated clubs. The Northern Clubs Federation Brewery, known as the 'Federation' or 'Fed', supplies many clubs in the North-East with a full range of bright, brewery-conditioned tank or keg beer, not cask-conditioned beer. In truth, it seems, the north-east taste (in spite of a vociferous minority demanding more 'real ales' for the area) leans more toward bright keg and bottled beers from Federation, Scottish & Newcastle and Vaux (though the latter two breweries do supply the area

with a certain amount of cask-conditioned ales as well). In particular, one unique style of beer reigns supreme here, brown ale. While brown ales (which are bottled versions of dark milds) are produced in other parts of the country, that associated with the city of Newcastle remains a classic, the most famous in the land. Newcastle Brown Ale – the Geordie's beloved 'broon' – in its distinctive clear-glass pint bottle, is a superb, strong reddish-brown beer available not only here but nationally. Double Maxim, brewed by Vaux in Sunderland, is a similar strong bottled brown ale, though its range of distribution is more local.

The North-West

Boddingtons' Breweries plc, Strangeways Brewery, Manchester. 'Boddies' has been trading in the North-West for over 200 years, and supplies its full-flavoured cask-conditioned bitter and mild to nearly 300 tied houses. Boddingtons also owns the Oldham Brewery, and 'Boddies' beers together with Oldham's own brews are available in some ninety additional Oldhams outlets.

Mild o.g. 1031–35
Bitter o.g. 1033–37

Forshaw's Burtonwood Brewery, Burtonwood, Warrington, Cheshire. This traditional family-controlled brewery near Warrington supplies its creamy, distinctive bitter and dark mild to some 280 tied public houses in the North-West and North Wales, as well as to a number of free trade outlets in the industrial North-West. Top Hat Strong Ale is a rich, full-flavoured bottled beer.

Dark Mild o.g. 1032
Best Bitter o.g. 1036

Greenall Whitley, Warrington, Cheshire. Greenall Whitley is one of the country's largest regional breweries, with a tied estate of well over 1000 public houses located mainly in the North-West. The company also owns Shipstone's of Nottingham and the Shrewsbury & Wem Brewery.

Mild o.g. 1034
Bitter o.g. 1038

Higson's Brewery plc, Liverpool. Higson's supplies Liverpudlian drinkers with cask- and brewery-

conditioned beers in over 150 tied outlets.

Mild o.g. 1032
Bitter o.g. 1038

Hydes, Anvil Brewery, Manchester. The founder of this independent Manchester brewing company was the great-grandfather of the present Chairman. Most of the production at the Anvil Brewery is traditional cask-conditioned Anvil ales, available in Hydes' tied houses located mainly in and around the city.

Mild Ale o.g. 1032
Best Mild Ale o.g. 1034
Bitter o.g. 1036

Joseph Holt Ltd, Manchester. Cask-conditioned mild and bitter are served in over eighty outlets mainly in and around Manchester.

Mild o.g. 1033
Bitter o.g. 1039

J. W. Lees & Co., Middleton Junction, Manchester. This small independent brewery supplies three cask-conditioned ales to some 150 pubs mostly in the north Manchester and North Wales areas. The brewery itself, built in 1876 by the grandson of the founder, is a fine example of Victorian architecture.

G B Mild o.g. 1032
Bitter o.g. 1037
Moonraker o.g. 1073

Matthew Brown plc, Blackburn, Lancashire. Matthew Brown began brewing ales in a Preston beer house over 150 years ago. Today this important north-west brewing company has some 550 tied public houses stretching from north Cheshire to the Scottish border, from the west coast to the Pennines. The company has a second brewery in Workington, Cumbria.

Lion Mild o.g. 1032
Lion Bitter o.g. 1036
John Peel Bitter o.g. 1040

Mitchell's of Lancaster, Lancaster, Lancashire. The North-West is a stronghold for independent breweries such as Mitchell's, a family firm that began by brewing beer for the Black Horse Inn, Lancaster, in 1871. Its roots today remain mainly in this town and the

A 'tight creamy head' is essential to beer drinkers in the North.

Wooden casks are being replaced by aluminium ones, but traditional breweries like Theakston's of Masham still persevere with the old ways.

surrounding area, supplying traditional beers to some seventy outlets.

> Country or Dark Mild o.g. 1034
> Bitter o.g. 1036
> Extra Special Bitter (ESB) o.g. 1045

Moorehouse's Burnley Brewery, Burnley, Lancashire. The Moorehouse Brewery has been in operation for over one hundred years, but until 1979 it produced only hop bitters, a type of beer primarily used for bottled beer shandy. Hop bitters are still produced, but now two cask-conditioned ales are brewed as well, mainly available in about one hundred free trade outlets as far apart as London and Glasgow.

> Premier Bitter o.g. 1036
> Pendle Witches' Brew o.g. 1050

Oak Brewery, Ellesmere Port, Cheshire. Oak is a new mini-brewery producing about twenty-five barrels of cask-conditioned ales each week, available mainly in Chester, Wirral and Liverpool.

> Best Bitter o.g. 1038
> Old Oak o.g. 1044
> Porter o.g. 1050

Oldham Brewery, Oldham, Manchester. Owned by Boddingtons (see above), Oldham's continues to brew its own beers, which are available in the company's tied houses along with 'Boddies'.

> Mild o.g. 1032
> Bitter o.g. 1037

Frederic Robinson, Stockport, Cheshire. Traditional draught beers have been brewed on the Unicorn site by this independent family company for well over a hundred years. While for many years, Robinson's Best Mild was the company's main seller, its sharp, creamy bitters are equally highly regarded by beer drinkers in the North-West, where most of Robinson's tied public houses are located. Robinson's Old Tom, a full-flavoured, winy old ale, is a classic. It has been brewed by Robinson's for the last ninety years.

> Best Mild Ale o.g. 1032
> Bitter Ale o.g. 1035
> Best Bitter Ale o.g. 1041
> Old Tom Ale o.g. 1080

Tetley Walker, Warrington, Cheshire. Though Tetley Walker and Joshua Tetley are both part of the national Allied Breweries group, the Pennines separate these two important and individual brewing companies. Tetley Walker was established in 1852 and the company operates more than 1000 public houses in Lancashire, Cheshire and the North-West.

> Tetley Mild o.g. 1032
> Tetley Bitter o.g. 1035.5
> Gold Cross (cask-conditioned lager brewed at Wrexham) o.g. 1040

Daniel Thwaites and Co., Blackburn, Lancashire. Beer drinkers in Lancashire and the North-West are spoiled for choice: Daniel Thwaites is another independent brewery supplying the area with fine traditional ales.

> Mild o.g. 1031
> Best Mild o.g. 1033
> Bitter o.g. 1035.5

Peter Walker Ltd, Liverpool. Peter Walker is part of the Allied Breweries group, and its beers are brewed at Tetley Walker's Warrington brewery. About seventy public houses on Merseyside, and in south Lancashire and Cheshire serve cask-conditioned ales.

> Mild o.g. 1031
> Bitter o.g. 1033
> Best Bitter o.g. 1035.5

Wilson's Brewery Ltd, Newton Heath, Manchester. The Newton Heath Brewery has been supplying Manchester and the North-West with beer since 1834. Wilson's is now part of the national Watney Mann & Truman brewing group, and its re-launched cask-conditioned ales are popular in the company's traditional north-west heartland.

> Wilson's Original Mild o.g. 1032
> Wilson's Original Bitter o.g. 1036

Yates & Jackson, Lancaster, Lancashire. This small, independent family brewery produces only two draught beers, both cask-conditioned, which are available in some forty tied public houses, seventeen of them in Lancaster itself.

> Mild o.g. 1030.8
> Bitter o.g. 1035.8

Yorkshire and Humberside

Bass North and Bass North West, Tadcaster and Sheffield. The national brewing company Bass UK (see p. 53) operates breweries at Tadcaster and Sheffield, producing cask-conditioned ales available in the company's vast tied estate in the North of England. The company also operates a second brewery at Sheffield and another one at Runcorn, Cheshire, both of which produce brewery-conditioned beers only. In the North-West, Bass has a reciprocal agreement with Jennings Brothers of Cockermouth whereby Stones BB is available in certain Jennings' outlets and Jennings' traditional cask bitter is available in selected Bass houses.

> Cask-conditioned ales brewed at Tadcaster:
>
> Best Mild XXXX o.g. 1031
> Extra Light o.g. 1031
> Blackpool Best Mild o.g. 1036
> Brew Ten o.g. 1036
> Cask Bitter o.g. 1036

> Cask-conditioned ales brewed at Sheffield
> (Stones Cannon Brewery):
>
> Stones BB o.g. 1038
> Cannon Special Ale o.g. 1050

H. B. Clark & Co. (Successors) Ltd, Wakefield, West Yorkshire. Clark's Bitter was first brewed in 1905, but the company ceased brewing during the 1960s. The brewery was re-opened in 1982, and two cask-conditioned ales brewed with only malt and hops are now in production.

> Clark's Traditional Bitter o.g. 1038
> Henry Boon's Wakefield Ale o.g. 1038

W. M. Darley Ltd, Thorne, near Doncaster, South Yorkshire. Darley's is an old established Yorkshire brewery, now a subsidiary of Vaux Breweries of Sunderland. The beers continue to be brewed at Thorne to suit local taste, and are available mainly in Yorkshire and Lincolnshire.

> Thorne Best Bitter o.g. 1038
> Chairman's (Dark Beer) o.g. 1039

Franklin's Brewery, Bilton, near Harrogate, North Yorkshire. This one-man brewery was started in 1979, and supplies Franklin's Bitter within a thirty-mile radius of Harrogate.

> Franklin's Bitter o.g. 1037.9

John Smith's Tadcaster Brewery, Tadcaster, North Yorkshire. John Smith's Tadcaster Brewery is the northern arm of the national brewing company Courage. A number of beers and lagers are brewed here, not just for distribution to the company's public houses in the region but throughout the country. John Smith's brews one cask-conditioned ale.

> J S Bitter o.g. 1034–38

Samuel Smith's Old Brewery, Tadcaster, North Yorkshire. Samuel Smith's is Yorkshire's oldest brewery, and continues to produce an excellent pint which satisfies the prodigious Yorkshire thirst: Old Brewery Bitter, known affectionately as 'Sam's' to regulars in the company's some 300 outlets.

> Old Brewery Bitter o.g. 1040.9

Timothy Taylor & Co., Keighley, West Yorkshire. Timothy Taylor is a highly regarded traditional brewery producing one of the largest ranges of cask-conditioned ales in the country.

> Golden Mild o.g. 1033
> Dark Mild o.g. 1033
> Bitter o.g. 1033
> Best Bitter o.g. 1037
> Landlord o.g. 1042
> Ram Tam (4X) o.g. 1043
> Porter o.g. 1043

Joshua Tetley, Leeds, West Yorkshire. Though a part of the national Allied Breweries group, and with over 1000 tied public houses, Joshua Tetley of Leeds remains very much a local traditional brewery, producing cask-conditioned ales to suit the Yorkshire taste. Tetley's has been in the brewing business since 1746 (originally the family began as maltsters at Armley, near Leeds, but Joshua did not begin brewing until 1822). At that time, he employed the famous Yorkshire system of fermentation in squares made from thick slabs of slate; today the Yorkshire squares are constructed from stainless steel, but this unique method of fermentation is otherwise unchanged.

Mild o.g. 1030–34
Bitter o.g. 1034–38
Falstaff Best o.g. 1030–34

T. & R. Theakston Ltd, Masham, North Yorkshire and Carlisle, Cumbria. Theakston's have been brewing in Masham (pronounced 'Massum') for over 150 years and though the company has grown considerably in recent years as the popularity of its traditional ales has spread throughout the country, the brewery here remains remarkably haphazard and unspoiled. A range of four traditional cask-conditioned ales are brewed in Masham and at Carlisle, formerly an old government brewery purchased by Theakston's in 1974. The company's most famous beer, Old Peculier, is a classic old ale: powerful, dark and sweet.

Mild o.g. 1032
Best Bitter o.g. 1038
XB o.g. 1045
Old Peculier o.g. 1058

Trough Brewery, Bradford, West Yorkshire. Trough is a small company established in 1980, and now the only brewery in Bradford, supplying its beers to three tied public houses and the free trade, exclusively in this city.

Trough Mild o.g. 1033
Trough Bitter o.g. 1035.5
Wild Boar o.g. 1039.9

S. H. Ward & Co., Sheffield, South Yorkshire. Ward's, an established Sheffield brewing company, merged with Vaux's of Sunderland in 1972. The majority of the company's public houses are in the Sheffield area.

Sheffield Best Mild o.g. 1034
Sheffield Best Bitter o.g. 1038

Samuel Webster & Sons Ltd, Halifax, West Yorkshire. Webster's, an established old Yorkshire brewery, is now part of the Watney Mann & Truman brewing organization. The Fountain Head Brewery produces not only traditional cask ales 'to meet the increasing demand for real ale' in this part of Yorkshire, but also Carlsberg and Fosters lagers which are supplied to the whole country.

Webster's Dark Mild o.g. 1032
Webster's Yorkshire Light o.g. 1033

Webster's Yorkshire Bitter o.g. 1036

Whitbread East Pennines, Sheffield; Whitbread Chesters, Salford, Manchester; Whitbread Castle Eden, Co. Durham. (see p. 152) Whitbread, like the other main national brewing companies, has acquired numerous old breweries in the North over the years. At the present, brewing is carried on at four different sites (the Salmesbury Brewery produces bright, brewery-conditioned beers only), supplying different trading areas with beers brewed to suit local tastes.

Cask-conditioned ales brewed at Sheffield:
Bentley's Yorkshire Bitter (BYB) o.g. 1031–35
Trophy o.g. 1035–39 (available nationally, but in cask form only in limited outlets)

Cask-conditioned ales brewed at Castle Eden:
Castle Eden Ale o.g. 1038–42
Durham Ale o.g. 1033–37

Cask-conditioned ales brewed at Salford:
Chester's Best Mild o.g. 1030–34
Chester's Best Bitter o.g. 1031–35

Cumbria

Hartley, Ulverston, Cumbria. Hartley has been brewing on the same site in Ulverston since 1755. It supplies three cask-conditioned ales 'draught from the wood' to over fifty tied houses mainly in Cumbria. Since 1982, Hartley's has been a subsidiary of the Stockport brewery Frederic Robinson.

Mild o.g. 1031
Bitter o.g. 1031
Best Bitter XB o.g. 1040

Jennings Bros, Cockermouth, Cumbria. This Lake District brewery produces cask-conditioned ales available in the North-West not only in the company's tied estate, but also in a select number of Bass outlets in the Burnley, Nelson, Colne and Barrow areas.

Mild o.g. 1033
Bitter o.g. 1035

The North-East

J. W. Cameron & Co. Ltd, Hartlepool, Cleveland. Cameron & Co., the largest supplier of cask-conditioned ales to the North-East, brews 'strong, high-quality beers appropriate to the thirsts of steel making and heavy engineering workers'. The company also brews Hansa lager.

Lion Bitter o.g. 1036
Strongarm o.g. 1040

Scottish & Newcastle Breweries, Tyne Brewery, Newcastle. Scottish Breweries and Newcastle Breweries merged over twenty years ago (see p. 210) and brewing is carried out in Edinburgh, Newcastle and Manchester (lager only). The Tyne Brewery in Newcastle, though it brews no cask-conditioned ales, is famous for the production of the classic drink of the North-East: Newcastle Brown Ale, first brewed in 1927 (bottles and cans, o.g. 1042–48). Cask-conditioned McEwans and Youngers ales are available in many S & N public houses, as well as in some free houses throughout the region.

Vaux Breweries, Sunderland, Tyne & Wear. Vaux Breweries, one of the largest regional brewing companies, began in 1837 and is now run by the sixth generation of the family. Two cask-conditioned ales brewed in Sunderland as well as Lorimer's Best Scotch (70/–) ale are available in many of the company's 650 tied houses, located throughout the north of the country from Carlisle to Berwick, and from Chester to Boston. A strong, smooth, bottled brown ale, Double Maxim, is particularly popular in the North-East.

Sunderland Draught Bitter o.g. 1040
Samson Ale o.g. 1042

Federation Brewery, Dunston, Tyne & Wear. The strength of clubs in the North-East and indeed throughout the country is evident by the fact that this unique brewery supplies some 1500 outlets, almost all of which are clubs. 'Fed' brews some 20,000 barrels of beer each week, including pale ale, dark mild, export bitter, brown ale, sweet stout and lager. None of these are conditioned in the cask.

Isle of Man

Okell and Son, Douglas, Isle of Man. The 1874 Isle of Man Brewers Act states: 'No

Brewery shall use in the brewing any article, ingredient or preparation whatever, for, or as a substitute for, malt, sugar or hops.' Okell's beers are brewed for sale on the island only.

Mild Ale (XXX) o.g. 1035
Bitter (PB) o.g. 1035

Castletown, Castletown, Isle of Man. The island's second brewery also produces pure traditional ales brewed only with malt, hops and sugar.

Mild o.g. 1036
Bitter o.g. 1036

The Holy Island of Lindisfarne.

Lindisfarne Mead

It seems fitting, perhaps, that mead is still produced in Northumberland, on the Holy Island of Lindisfarne: an ancient drink for an ancient region that has the remains of more castles than any other part of Britain. Mead, in its simplest form, is a drink made from fermented honey. Bees were kept in this region from earliest times (Beal, a village on the mainland, is named from the Saxon word for bee-hill), and it is probable that the monks who established the monastery on Holy Island over thirteen centuries ago produced some sort of equivalent beverage. Today, the modern Lindisfarne Winery stands opposite the ancient ruins of the monastery, and the mead produced here is served at mediaeval banquets throughout the country, as well as in private homes. The Winery can be visited, but it is essential to check tide times before

crossing the causeway which separates Lindisfarne from the mainland. Further north, in Berwick-upon-Tweed the Lindisfarne Wine & Spirit Museum is also worth visiting.

Lindisfarne Wine & Spirit Museum
Palace Green
Berwick-upon-Tweed
Northumbria
Open Monday–Saturday, 10.00–17.00, Easter to October.

Some Useful Addresses

Cumbria Tourist Board
Ellerthwaite
Windermere
Cumbria

Northumbria Tourist Board
9 Osborne Terrace
Jesmond
Newcastle-upon-Tyne

North West Tourist Board
The Last Drop Village
Bromley Cross
Bolton

Yorkshire and Humberside Tourist Board
312 Tadcaster Road
York

Upper Dales Folk Museum
Station Yard
Hawes
North Yorkshire
Open: Easter or April 1 to September 30
Monday–Saturday, 11.00–17.00; Sunday, 14.00–17.00

R. Woodall Esq.
Lane End
Waberthwaite
near Millom
Cumbria
Cumberland ham, Cumbria Royal ham (sweet-pickle cure) and Cumbria ham (Parma-style), Cumberland sausage and home-cured bacon. Mail order service.

Sarah Nelson's Gingerbread Shop
Grasmere
Cumbria
Grasmere gingerbread made to a world famous but very secret recipe.

Calthwaite Dairies
Calthwaite Hall
near Penrith
Cumbria
Cumberland rum butter, cream and dairy products from Calthwaite's own herd of Jersey cattle. Mail order service.

Harry Ramsden's
White Cross
Guiseley
near Leeds
West Yorkshire

Betty's Tea Rooms
1 Parliament Street
Harrogate
and
6–8 St Helens Square
York
North Yorkshire
Traditional Yorkshire baked goods and cakes.

L. Robson & Sons Ltd
Craster
Alnwick
Northumberland
Craster kippers. Mail order service.

The Lion Salt Works
Marston
Northwich
Cheshire
Ancient salt pans still in use producing natural Cheshire salt. Visitors welcome.

Morris's Pork Butchers
120 Market Street
Farnworth
near Bolton
Gold-medal-winning black puddings.

Hinton Bank Farm
Whitchurch
Shropshire
Blue Cheshire cheese made on this farm only. International mail order service from Alkington Cheese Supplies, 10 Chester Avenue, Whitchurch, Shropshire.

Lower Barker Farm
Inglewhite
near Preston
Lancashire
Farmhouse Lancashire cheese available from the village Post Office and General Store.

THE MIDLANDS

Like a wide girth across John Bull's belly, expanding from Lincolnshire across to Gloucestershire, separating North from South (though unable to enclose the unwieldy bulges formed by Wales and East Anglia), the Midlands supports the country. This extensive section of England remains today its major centre of manufacturing. Birmingham, Coventry, Stoke-on-Trent, Leicester and Derby are all important engineering centres. Yet though at first glance the character of the Midlands may appear essentially industrial, this large region contrasts its concentration of inner cities with wide expanses of long-established rural countryside.

Strike out in any direction from any of the major industrial centres and one quickly enters the country. Not for Birmingham, second largest city in England, those endless mile after mile of terraced suburbs which seem almost to suffocate London; leave its Bull Ring and its 'spaghetti junction' of motorways behind, and the oaken copses of Warwickshire, the rich fields of Staffordshire, the lush meadows and dairylands of Shropshire soon begin. What a contrast to the urban concrete, the factories with their belching, filthy chimneys, this gentle, pastoral countryside of half-timbered villages, where the hills still resound to the blast of the horn, the gallop of hoofs! Even the old names of the counties themselves suggest long-established country England: Warwickshire, Staffordshire, Herefordshire, Worcestershire, Gloucestershire, Shropshire, Leicestershire, Lincolnshire, Northamptonshire, Derbyshire and Nottinghamshire.

Rich farmlands, famous dairies producing the milk for some of England's greatest cheeses, lush market gardens yielding the finest fruits and vegetables, cider orchards and hop gardens: all provide a wealth of food and drink for city and country alike; in return, the city provides metal-stampings, automobiles, electronic equipment, plumbing fittings and plastic mouldings – literally the nuts and bolts, the unromantic hardware that helps keep the country running.

In the past, certainly, those workers who flooded into the cities to take jobs in the new factories that developed after the onset of the Industrial Revolution which began in the Ironbridge Gorge must have lived, at times, on an exceedingly frugal and monotonous diet. Documents speak of difficult working and living conditions in Staffordshire towns such as Longton and Stoke during the mid-nineteenth century, when the potters and their families subsisted on such foods as lobby (probably related to Liverpool's lobscouse), hasty pudding (a mixture of oats or barley, water, suet and treacle, eaten hot or cold), pobs (breadcrusts merely soaked in water or milk, and sprinkled with sugar and tea), frumenty (a special treat made with soaked wheat, fruit and spices) and chicklings (chitterlings). Such foods today may seem only historical curiosities, but throughout the Midlands other favourites remain whose origins were in this same harsh past: faggots or savoury ducks (liver meatballs wrapped in caul fat), polonies and other sausages, haslet, brawn, jellied chitterlings, tripe and pig's feet. Pork scratchings (like the crackling on roast pork) are still the popular snack in pubs here, while mild, an inexpensive low-gravity beer, remains the favourite working man's pint.

Working and social conditions, certainly, have improved over the centuries. Industry has brought prosperity to the Midlands, and today manual workers do not appear to fare too badly (those fortunate enough to be in work, at any rate). Jobs and industry have also brought people from a variety of communities to the Midlands, so that the region today reflects the heterogeneous diversity of modern Britain.

Thousands of bottle ovens once dotted the Potteries of Staffordshire: the production of fine bone china continues here today, one of many traditional Midlands' industries.

The Iron Bridge, symbol of England's Industrial Revolution: it was here that Abraham Darby first smelted iron using coke as fuel.

Outside the confusion of the cities, the countryside of the Shire counties continues to present a uniform aura of long-established satisfaction. This, after all, is hunting country *par excellence* with all the social conventions that this favourite activity of the landed gentry and nobility implies. The Quorn and the Belvoir (pronounced 'Beever') are two of the most famous hunts in the country, and this activity has directly and indirectly contributed a number of important regional foods. Riding after a pack of hounds all day is strenuous to say the least, though the local custom of breakfasting on pork pies must go some way to holding hunger at bay. Indeed, Melton Mowbray, a rather unexceptional Leicestershire market town located in the heart of the Shires,

has gained fame through the excellence of its pork pies, primarily because the society folk who came here to hunt enjoyed these hand-raised savoury pies and then requested them on their return to London. Melton hunt cake, made to a well-guarded recipe, is eaten after the day's outings, preferably with a glass of rich ruby port. The Quorn bacon roll is another hunt speciality, though perhaps this humble suet pastry filled with bacon and onions is enjoyed more by the hunt attendants and by local farmers after a day's rough shooting for rabbit and hare than by those who dress in bowlers and riding breeches to follow the hounds.

To the south, other important hunts are to be found in Gloucestershire, including the Berkeley and the Beaufort. Indeed, the region known as the Cotswolds, with such villages as Broadway, Stow-on-the-Wold, Chipping Camden and elegant Cheltenham Spa, is another area of long-

established affluence, and the mellow golden glow of weathered limestone attests to centuries of prosperity among the landed gentry. The Vale of Evesham, an area of numerous small market gardens, reflects this richness and fertility; throughout the year, roadside stalls around Badesey, Offenham, Wickhamford and Evesham itself offer an overflowing abundance of the finest English fruits and vegetables.

Asparagus and strawberries, those two favourite seasonal delicacies, herald the summer, though other produce follows in an unending profusion: cherries, blackberries, gooseberries, raspberries, blackcurrants, redcurrants, numerous varieties of fine English apples and pears, plums, tomatoes, lettuces, cabbages, potatoes, sprouts, turnips and other root vegetables. Such produce is grown commercially here, but on a comparatively small horticultural scale rather than an intensive agricultural one. On a purely private scale, too, people in the Midlands take great pride in growing their own vegetables, whether on city allotments or in their own back gardens. Vegetables such as tiny freshly-picked broad beans, runner beans topped and tailed only, Webb's lettuce and garden-grown courgettes form the cornerstone of good English eating at its simplest and best.

This simpler, homely character is evident elsewhere in the region, too, particularly in the west, in those ample rural lands bordering Wales and the South-West. They, too, are rich and prosperous, with more than their share of fine natural produce. Rivers such as the Severn and the Wye, for example, are full of salmon as fine as can be caught on a rod in Britain, and this great delicacy is enjoyed in homes and hotels and restaurants. Lampreys are an unusual speciality of the area not widely encountered elsewhere, while elvers are eaten in great quantity here during their brief season. The region, too, has rich dairy land, while fresh pork and locally-cured bacon are both plentiful and good. Such foods, simply prepared, accompany good local ales and traditional farm ciders and perrys for which the western counties of Gloucestershire and Hereford and Worcester are so famous.

The Midlands is a vast region of considerable contrast. From the Ironbridge Gorge through Birmingham and Aston to Coventry and Leicester, the yellow-orange glow of a thousand factories and foundries hangs over the cities at dusk like an end-of-day exhalation. Yet the countryside of the Shires, Gloucestershire, Warwickshire, Shropshire and elsewhere remains gloriously fresh, well-established and unpolluted. Food and drink here is a similar contrast: plates of black pudding and pints of mild at working men's public houses; sideboards groaning with joints of spiced hunt beef, hams and raised pies at formal hunt balls; rabbit stew and cider enjoyed in flag-stoned farmhouse kitchens; ample joints of roast beef and fine clarets served for boardroom luncheons; curry and chapatis eaten on the factory shop floor. The Midlands in all its diversity and complexity reflects the nation today.

Cheeses of the Midlands

Stilton Creamy and open-textured, with a green-blue mould radiating from its centre and a characteristic rough orange-brown coat, Blue Stilton is the supreme English cheese. The only English cheese to have its name protected by law, Stilton may only be produced from milk from the three shires of Leicester, Derby and Nottingham. Traditionally Melton Mowbray, in the Vale of Belvoir, is considered the centre of this famous industry, for indeed it was near this market town that the first such cheeses were produced, some three hundred years ago. They were sent to the cheese maker's brother-in-law, the landlord of the Bell Inn, a coaching inn on the Great North Road in the village of Stilton. The cheeses were extremely popular with visitors and travellers; by 1727 Daniel Defoe remarked that he 'passed through Stilton, a town famous for cheese'. Thus, though the village itself does not and never has made cheese, it gave its name to one of the greatest in the world.

Today only half a dozen creameries and dairies belong to the Stilton Cheese Makers' Association, but every cheese which bears this treasured name has been produced by time-honoured methods. Each producer naturally has its own particular way of doing things, and the resulting cheeses from different creameries and dairies remain distinct and individual. The basic Stilton method, nevertheless, is unique. Fresh milk from surrounding farms comes to each creamery or dairy daily. It is generally pasteurized (though one dairy still makes cheese from unpasteurized milk), and then the starter and penicillin cultures and the rennet are added, causing the milk solids to form into curds. The resulting vat of junket is cut by hand vertically and horizontally with knives to allow the drainage of whey (the whey in turn is fed to pigs, whose flavourful meat is used in the region's renowned pork pies). The curds are then ladled gently into a trolley and left overnight, allowing further drainage of whey. This delicate work by hand is essential to maintain the creamy open texture which is the hallmark of Stilton.

The next morning the curds are cut into squares, milled into walnut-size pellets, salted and packed into cylinders, again by hand. About twenty-six pounds of curds will eventually result in a mature sixteen-pound Stilton – that is, about seventeen gallons of milk, or over a gallon, for each pound of cheese. Unlike many other English cheeses, Stilton is not pressed, again an important difference which contributes to its creamy texture. The cylinders of cheese are left for a week, turned daily, then scraped and smoothed down by hand and wrapped in clean muslin. The cheeses at this early stage are white and quite firm; they look rather like cylinders of butter. White Stilton, in fact, can be eaten after only ten days, while the maturation of prime Blue Stilton takes a further ten weeks at least.

The cheeses destined to become Blue Stilton are next transferred to the maturing room, where, in this moist, carefully-controlled atmosphere, the crust slowly develops, while the blue veining process begins within the cheese. The wetness and the warmth of the Vale of Belvoir provides the ideal conditions for this natural process. After six weeks, the cheeses are pierced with stainless steel needles, a process which further encourages the blue veins to spread evenly from the centres of the cheeses. The cheeses develop for a further four weeks, at which time they are graded by the cheese maker on the basis of blueness, texture, flavour and general quality, thus ensuring that first-grade Stilton maintains its deservedly high standard and reputation.

A word about serving Stilton: it should never be scooped out with a spoon. Here in the Vale of Belvoir they say 'cut high, cut low, cut level'. The cheese makers themselves, moreover, are the first to agree that port is superb with Stilton, not, they stress, *in* it.

Leicester Leicester is the deepest coloured of all English cheeses, traditionally made in large, flat cartwheels up to forty-five pounds in weight. Mild in flavour, with a granular texture, it is generally eaten within a few months of its manufacture. It is an excellent cheese for toasting.

Derby This old-established English cheese is now made in limited quantities by a process similar to Cheddar, but resulting in a softer, lower-acid cheese traditionally formed into flat cartwheels. Sage Derby, available primarily at Christmas, is produced by colouring the curds with chlorophyll

The cheese maker at Long Clawson Dairy grading mature Blue Stilton.

and adding powdered sage prior to milling. This results in an attractive marbled effect and a cheese with a surprisingly assertive flavour of the herb.

Gloucester Cheese rolling, an ancient Gloucestershire custom, takes place in certain villages such as Brockworth, Randwick and Birdlip, and presumably is an indication that Gloucester cheeses have always been both round and relatively tough. Double Gloucester is the most widely available, made traditionally on farms as well as in creameries, not all or even most of which are located in this old county. It is manufactured in a process similar to Cheddar, but the curds are twice-milled to fine pellets rather than large chips. The cheese, which is dyed pale orange, matures more quickly than Cheddar, and has a smooth waxy texture and a moist buttery flavour. There is some confusion concerning the differences between Double and Single Gloucester cheeses; the latter, apparently,

were both smaller and made with the cream of only one milking. Gloucester cheeses were originally made with the rich milk from the old Gloucester herd of cattle, a breed which has been revived by one farm in Dymock making both the Double and the much rarer Single varieties.

Cheeses with added flavourings For centuries, cheese makers and cheese lovers have 'improved' their products either by adding flavourings direct to the curd or by pouring wine or beer into the cheese once it had been made. The practise of adding crushed sage leaves to Derby and Lancashire cheeses is an ancient one, while Stilton producers used to pour port over their cheeses as they matured (this led to the custom of pouring port into Stilton at home). Cheese makers today sometimes add a variety of ingredients to their cheeses, including chives, sweet pickle, beer or wine.

Recipes from the Midlands

Savoury Ducks   (Serves 4)

Savoury ducks, or faggots, a rich highly-seasoned paste of liver made into balls, is a typical Midlands' favourite, served hot with gravy and peas for supper or high tea.

350 g/12 oz pig's liver	Freshly-chopped thyme
225 g/8 oz belly pork	Knob of butter
1 large onion, finely chopped	1 egg, beaten
Salt	100 g/4 oz/3 cups fresh white breadcrumbs
Freshly-ground black pepper	Pig's caul, cleaned and soaked
Pinch of freshly-grated nutmeg	150 ml/¼ pt/⅔ cup rich home-made stock
Freshly-chopped sage	

Mince the liver and belly pork together and mix with the onion, salt, pepper, nutmeg, sage and thyme. Melt the knob of butter in a saucepan and add the liver mixture. Cook gently over a low heat for 30 minutes, covered. Drain off the fat. Allow to cool slightly, then add the beaten egg and breadcrumbs. Mix thoroughly, then form into small balls. Cut the caul into squares and wrap up each faggot ball. Arrange them side by side in a baking dish, add the stock, and bake in a moderately hot oven (190°C/375°F/Gas Mark 5) for about 30 minutes, or until browned. Serve with the gravy, peas and potatoes.

Quorn Bacon Roll   (Serves 4)

A huntsmen's favourite to eat after a very cold day spent outdoors.

225 g/8 oz plain flour	1 large onion, chopped
Pinch of salt	Handful freshly-chopped sage
1 tsp baking powder	Salt
100 g/4 oz/½ cup suet, shredded	Freshly-ground black pepper
Cold water to mix	Freshly-chopped parsley
350 g/12 oz lean bacon rashers	

Sieve the flour, salt and baking powder into a large mixing bowl and stir in the suet. Add enough cold water to make a firm dough. Roll out on a floured board into a rectangle about 1.3 cm/½ in thick. Lay the bacon rashers on the pastry and sprinkle with onion and sage. Season with salt and pepper. Roll up like a Swiss roll, wrap in a pudding cloth or foil, and boil for about 2 hours. Serve on a hot platter, garnished with parsley, and surrounded with boiled vegetables such as potatoes, carrots and swede.

Potted Stilton   (Serves 4–6)

Potted Stilton is an excellent way of using left-over or odd bits of cheese, for it makes a rich creamy spread that can be eaten as a first course, or after a meal with fruit and biscuits.

225 g/8 oz Blue Stilton	Pinch of mace
50 g/2 oz/½ stick unsalted butter	¼ tsp freshly-prepared English mustard
2 tbsp port	

Mix the cheese and butter to a paste. Add the port, mace and mustard and mix well. Pack into earthenware or china pots. If the potted Stilton is to be kept for any length of time, cover with clarified butter (see p. 16).

Gloucester Cheese and Ale   (Serves 4)

This traditional country method of serving Gloucester cheese is excellent sampled in local pubs with pints of Cheltenham-brewed Flowers Original, though of course it can also be made easily at home.

225 g/8 oz Double Gloucester cheese	4 thick slices of wholemeal bread, toasted
1 tbsp mild mustard	
300 ml/½ pt/1¼ cups strong ale	

Slice the cheese very thinly and place in an ovenproof dish. Spread each layer with mustard and pour on enough ale to cover. Bake in a moderate oven (180°C/350°F/Gas Mark 4) until the cheese has melted, then pour on to the slices of toast. Serve immediately, with mugs of ale.

Melton Mowbray Pork Pie

(Makes 1 large pie)

Leicestershire has always been famous for its pork pies, partly because the pigs here thrive on a diet of whey, one of the main by-products of cheese making. Also, of course, pork pies are a portable food, and the local hunts found them easy to carry around the countryside. Melton Mowbray pork pies are distinctive because of their hand-raised hot water crusts, baked without a tin or hoop. The oldest remaining pork pie bakery in the town is Dickinson & Morris, where pies have been produced since 1850; they explained to us their careful method of manufacture. While Dickinson & Morris hand-raise their pies on age-old wooden blocks, a well-floured jam jar will also do the job.

Hot Water Pastry

300 g/10 oz/2 cups plain flour	75 g/3 oz/$\frac{3}{8}$ cup of lard
Pinch of salt	150 ml/$\frac{1}{4}$ pt/$\frac{2}{3}$ cup milk and water combined

For the filling

450 g/1 lb lean coarsely-minced pork	Handful freshly-chopped herbs
Salt	Bones and pork trimmings
Freshly-ground black pepper	Beaten egg to glaze
	Water

Sieve the flour and salt into a large warmed mixing bowl, and make a well in the centre. Heat the lard and milk and water together until boiling, then pour into the mixing bowl. Stir in well with a wooden spoon until cool enough to knead with the hands. Form into a ball and chill in a refrigerator. Meanwhile, season the coarsely-minced pork liberally with salt and plenty of black pepper and add the chopped herbs. Put the bones and pork trimmings in a saucepan, season with salt and pepper, and cover with cold water. Bring to the boil and simmer for 2 hours to make a concentrated jelly which will set when cold.

Ensure that all surfaces, the wooden pie block or jam jar for raising, and hands are well floured. Divide the pastry, reserving about a quarter for the pie lid. Take the main ball of pastry and shape it into a 'top hat' shape with the edge of the hand. Turn it upside down, and with the thumbs and fingers form into a cup shape. Place the floured wooden block or a floured jam jar into this cup of pastry, and raise the paste up the sides, turning the block or jam jar with the thumbs.

Fill the pastry case with the minced pork mixture

and place back in the refrigerator to firm. Roll out the remaining pastry to make a lid. Dampen the pie edges and place and seal the pastry lid. Pinch the edges together and make a small circular vent in the top. Brush with beaten egg. Pin three or four folds of greaseproof paper around the pie to preserve its shape and to prevent it from becoming too brown. Place in a hot oven (220°C/425°F/Gas Mark 7) for 30 minutes, then reduce to a moderate heat (180°C/350°F/Gas Mark 4) for a further 1$\frac{1}{2}$ hours. Remove the greaseproof paper for the last $\frac{1}{2}$ hour and brush the sides with beaten egg.

Reheat the stock, and while the pie is still hot pour enough through a funnel into the circular vent to fill the pie. Allow this jelly to set and serve the pie cold with English mustard and chutney.

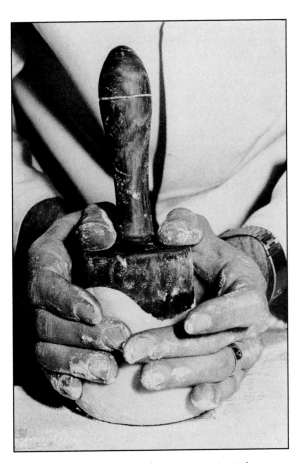

Hand-raising pork pies at Dickinson & Morris, Melton Mowbray.

Gloucestershire Elvers

Elvers are immature young eels only two or three inches in length. Spawned in the Sargasso Sea, they are carried across the ocean by the Gulf Stream, a remarkable journey which takes up to three years. Once here, they make their way up the Severn on high spring tides and fishermen catch the tiny fish with ultra-fine nets. The elver season lasts only from February until the end of May. In season, they are available from local fishmongers in the Severn area, and in the market in Gloucester. But they have become expensive owing to their scarcity.

Every Easter Monday, an annual elver-eating contest takes place on the ample village green of Frampton-on-Severn. The object is to eat a pound of elvers as quickly as possible. Not being squeamish, we nevertheless feel that elvers are a delicacy so rarely encountered that they should perhaps be treated with rather more respect. In the Basque country of Spain elvers are much loved fried in copious amounts of olive oil and garlic, then eaten with wooden forks. In Italy, the Pisans are exceedingly fond of these small fry flavoured with fresh sage. In Gloucestershire, too, they are highly regarded: the favourite local method here is to fry the elvers in bacon fat, then bind them with beaten egg.

Gloucestershire Elvers (Serves 2–4)

450 g/1 lb elvers	2 eggs, beaten
4 rashers bacon	Splash of malt vinegar

Wash the elvers thoroughly, and pat dry. Fry the bacon and when crisp, remove from the pan. Add the elvers to the hot bacon fat, and fry briskly, turning with a spatula. If the elvers throw off a lot of liquid, drain this. Continue to fry for about 5–7 minutes. A minute or two before the elvers are done, add the beaten egg, mix well, and cook until the egg is set. Sprinkle with malt vinegar, and serve immediately with the bacon, for breakfast, tea or supper.

Opposite: Elvers being prepared at the village green at Frampton-on-Severn for the annual contest.

Rabbit Stew (Serves 4–6)

While pheasant and other wild fowl are shot throughout the Midlands in season, farmers in Staffordshire, Warwickshire, Leicestershire, Gloucestershire and elsewhere have never been averse to bagging the odd rabbit or hare they happened to come across on a weekend's rough shooting.

1 large rabbit or two small ones, skinned and cleaned	Seasoned flour
150 ml/¼ pt/⅔ cup red wine	50 g/2 oz/¼ cup lard
1 large onion, finely sliced	4 rashers bacon, coarsely chopped
4 juniper berries, crushed	2 sticks celery, coarsely chopped
1 bay leaf	4 small carrots, coarsely chopped
Sprig of fresh thyme	300 ml/½ pt/1¼ cups chicken stock
Handful of fresh parsley	Dash of port
Salt	3 tbsp redcurrant jelly
Freshly-ground black pepper	

Joint the rabbit and divide into small pieces. Rinse well under running cold water. Pat dry and place in a large bowl. Add the wine, onion, juniper berries, bay leaf, thyme, parsley and salt and pepper. Turn the pieces so that they are well coated in this marinade. Cover and set aside for 12–24 hours. Remove the rabbit and pat dry. Coat with the seasoned flour. Brown the bacon in the lard in a large casserole. Add the rabbit and brown on all sides. Add the celery and carrots and allow to coat in the fat. Pour on the marinade and chicken stock. Bring to the boil, cover, and simmer for about 1 hour. Add the port and redcurrant jelly, and adjust the seasoning. Cover again and continue to cook for a further 45 minutes–1 hour, or until the meat is tender, but not falling apart. Serve at once.

Worcestershire and Other Sauces

England's most famous bottled sauce originated when an aristocrat from Worcester, Lord Sandys, returned from the East where he was Governor of Bengal and asked his local chemists, John Lea and William Perrins of Broad Street, Worcester, to make up a recipe that he had acquired in India. The resulting sauce, however, was highly unpalatable, so the chemists abandoned it in their cellars. When they chanced to come across it again several months later, they sampled it and found that it had matured splendidly. Thus the Original and Genuine Worcestershire Sauce, was born and continues to thrive today, matured in oak hogsheads for several months, then bottled and despatched throughout the country and the world.

The English are exceedingly fond of bottled sauces with strong, sharp, fruity, spicy and sweet flavours, made with exotic fruits, peppers and spices from around the world. In addition to Worcestershire sauce, other popular bottled sauces include HP Sauce, Daddy's Sauce, brown sauce, tomato ketchup and others. Though they may lack the subtlety of home-made sauces, nevertheless they are essential English condiments, at home almost anywhere.

Nottingham Roast Goose   (Serves 8)

The Nottingham Goose Fair takes place annually in the first week of October. It was originally a Michaelmas Fair, and goose was traditionally eaten at this time of year. Though there are no geese at the Fair today, it remains a popular event. Goose, too, is enjoyed in the Midlands, especially at Christmas.

1 oven-ready goose, about 4 kg/9 lb
Salt
Freshly-ground black pepper
4 large cooking apples, peeled, cored and chopped
Freshly-chopped sage
350 g/12 oz/4 cups fresh white breadcrumbs

Remove the giblets and wipe the goose inside and out. Mix together the salt, pepper, apples, sage and breadcrumbs, and spoon into the cavity of the bird. Rub the skin of the goose well with salt and pepper, and place on a rack in a roasting tin. Roast in a moderately hot oven (200°C/400°F/Gas Mark 6) for 30 minutes. Remove from the oven and lightly prick all over. Reduce the heat (180°C/350°F/Gas Mark 4) and return the goose to the oven for a further 1 hour. Remove and prick the skin again. Drain off the excess fat from the roasting tin. Cook for a total of 3–3½ hours, depending on size. If the breast becomes too brown, cover with foil or greaseproof paper. When done, place the goose on a warmed serving platter and keep hot. Strain off the excess fat from the roasting tin, and make a gravy with the pan juices. Carve the goose and serve, together with roast potatoes and home-made apple sauce.

Spiced Pears in Cider   (Serves 8)

Hereford and Worcester is an important centre for fruit-growing, particularly for fine English apples and pears. Both Comice and Conference pears come from this orchard area; the latter is superb for eating as well as cooking, and should be used in this recipe, together, preferably, with Hereford cider.

8 Conference pears	Squeeze of lemon juice
250 g/8 oz/1 cup granulated sugar	150 ml/$\frac{1}{4}$ pt/$\frac{2}{3}$ cup dry Hereford cider
4 tbsp water	2 cloves
Cinnamon stick	Strip of orange rind

Peel the pears, leaving them whole and their stems intact. Sprinkle the pears with lemon juice to prevent them from discolouring. In a small deep pan dissolve the sugar in the water and bring to the boil with the cinnamon stick. Add the pears, cider, cloves and orange rind. Bring to the boil, cover, and simmer very gently until the pears are tender but not overcooked. Transfer the pears to a deep serving dish and boil down the liquid to a thick syrup. Strain this syrup over the pears, chill and serve with cream.

Nottingham Apple Batter Pudding   (Serves 6)

The Bramley cooking apple came from Southwell, Nottinghamshire, where the original tree, apparently, is still flourishing.

175 g/6 oz/1 cup plain flour	50 g/2 oz/$\frac{1}{2}$ stick butter
Pinch of salt	50 g/2 oz/$\frac{1}{3}$ cup sugar
4 eggs, separated	Pinch of freshly-grated
300 ml/$\frac{1}{2}$ pt/1$\frac{1}{4}$ cups milk	nutmeg
6 small Bramley cooking apples	1 tsp cinnamon
	Castor sugar to sprinkle

Sieve the flour and salt into a large mixing bowl. Make a well in the centre and stir in the egg yolks one at a time. Gradually add the milk to make a smooth batter. Beat well and set aside for an hour.

Peel and core the apples but leave them whole. Place them in a deep, buttered pie dish. Mix the butter with the sugar and spices and stuff each apple with the mixture. Whisk the egg whites until stiff and gently fold them into the batter. Pour this over the apples and bake in a moderately hot oven (190°C/375°F/Gas Mark 5) for about 45–50 minutes. Sprinkle with castor sugar and serve hot with double cream.

Oldbury Gooseberry Tarts   (Makes 6)

These tarts were often made at Whitsuntide in and around Oldbury-on-Severn in Gloucestershire. They are unusual in that they are made with a hot water pastry such as that used for savoury pork and other meat pies.

1 lb hot water pastry (see p. 43)	Demerara sugar
	Beaten egg
About 450 g/1 lb of small gooseberries, cleaned	

Roll out the pastry. Cut out an equal number of large and small circles using a saucer and a teacup as a guide. As the large circles become firm enough to handle, form into self-supporting cup shapes by turning the edges up with the thumb and forefinger. Fill each with gooseberries, and sprinkle with plenty of sugar to taste. Place the lids over each tart, and pinch to close. Leave overnight in the refrigerator to become firm, then glaze with beaten egg before baking in a hot oven (220°C/425°F/Gas Mark 7) for about 20–25 minutes, until golden brown.

Stilton Savoury   (Serves 4–8)

The savoury course is a peculiarly English one, a hot, highly-flavoured mouthful that follows the sweet course but precedes the port and cigars. In wealthy country houses throughout the Midlands, such savouries as this one, together with angels on horse-back, gentleman's relish on toast fingers and others were often enjoyed after long meals: it is a custom worth reviving.

4 slices wholemeal bread	225 g/8 oz Stilton cheese, thinly sliced
1 large bunch of watercress	Pinch of cayenne pepper
4 Comice or Conference pears, peeled, cored, and thinly sliced	

Toast the bread and place in a buttered ovenproof dish. Cover each slice with watercress, slices of pear and slices of cheese. Bake in a moderate oven (180°C/350°F/Gas Mark 4) for 5–10 minutes, or until the cheese has begun to melt. Sprinkle with cayenne pepper, cut into fingers and serve piping hot as a savoury.

Bakewell pudding, made to the original secret recipe, in this Derbyshire town.

Bakewell Pudding (Serves 4–6)

This famous pudding (the real thing here is never called a tart) was first created by accident at a local inn in Bakewell, a small Derbyshire village. Perhaps the cook had drunk one too many the night before, for instead of stirring an egg mixture into the pastry, he spread it on top of the strawberry jam. The result was a hit: so popular were these puffy, chewy puddings that Mrs Wilson, wife of the local tallow chandler, obtained the recipe and began making and selling them from what still remains 'The Old Original Bakewell Pudding Shop'. That recipe, not surprisingly, remains a well-guarded secret, but it is widely imitated.

225 g/8 oz rough puff pastry (see p. 66)
3 tbsp strawberry jam
100 g/4 oz/1 stick butter
75 g/3 oz/½ cup castor sugar
4 eggs, beaten
100 g/4 oz/⅔ cup ground almonds

Roll out the pastry and line a deep 22 cm/9 in oval pie dish. Spread the jam evenly over the pastry base. Cream the butter and sugar together until white and fluffy and gradually stir in the beaten eggs and ground almonds. Pour this mixture over the jam. Bake in a moderately hot oven (200°C/400°F/Gas Mark 6) for about 30 minutes or until the filling is set. Serve hot with custard or cream.

Fine English Bone China

Fine English bone china is an indispensable part of good living in Britain. Full dinner services richly decorated with gilt and hand-enamelling; beautifully-shaped soup tureens, jugs and gravy boats; flowered teapots, matching plates and delicate cups: all adorn polished mahogany tables and well-scrubbed farmhouse sideboards alike, proud foils to enhance the finest in English food and drink. Bone china remains virtually a unique British product, unrivalled above all for its strength, purity of whiteness, translucency and fineness of forms and decorations. Such bone china is in great demand not only in Britain itself, but throughout the world. The centre of this remarkable industry remains where it began, in North Staffordshire around six towns known collectively as the Potteries: Burslem, Hanley, Fenton, Tunstall, Stoke-on-Trent and Longton.

Though English bone china is noted for its whiteness, the development of the china industry here came about early in the seventeenth century because of the discovery of great deposits of red clay, coupled with an abundant source of coal to fire the kilns. Refinements and innovations rapidly revolutionized a cottage pursuit turning out simple red and brown ware into a highly-skilled, progressive industry which reflected the confidence of a prosperous age. New methods of glazing were discovered to decorate elaborate rococo leaf- and vegetable-shaped teapots, plates and cups, and Josiah Wedgwood perfected a pale cream-coloured earthenware with a rich, brilliant glaze that rivalled even Chinese and European porcelain. So fine was this new 'Queen's Ware', so advanced had the industry become, so unique and so famous was this new English china, that by 1774 a dinner and dessert service of over 950 pieces, all hand-decorated with different English scenes, had been commissioned and supplied to Catherine II, Empress of Russia. This famous Catherine Service cost some £3000, yet the advances in methods of production were such that fine earthenware dinner and tea services could now be bought by all but the very poorest classes.

By 1800 there were thousands of brick bottle-ovens concentrated in potbanks (pottery factories) around these six towns, and the industry, its avenues of supply for raw materials, its outlets for sale opened by the Trent and Mersey Canal, continued to expand, culminating in the perfection of the finest – and most refined – tableware of all: bone china. Bone china is so very special because it is made with a unique mix of up to fifty per cent animal bone ash added to china clay and china stone. The calcined bone content gives bone china its extreme strength, and results in china that is both translucent and dazzlingly white, and which can be shaped and decorated in any number of refined forms and shapes. The finest and most elaborately-decorated bone china remains, today as in the past, fit for royalty. Yet the English genius of the Potteries was manifested in its success at producing objects at once beautiful and practical, not only – or even mainly – for the top end of society, but primarily for ordinary people. Today, there are probably few houses in Britain without at least some pieces of fine English bone china – whether special tea cups brought out for special guests, or full, elaborate dinner services. It is an essential part of the national heritage.

Coventry Godcakes

In the past, these small cakes were given by godparents to their godchildren for good luck. Their triangular shape is said to represent the Holy Trinity. They varied in size according to the wealth of the godparent.

450 g/1 lb rough puff pastry (see p. 66)
350 g/12 oz mincemeat

1 egg white, beaten
Granulated sugar to sprinkle

Roll out the pastry to about 3 mm/$\frac{1}{8}$ in thickness and cut into 10cm/4in squares. Cut each square to make two triangles. Place a spoonful of mincemeat in the middle of half of them. Moisten the edges and cover with the remaining triangles. Press the edges together well to seal. Make three small slits in the top of each and brush with beaten egg white. Place on a greased baking tray and sprinkle with sugar. Bake in a hot oven (220°C/425°F/Gas Mark 7) for about 20 minutes or until golden brown.

Grantham Gingerbread

This unusual white gingerbread comes from Grantham in Lincolnshire.

225 g/8 oz/1⅗ cups plain flour
1 tsp baking powder
2 tsp ground ginger

100 g/4 oz/1 stick butter
100 g/4 oz/½ cup castor sugar
2 large eggs

Sieve the flour, baking powder and ginger into a large mixing bowl. Cream the butter and sugar together and beat in the eggs. Stir in the remaining dry ingredients and knead until a smooth dough is formed. Break off small pieces and roll into walnut-size balls. Place on a large well-greased baking tray, leaving room for expansion, and bake in a slow oven (150°C/300°F/Gas Mark 2) for about 1 hour. Allow to cool and harden on the baking tray.

Right: A pint of home-brew and a plate of black pudding at the Old Swan, Netherton.

Pikelets (Makes about 24)

Pikelets, fresh off the griddle, served hot with lashings of butter and mugs of strong tea: hungry boys home from school or working men alike can pack away this Midlands' tea-time staple by the dozen.

450 g/1 lb plain flour
Pinch of salt
10 g/⅓ oz dried yeast

1 tsp sugar
600 ml/1 pt/2½ cups milk
2 eggs, beaten

Heat the milk until tepid, remove from the heat, and dissolve the sugar in it. Sprinkle on the yeast and set aside in a warm place until frothy, about 15 minutes. Meanwhile, sieve the flour and salt into a large mixing bowl. Make a well in the flour and pour in the yeast liquid. Mix well and add the beaten eggs. Beat vigorously for 5–10 minutes. Set aside in a warm place for 1 hour.

To cook the pikelets, lightly grease a griddle or heavy-based frying pan. Heat until a drop of the batter sizzles as it hits the pan. Then drop tablespoons of the batter into the pan and cook until the tops are firm; turn over with a palette knife or spatula and brown the other sides. Continue until all the batter is used. Eat hot with butter and jam for tea. Left-over pikelets can be toasted.

Stop for tea.

49

Home-grown produce from gardens and allotments provide many with fresh, tasty vegetables throughout the year.

Blossom time in the Vale of Evesham.

Herefordshire harvest time.

Opposite: Wye salmon, caught and prepared by the chef at the Royal, Ross-on-Wye.

Drink in the Midlands

Burton-upon-Trent is generally acknowledged as the brewing capital of Britain, a town renowned for the quality of its beers for several centuries; breweries located in this small Staffordshire town and elsewhere supply cities such as Birmingham, Leicester, Derby, Coventry and Stoke with ample casks and kegs of bitter and mild. In the cleaner, quieter countryside of Hereford and Worcester, traditional ciders and perries are produced on small farms and large factories alike, while there are now additionally a number of English vineyards in the region, particularly in these western counties, but also as far north even as Derbyshire. The consumption of bottled mineral water in Britain may well seem a modern habit picked up from the Continent, but in fact the British have 'taken the waters' since before Christianity came to Britain and spa towns such as Droitwich and Buxton were popular with the Roman legions.
Hours: see page 30.

Traditional Beer

The pale amber colour, pronounced hop aroma and palate, and the dry stinging bitterness of Burton ales may well be a national favourite, but in the Midlands this is only one of many styles of beer, all of which have their own fervent and opinionated devotees. Draught Bass, available nationally, certainly remains a classic, while Marston's Pedigree (the only brewery in Burton still using the famous Burton Union system of fermentation) is equally highly regarded. Drinkers in Birmingham seem to prefer somewhat sweeter, softer ales such as Mitchell & Butler's Brew XI, while in the Black Country between the nation's second city and Wolverhampton, dark, medium-dark and light milds from M & B's Highgate Brewery and from Banks's, Hanson's and other local breweries are preferred. To the south, Whitbread's Flowers Original is a fruity, full-flavoured strong ale brewed in Cheltenham.

If the beers of the Midlands defy

Assorted mats and labels of the region.

categorization, it should also be pointed out that not all beer drinkers here are unanimous in their appreciation of the merits of cask-conditioned real ales. Indeed, many actually prefer the consistency, flavour and carbonation of brewery-conditioned keg beers. Contrary to what real ale enthusiasts would have many believe, not all such beers are necessarily weak, tasteless drinks to be scorned; brewers themselves even at the most traditional breweries are often as proud of their keg beers as of their cask brews.

Incidentally, though elsewhere in the country cask-conditioned beers are most often dispensed by traditional beer engines (tall hand pumps operated manually), many Midlands' breweries prefer electric pumps. Thus it is not always immediately apparent from the dispensing equipment whether or not one is drinking cask- or brewery-conditioned ale.

Staffordshire

Bass plc, Burton-upon-Trent, Staffordshire. If Burton ale is a classic British style of beer, then Draught Bass is the classic Burton ale. This famous company was founded in 1777; today the nucleus of a brewing and leisure empire remains on that same original site. Bass operates some thirteen group breweries throughout Great Britain and Northern Ireland, ranging from the immense, highly-modern complex at Burton to the remarkably antiquated Highgate Brewery at Walsall, where the brewing of mild is carried out on equipment and by methods virtually unchanged for generations. The famous Burton Union system, a unique method of continuous circulating fermentation in wooden casks, however, has ceased, though Draught Bass and Worthington White Shield (a strong, bottle-conditioned ale) continue to be produced in Burton and distributed nationally. In common with other national breweries, Bass has amalgamated many other famous names in the industry, including, in this region, Worthington and Mitchell & Butlers. Thus, in most of the Midlands the company operates under the Mitchell & Butler's banner, though in the northern and north-eastern sections, it operates as Bass Worthington, and in parts of Gloucestershire as Welsh Brewers.

Draught Bass o.g. 1044
Draught Worthington o.g. 1037

Bottled-conditioned ale:

Worthington White Shield o.g. 1051

Ind Coope Ltd, Burton-upon-Trent, Staffordshire. Allied Breweries, another national brewing group, has strong brewing links in the Midlands. When pale ale began to supersede porter as a favourite beer style, the firm of Ind Coope, already brewing at Romford, Essex, purchased the Allsop brewery in Burton, and soon began brewing its own pale ales, its double diamond trademark in competition with the red triangle of Bass. Today Ind Coope's Burton brewery is adjacent to Bass's, together dominating this otherwise rather ordinary market town. The connection with the Midlands was further strengthened when Allied Breweries was formed in 1961 through a merger between Ind Coope, Ansell's (a famous Birmingham brewery) and Tetley Walker. Ansell's remains an important name in the Midlands today, with numerous public houses throughout Birmingham and the surrounding areas, but brewing at Ansell's Aston site ceased in 1981. Ansell's beers are now produced at the super-modern complex at Burton. Beers are also brewed here for two other group companies, Hall's of Oxford, and the Aylesbury Brewery Company.

Ind Coope Bitter o.g. 1037
Ind Coope's Draught Burton Ale o.g. 1047

Ansell's Mild o.g. 1035
Ansell's Bitter o.g. 1037

Marston, Thompson & Evershed Ltd, Burton-upon-Trent, Staffordshire. In a town with two huge brewing concerns such as Bass and Ind Coope, Marston's seems very much the small cousin, but the company does have some 700 public houses, concentrated in this region as well as located throughout the country. Now that Bass has ceased using the Burton Union system, Marston's remains the only brewery maintaining this unique method of fermentation. Its Pedigree ale is a classic premium Burton ale.

Mercian Mild o.g. 1032
Burton Bitter o.g. 1037
Pedigree Ale o.g. 1043
Merrie Monk (dark mild) o.g. 1043
Owd Roger o.g. 1080

Five Towns Brewery Ltd, Hanley, Stoke-on-Trent, Staffordshire. This new family-owned brewery located in central Stoke brews three cask-conditioned ales available in the Staffordshire Potteries towns after which it is named, as well as in parts of Shropshire, Derbyshire and Cheshire. The brewery owns one tied house, the Globe Inne at Hanley.

Mild Ale o.g. 1035
Bursley Bitter o.g. 1039
Bennet Ale o.g. 1052

Mild

The Midlands remains a bastion for traditional draught mild, an old style of beer that elsewhere has declined drastically in popularity in recent years. Cheaper than bitter, lower in gravity, and less highly-hopped, mild is the straightforward drink of the public bar, served in a straight-sided glass, the honest, easy-to-down working man's 'jar'. Today mild is considered by many to be an old man's drink; lager, on the other hand, is hyped as the drink of the young. Yet mild resolutely remains, a classic style of beer unique to Britain.

In addition to dark milds, light milds are also popular in the Midlands and in Manchester and the North-West. It is sometimes difficult to distinguish between light (in colour) milds and light (low-gravity) bitters. Some light milds have a soft, almost soapy character, but others are pleasantly sharp and bitter. We suspect that in those parts of the country where bitter does not sell well, such beers are called light milds, while in those parts where mild is hardly drunk, they are sold as light bitters. An age-old example of clever marketing.

West Midlands

Mitchell & Butler's, Birmingham, Wolverhampton and Walsall. Mitchell & Butler's, part of the Bass brewing group (see above) operates three breweries in the West Midlands (Cape Hill, Birmingham; Springfield Brewery, Wolverhampton; and the Highgate Brewery, Walsall) all producing bitters and milds to suit local tastes. The Highgate Brewery is the only one in the world to brew mild exclusively.

> M & B Brew XI o.g. 1040
> M & B Mild o.g. 1036
> M & B Springfield Bitter o.g. 1036
> Highgate Mild (dark mild)
> o.g. 1036
> Highgate Best Mild (light mild)
> o.g. 1036
> Highgate Old Ale (Christmas only) o.g. 1055

Banks's, Park Brewery, Wolverhampton; Hanson's, Dudley Brewery, Dudley. These two well-loved Black Country breweries, both producing traditional milds and bitters, together form the independent company known as Wolverhampton & Dudley Breweries. The company's public houses are located primarily within fifteen miles of the breweries, in and around Wolverhampton, Dudley, West Bromwich, Stourbridge and Halesowen.

> Banks's Mild o.g. 1035.5
> Banks's Bitter o.g. 1038.5
> Hanson's Mild o.g. 1035.5
> Hanson's Bitter o.g. 1038.5

Daniel Batham & Sons Ltd, Brierly Hill, West Midlands. Batham's is a small independent family company brewing mild and strong premium bitter for the Black Country taste. One of the best places to sample Batham's beers is The Vine (also known as the 'Bull and Bladder') located in front of the brewery.

> Mild o.g. 1036
> Bitter o.g. 1043

Davenport's, Birmingham, West Midlands. Davenport's Brewery is an independent Birmingham company with over one hundred tied public houses, most serving cask-conditioned mild and bitter.

> Mild o.g. 1034
> Bitter o.g. 1039

Holden Brewery, Dudley, West Midlands. Another small Black Country brewery, Holden brews a good range of cask-conditioned ales, including a fine winter warmer, available in some fifteen tied public houses located in this region's industrial towns.

> Mild o.g. 1036
> Bitter o.g. 1039
> Special o.g. 1052
> Old Ale (winter only) o.g. 1080

Simpkiss Brewery, Brierly Hill, West Midlands. This family company brews cask-conditioned ales available in some fifteen tied houses as well as in free outlets mainly in the Black Country.

> Bitter o.g. 1037
> Old Ale o.g. 1050

Nottinghamshire

Hardy's & Hanson's, Kimberly Brewery, Nottingham. Deep local sources of water percolated through a subterranean strata of limestone provides liquor ideal for brewing, and the firms of Hardy's and Hanson's have tapped these wells for over 150 years. Rivals for much of that time, these two independent breweries merged in 1930, and continue to supply traditional mild and bitter to the Nottingham area.

> Mild o.g. 1035
> Bitter o.g. 1038

Home Brewery, Nottingham. The Home Brewery is an established East Midlands company brewing cask-conditioned mild and bitter for a tied estate of some 400 public houses.

> Mild o.g. 1036
> Bitter o.g. 1039

Priory Brewers Ltd, Newark-on-Trent, Nottinghamshire. This small brewery was formed in 1980, and supplies the East Midlands free trade.

> Priory Pride Bitter o.g. 1035
> Ned Belcher's Bitter o.g. 1040

J. Shipstone & Son, Star Brewery, Nottingham. Shipstone's is a long-established Nottingham brewery, serving the East Midlands with traditionally-brewed mild and bitter.

> Mild o.g. 1034
> Bitter o.g. 1038

Leicestershire

Everard's Brewery Ltd, Tiger Brewery, Leicester. Though Everard's began as a Leicester brewery in the last century, the merits of the brewing liquor at nearby Burton-upon-Trent led the company to acquire a brewery in that Staffordshire town. The Leicester brewery was closed in 1931, and today, though Everard's headquarters remain in Leicester, all brewing continues in Burton. The company's tied trade is concentrated in Leicester and the surrounding Midlands.

> Mild o.g. 1032.6
> Beacon o.g. 1034.2
> Tiger o.g. 1040.7
> Old Original o.g. 1049.4

G. Ruddle & Company plc, Langham, Oakham, Rutland. Ruddle's of Rutland, the only brewery in what was once the smallest county in England, produces two cask-conditioned ales supplied almost entirely to the free trade throughout the country. Unusually, Ruddle's took the decision in 1977 to sell off their tied public houses (the company now owns only one, the Noel Arms at Langham) to concentrate on the take-home trade, which now represents some seventy per cent of its business. Thus Ruddle's beers in cans and bottles (carbonated at a 'particularly low level so that the flavour is as similar as possible to their draught counterparts') are now widely available, particularly from supermarkets.

> Rutland Bitter o.g. 1032
> Ruddle's County o.g. 1050

Gloucestershire

Whitbread & Co., Cheltenham, Gloucestershire (see p. 152). This national brewing company produces fine traditional ales at its regional brewing headquarters at Cheltenham, formerly the West Country Brewery Holdings, acquired by Whitbread in 1958. Like other national brewing companies, Whitbread has taken over numerous smaller companies, and brewing has been centralized. Nevertheless, famous names such as Flowers (originally of Stratford-upon-Avon) have been maintained.

> West Country Pale Ale
> o.g. 1030–34
> Flowers IPA o.g. 1036–40

Flowers Original o.g. 1043–47

Donnington Brewery, Stow-on-the-Wold, Gloucestershire. The Arkell family have been brewing Donnington beers since 1865. The brewery is located in an idyllic setting, with a mill pond and two water wheels that still drive small pumps and machines. The brewing liquor is drawn from the spring beside the mill pond, and the beers are still brewed to much the same recipes that have always been in use. The beers can be sampled in seventeen Cotswolds inns located in the countryside and villages around the brewery.

XXX (dark mild) o.g. 1033
BB o.g. 1035
SBA o.g. 1040

Hereford & Worcester

Fox & Hounds, Stottesdon, near Kidderminster, Worcestershire. Although this small pub which began brewing in 1979 has a Worcestershire postal address, it is actually located well into Shropshire. About 150 gallons of Dasher's Draught are brewed once or twice a week, available as a 'guest beer' in a few other outlets, as well as in the Fox & Hounds itself.

Dasher's Draught o.g. 1039–40

Malvern Chase Brewery, Sherridge, near Malvern, Worcestershire. This small brewery supplies the free trade within a twenty-five mile radius of the brewery, as well as outlets in London.

Malvern Chase Ale o.g. 1041

Northamptonshire

Mann's, Northampton, Northamptonshire. Mann's, part of the Watney Mann & Truman brewing group, itself a subsidiary of Grand Metropolitan, operates a tied estate of some 600 public houses mainly in Northamptonshire and Lincolnshire, as well as in the borders of surrounding counties. While the old brewery site is now used to brew Carlsberg lager, Mann's Best Bitter and IPA are brewed ('specially for the Midlands') at the group's Norwich Brewery. Other cask-conditioned ales available in some Mann's outlets include Wilson's Original Bitter (from Manchester) and Stag Bitter (from London).

Mann's Traditional Mild

Stilton and port: a classic combination (with, *not* in, the cheese).

Pies from Broadway make a delicious picnic to take to local point-to-points.

o.g. 1034–38
Mann's Traditional Bitter
o.g. 1038–42
Mann's IPA o.g. 1037–41

Derbyshire

Winkle's Saxon Cross Brewery, Buxton, Derbyshire. This small Derbyshire brewery was only started in 1979, but its popular cask-conditioned ales are available across the county in free houses as well as in a limited number of tied houses.

Saxon Cross Mild o.g. 1037
Saxon Cross Bitter o.g. 1037
House Bitter o.g. 1037

Shropshire

Wood Brewery Ltd, Craven Arms, Shropshire. A family brewery begun in 1980 supplying about fifty outlets with cask-conditioned ales.

Parish Bitter o.g. 1038
Wood's Special Bitter o.g. 1043

Shrewsbury & Wem, Shrewsbury, Shropshire. This subsidiary of Greenall Whitley, serves cask-conditioned Wem ales in many of the companies 200-plus tied public houses.

Wem Pale Ale o.g. 1034
Wem Mild o.g. 1036
Wem Best Bitter o.g. 1039

Lincolnshire

George Bateman & Son Ltd, Wainfleet, Lincolnshire. Lincolnshire's only established brewery produces traditional ales available mainly in the east coast and surrounding areas.

Mild o.g. 1032
XB o.g. 1037
XXXB o.g. 1048

Hereward Brewery, Market Deeping, Lincolnshire. Located just inside Lincolnshire, this new mini-brewery was established in 1983 and produces cask-conditioned ales mostly available outside the local area. The largest concentration of outlets is in clubs and hotels in Peterborough.

Hereward Bitter o.g. 1038
Hereward Warrior o.g. 1055

Home-brew Pubs in the Midlands

Most public houses in the country once brewed their own beers. Though this practice is being revived by many pub breweries which in some cases also supply the free trade, the following three historic home-brew pubs in the Midlands deserve to be singled out, for, together with the Blue Anchor at Helston, Cornwall, they were the only public houses in the country to maintain this centuries-old tradition when all others had ceased brewing.

The Old Swan
Halesowen Road
Netherton
West Midlands
Beer is also brewed here for the family's other pub, The White Swan, Holland Street, Dudley.

All Nations
Coalport Road
Madeley
Shropshire

Three Tuns
Bishop's Castle
Shropshire
Three draught beers are brewed on the premises, XXX Bitter, Mild and Steamer, available not only here but also in about half a dozen pubs around the area. Local records first mention brewing at the Three Tuns in the mid-1600s.

Mineral Water

The Midlands gained eminence as a brewing centre because of its numerous sources of spring water rich in mineral salts and other chemicals ideal for brewing. Such underground springs also became the centres for spas where people came to restore themselves by 'taking the waters'. Some of the most famous and fashionable spa towns in Britain are located in this region, towns frequented since Roman days, and which retain the atmosphere of Regency, Victorian and Edwardian times: Cheltenham, Malvern, Royal Leamington Spa, Droitwich, Buxton and Woodhall Spa. Bottled English mineral water, both still and sparkling, from sources such as Ashbourne in Derbyshire, Malvern and Buxton are popular throughout the country, both as drinks on their own, as well as mixers with spirits or juices. Indeed, in these health-conscious days, the concept of spa holidays is even enjoying something of a revival.

Cider and Perry

Herefordshire, Gloucestershire and Worcestershire are important fruit-growing areas so it is not surprising that this western section of the country is also an important area for the production of ciders and perries. As cider is an alcoholic drink made from the fermented juice of apples, so perry is a similar beverage made with the juice of pears. It is less widely available than cider, but it is well worth seeking: an ancient, mellow drink, less sharp than the former, and easy to acquire a taste for.

Special fruits are cultivated for the production of these time-honoured drinks. Though some single variety ciders and perries are produced by farmers for their own use, most that are sold commercially are made from a blend of a number of varieties of either apples or pears. In the case of cider, bittersweet cider apples (high in tannin but low in acid) such as Yarlington Mill, Dabinet, Strawberry Norman, Brown Snout and others are generally blended with bittersharp cider apples (high in both tannin and acid) such as Kingston Black, Stoke Red and others, as well as with sweets and sharps. There are even more varieties of perry pears than cider apples, grown throughout the region on huge, ancient trees that reach remarkable heights and which must be harvested from tall ladders. Oldfield, Huffcap, Mumblehead and Taynton Squash are just a few of the many varieties.

Methods of production and styles of ciders produced vary considerably in the region. H. P. Bulmer is the largest cider company in the world, and its operation is necessarily on an immense scale, resulting in a full range of ciders. Elsewhere, individual farmers still mill and press their own fruit to make cider or perry mainly to drink themselves during the year, a carry-over from the days when farm labourers were paid 'in truck', that is with a daily ration of cider to be drunk out of wooden 'costrels'. Today, even the largest cider companies still follow traditional methods, and supply local public houses in the region with draught ciders to be drawn from the wood. Perry, less widely available, is generally sold in bottles or flagons.

Surprisingly, perhaps, there is no tradition of distilling cider in Britain (in Normandy, French cider is distilled into brandy known as Calvados). However, the Museum of Cider in Hereford may soon begin distilling cider into apple brandy on a small scale. This museum is well worth visiting (address below).

Some Cider and Perry Makers in the Region

H. P. Bulmer Ltd
The Cider Mills
Plough Lane
Hereford
Herefordshire

H. Weston & Sons
Much Marcle
Ledbury
Herefordshire

Symonds' Cider and English Wine Co.
Stoke Lacy
Hereford
Herefordshire

The Cider Mill Gallery
Blanchworth
near Stinchcombe
Dursley
Gloucestershire

English Wine in the Midlands

English vineyards are planted throughout the Midlands, mainly in the southern and western counties such as Gloucestershire, Hereford and Worcester, but even as far north as Derbyshire. Some individual properties in the Midlands do make good wines; viticulture in the region as a whole, however, is probably not yet as organized or as significant as in areas such as the West Country, East Anglia and the South. Three Choirs Vineyards is the largest vineyard in the Midlands and receives visitors for conducted tours by appointment.

Three Choirs Vineyard
Newent
Gloucestershire
The largest vineyard in the Midlands ($17\frac{1}{2}$ acres), it was established in 1973 and is planted mainly with Reichen-

steiner and Müller-Thurgau vines to produce quality white wines that have been awarded honours in competitions at home and in Bordeaux. An apple wine produced from Cox's Orange Pippins and other English varieties is also produced in the Three Choirs winery.

Conducted tours of the vineyard can be arranged by appointment from August to Christmas.

The following vine growers are also members of the English Vineyards Association. Many sell wine direct.

Gloucestershire

Cotswold, Wotton-under-Edge
Charlton Court, Tetbury
Tapestry, Ampney Crucis
Solomon's Tump, Huntley
North Cotswold, Weston Subedge

Hereford and Worcester

Bredon Hill, Bredons Norton
Baughton Vines, Baughton
Stocks, Suckley Orchard
Farmhouse, Droitwich
The Homestead, Droitwich
Astley, Stourport-on-Severn
Kinver, Stourbridge
Broadfield, Bodenham
Croft Castle, Leominster

Leicestershire

Chevelswarde, South Kilworth

Lincolnshire

City of Lincoln, Lincoln

Derbyshire

Renishaw, Renishaw

Some Useful Addresses

Heart of England Tourist Board
P O Box 15
Worcester
Worcestershire

East Midlands Tourist Board
Exchequergate
Lincoln
Lincolnshire

Bass Museum of Brewing
Horninglow Street
Burton-upon-Trent
Staffordshire
Open: Monday–Friday,
10.30–16.30; Saturday and Sunday
(October 1–March 31), 14.00–17.00;

Saturday and Sunday (April 1–September 30), 11.00–17.00

Black Country Museum
Tipton Road
Dudley
West Midlands
Open: Daily (except Saturday),
April–November, 10.00–17.00

Ironbridge Gorge Museum
Ironbridge
Telford
Shropshire
Open: All sites are open daily from
10.00; closed Christmas Day

Gladstone Pottery Museum
Uttoxeter Road
Longton
Stoke-on-Trent
Staffordshire
Open: Daily throughout the year
(closed Mondays October–March)

Museum of Cider
The Cider Mills
Plough Lane
Hereford
Herefordshire
Open: Daily except Tuesdays and
Christmas Day

Rackhams
Corporation Street
Birmingham
The Food Hall in this House of
Fraser store is one of the best in the
Midlands.

Dickinson & Morris Ltd
Melton Mowbray
Leicestershire
Melton Mowbray pork pies.
Ye Olde Original Melton Hunt Cake
is available by mail-order.

Ashbourne Gingerbread Shop
26 St John Street
Ashbourne
Derbyshire

H. H. Collins
Broadway
Worcestershire
Handmade Broadway pies; custom
pies made to order.

Curtis's of Lincoln
164 High Street
Lincoln
Lincolnshire
Lincolnshire and other sausages
made to recipes passed down for
generations.

57

THE THAMES & CHILTERNS AND THE HOME COUNTIES

'I beg your pardon,' said the Mole, pulling himself together with an effort. 'You must think me very rude; but all this is so new to me. So—this—is—a—River!'

'*The* River,' corrected the Rat.

'And you really live by the river? What a jolly life!'

from Kenneth Grahame's *The Wind in the Willows*

England's greatest river, the Thames, starts life high in the Cotswolds, near Cirencester, then descends gently through a most prosperous belt of the country, winding through lush fields and old established upriver towns down to Oxford, Pangbourne, Henley-on-Thames, Marlow and Windsor before reaching the outskirts of the capital itself. Those lands watered by the Thames, and the surrounding country around London known as the Home Counties, share a character that is quintessentially English: at once prosperous, extremely civilized (perhaps even a trifle arrogant), certainly well-fed and generous. Splendid mansions, palaces such as Windsor and Blenheim, smug weekend 'cottages' with vast, striped lawns extending down to the river's edge, royal parks, woodlands, hunting lodges and country estates all testify to the past and continued affluence of this influential section of the country made up of the counties of Surrey, Buckinghamshire, Royal Berkshire, Middlesex, Hertfordshire, Bedfordshire and Oxfordshire.

In the past, nobles, aristocrats and the wealthy who owned town houses in London also kept country houses within easy reach. Kensington Palace, after all, was originally acquired by William III who, tired of life in Whitehall, desired the 'peace of the country' for reasons of health (Kensington was then a village lying outside London). The Palladian Chiswick House, Kew Palace and other splendid mansions once similarly located in the peaceful country are also now virtually within London itself, though in the surrounding areas many other substantial country dwellings (such as Chequers in Buckinghamshire, country residence for prime ministers in office), palaces and more modest homes, too, still manage to provide refuge from the city. Many today who live in this part of the country (dubbed by some 'England's stockbroker belt') work in London, travelling each morning (buried behind the *Financial Times* or *Daily Telegraph*) on the frequent trains which converge on the city centre; if they have second homes – and many do – they are more apt to be cottages in Cornwall, or villas in the Algarve or Costa del Sol rather than country mansions. Such have the times changed.

Yet in other ways, this region itself remains timeless, for it epitomizes, above all, a certain way of English life that will, one senses, never change. The picnic hampers from Fortnum's taken to the Derby, the countless glasses of Pimm's sipped languidly while watching (now and then, but who does, really?) the Henley boat races, the strawberries and champagne at Wimbledon, the luncheon out of the boot of the Rolls at Royal Ascot: these classic English experiences have been enjoyed similarly for generations, by people whose very attire has changed little over the years (blazers and boaters, long dresses and outrageous hats, morning suits, frock coats and toppers).

What, then, do people eat and drink in this heartland of the country? Regional foods, perhaps, are not so immediately apparent here, amidst the magpie affluence of this influential area, as they are in more rural areas or areas with hard-working roots (for the true foods of the country are often born from the land itself or out of necessity). Nevertheless, certain specialities are associated with the region. Aylesbury duck is the most famous, often served simply roasted with an orange or apple sauce. As in many other parts of Britain, a number of baked delicacies are associated with certain towns or localities. Ban-

Butcher in the Oxford Market.

Below: The Thames at Pangbourne.

bury cakes, for instance, are as famous as that small town's market cross. Richmond Maids of Honour have been enjoyed in that Surrey town (now virtually part of London) since the days of Henry VIII. The Bedfordshire clanger is a hefty suet pasty with a savoury filling at one end and a sweet one at the other, thus giving farm labourers a complete meal in one. Poor Knights of Windsor is another venerable old pudding, while Hollygog, New College pudding and Oxford pudding are all associated with that famous University town.

It is not surprising that Oxford should have a number of foods associated with it, for one senses a comfortable, affluent way of living in this town of dreaming spires which has been a centre for learning since the twelfth century. Dons and undergraduates alike relax after their studies with substantial meals, and the University wine society is meticulous in its study of the world's finest vintages.

Butchers in Oxford's indoor market have long associations with particular colleges, supplying them year after year with the finest meat, poultry and game, and with particular specialities such as Oxford john (a lamb steak cut from the leg), Oxford brawn (also called head cheese since it is made from the meat of the pig's head), sausages, quail eggs and the best game in season. Breweries, too, identify strongly with the University. Oxford, not surprisingly with its substantial student body, has always been a significant beer-drinking centre. Indeed, in the past, the colleges themselves once brewed their own beers (Merton, for example, employed a brewer as long ago as the thirteenth century), a practice which did not die out until this century. Morrell's, the only commercial brewery remaining in Oxford, has been trading with some of the colleges for well over a hundred years. Morrell's head brewer, in fact, was the last to brew Chancellor's Ale in the ancient brewhouse of Queen's College (it was fermented in cask, with a potent, mind-expanding original gravity of 1100).

If Morrell's is the only brewery remaining in Oxford (there were once so many that the University was invested with the power to control by rota when each could brew to ensure that there were no gluts of beer to disrupt college

life), the region itself is well represented with fine independent breweries producing distinctive traditional ales. English vineyards thrive in this favoured land, too, in Berkshire, Oxfordshire, Surrey and Hertfordshire (such is the confidence of this region that one grower tells us, with insistent belief, that English wine — his in particular — will soon take its place alongside the very greatest in the world).

English wine — some of it at least — may be good, or even very good, but we suspect that rather more claret is still drunk here than home-produced wines. It seems also somewhat unlikely (though not impossible) that those living in this frightfully proper affluent region would indulge regularly in hefty rural foods like Bedfordshire clangers. Such generalizations, granted, are dangerous, and there is naturally more to this complex area (contrast Oxford's colleges with British Leyland's Cowley factories, for example). Nevertheless, we sense that here, for many, it is as much a question of style as of substance. The sets of bone china handed down for generations, the cut-glass claret jugs and port decanters, the solid silver cutlery are as important as what is actually served and consumed. In villages beside the Thames or nestling in the folds of the Chilterns, in Hertfordshire or in Surrey, an English way of life endures that seems almost from another age — an age, perhaps, when the evenings were that much longer, made for sipping Pimm's or lemonade beside the lawn tennis court. The region also recalls, inevitably, an age of childhood, when we were very young, and the Wide World lay beyond the Wild Wood, when summer days were meant to be spent – with Mole and Ratty – 'simply messing about' by the river.

The unhurried Thames flows today as serenely and majestically as ever, through this comfortable, essentially middle-class swath of the country.

Opposite: Summer evening on the Thames.

Recipes from the Thames & Chilterns and the Home Counties

Melon and Pimm's Cocktail

(Serves 4)

Pimm's may be produced in the City of London, but it is our guess that more than its fair share of this frivolous thirst-quencher is drunk in this part of the country. Melon and Pimm's is a delicious combination.

4 ripe Ogen melons	Orange slices
Black grapes, split in half and de-seeded	Pimm's No. 1 Cup

Cut about a third off the tops of the melons, and scoop out the seeds. Scoop out the melon flesh from the tops into balls, and return to the melons, together with sufficient grapes and orange slices to fill. Add a generous measure of Pimm's to each melon, and chill.

Brown Windsor Soup   (Serves 4)

This smooth, meaty soup, in spite of its rather uninspiring name, is tasty and warming, but only when made with good stewing steak and home-made stock. It was a favourite in Victorian times, but like so many other good solid English foods, it has been sorely wronged by indifferent (or downright tasteless) fare masquerading under the same name in second-rate restaurants and boarding houses.

25 g/1 oz/$\frac{1}{4}$ stick butter	1.2 l/2 pt/5 cups home-made beef stock
1 small onion, finely chopped	Bouquet of fresh herbs
1 small carrot, diced	Salt
Green of leek, chopped	Freshly-ground black pepper
350 g/12 oz stewing steak, trimmed and diced	2 tbsp brown or cream sherry
1 tbsp flour	

Melt the butter in a large saucepan and sauté the onion, carrot and green of leek. Add the beef and brown well. Sprinkle on the flour and stir and cook for a further 5 minutes. Gradually stir in the stock and bring to the boil. Skim and add the bouquet of fresh herbs, and season with salt and pepper to taste. Cover and simmer for about 2 hours. Remove the herbs, liquidize the soup, and strain. Return to a clean saucepan, re-heat and add the sherry. Adjust the seasoning and serve hot.

Roast Aylesbury duck at the Bell at Aston Clinton, near Aylesbury.

Below: The Henley Royal Regatta.

No cheese is made in this region, but one of the very best selections of English farmhouse varieties can be found at Well's Stores, Streatley.

Below: Oxford marmalade, a dark, bittersweet classic.

Oxford Marmalade

Marmalade has been associated with this University town since 1874, when Mrs Sarah Jane Cooper used her mother's recipe to make this breakfast preserve in the kitchens of the Angel Hotel. It was sold from Frank Cooper's shop at 83, The High in distinctive earthenware crocks that have now become collectors' items. Dons, noblemen, clergymen and dignitaries all praised the virtues of this unique preserve (two qualities, apparently, which made it so highly regarded in those days were its supposed laxative and digestive properties). Oxford marmalade never needed to be advertised, but rather was sold through personal recommendation, and was taken to the top of Everest, the jungles of Malaya, even to the South Pole.

While marmalades are made throughout Britain, Oxford marmalade remains special for its particular chunky, coarse, thick pieces of aromatic orange peel set in a darker than normal jelly. The use of bitter Seville oranges is essential. It is interesting to note that some ninety-five per cent of the bitter orange crop grown around that city in Andalusia comes to Britain, for it is primarily only the 'mad English' who so love this unique bittersweet preserve.

'Oxford' Marmalade

(Makes about 4.5 kg/10 lb)

1.35 kg/3 lb Seville oranges	Juice and pips of 2 lemons
3 1/5 pt water	1.35 kg/3 lb castor sugar
	1.35 kg/3 lb brown sugar

Scrub the oranges and put them in a large pan with the water. Bring to the boil and simmer covered for 2 hours. Remove the oranges and set aside the water in which they boiled. Cut the oranges in half and scoop out the pips. Return the pips and the lemon juice and pips to the cooking liquid and boil rapidly for 15 minutes. Sieve into a large heavy-based pan, pressing a wooden spoon into the sieve to squeeze out all the pectin. Cut the oranges into chunks about 6 mm/$\frac{1}{4}$ in thick with a sharp knife. Add the orange chunks to the pan and over a gentle heat stir in the castor and brown sugar. Bring to the boil until setting point is reached. Remove the scum and allow to cool for 5 minutes. Stir well to distribute the fruit, then pour into warm, sterilized pots, seal, cover and label.

Oxford Sausages (Makes about a dozen)

Oxford sausages are rather unusual as they are not made in skins. They are simple and delicious to make at home. Serve them for breakfast with (what else?) hot buttered toast and Oxford marmalade.

225 g/8 oz lean pork	$\frac{1}{2}$ tsp thyme
225 g/8 oz veal	$\frac{1}{2}$ tsp marjoram
75 g/6 oz/$\frac{3}{4}$ cup shredded suet	Pinch of freshly-grated nutmeg
100 g/4 oz/3 cups fresh white breadcrumbs	Salt
Grated rind of 1 lemon	Freshly-ground black pepper
$\frac{1}{2}$ tsp sage	Butter or oil for frying

Trim the pork and veal and mince finely with the suet. Add the breadcrumbs, lemon rind, sage, thyme, marjoram, nutmeg, salt and pepper and mix well. Roll the mixture into sausages on a floured board, and fry in hot butter or oil for about 10 minutes or until cooked through and golden brown. Serve at once.

Bedfordshire Clanger (Serves 4)

This unique complete meal – savoury at one end, sweet at the other – was made for Bedfordshire farm workers to sustain them through long, hard days out in the fields. This boiled suet meal is best eaten hot, with gravy and vegetables with the savoury, and home-made custard with the sweet.

25 g/1 oz/$\frac{1}{4}$ stick butter	Freshly-ground black pepper
1 onion, finely chopped	
450 g/1 lb stewing steak, diced	450 g/1 lb suet crust (see p. 102)
100 g/4 oz ox kidney, cleaned, skinned, cored and diced	2 large cooking apples, peeled, cored and diced
Salt	75 g/3 oz/$\frac{1}{2}$ cup raisins
	2 tbsp sugar

Melt the butter in a frying pan and gently brown the onion, steak and kidney. Season well with salt and pepper. Roll out the suet crust into a rectangle and cut off a thin strip from the shorter side and place in the middle to divide the pastry into two equal parts. On the one half, spread the meat mixture, and on the other, the apples, raisins and sugar. Roll up gently like a Swiss roll, moisten and seal each end. Wrap loosely in greased foil, and place in a large saucepan. Simmer for $1\frac{1}{2}$ hours, adding more water if necessary. Serve the savoury end first, with vegetables and gravy. Re-wrap the remaining end and keep warm until required, then serve with home-made custard.

A Victorian Roller Mill

A hundred years ago or so, nearly every village in the country had its own mill, grinding local grains into flour and animal feed. In Bedfordshire, a county that still remains an important corn-growing centre, there were 400 independent mills in 1855, the year when the Jordan family took over Holme Mills, on the banks of the Ivel River, a tributary of the Ouse; today, they are the only one remaining. The flour mill itself is remarkable, for it remains virtually unchanged since 1896, when rollers were installed in place of the old millstones. At that time, Jordan's must have been a progressive, modern company, for the roller system was an innovation, both faster and more efficient, producing purer, finer, whiter flour than by previous methods. Today, this family company's image is virtually the opposite, for what was then a progressive factory, has now become a charming anachronism, with its water wheel, wooden shutes, wooden channels, gyrating sieves, and leather pulleys; moreover, the flour produced by the slow, water-powered rollers is infinitely purer and more wholesome than that produced by the ultra-high-speed modern mills of today.

Jordan's Wholewheat Bread

(Makes 3 loaves)

1 tbsp malt extract	900 g/2 lb Jordan's
600 ml/1 pt/2½ cups warm water	Wholewheat Flour
	3 tsp salt
1 tbsp dried yeast	50 g/2 oz/½ stick butter

Dissolve the malt extract in the warm water. Sprinkle the dried yeast on the top, and set aside in a warm place until the mixture is frothy. Meanwhile, mix together the flour and the salt, and rub in the butter. Pour the yeast and malt extract liquid into the flour and mix well. Turn out on to a floured board and knead. Divide the dough into three equal parts, and place in loaf tins. Cover with a damp cloth, and place in a warm spot until doubled in size. Bake in a pre-heated moderately hot oven (200°C/400°F/Gas Mark 6) for 10 minutes, then reduce temperature to a moderate heat (180°C/350°F/Gas Mark 4) for a further 25–35 minutes (when done, the loaves should sound hollow when tapped).

Oxford John   (Serves 4)

The origin of this delicious lamb steak is uncertain. Some Oxford butchers we spoke to were unaware of this cut of meat, yet it is served in restaurants in the area and riverside pubs along the Thames, where people in river- and narrow-boats tie up for an evening's drinking and eating. This timeless holiday pursuit epitomizes the civilized pace of this region, when your only concern is getting through the next lock and deciding at which pub to moor for the night.

4 lamb steaks, cut from the leg	2 shallots, finely chopped
Salt	75 g/3 oz/¾ stick butter
Freshly-ground black pepper	1 tbsp flour
Pinch of grated nutmeg	300 ml/½ pt/1¼ cups home-made brown stock
1 tbsp freshly-chopped parsley	2 tsp lemon juice
1 tbsp freshly-chopped thyme	Dash of port

Trim the lamb steaks and season with salt, pepper and nutmeg. Mix the parsley, thyme and shallots together and coat the steaks with the mixture. Melt the butter in a large frying pan and fry until the steaks are gently browned on both sides. Remove to a warmed dish, then stir the flour into the frying pan. Cook for about 3 minutes, then gradually add the stock. Add the lemon juice and port and stir until the sauce begins to thicken. Return the lamb steaks to the frying pan and bring back to the boil. Simmer for a further 5 minutes or until lamb is done to liking. Transfer to a serving dish, and serve immediately.

Aylesbury Duck with Orange Sauce (Serves 2)

The country around Aylesbury is noted for its large number of duck ponds, and locals used to bring their ducks to the town market to sell them. The Aylesbury duck is no longer produced on any scale for the table (most commercial duck breeders use hybrids developed from the Pekin duck), but the Aylesbury Club is a private society formed to preserve the tradition of eating duck in this area.

1 oven-ready duck, 1.125–1.35 kg/2½–3 lb with giblets	5 or 6 oranges
Salt	1 tbsp brown sugar
Freshly-ground black pepper	2 tbsp sherry

Place the duck on a rack in a roasting tin and prick all over with a fork to pierce the skin only. Season well with salt and pepper. Peel one of the oranges and cut it into thick slices. Place these inside the duck. Roast in a pre-heated moderately hot oven (200°C/400°F/Gas Mark 6) for 20 minutes, then reduce to moderate heat (160°C/325°F/Gas Mark 3) and cook for a further 20 minutes. Remove from the oven, lightly prick again, and baste with the pan juices. Cook for a further 30–45 minutes, depending on the size of the duck.

Meanwhile, boil the giblets in water to make about 300 ml/½ pt/1¼ cups of stock and strain. When the duck is ready, transfer to a serving platter and keep warm. Skim off the fat from the roasting tin. In a saucepan, add the juice and the grated rind of 3 oranges. Add the giblet stock and the meat juices, stir in the sugar and sherry. Season and bring to the boil. Simmer for about 5 minutes. Decorate the duck with the remaining orange slices, and serve with the sauce separately.

Poor Knights of Windsor (Serves 4)

The name of this exceedingly simple pudding has a certain frugal grandeur which is in keeping, for it transformed meagre stale bread into a delicious rich dessert. The Poor Knights of Windsor, incidentally, was a military order founded by Edward III in the fourteenth century.

8 slices stale white bread	75 g/3 oz/¾ stick butter
1 tbsp castor sugar	Castor sugar to sprinkle
150 ml/¼ pt/⅔ cup milk	1 tsp ground cinnamon
1 tbsp cream sherry	Strawberry or raspberry jam
4 egg yolks, beaten	

Cut off the crusts from the stale bread and cut each slice in half. Dissolve the sugar in the milk in a shallow dish and stir in the sherry. Dip each slice of bread in this mixture and then into the beaten egg yolks. Melt the butter in a large frying pan and fry the bread until golden brown on both sides. Drain well and keep warm while the remaining pieces are fried. Sprinkle with sugar and cinnamon and serve hot, with strawberry or raspberry jam.

Rough Puff Pastry

(To make 350 g/12 oz pastry)

350 g/12 oz/2½ cups plain flour	75 g/3 oz/⅜ cup lard, chilled
Pinch of salt	2 tsp lemon juice
175 g/6 oz/1½ sticks butter, chilled	150 ml/¼ pt/⅔ cup chilled water

Sieve the flour and salt into a large cold mixing bowl. Cut the butter and lard into small lumps and mix them into the flour with a knife. Add the lemon juice and slowly stir in the chilled water. Mix it in very lightly so as not to break down the fat. Firm into a ball and turn out on to a floured board. Lightly roll the pastry out into a rectangular shape about 6 mm/¼ in thick. Fold it in three and press the edges together firmly to seal in the air. Turn the pastry around 90 degrees, and roll into a rectangle again. Do not roll out beyond the edges as this will force out the air. Fold the pastry in three, seal the edges, and turn, and roll once more. Repeat this operation twice. Finally, roll out the pastry to the required size. Take care not to stretch it, or it will shrink when baked.

Banbury Cakes (Makes about 6)

The original Banbury cake shop has gone, but you can still buy Banbury cakes from most bakers in this small town, as well as in some pubs, too.

225 g/8 oz rough puff pastry	100 g/4 oz/⅔ cup currants
50 g/2 oz/½ stick butter	1 tsp mixed spice
1 tbsp honey	1 tsp cinnamon
50 g/2 oz/½ cup finely-chopped mixed peel	1 tbsp rum
	Milk to brush
	Castor sugar to sprinkle

Roll out the pastry thinly and cut into oval shapes about 15 cm/6 in by 10 cm/4 in. Soften the butter and beat in the honey, then add and mix in the peel, currants, spices and rum. Put a tablespoon of the mixture in the middle of each oval. Fold the pastry over to enclose the filling, and seal the sides together with a little water. Flatten slightly with a rolling pin and make 3 parallel slits in the top. Brush with milk and sprinkle with plenty of castor sugar. Bake in a moderately hot oven (200°C/400°F/Gas Mark 6) for about 20 minutes, or until golden. Serve warm.

Banbury cakes, as famous (almost) as the town's cross.

Richmond Maids of Honour

(Makes about a dozen)

Henry VIII was strolling through the grounds of Hampton Court (so the story goes) when he chanced to encounter a group of Maids of Honour who were eating cakes. Not one to miss an opportunity, he sampled one (of the cakes) and declared it so delicious that they were thereafter called Maids of Honour. They are now made to the well-kept secret traditional recipe at a tea shop near Kew Gardens. Here is one variation.

225 g/½ lb curd cheese
75 g/3 oz/¾ stick butter, softened
1 egg
1 tsp brandy
2 tbsp sugar

3–4 tbsp ground almonds
Grated rind of ½ lemon
A little freshly-grated nutmeg
225 g/½ lb rough puff pastry

Mash the curd cheese with the softened butter. Beat in the egg, brandy, sugar, ground almonds, lemon rind and nutmeg. Roll out the puff pastry and use to line a dozen greased patty tins. Spoon the mixture into the pastry cases about half full and bake in a pre-heated moderately hot oven (200°C/400°F/Gas Mark 6) for 15–20 minutes, until the pastry is golden brown and the filling set.

Hollygog Pudding   (Serves 4–6)

Oxfordshire is a varied county, with a rural character that contrasts with the sophistication of its principal town. This is a typical simple, robust Oxfordshire farm pudding.

225 g/8 oz/1⅗ cup plain flour
Pinch of salt
100 g/4 oz/½ cup lard

300 ml/½ pt/1¼ cups milk
4 tbsp golden syrup

Sieve the flour and salt into a large mixing bowl. Rub in the fat until it resembles fine breadcrumbs. Add enough milk to form a stiff dough. Turn out on to a floured board and roll into a long rectangle. Spread with golden syrup and roll up. Place in a greased deep dish and pour the remaining milk over the roll to about half-way up. Bake in a moderately hot oven (200°C/400°F/Gas Mark 6) for 30–45 minutes, or until golden. Slice and serve with home-made custard.

Home-made Lemonade

(Makes 2.4 l/4 pt)

Home-made lemonade is the perfect drink to sip beside the tennis court or croquet lawn, on those long, balmy midsummer evenings when the sun stays out until eleven o'clock or so.

8 large lemons
675 g/1½ lb/3½ cups sugar
2.4 l/4 pt/10 cups water
Pinch of salt

Lemon slices and fresh spearmint sprigs to decorate

Peel the lemons, and squeeze the juice from them. Add the peel to a large saucepan, together with the sugar, water and salt, and boil vigorously for 5 minutes. Remove the lemon peel, add the lemon juice, mix well, and chill. Serve as it is, or diluted to taste with water, in tall glasses with plenty of ice, decorated with lemon slices and sprigs of fresh spearmint.

Sporting Events

There is nothing quite like the start of summer in England, and in this part of the country, it is heralded not only with strawberries and asparagus, but with unique sporting events that are followed the world over. Such events are important, certainly, for keen followers of racing, tennis and rowing, yet to most people, they really have very little to do with sport.

The Derby, possibly the greatest horse race in the world, is quite simply a great day out for all. Those in morning coats may well enjoy their picnic hampers from Fortnum's, but for our money, we'd rather be on the hill, with the touts and fortune-tellers and good-natured East Enders, munching on bowls of jellied eels, sandwiches and beer, watching the race now and then, but mainly keeping an eye on all the other carry-ons.

Tennis may not be the nation's most popular sport, but during its fortnight duration, Wimbledon grips the nation. For those who actually attend, just as Wimbledon marks the summer, so does a bowl of Wimbledon strawberries and cream,

Pimm's No. 1 Cup, the popular refresher at the Henley Royal Regatta.

and a glass of champagne round off a perfect day at the All England Lawn Tennis and Croquet Club.

Royal Ascot, a four-day meeting, is to many the highlight in the summer social calendar. Women in their most spectacular hats and finest dresses look one another over on Ladies' Day. In the raceground car-parks, visitors enjoy elegant knife-and-fork picnics, while in the modern boxes in the lower, middle and upper tiers of the grandstand, private race-goers and businessmen, their wives and clients, sit down to long, elaborate three-course luncheons served by uniformed waitresses.

The Henley Royal Regatta is another unique sporting and social event. Who, after all, comes to this four-day meeting to watch the rowing? The rowing, like the pretty town of Henley itself, makes an agreeable enough backdrop to the proceedings, but this event, to many, we suspect, is really about dressing up in school blazers and boaters and cotton summer frocks, walking barefoot down the towpath, enjoying long, elaborate picnics in the car-park, even, occasionally, watching a boat or two glide past. The Henley Royal Regatta is a perfect example of the English attitude both to sport and to summer.

A 'simple' picnic before the races.

Ladies' Day at Ascot: showing off in the afternoon sun.

Drink in the Thames & Chilterns and the Home Counties

Both traditional beers and English wines are produced throughout this area, but it is our guess that people here also consume fair amounts of those essentially British drinks such as claret, port and other fine wines, gin and tonic, and, of course, Pimm's No. 1 Cup.
Hours: See p. 30.

Traditional Beer

This relatively small central heartland of the country is particularly fortunate to have a number of fine traditional breweries producing individual and distinctive cask-conditioned beers available generally only within a small radius of the brewery. Morrell's of Oxford, Hook Norton of Banbury, Morland's of Abingdon, Brakspear's of Henley-on-Thames, McMullen's of Hertford are all independent companies producing highly-regarded beers. Additionally, the central position of these diverse counties has enabled other breweries from East Anglia, Kent, the South and West, to supply their traditional beers to a number of free trade outlets. It is always difficult to generalize about styles of beer, but even more so in this diverse region: Morrell's tasty, well-attenuated light ale, for example, contrasts interestingly with Brakspear's richer, sweeter Henley Special, while McMullen's unique light mild, AK, is virtually opposite in character to Hook Norton's potent, dark old ale, Old Hookey. What is indisputable, however, is that the beer drinker here has an exceptional range of styles to choose from, to enjoy in elegant riverside pubs, country inns, riotous students' taverns, and straightforward city 'boozers' and public bars.

Allied Breweries: Aylesbury Brewery Co., Aylesbury and Hall's Oxford and West Brewery, Oxford, Oxfordshire; Ind Coope Benskins, Watford, Hertfordshire; Ind Coope Friary Meux, Godalming, Surrey. Allied Breweries, formed by a merger between Ind Coope, Ansell's and Tetley

Assorted mats and labels of the region.

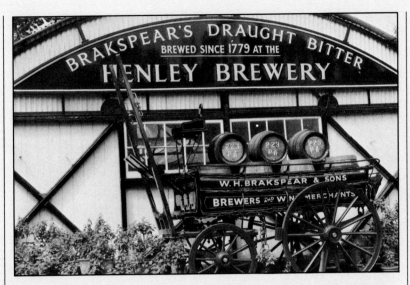

Brakspear's Henley Brewery supplies the Thames area with a fine range of traditional cask-conditioned ales.

Walker, has, like the other national brewing companies, absorbed a large number of regional brewing companies over the years. In this region in particular several marketing companies continue to operate tied house estates under the old breweries' names, even though they are no longer brewing beers. Individual cask-conditioned beers are produced in the company's Romford and Burton breweries, however, to suit local tastes.

ABC Bitter o.g. 1037 (brewed in Burton)
Hall's Harvest Bitter o.g. 1037 (brewed in Burton)
Benskins Bitter o.g. 1037 (brewed in Romford)
Friary Meux Bitter o.g. 1037 (brewed in Romford)

Berkshire

Courage Ltd, The Berkshire Brewery, Reading, Berkshire. Courage, one of the major six national brewing companies and part of the Imperial Group, has an extremely modern brewing complex located on the outskirts of Reading. The complex was developed in the early 1970s to meet the rising demand for English ales and lagers throughout the country as a whole. Though no cask-conditioned beers are produced at Reading, Courage's range of fine traditional ales brewed in Bristol (see p. 135) are available in a number of the company's public houses in the region. Courage produce a unique bottle-conditioned brew, Imperial Russian Stout (o.g. 1104). The Courage Shire Horse Centre is one of the region's popular attractions.

Buckinghamshire

Wethered's Brewery, Marlow, Buckinghamshire Thomas Wethered established the Marlow brewery in 1788, and beers have been brewed continuously on the same site since that time. Wethered's is now part of the Whitbread group (see p. 152), and its distinctive cask ales are available in a number of pubs in the Thames area.

Cask-conditioned ales:

Wethered's Bitter o.g. 1034–37
S.P.A. o.g. 1038–42
Winter Royal o.g. 1050 +

Oxfordshire

Morrell's Brewery Ltd, Oxford, Oxfordshire. Morrell's is an independent family company which has been supplying Oxford and the surrounds within a thirty-mile radius with a full range of traditional ales for over 200 years. Seven traditional draught beers are brewed by Morrell's (Celebration Ale and College Ale are occasional brews, sometimes available in cask), possibly the largest range of cask-conditioned beers produced by an independent brewery in the country.

Light o.g. 1032
Dark Mild o.g. 1032
Bitter o.g. 1036
200 Ale o.g. 1038
Varsity Bitter o.g. 1041
Celebration Ale o.g. 1066
College Ale o.g. 1073

W. H. Brakspear & Sons, Henley-on-Thames, Oxfordshire. The comforting smell of brewing wafts over the Thames during the annual Regatta, and at all other times of the year, in this lovely Oxfordshire riverside town. Brakspear's produces a good range of traditional cask-conditioned ales, served in some of the most pleasant public houses in the land, many located alongside the river.

Mild XXX o.g. 1031
Draught Bitter o.g. 1035
Special Bitter o.g. 1043
Special Bitter XXXX o.g. 1043

Morland & Co. Ltd, Abingdon, Oxfordshire. The Morland family started brewing in West Ilsley during the eighteenth century and acquired the present site in 1861. The present brewhouse was built in 1911 and provides cask-conditioned ales to outlets throughout the Thames Valley area.

Morland Mild (XX) o.g. 1030–34
Morland Bitter (PA) o.g. 1033–37
Morland Best Bitter (BB) o.g. 1040–44

Hook Norton Brewery Co., Banbury, Oxfordshire. One of the few remaining breweries powered by steam, Hook Norton is a small family company where brewing continues as a master craft, using traditional methods and equipment virtually unchanged since the turn of the century when the brewery was re-built and re-equipped. The company's main trading area remains in a radius around Banbury, but Hook Norton ales are also available in a number of free outlets throughout the country.

P.A.B. (Mild) o.g. 1032
Best Bitter o.g. 1036
Old Hookey o.g. 1049

The Glenny Brewery Co., Witney, Oxfordshire. Established in 1982, the Glenny Brewery claims to be the first independent commercial brewery opened in Ox-

Geneva Double Curtain

Britain may be an infant in the wine-producing world, but the country's new and fledgling vine growers and wine makers have set to their task with the fervour and enthusiasm that built an empire. The latest techniques in viticulture and vinification are assiduously studied and employed and great debates take place over the advantages of particular systems or methods.

One of the most significant developments in English viticulture is the use of the Geneva Double Curtain (GDC) system of training vines. The first vineyard in Europe to be planted by this system (pioneered in Geneva, New York not Switzerland) was Westbury Vineyard in Berkshire, and a number of other English vineyards have now followed suit. The GDC system, basically, is a high wire trellis system whereby far fewer vines per acre are trained on high wires to a height of about five feet, resulting in a canopy of increased foliage which allows optimum photosynthesis to take place, even on overcast days (thus the obvious advantage of this system in England). There is a considerably higher cropping density per plant than with conventional systems such as Double Guyot; moreover, because each plant grows large enough to place it under stress, the quality of the fruit is enhanced, say the exponents. Another advantage of the GDC system is that it requires only about 450 vines per acre as opposed to 1500 or more needed by other methods, and thus the initial cost of planting a vineyard is considerably cheaper. The GDC system, like Lenz Moser's high-culture system used in Austria and elsewhere with great success, furthermore allows considerable mechanization in the vineyard, which perhaps makes it more viable for the larger vineyards than for one- or two-acre sites. In spite of these advantages, however, many vineyard owners remain equally convinced of the super-

Westbury Vineyard, Purley, was the first in Europe to be planted using the Geneva Double Curtain system of training vines.

iority of training vines along more conventional lines, like the Double Guyot. The debate, therefore, will no doubt continue – evidence, if any is needed, of the serious commitment to growing grapes in Britain.

---

fordshire this century. One cask-conditioned ale is brewed, available in free outlets and clubs within a fifteen-mile radius of the brewery.

Witney Bitter o.g. 1037

Phillips Brewing Co., Marsh Gibbon, Bicester, Oxfordshire. This new brewery located in an old village has revived a brewing tradition at the Greyhound Inn which dates back at least to the seventeenth century. The beers are available both at the Greyhound, as well as in free outlets within a forty-mile radius.

Heritage Traditional Beer
o.g. 1036
Ailric's Old Ale o.g. 1045

Hertfordshire

Rayment & Co., Furneux Pelham, Buntingford, Hertfordshire. Rayment's is a wholly-owned subsidiary of the Greene King Group, producing one cask-conditioned ale available in Rayment's pubs in east Hertfordshire and north-west Essex, as well as in free outlets further afield.

BBA (Best Burton Ale) o.g. 1036

McMullen & Sons, Hertford, Hertfordshire. In 1904 there were some thirty-five different breweries in Hertfordshire, but today McMullen's are the only major independent remaining, a traditional brewery founded in 1827, supplying beers to 160 pubs in Hertfordshire, Middlesex and Essex. AK Best Mild and Country Bitter are both highly regarded, while Mac's No. 1 is a popular bottled beer (now available in draught, brewery-conditioned form).

AK Best Mild o.g. 1033
Country Bitter o.g. 1041

Victoria Brewery, Ware, Hertfordshire. The Victoria Brewery was established in 1981, the first new brewery in Hertfordshire this century. The brewery is located in an old maltings in Ware, an area which was once Europe's largest malting centre. Three cask-conditioned ales are produced, available throughout Hertfordshire, parts of Cambridgeshire and Essex, and north London.

Victoria Bitter o.g. 1037
Victoria Special o.g. 1043
Hellfire o.g. 1063

Bedfordshire

Charles Wells, Bedford, Bedfordshire. This privately-owned Bedford brewing company owns some 265 public houses, mainly in the country and towns surrounding the brewery in a circle made approximately by Aylesbury and Hertford to the south-west and south-east, and Northampton, Huntingdon and Cambridge to the north-west, north, and north-east.

Eagle Bitter o.g. 1035
Bombardier Bitter o.g. 1042

Surrey

The Pilgrim Brewery, Woldingham, Surrey. Surrey's only brewery began in 1982, and is now supplying the free trade with two cask-conditioned ales.

Surrey Bitter o.g. 1038
Progress Bitter o.g. 1042

English Wine in the Thames & Chilterns and the Home Counties

Vines have been grown in the Thames River Valley since Roman times, but commercial viticulture in the area ceased after the outbreak of World War I. Today, as elsewhere in the country (see pp. 110–111), there has been a considerable revival, indeed a renaissance in growing grapes in Britain. There are a number of vineyards now in the Thames and Chilterns and the Home Counties, and some of the most exciting developments in English viticulture are being carried out here. One vine grower in Berkshire, Bernard Theobald of Westbury Farm, explains, 'The quality of English fruit is superior to any in the world. Cherries from Kent, Cox's Orange Pippin apples, Hampshire strawberries, soft fruit from Evesham are better than any fruit in the world. There is no reason why our climatic conditions should not produce the very best wine grapes. In ten years time,' he confidently adds, 'English wine will be the finest in the world.' This may sound like outrageous braggadocio, but the belief is undoubtedly sincere, and the approach to vine growing, wine making, and wine marketing is both empirical and realistic.

Westbury Farm
Purley
Near Reading
Royal Berkshire
Westbury Vineyard was the first vineyard in Europe to be planted with the Geneva Double Curtain training system for vines (opposite). A number of grape varieties are cultivated, including Müller-Thurgau, Madeleine Angevine, Siegerrebe, Reichensteiner, Seibel, Pinot Noir, Pinot Meunier, Seyval Blanc and others. The Westbury style of white wine is distinctly English (the use of sweet reserve, for example, is frowned upon) producing dry, relatively strong wines that need at least two or three years bottle age (or longer) to develop complexity and to mellow an initially aggressive character. Red wines are also commercially produced here, while the Westbury rosé, produced by fermenting black grapes briefly on the skin to draw out the required amount of colour, is, says Bernard Theobold, 'the finest rosé in the world'. Westbury Farm is a mixed commercial farm, with traditional crops, orchards and fishing.

Group visits with wine tasting and a vineyard meal by appointment only.

Gamlingay Vineyard
Gamlingay
Sandy
Bedfordshire
Gamlingay is one of the driest spots in England, one reason the owners chose this area between Bedford and Cambridge to plant their vineyard in 1969. Today the ten-acre site, consisting of light sandy well-draining soil, is planted with Müller-Thurgau, Reichensteiner and Scheurebe grapes, and the wines produced are exported as far away as the USA and Japan.

Wines can be purchased direct from the vineyard or by post, and guided tours are available by appointment.

Hascombe Vineyard
Hascombe
Godalming
Surrey
This Surrey vineyard, first planted in 1969, now comprises eight acres of fruit-bearing vines, two-thirds of which are Müller-Thurgau, and the remaining third Seyval Blanc. In addition to the dry and medium-dry wines produced, Hascombe also produces vintage ciders and Surrey 'scrumpy'.

In addition to the above vineyards, the following are members of the English Vineyards Association. Many sell wine direct.

Bedfordshire

Woburn, Woburn
Merton Grange, Gamlingay

Berkshire

Joyous Garde, Wargrave
Ascot Farm, Ascot
Stanlake Park, Twyford
Bowden, Pangbourne
Frogmore, Bradfield
Hillfoot, Beenham
Holt, Newbury
Kirby, Inkpen
Northbourne Manor, Chievey

Hertfordshire

Rowney, Sawbridgeworth
Saint Giles, Welwyn
Felden Grange, Felden
Frithsden, Berkhamsted

Oxfordshire

Hendred, Wantage
The Bothy, Abingdon
Wychwood, Shipton-under-Wychwood
Newington Grounds, Newington

Surrey

Hembury, Woking
Whitethorne, Oxted
Ockley, Ockley

Some Useful Addresses

Thames & Chilterns Tourist Board
8 The Market Place
Abingdon
Oxfordshire

Wells Stores
Streatley-on-Thames
near Reading
Berkshire
One of the best selections of English cheese in the country in a village shop run by acknowledged cheese expert and author Patrick Rance. International mail order service.

W. Jordan & Son Ltd
Holme Mills
Biggleswade
Bedfordshire
Jordan's range of flours and cereals is available nationally as well as from the shop at Holme Mills.

Loseley Park Farms
Loseley Park
Guildford
Surrey
High-quality dairy products from the rich milk of Loseley's pedigree Jersey herd. Loseley House is an Elizabethan stately home open to the public from June to September, Wednesday to Saturday, 14.00–17.00.

EAST ANGLIA

East Anglia seems remote, despite the evidence to the contrary. The arteries of the country – the main railway lines, motorways and roads which pump lifeblood to those areas they connect – somehow bypass this land mass which juts alone into the cold North Sea. Because it is so close to London, compared, say, to Cornwall, Dyfed or Ross & Cromarty, its remoteness is intensified. Armless windwills punctuate a flat horizon – too flat, one thinks, to be England. The rich, peaty, reclaimed earth of the fens is criss-crossed by wide channels with names such as Sixteen-Foot Drain, Vermuden's Drain and South Holland Main Drain. This is a remarkable below-sea-level landscape where tulips are cultivated alongside barley, wheat and blue-green rye, the flat fields extending right up to the very edge of villages such as Marshland St James, Friday Bridge, and Walton Highway.

Elsewhere, in Norfolk, the Broads – those vast inland lakes whose reed-covered banks provide sanctuary for wildfowl – remain a secret world, closed and inaccessible to those of us marooned on land. The docks of Great Yarmouth, where over a thousand herring boats once tied up – so many, they say, that a man could walk across them to the other side – are now silent, a bizarre contrast to the bingo halls and neon amusement arcades just across on the Marine Parade. Below Yarmouth and Lowestoft, Suffolk villages such as Southwold and Aldeburgh stand at the end of small roads some miles off the main road, separated from the rest of the county by wide shallow marshes. The main street of Aldeburgh is lined with elegant, well-kept town houses. Yet it trails lamely off into nowhere, a curious dead end. Inland, small villages such as Debenham and Woodbridge seem just as remote: insular and proudly self-contained.

The region throughout is hard-working, essentially a rich, agricultural land with a favoured stretch of coast, a land which gives a plentiful yield to an enterprising people who take full advantage of its bounty. Samphire, for example, grows throughout Britain, but nowhere else except East Anglia is this succulent marsh plant harvested and enjoyed on any regular scale. The fields of grain, coastal marshes and flat fens provide shelter for a profusion of game birds: partridge, quail, woodcock, wild duck and pheasant. Rabbit and hare, too, remain traditional East Anglian fare, a carry-over from the days when beef or lamb were not so plentiful (such 'butcher's meat' was purchased only for special occasions). Just as samphire and seakale are gathered from the shore – a gift from nature accepted with pleasure – so do many people stalk their fields with a gun, not for mere sport, but for the end result which finds its way into the pot.

Each coastal village or town has developed its own special industry. Cromer is famous for its small, weighty crabs. Come to this village in summer and houses by the road have their front windows open, displaying trays of boiled crab just off the boats and freshly cooked. Fishermen from nearby Stiffkey (pronounced 'Stookey'), on the other hand, gather some of the best cockles in the British Isles (though this might be disputed by fishermen from Leigh-on-Sea in Essex, where these inexpensive bivalves are gathered from the mouth of the Thames, unloaded with primitive man-yokes, and boiled in tin shacks along the shore). Wells-next-the-Sea specializes in whelks, the large chewy gastropods so popular at shellfish bars and stands throughout the country (some eighty per cent of whelks in England come from this small village), while Southend, next to Leigh, is famous for its whitebait (an annual Whitebait Festival is held every September to bless the catch). The oyster beds of Colchester have been exploited since Roman times, while a daily harvest of sea salt is still gathered from the Blackwater at Maldon, Essex.

Inland, the fields of East Anglia, set under a

Cockles at Leigh-on-Sea.

wide eastern sky, dance lightly in the wind, a waving vista of wheat, barley and rye. This has always been a corn-growing area, a fact reflected in simple, ample foods such as Norfolk and Suffolk dumplings. Local barley, too, is important for this region's brewing industry. While grain remains the staple agricultural crop, East Anglia is equally well-known as a centre for soft fruit farming, especially around areas such as Wisbech and Tiptree. Redcurrants and blackcurrants, succulent strawberries, raspberries, giant blackberries, cherries and plums are sold from roadside stands, and many come here to pick the fruit themselves, eating as much as they gather. This rich profusion of fruit is made into jam in households throughout the region, while towns such as Tiptree and Elsenham are associated with the commercially-made product. The Elsenham firm, though well-known throughout the world, still remains very much a 'cottage industry', its Norfolk strawberry preserves hand-made in small batches in old copper pans.

A certain spirit of enterprise is apparent throughout the region, for both natives and newcomers display a pride in local products and produce combined with a welcome willingness to exploit their natural riches. Local industries have long made use of the region's heritage. The abundant herring landed at Great Yarmouth led to the rise of large and numerous smokehouses in the dock area of that town, for example, and this indigenous industry remains today, even though the local herring have long gone (a situation which may shortly change, for the traditional North Sea grounds have reopened). Red herrings, left in brine for a week, then smoked over oak dust and shruff, or very fine wood shavings, until hard, dry and pungent, were once a daily staple (today they are mainly exported), but it was the milder Yarmouth bloater that was even more loved. Indeed, generations of holiday-

Herrings & Holidays

Great Yarmouth is famous for two things: herrings and holidays. Stroll around the Marine Parade, and you will see plenty of evidence of the latter: amusement arcades, bingo halls, shops selling rock, T-shirts, candy floss and ice-cream, 'caffs' and chip shops, holiday parks and caravan sites. But as for the former, the Yarmouth herring trade is not what it was at the beginning of this century when over a thousand boats worked out of the harbour. The traditional North Sea herring grounds have been closed this past twenty years, but they have now reopened; perhaps we will see a re-emergence of this traditional East Anglian industry.

In the past, herring was the everyday staple, and a monotonous diet it must have been: herring and tatties – boiled potatoes and red herring – day in and day out. Reds, cured in brine, then smoked for five days until strong and hard as a rock, were a necessary staple in the days before refrigeration. Though they are still produced commercially in Yarmouth, few are eaten in this country today. Rather, they are sold to traditional markets such as Egypt, Greece and the Caribbean. A well-cured Yarmouth bloater, however, is another kettle of fish, and a rare treat it is for those who don't live in this part of the country.

Bloaters are much milder than red herrings. To produce them, fresh ungutted herring are put in brine for only eighteen to twenty minutes. Then they are threaded on to spits and placed in the smokehouse over a very slow fire of oak billets and oak dust. They stay in the smokehouse for twenty-four hours, and as the smoke slowly cures them, they swell up and become 'bloaters'. Bloaters, like kippers, are cold-smoked, so they must be cooked before eating. Cut the head off, split the fish and clean, then run your thumb under the backbone to remove it. Fry or grill the bloater with a bit of butter. Beautiful.

Bloaters.

The trough mill at the Aspall Cyder House was built in 1728 from granite stones from Normandy.

makers paid half a crown to send home as souvenirs a small wooden box containing this gamy smoked fish: 'A present from Yarmouth.'

Ham and bacon curing is another traditional East Anglian industry whose fame has spread beyond the borders of the region. Suffolk sweet-pickled hams are among the finest in the land, available in Harrods and other such prestigious establishments. And when it comes to publicizing local products, what marketing man could have conceived of a better promotion for local bacon than the traditional Dunmow Flitch Trial (see p. 80), a famous annual custom carried on in Great Dunmow since the thirteenth century!

Norfolk is well-known for its turkeys (they used to be marched to London in order to reach the market for Christmas, a journey which took three months) and now boasts the largest turkey farm in Europe. Asparagus, once considered mainly a market crop grown in the gardens of Evesham, is cultivated here on a large agricultural scale, making East Anglia one of the most important regions for this great English delicacy.

Hot English mustard, produced from seed grown in brilliant yellow fields surrounding the region's capital, Norwich, is another world-renowned product from this rich land. Commercial oysterages in East and West Mersea and Orford continue to exploit this great native delicacy as they have for centuries, while in recent years a number of successful English vineyards have been planted, in Essex, Cambridgeshire, Suffolk and Norfolk.

And yet, despite all this activity, a glorious, slow pace still remains, like the luxurious indolence of a punt poled languidly down the slow, lazy Cam. For East Anglia, after all, *is* remote. Somehow the pace and the attendant worries of the modern age have passed by, sped elsewhere on motorways and highways which never came here. It remains essentially a land of rural simplicity, of cottages and churches thatched with Norfolk reed, of insular villages where locals look twice at strangers who enter the public bar, of landscapes with the pastoral quietude of a canvas by Constable: a land where food can be had for the gathering, where life remains as easy-going, as unhurried as is ever possible.

Recipes from East Anglia

Grilled Norfolk Herrings with Mustard   (Serves 4)

When the Colmans began milling mustard in Norwich, the Norfolk herring industry was at its peak, and the resulting combination of mustard and fresh herring became a popular one.

4 fresh herrings, cleaned and scaled	1 tsp vinegar
1 tsp English mustard powder	1 tsp sugar

Cut a few slashes into the sides of each cleaned herring. Mix the mustard powder, vinegar and sugar, and spread over the herrings. Place on a grill pan, and grill for five minutes each side. Serve at once.

Angels on Horseback   (makes 1 dozen)

Native oysters from Colchester (available only in months with an 'r') are among the best in the land. Pacific *gigas* oysters are plentiful all the year, and those from Butley Orford are particularly tasty. While *aficionados* prefer their oysters in the simplest way possible, that is, raw on the half shell, this recipe is a traditional favourite; in the past it would have been served as a 'savoury' after the meal, but it is equally suitable as an appetizer.

1 dozen oysters, shelled	Tabasco sauce
Lemon juice	12 rashers streaky bacon
Salt	Watercress to garnish

Dip the oysters in lemon juice and sprinkle with salt and a drop of tabasco. Cut off the rind from the bacon, and roll each oyster up in one rasher. Secure with a cocktail stick. Just before serving, place under a hot grill for 4–6 minutes, until the bacon is crisp. Be careful not to overcook as the oysters will toughen. Garnish with watercress and serve at once.

Cockles, whelks and prawns at a shellfish stand at Leigh-on-Sea.

Pacific oysters raised in the Butley River are sorted for the table.

Baked Cromer Crab   (Serves 2)

The crabs caught by fishermen at Cromer are considerably smaller than those from the West Country, but they are particularly succulent and fleshy, with a high proportion of rich, dark meat. Because they are too small to fetch good prices in London's Billingsgate, almost the entire catch is sold locally by fishermen and fishwives, in roadside stalls, or from displays set up inside front room windows. To tell if a crab is full, feel it for its weight, and examine its tail end: a full shell will separate from its bottom half, exposing a white section.

2 boiled crabs	2 tbsp malt vinegar
4 tbsp fresh white	Salt
breadcrumbs	Pinch of cayenne
Juice of 1 lemon	50 g/2 oz/$\frac{2}{3}$ cup grated
	cheese

Lay the crabs on their backs and twist off the claws and legs and set aside. Pull the body and shell apart and discard any green matter and the so-called 'dead man's fingers' (the greyish gills). Scoop out all the meat from the shells and put in a mixing bowl. Crack the claws with a hammer to obtain all the white meat, and add to the dark meat. Mix the breadcrumbs with lemon juice, vinegar, cayenne and salt. Add half this to the crab meat and mix well. Clean the shells, and pile in the crab mixture. Top with remaining breadcrumb mixture and grated cheese, and bake in a hot oven (220°C/425°F/Gas Mark 7) for 10–15 minutes, until cheese is brown.

Cromer crabs for sale.

Asparagus

There is hardly anything which the English await more eagerly than the year's first taste of asparagus: picked up and eaten with the fingers, dripping with melted butter or rich hollandaise. When it finally comes, the asparagus season is maddeningly brief, but for a short period anyway – in spite of what the weather is doing – it is evidence (together with Wimbledon, the Test match at Lord's, and strawberries) that the English summer has arrived.

Asparagus is grown in many private gardens, but the main commercial centres are East Anglia and, to a lesser degree, the Vale of Evesham. The plant, which is a member of the lily family, consists of a base 'crown' which throws out some thirty to forty spears of asparagus in a season. The cutting must stop around the end of June to allow the crowns to go to fern and thus regenerate. Asparagus is sold mainly in four grades, depending on its size. The largest grade, Jumbo, is the most expensive; Extra Select, Select and Choice are correspondingly smaller and cheaper.

Norfolk Turkey Breast with Asparagus   (Serves 4)

Norfolk, once famous for its small black-plumed turkeys, today remains an important turkey-rearing centre, though the days when hundreds of birds could be seen walking to market in London are long gone. While roast turkey is the traditional Christmas favourite, smaller turkey joints or breasts can be enjoyed all the year round. This recipe combines two superb East Anglian products.

4 portions skinned turkey	150 ml/$\frac{1}{4}$ pt/$\frac{2}{3}$ cup cream
breast	Freshly-chopped sage
Salt	50 g/2 oz cooked ham, diced
Freshly-ground black	1 bundle cooked asparagus
pepper	or 1 small tin of
Flour to coat	asparagus tips
25 g/1 oz/$\frac{1}{4}$ stick butter	

Season turkey breasts and lightly coat with flour. Heat butter in frying pan, and sauté turkey until firm. Add the cream and sprinkle with freshly chopped sage. Cover and simmer gently for about 15–20 minutes. Uncover, adjust seasoning, and lay diced ham and cooked asparagus over the turkey. Cover and heat for a few more minutes, then serve at once.

The Dunmow Flitch Trial

The Dunmow Flitch Trial is a curious custom dating back to the thirteenth century, held in the town of Great Dunmow, Essex, every third year on Whit Monday. A flitch – that is, a side of bacon – is awarded to a local couple who prove to a jury of villagers that they have not argued during the previous year. Traditionally, the flitch of bacon has been supplied by a local curer; although the local bacon factory recently ceased trading, a new Dunmow bacon company has been started, and they will participate in the next trials.

Norfolk Salt Beef and Dumplings   (Serves 6–8)

In Norfolk and Suffolk, dumplings are called 'swimmers' or 'floaters' because they are traditionally made with bread dough, not suet, and thus they float rather than sink. In hard times, they were a staple, served on their own with just a bit of gravy but they are an excellent accompaniment to Norfolk salt beef.

450 g/1 lb Maldon sea salt	1.35–1.8 kg/3–4 lb
225 g/8 oz/1 cup brown	silverside of beef
sugar	4 carrots, sliced
3.6 l/6 pt/15 cups water	2 bay leaves
50 g/2 oz saltpetre	2 onions, chopped
(obtainable from most	12 black peppercorns
chemists)	Bouquet garni

Norfolk Dumplings

900 g/2 lb plain flour	50 g/2 oz/$\frac{1}{2}$ stick butter
Pinch of salt	2 tsp sugar
600 ml/1 pt/2$\frac{1}{2}$ cups milk	25 g/1 oz dried yeast

In a very clean, large pot or plastic tub, mix the brine ingredients (salt, sugar, saltpetre and water). Place the meat in the brine, and keep submerged with a clean plate. Cover the tub, and leave in a cool place for 5–7 days, turning periodically. To cook, place the salt beef in a large saucepan, together with carrots, onions, bay leaves, peppercorns and bouquet garni. Cover with water and bring to the boil, skim, and leave to simmer for 2$\frac{1}{2}$–3 hours, or until tender.

To make the dumplings, sieve the flour and salt into a large mixing bowl. Gently heat the milk and butter until the latter has melted. Add the sugar to the milk and butter and allow to cool until lukewarm, then sprinkle on the dried yeast. Set aside for 15 minutes until frothy. Pour this mixture into the flour, and mix to a firm dough. Turn out on to a floured board and knead until smooth and elastic. Return to the bowl, cover with a damp cloth, and set aside in a warm place until the dough has doubled in size. Knead again and form into small balls. Leave to rise in a warm place for a further 15 minutes.

To cook, drop the balls into a large pan of fast-boiling salted water (the cooking liquid left from the salt beef is ideal, but make sure that there is sufficient room in the pot). Cover and boil for 10–15 minutes, until the dumplings rise to the surface. Strain and serve with salt beef, together with English mustard.

Huntingdon Fidget Pie   (Serves 4–6)

This typical country pie, consisting of meat, onions and apples, is a combination that has been popular since the Middle Ages. Rather runny in consistency, the pie does indeed seem to 'fidget' on the plate.

675 g/1$\frac{1}{2}$ lb thick bacon,	2 tsp sugar
diced	150 ml/$\frac{1}{4}$ pt/$\frac{2}{3}$ cup stock
2 onions, sliced	Freshly-chopped thyme
3 cooking apples, peeled	225 g/$\frac{1}{2}$ lb shortcrust pastry
and sliced	(see p. 25)
Salt	A little milk
Freshly-ground black	
pepper	

Grease a large pie dish, and layer alternately with bacon, onion and apple. Season each layer well, sprinkle with a little sugar, and end with a layer of bacon. Pour on enough stock to cover the filling, and add the thyme. Roll out the pastry to make a lid for the pie, and brush with milk. Bake in a pre-heated moderately hot oven (190°C/375°F/Gas Mark 5) for 20 minutes, then lower the heat (180°C/350°F/Gas Mark 4) and cook for a further hour. Cover with foil if pastry is browning too much. Serve hot with East Anglian cyder or beer.

Jugged Hare   (Serves 4)

Hare, like rabbit, is traditional East Anglian fare, the sort of field game hunted by farmers as much to keep their fields from being overrun as for the pot. Today both are available in numerous game shops throughout the region. Jugged hare is a classic English dish, so-called because the hare was originally cooked in a tall jug set in a deep pan of water. Ask your butcher to preserve the hare blood.

1 hare, jointed
Seasoned flour for coating
Bouquet of fresh herbs
4 rashers of bacon, chopped
2 onions, chopped
6 cloves
1 tsp allspice
Grated rind of 1 lemon
Salt
Freshly-ground black
  pepper
1 tbsp butter
1 tbsp flour
Blood from the hare
Splash of port

Lightly flour the joints of hare and place in a casserole. Add the herbs, bacon, onion, spices and lemon rind. Season with salt and pepper. Cover with water, slowly bring to the boil, then cover and transfer to a slow oven (160°C/325°F/Gas Mark 3) for 2–2½ hours or until the hare is tender. When cooked, remove the hare, onions and bacon with a slotted spoon, and keep hot on a warmed serving dish. Discard the bouquet of herbs and cloves. In a small saucepan, melt the butter and stir in the flour. Gradually add the cooking liquid, and mix well until thickened. Stir in the hare blood, and add a splash of port to taste, mix well and adjust seasoning. Pour this sauce over the hare, and serve with redcurrant jelly.

Casserole of Pheasant   (Serves 6)

Game is plentiful throughout the region, and wild-fowling for mallard, teal, partridge and pheasant are timeless East Anglian activities.

25 g/1 oz/¼ stick butter
A brace of pheasant,
  prepared and jointed
225 g/8 oz button
  mushrooms
225 g/8 oz baby onions
2 tbsp flour
1 glass red wine
Grated rind and juice of 1
  large orange
1 tbsp redcurrant jelly
600 ml/1 pt/2½ cups stock
1 bouquet garni
Salt
Freshly-ground black
  pepper
Freshly-chopped parsley

Melt the butter in a large casserole and brown the pheasant pieces. Remove and add the onions and mushrooms. Fry until the onions are golden. Remove from the pan and add the flour, stirring to take in the fat. Add the rest of the ingredients except the parsley and bring to the boil. Return the pheasants to the pot and surround with mushrooms and onions. Cover tightly and cook in a moderate oven (160°C/325°F/Gas Mark 3) for 1½–2 hours. Remove the pheasant pieces, mushrooms and onions to a warmed serving platter. Skim the cooking liquid and reduce if necessary. Adjust seasoning, pour over the pheasants, and garnish with parsley.

Norfolk Partridge Pot   (Serves 4)

4 partridge, jointed
Salt
Freshly-ground black
  pepper
100 g/4 oz/1¼ cups fine
  oatmeal
175 g/6 oz cooked ham,
  diced
1 bay leaf
3 cloves
Sprig of thyme
1 onion, chopped
225 g/½ lb tomatoes, skinned
  and pulped
175 g/6 oz mushrooms,
  sliced
300 ml/½ pt/1¼ cups port or
  red wine

Season the partridge pieces and coat with fine oatmeal. In a large casserole, lay them on a bed of diced ham. Add the herbs and other ingredients, and pour over sufficient port or red wine to cover. Put on lid and place in a slow oven (140°C/275°F/Gas Mark 1) for 2½ hours. Serve at once, or – even better – leave for a day, then re-heat for another hour or so.

The marshlands of East Anglia harbour a profusion of game.

Suffolk Sweet-pickled Hams

'I know my hams like my women,' the butcher told us. 'Some you think, "oh what a lovely leg"; others you say, "no, don't like the look of that one".' He was fondly holding one of his shiny black sweet-pickled Suffolk hams, 'a little one,' he said, 'not a bad leg'. Flitches of sweet-pickled bacon, and black, treacly chaps were hanging from a rail in the open air of the butcher's yard. 'But it's dying out.' He shook his head sadly. 'Young people today, they don't want to know. I spent Sundays out there looking after my hams. Today, they won't do it.'

Indeed, there are few remaining butchers who still make the old-fashioned sweet-pickled hams of Suffolk; few, for that matter, throughout the country who take the time and trouble to cure hams to traditional regional recipes. It takes nearly ten weeks to cure a Suffolk ham properly. The best butchers are meticulous in choosing their hams, buying 'on the hoof' and slaughtering themselves.

The hams are first soaked in brine for four weeks or more, then placed in a thick, black treacly solution, the recipe for which is a well-guarded secret (the prime ingredients, we are told, are Barbados and demerara sugars, salt and saltpetre). The hams stay in this sweet pickle for three weeks to a month, during which time they must be turned daily, for if they 'kiss' then the cure will not take. Finally, the hams are removed from this sticky solution, and smoked over a low fire of applewood, oak and oak sawdust kept barely smouldering for four or five days.

The result is splendid, both to look at and to taste. Well-made hams have a deep black sheen, and will keep and improve for up to a year, if kept in a cool, well-ventilated store. To cook a ham, place it in a large pot, cover it with water and barely simmer for 20 minutes to the pound. A tip for bringing flavour to hams: the night before

Oysters are never fresher than those at the Butley Orford Oysterage.

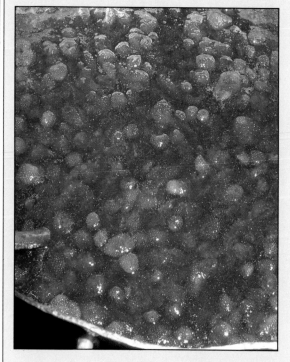

Strawberry jam at Elsenham's.

cooking a ham, take it from the larder, put it in a ham bag or pillow case, and hang it outside, 'in God's given air, as high as you can – but mind the cats'. Once a whole ham is carved down to the bone, scrape all the remaining meat off and mince it twice, add some stock or cooking liquor to it and season well with salt and pepper, then pack into small pots and seal with melted butter.

Though Suffolk hams are a traditional Christmas speciality, less expensive Suffolk sweet-pickled bacon and chaps are regional delicacies that can be enjoyed throughout the year.

A butcher in Debenham displays his Suffolk sweet-pickled ham.

Fruit Preserves

Fruit farming is carried on throughout East Anglia. For Londoners and many from further afield, picking fruit direct from the farms provides a perfect outing.

English fruit is possibly the best in the world, for it combines a ripe sweetness with an underlying fruity acidity, qualities which make it ideal for preserving. Not surprisingly, with the abundance of fruit here, the region has become a centre for the commercial production of jams and preserves. Three of the best-known firms in the country are located here, Wilkin's & Sons of Tiptree, Chivers Jams and Elsenham Quality Foods. At Elsenham, numerous varieties of preserves are still prepared by hand, in old copper pots hardly larger than a housewife's. But there is really nothing more satisfying than making your own: stirring the sticky, bubbling pot of fruit, watching the dab on the saucer wrinkle, bottling and labelling with hand-written stickers, and storing on a larder shelf – then, in the dead of winter, enjoying fruits you picked yourself in the heat of summer, now preserved in a rich, dark, sweet jelly.

Strawberry Jam

(Makes about 2.5 kg/5 lbs)

1.35 kg/3 lb fresh, firm strawberries
Juice of 1 lemon

1.35 kg/3 lb granulated sugar

Hull the strawberries. Place in a large heavy-bottomed pan with the lemon juice and heat gently for 5–10 minutes. Meanwhile, put the sugar into an ovenproof dish and gently warm in a low oven for 10–15 minutes. Add the warmed sugar to the pan of strawberries, and stir continuously until the sugar dissolves. Bring this mixture slowly to the boil, and cook briskly until the setting point is reached (a drop on a cold saucer will solidify in one minute and have a wrinkled skin). Be careful not to overboil, as the fruit will lose its bright colour. Skim and leave aside to cool for 20 minutes, or until a skin starts to form on the surface. Pour into hot sterilized jars and seal.

83

Suffolk Stew (Serves 4–6)

Stone-ground bread and hard Suffolk cheese was once the daily diet of the field and farm workers, but at weekends, there was always a hearty country spread. This rustic stew (which comes from the elegant Le Talbooth Restaurant) is the sort of food to have on a cold February day, when harsh winter winds drive across open fenlands and marshes.

50 g/2 oz/$\frac{1}{3}$ cup brown lentils	2 onions, chopped
25 g/1 oz/$\frac{1}{4}$ cup haricot beans	900 g/2 lb best-end-of-neck or breast of lamb
25 g/1 oz/$\frac{1}{4}$ cup pearl barley	2 bay leaves
2 large potatoes, peeled and roughly chopped	Salt
1 large turnip, peeled and roughly chopped	Freshly-ground black pepper
4 carrots, chopped	Sprig of fresh parsley
	Sprig of thyme
	1.8 l/3 pt/7$\frac{1}{2}$ cups water

Soak the lentils and beans in cold water overnight. The next day, put all the prepared vegetables in a large saucepan. Trim the excess fat from the lamb, and cut into pieces (either chops or ribs). Add lamb and herbs to pot, and season well. Drain the lentils and beans, and add together with the pearl barley. Pour on water, gently bring to the boil, cover and simmer for 3 hours. Serve with dumplings.

Marlborough's Ipswich Almond Pudding (Serves 4)

An eighteenth-century recipe adapted by a Suffolk hotel, this traditional dessert is excellent served with a fruit *compote* made with the abundance of soft fruit grown in East Anglia, such as cherries, plums, blackcurrants and redcurrants, or raspberries.

450 ml/$\frac{3}{4}$ pt/2 cups milk	50 g/2 oz/$\frac{1}{4}$ cup sugar
150 ml/$\frac{1}{4}$ pt/$\frac{2}{3}$ cup double cream	175 g/6 oz/1 cup ground almonds
50 g/2 oz/$\frac{2}{3}$ cup fresh white breadcrumbs	3 eggs, beaten
	25 g/1 oz/$\frac{1}{4}$ stick butter

Warm the milk and cream and pour over the breadcrumbs. Stir in the sugar and almonds and leave to soak for 5 minutes. Pour on the beaten eggs and blend well. Turn into either a greased pie dish or individual buttered pots. Dot with butter, place in a water bath, and bake in a slow oven (150°C/300°F/Gas Mark 2) for 30 minutes. Serve with fruit *compote*.

Summer Pudding (Serves 6)

The soft fruit of East Anglia is ideally shown off in this glorious, colourful English pudding. Most soft fruits can be used, such as raspberries, redcurrants, black-

Essex Sea Salt

Way out on the wide marshes of the Blackwater estuary, black-headed gulls, lapwings and coots nest in the tall grasses of numerous creeks and inlets. Twice a day these mud-flats and marshes are flooded, leaving behind salt deposits that are concentrated further through rapid evaporation by sun and wind. The returning tide washes over them, making this Essex estuary one of the saltiest in Britain. This bounty of pure salt from the sea has been harvested for millennia. The Saxons gathered the salty water in clay pans embedded in the river banks. This was allowed to evaporate partially, and the resulting brine was transferred to pots, then heated to evaporate it further. In 1086 the Domesday Book recorded forty-five salt pans in the Maldon area, and salt production remained a vital local industry through the Middle Ages.

Today Maldon sea salt is still harvested by methods virtually unchanged for hundreds of years. Water is drawn from the river after a period of dry weather. Once it has settled and has been filtered, it is pumped directly into salt pans where it is carefully heated, causing crystals to form. As the water evaporates, the pans fill with salt, which settles and cools overnight. The next morning, the salt is dragged to the sides of the pans with wooden rakes. The result is pure salt gathered from the sea, with no additives whatsoever. Crystal sea salt crumbles in the fingers; it has an intense, clean and more pronounced flavour than ordinary salt, and you therefore need use less of it.

berries, loganberries or bilberries. Use at least three types, and prepare a day in advance to allow the fruit juices to steep.

900 g/2 lb mixed soft fruit, hulled and washed	About 8 slices stale white bread with crusts removed
100 g/4 oz/$\frac{1}{2}$ cup castor sugar	

Put the fruit in a heavy-based saucepan with sugar and gently cook until sugar has dissolved and the juices begin to run. Line the base and sides of a 1.2 l/2 pt pudding basin with the bread, cutting it into slices so that it fits neatly together with no gaps. Reserve a couple of slices for the top. Fill the mould with the fruit and most of the syrup and pack down well. Cover with the remaining bread slices and spoon over a little syrup. Put a plate over the top and weigh down with a heavy object. Allow to stand overnight in a cool place. Turn out on to a plate. Cut into slices and serve with cream.

Norfolk Treacle Tart   (Serves 6)

Treacle tart is a typical 'pud' enjoyed by sweet-tooths throughout the country: sticky, chewy and preferably bathed in creamy home-made custard.

225 g/$\frac{1}{2}$ lb shortcrust pastry (see p. 25)	Grated rind of 1 lemon
6 tbsp golden syrup	1 egg, lightly beaten
35 g/1$\frac{1}{2}$ oz/1$\frac{1}{4}$ cups fresh white breadcrumbs	

Lightly butter a round sandwich tin, and line with the shortcrust pastry. Prick all over the base with a fork. Warm the golden syrup until runny, but not hot. Stir in the breadcrumbs, lemon rind and beaten egg. Pour this mixture into the pastry shell, and bake in a moderate oven (180°C/350°F/Gas Mark 4) for 35–40 minutes, or until set. Serve hot with home-made custard or cream.

Syllabub   (Serves 4)

Originally this favourite dessert was made by milking the cow directly into a pail of cider or beer.

150 ml/$\frac{1}{4}$ pt/$\frac{2}{3}$ cup white wine	1$\frac{1}{2}$ tbsp castor sugar
1 tbsp sherry	300 ml/$\frac{1}{2}$ pt/1$\frac{1}{4}$ cups double cream
2 tbsp brandy	Freshly-grated nutmeg
1 bitter (Seville) orange	

Samphire

Samphire, an edible dark green fleshy marsh plant, grows throughout Britain, but is particularly common in East Anglia. It is harvested along the north Norfolk coast in July and August. In Norwich, the fish stalls in the open market in the centre of the city sell samphire in season. It is called by some 'poor man's asparagus', but its flavour is in no way inferior. The favourite local way to eat this unusual delicacy is pickled in vinegar.

Pour the wine, sherry and brandy into bowl. Peel the orange very thinly and squeeze out the juice. Add the peel and juice to the wine mixture and set aside overnight. Remove the peel and stir in the sugar until dissolved. Pour in the cream very slowly and whip with a wire whisk until the mixture forms peaks. Spoon into 4 glasses and sprinkle with a little nutmeg.

Cambridge Burnt Cream   (Serves 4–6)

Cambridge burnt cream came to the Trinity College kitchens by way of an enthusiastic nineteenth-century academic gastronome. Similar to French *crème brulée*, it requires care in preparation, though its ingredients are simple.

600 ml/1 pt/2$\frac{1}{2}$ cups double cream	4 egg yolks
1 tsp vanilla essence	3 tbsp sugar

Put the cream and vanilla essence in a saucepan and bring to the boil. Meanwhile, beat the egg yolks in a large mixing bowl with 1 tbsp of sugar until they are thick and pale yellow. Remove the cream from the heat, allow to cool slightly, then pour over the egg yolks in a slow, steady stream, whisking constantly. Transfer this mixture into an ovenproof dish or individual ramekins, and bake in a slow oven (150°C/300°F/Gas Mark 2) for about 30 minutes, until set. Leave to cool and refrigerate for a couple of hours. A couple of hours before serving, pre-heat the grill to its highest temperature. Sprinkle the remaining sugar over the top of the cream, coating the surface evenly and thickly. Place the dish or dishes under the grill as close to the heat as possible and allow the sugar to caramelize to a deep brown. Be careful not to burn it. Allow to cool, and serve chilled.

English Mustard

Those who think English food plain or bland should consider English mustard, an everyday table condiment which is exceedingly hot, far more fiery than French or German equivalents. A mere tip-of-the-knife on the edge of a plate is probably sufficient quantity for a platter of rare roast beef; indeed, it has often been said that Messrs Colman of Norwich made their fortune from what people left behind on their plates.

Mustard has been used in Britain since at least Roman times, though until the eighteenth century it was probably prepared in the home in a rather coarse fashion, just roughly pounded into a paste. A commercial mustard factory began operation in 1742 at Garlick Hill, London, run by the Keen family (thus the saying 'keen as mustard'?), while the Colmans began their first mustard mill near Norwich in 1814. Mustard seed is a traditional East Anglian crop, grown in the fens of Cambridgeshire and Lincolnshire and throughout Norfolk, as well, to a lesser degree, in Suffolk and Essex. There are few sights more breathtaking and vivid than a field of mustard in flower; numerous fields around the

city of Norwich, traditionally under contract to Colman's, are a blaze of brilliant yellow during the last two weeks of June. Two types of mustard for condiment use are cultivated: brown mustard (*Brassica juncea*) and white mustard (*Sinapis alba*). The mustard crop is harvested in late August and September, and the dressed seed taken to the plant at Carrow.

Jeremiah Colman first began his business in an old water mill, grinding crushed seed into a fine mustard powder which his wife and daughter helped pack and label in casks. Today the Carrow factory is ultra-modern, but the milling of mustard seed is basically unchanged, resulting in extremely fine mustard flours from both the brown and white seeds which are then blended together, for each contributes its own character. When mixed with water, dry mustard powder releases its volatile strength and heat by enzyme action. While Colman's normal-strength English mustard is hot enough for most, an even fiercer powder, Genuine Double Superfine, is available, but only from the Mustard Shop in Norwich.

Above: A collection of old mustard tins at Colman's Mustard Shop, Norwich.

Opposite: A field of mustard in bloom outside Norwich in late June.

Drink in East Anglia

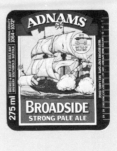

East Anglia, with its wide, expansive fields, has long been a grain-growing centre, so it is not surprising that fine and distinctive beers are produced here. Britain's national drink, after all, is no more than a beverage made from fermented grain, and East Anglian brewers are proud of the quality of their local barley. As befits this rural region, cyder (spelled here with a 'y') is also an important drink of the land, though its production has declined considerably since the days when it was rationed liberally to farmworkers. East Anglia today, however, is developing as one of the foremost English wine-producing regions, and some of its vineyards are among the best in the land.

Hours: see p. 30.

Traditional Beer

Beer drinkers in East Anglia are offered the choice of plenty of fine traditional ales, served in free and tied houses alike. Adnams, Tolly Cobbold and Greene King are all highly-regarded independent breweries with strong local followings, while breweries linked to national combines (Ind Coope in Essex and the Norwich Brewery, part of the Watney Mann brewing group) also serve cask-conditioned ales in many outlets. To risk generalization, the regional taste in East Anglia seems to lean to strong bitter beers with a pronounced hop character, served preferably by direct dispense from the barrel, or by hand pump. Dark milds are not as popular here as bitter, but they do have a strong following in certain areas, and they are available in traditional form in many pubs. A good head of foam, incidentally, is not particularly important to beer drinkers in East Anglia. As one brewer put it: 'our customers like to see a full glass.'

Suffolk

Adnams & Co., Southwold, Suffolk. Adnams, an immaculate traditional brewery, has been brewing in this picturesque Suffolk coastal town for about 110 years. Some eighty-five per cent of the company's production is sold

Assorted mats and labels of the region.

through the free trade, primarily in Suffolk and Norfolk, although its much-sought beers are now available in outlets throughout the eastern quarter of the country, including nearly fifty public houses in London. In addition to three cask-conditioned ales, Adnams produces a range of distinctive bottled beers, such as Fisherman and Broadside.

> Bitter o.g. 1036
> Mild o.g. 1034
> Old Ale o.g. 1038

Tollemache & Cobbold Breweries, Ipswich, Suffolk. Founded in 1723 by the Cobbold family, this Ipswich brewery's beers (the company did not merge with the equally long established Tollemache family until this century) were enjoyed by, among others, John Constable, a friend of the family who often painted in the grounds of the Cliff Brewery. While Tolly's Bitter remains the company's biggest selling beer, the East Anglian thirst for strong hoppy traditional ale is aptly quenched by the stronger, popular Tolly's Original. Tolly's Old Strong is a high-gravity dark mild brewed only during the winter months. Though Tolly Cobbold is very much identified as an East Anglian establishment, its beers are increasingly available outside the traditional Tolly heartland of Suffolk, Norfolk, Essex and Cambridgeshire.

> Tolly's Bitter o.g. 1034
> Tolly's Original Bitter o.g. 1036
> Tolly's Mild o.g. 1032
> Tolly's Old Strong (winter only) o.g. 1046

Greene, King & Sons, Bury St Edmunds, Suffolk. Another long-established independent East Anglian brewery, Greene King began trading in 1806 in Bury St Edmunds. Today the company brews in Biggleswade as well as Bury, while a subsidiary, Rayment's, brews traditional beer at Furneux Pelham. Greene King beers are available in over 800 outlets, mainly in East Anglia (the Nutshell Inn in Bury, incidentally, claims to be the smallest in Britain). Abbot Ale is another favourite example of the East Anglian preference for robust, full-bodied, hoppy beer. Greene King brews both dark and light cask-conditioned milds.

> IPA o.g. 1034–38
> Abbot Ale o.g. 1046–52
> BBA o.g. 1034–38 (brewed at Rayment's)
> XX (dark mild) o.g. 1030–34
> KK (light mild) o.g. 1030–34

Norfolk

Norwich Brewery Co., Norwich, Norfolk. A part of the Watney Mann & Truman national brewing group, the Norwich Brewery nevertheless retains individual roots very firmly planted in East Anglia. The company, an amalgamation of four main East Anglian breweries (Steward and Patteson, Bullard's, Morgan's and Young's, and Crawshay and Young's), has an estate of over 800 tied public houses, mainly in such centres as Norwich, Great Yarmouth, Lowestoft, Ipswich, Colchester, King's Lynn, Ely, Wisbech and Cambridge, as well as throughout the East Anglian countryside and rural areas. A range of brewery-conditioned beers is complemented with two new cask-conditioned beers, a mild and a bitter, while other beers brewed in the group's breweries elsewhere are also available.

> Bullard's Mild o.g. 1034
> S & P Best Bitter o.g. 1038

Woodeforde's Norfolk Ales, Erpingham, Norwich. This cottage brewery (named after the eighteenth-century Norfolk parson who championed 'home brew') is located in a converted stable block adjacent to the Spread Eagle Inn. Six traditional cask beers are presently brewed, available throughout Norfolk in select free houses only.

> Broadsman Bitter o.g. 1035–37
> Wherry Best Bitter o.g. 1040–42
> Norfolk Porter o.g. 1041–45
> Festival o.g. 1052
> Spread Eagle Bitter o.g. 1036 (available only at the Spread Eagle Inn)
> White Lion Bitter o.g. 1036–37 (brewed for the White Lion Inn, Norwich)

Cambridgeshire

Elgood & Sons, Wisbech, Cambridgeshire. The North Brink Brewery is an important landmark in this fenland market town in the north-east of the county. About half of Elgood's fifty-five tied houses serve cask-conditioned bitter by hand pump.

> Elgood's Bitter o.g. 1037

Essex

Ind Coope, Romford, Essex. Ind Coope, one of the great names in British brewing, is now part of the Allied Breweries group. The Romford Brewery has been supplying the capital and surrounds with beers for centuries, though Ind Coope's main brewery is now located in Burton. Traditional beers are brewed here for Allied's marketing companies which operate their own tied estates, including Taylor Walker, Benskins and Friary Meux.

> Benskins Bitter o.g. 1037
> Friary Meux Bitter o.g. 1037
> Taylor Walker Bitter o.g. 1037
> Taylor Walker Mainline o.g. 1041

T. D. Ridley & Sons, Chelmsford, Essex. Working from an old-fashioned tower brewery built in 1840 in a rural setting surrounded by fields and river, Ridley's supplies traditional bitter and mild to pubs mainly in Essex.

> XXX Mild o.g. 1034
> Pale Ale o.g. 1034

Crouch Vale Brewery, South Woodham Ferrers, Chelmsford, Essex. This small company begun in 1981 brews cask-conditioned ales available in an area from Essex to London. Special house beers are brewed for a few pubs.

> Woodham Bitter o.g. 1033–36
> Best Bitter o.g. 1036–41
> SAS o.g. 1046–51
> Advocate Ale o.g. 1032 (The Sun and the Moon, London WC1)
> Towngate Special o.g. 1043 (Towngate Theatre, Basildon, Essex)

English Wine in East Anglia

East Anglia is one of the most important areas for growing grapes in Britain, with its own regional association, the East Anglian Wine Growers' Association. There are presently over forty vineyards here that belong to members of the parent organization, the English Vineyards Association. East Anglia has an almost continental climate of warm

A Look Inside a Traditional Brewery

Anyone who lives near a traditional brewery is familiar with the pungent, porridgy smell which billows out with the steam on days when brewing is taking place. Some might find this distinctive exhalation rather overpowering, but to the beer drinker it is a year-round source of comfort, a homely aroma which promises a satisfying pint, drawn from the cellar of the local with the steady pull of an old-fashioned hand pump.

The process of brewing that pint is really rather remarkable, for the raw ingredients from which beer is produced hardly suggest the drink that results. The traditional brewer begins with basic ingredients, yet he chooses them with the utmost care. Throughout the year, he keeps an eye on the weather and other conditions which might affect the quality of the barley and hop crops. He purchases his malted barley from reliable maltsters (the days when breweries malted their own are largely a thing of the past) to a very stringent specification which will yield the best results for his brewery's conditions and individual styles and types of beer. The brewer likewise chooses his hops to suit his needs, for different varieties have different degrees of bitterness and aroma. His strain of yeast is carefully nurtured, a portion kept back from each brew. Many breweries are exceedingly proud of the longevity of strains kept going for as long as anyone can remember. The individual character of each brewery's yeast is an extremely important factor in regional brewing, some brewers say *the* most important single factor. Local brewing liquor was once equally critical. Many breweries even today remain sited over wells and boreholes. In fact, although many regional breweries continue to use a local source, water technology is so advanced that breweries can now adjust their liquor composition to suit individual brewing requirements.

To begin a brew, the grains of malted barley are first cracked and crushed in a mill to produce grist. This grainy cereal is transferred to a vessel called a mash tun, where it is mixed with hot brewing liquor. The porridgy mash infuses for a period, and in the process, the natural maltose is extracted, resulting in a rich, sweet, sugary liquid known as wort. The wort is drained through a perforated base in the mash tun and transferred to another vessel called the copper as the remaining grains are sprayed, or sparged, with hot liquor to extract the remaining sugar. The spent grains are finally sold to farmers for cattle food.

Sacks of whole cone hops (or, in some breweries, manufactured hop pellets) are added directly to the copper. The wort and hops are boiled vigorously together for one or two hours to extract the bitter resins from the hops. If necessary, additional sugar is added at this stage to help increase the alcohol level and characteristics of the finished beer. Once boiling is complete, the hops must be separated from the wort, so the mixture is transferred to another vessel known as the hop back. This vessel, like the mash tun, has a perforated base that allows the wort to be filtered through the natural bed of spent hops.

The hopped wort is cooled as it is transferred to fermenting vessels, which may be made from a variety of materials, including slate, wood, concrete, copper, stainless steel or plastic, and in an equal variety of shapes and sizes. Fermentation begins when the yeast is pitched. British beers are traditionally made with top-fermenting yeasts, which form a slowly-bubbling froth on top of the liquid wort, feeding on the sugars to produce alcohol and carbon dioxide, a process which takes anywhere from three days to a week. Once fermentation is complete, the finished beer is run into storage tanks to condition or mature.

While beer destined for pressurized kegs, tanks or bottles is usually filtered and pasteurized (a process which stabilizes beer but results in an inevitable change in character), traditional cask-conditioned beer is filled directly into the wooden or aluminium containers from which it will be drawn. Because such real ale still contains working yeast which has not been filtered out, a secondary fermentation in the cask occurs, sometimes aided by the addition of priming sugar. A handful of dry hops might also be added to the cask at this point to add a fresh distinctive hoppy aroma which is the hallmark of certain bitter beers. Isinglass finings are also added to precipitate any solids in suspension and thus leave the beer clear. Cask-conditioned beer is a living product which continues to mature and develop even after it has been delivered (sometimes by horse-drawn dray) to the publican's cellar. It is one of the finest drinks in the world.

Top left: British and Irish ales, as opposed to lagers produced here and elsewhere, are top-fermenting, that is, the yeast rises to the surface and forms a thick layer, feeding on the nutrients and sugars of the wort below. The brewer ends up with about five times as much yeast as he starts with, and some is always kept back for future use. (Eldridge Pope's Dorchester Brewery)

Top centre: Natural real ales are racked into wooden or aluminium casks where they continue to develop and come into condition in the publican's cellar. (T. & R. Theakston's Masham Brewery)

Top right: Pale ale malt is ground into grist and mashed with hot brewing liquor to extract its fermentable sugar.

Bottom left: Pockets of native hops from Kent and Hereford & Worcester. (Young & Co's Brewery, Wandsworth)

Bottom right: Wort and hops are added to the copper, and boiled together vigorously. (Adnams' Sole Bay Brewery, Southwold)

summers and cold, hard winters which allow the vines to rest. A relatively low rainfall, and subsequent increase in sunshine hours, combine with warm late autumns to make the region one of the most favourable for growing grapes. Soils throughout the region vary, ranging from sandy clay and flinty loam to gravel and chalk, and a variety of grapes are grown, resulting in a range of individual wines. However, to generalize, the conditions of the East Anglian vineyard do seem to produce wines that are somewhat rich and spicy in character, with at times an intense concentration of flavour. As elsewhere, many English vineyards in the region are well suited to receive visitors; they provide the best opportunity both to taste and purchase wine. Though some establishments keep 'open house' in summer, it is wise (and in some cases essential) to make arrangements in advance. The following is a selection of some East Anglian vineyards.

Bruisyard St Peter
Church Road
Bruisyard
Saxmundham
Suffolk
Bruisyard is a ten-acre vineyard planted entirely with Müller-Thurgau vines on a south-facing slope near Bruisyard Church. The wine is made and bottled in the winery (converted from the old milking parlour) and is not generally released until the previous vintage is finished.
    Visitors welcome.

Elmham Park Vineyards
Elmham House
North Elmham
Dereham
Norfolk
About ten acres of vines are planted in three sites, forming part of an estate where dessert apples, giant blackberries, strawberries, raspberries and gooseberries are also cultivated. Madeleine Angevine and Müller-Thurgau are the main grape varieties grown, together with some twenty experimental vines. Elmham Park is a crisp, fresh wine particularly suited to shellfish and seafood from the nearby Norfolk coast. Vintage cider for the 'wine drinker' is also produced.

Cavendish Manor Vineyard
Nether Hall
Cavendish
Sudbury
Suffolk
The lovely Stour Valley behind Cavendish village green is the site for this ten-acre vineyard planted with Müller-Thurgau.
    Visitors welcome.

Highwayman's
MacRae Farms Ltd
Hatchery House
Barrow
Bury St Edmunds
Suffolk
Highwayman's vineyard is planted with twenty-four acres of Müller-Thurgau, Huxelrebe and Pinot Noir, as well as with other experimental varieties.

The Felstar Wine Estate
The Vineyards
Crick's Green
Felsted
Essex
When the Barretts planted their vineyard in 1966 it was probably the first commercial vineyard in Essex since the Middle Ages, though vines had been grown in the immediate area at the time of the Norman Conquest as recorded in the Domesday Book. Today ten and a half acres planted with some thirteen grape varieties result in six to nine single-grape varietal wines, pressed, vinified and bottled in the small traditional winery.
    Parties and groups welcome by prior arrangement.

Chilford Hundred Wines Ltd
Chilford Hall
Linton
Cambridge
Cambridgeshire
The Chilford Hundred vineyard (the Saxons divided most of England into administrative areas known as 'hundreds') is planted on the Lenz Moser high-culture system of wide spacing between the rows of vines, fewer vines per acre, and training on high wires. Eighteen acres are planted with Müller-Thurgau, Ortega, Huxelrebe, Siegerrebe and Schönburger on soil which is flinty loam and gravel.

Lexham Hall Vineyard
Lexham Hall
King's Lynn
Norfolk
Lexham Hall Vineyard, consisting of eight acres half a mile downstream from the village of East Lexham planted with Müller-Thurgau, Scheurebe, Reichensteiner and Madeleine Angevine, is open to parties of ten or more persons by appointment.

Chickering Vineyards
Chickering Hall
Hoxne
Suffolk
Chickering Rivaner wine is produced from Müller-Thurgau grapes grown on the Geneva Double Curtain system of training (see p. 72).

Boyton Vineyards
Boyton End
Stoke-by-Clare
Suffolk
The vineyard consists of four and a half acres planted with Müller-Thurgau and Huxelrebe. The estate winery has been converted from an original stable and barn, parts of which date back to the fifteenth century.
    Visitors welcome.

In addition to the above, the following East Anglian vine growers are members of the English Vineyards Association. Many sell wine direct.

Cambridgeshire
Fenlandia, Cottenham
Paxton Hill Fields, St Neots

Essex
Saffron Walden, Saffron Walden
Wendon Vineyard, Saffron Walden
Nevards, Boxted
Langham, Langham
Crown Lane, Ardleigh
Erdelega, Ardleigh
Heath Lodge, Alresford
Owls Hall, Braintree
Coral Lodge, Chelmsford
New Hall, Purleigh
Fyfield Hall, Fyfield
Envilles Farm, Moreton

Norfolk
Islington Lodge, Tilney All Saints
Silver Green, Silver Green

Bunwell, Bunwell
Pulham, Pulham Market
Woodfarm, Fressingfield
Heywood, Hoxne
Warwick Lodge, Hoxne
Harling, East Harling

Suffolk

Barningham Hall, Barningham
Bardwell, Bardwell
Tuddenham Mill, Tuddenham St Mary
Kings Forest, Bury St Edmunds
Peasenhall, Peasenhall
Kelsale, Kelsale
Helions Vineyard, Helions Bumpstead
Henny, Little Henny
Constable Country, Bures
Brandeston Priory, Woodbridge
Snipe, Woodbridge

Cyder

Cyder was once the main country drink here, as in most parts of rural England. Norfolk and Suffolk cyders in particular were much favoured, made primarily with the juice not from bittersharp or bittersweet cider apples as in the West Country, but from culinary fruit such as the Bramley seedling. Today, there are only two major firms in the region who are members of the National Association of Cidermakers.

The Chevalliers, a Huguenot family from France, came to Suffolk some 250 years ago. They soon began making cyder both for themselves and for sale. A cyder press was made in 1729 of oak from the Aspall Hall estate, while an enormous stone mill was brought over from France. It cost six pounds just for transport alone, a considerable sum in those days. Such a traditional stone trough mill consists of a circular hollowed-out trough and an upright millstone, connected to a wooden yoke. Thus, a horse can be harnessed to the yoke, and as it walks around the trough, the stone mill crushes the apples. The trough mill at Aspall's was used commercially until 1947, when their last working horse died; the original wooden press was used up to 1970. Today, this family firm has modern equipment, but the cyder made is still traditional: a good, strong, unsparkling drink made only from the fermented juice of crushed and pressed apples grown organically in Aspall's sixty-five acres of orchards. Organic cyder

vinegar is also made here (in fact, it has become the dominant product). Both cyders and vinegars can be purchased direct from the 'Cyder House', which still contains both the original trough mill and wooden press.

Robert Gaymer began making Norfolk cyder in the mid-eighteenth century at the family farmhouse at Banham. Today, at nearby Attleborough, outside Norwich, cyder is manufactured on a large scale. The family firm of William Gaymer & Son merged with R. N. Coate & Co. of Somerset, thus linking two important cider-making counties. In Attleborough, Gaymer's produce bottled cyders such as Gaymer's Norfolk Dry and Gaymer's Olde English Cyder, both available nationally.

Aspall Cyder House
Debenham
Stowmarket
Suffolk

William Gaymer & Son Ltd
Attleborough
Norfolk

Additionally, as in the South and South-East, some wine makers are also using their equipment and expertise to produce quality ciders which are, in fact, more like apple wines: fine, pale drinks with a delicate fragrance and relatively high alcohol content, sold in corked bottles with carefully drawn labels. Such ciders are made from culinary fruit, and the result is a far cry either from carbonated bottled cider, or from 'scrumpy' tasted from the wood in the West Country. Two such East Anglian wine establishments producing vintage cider for the wine drinker are Elmham House and the Felstar Wine Estate (see addresses above).

Some Useful Addresses

East Anglia Tourist Board
14 Museum Street
Ipswich
Suffolk

F. E. Neave & Son
Debenham
Suffolk
This traditional butcher still
prepares Suffolk sweet-pickled

hams, sweet-pickled chaps and bacon by the old, time-honoured methods.

The Bloater Depot
Regent Road
Great Yarmouth
Norfolk
Bloaters and kippers by post: 'a present from Yarmouth.'

Sutton's
Sutton Road
Great Yarmouth
This 140-year-old company cures bloaters, kippers and red herring.

The Butley Orford Oysterage
Market Hill
Orford
Suffolk
Pacific oysters raised in the Orford and home-smoked salmon can be enjoyed in this popular restaurant or purchased from the shop.

The Colchester Oyster Fishery
North Farm
East Mersea
Colchester
Essex
Native Colchester oysters are reared here, and supplied to shellfish wholesalers as well as sold direct. Open days are held the first Friday of every month.

Michael Paske Farms Ltd
Barnston
The Spinney
Hartford
Huntingdon
Cambridgeshire
Farm-fresh asparagus available by mail order.

The Mustard Shop
3 Bridewell Alley
Norwich
Norfolk
Mustards, mustard pots and other related items available by mail order, or to personal callers to this unique reconstructed Victorian shop which celebrates the history of English mustard and the famous Norwich firm of J. & J. Colman.

THE SOUTH

In 1066 a Norman duke named William crossed 'La Manche' to Sussex, drew up his force of fighting men on the field where Battle Abbey now stands, and there defeated the Saxon king, Harold, thus claiming the English throne. It was to be (as every schoolboy knows) the last successful invasion of England. The Norman Conquest brought changes to Britain, for William administered the country as a feudal fiefdom. The Domesday Survey that he commissioned was compiled in 1086, a meticulously detailed survey of the English counties, listing land settlements, ownership of estates, local customs and practices, and much else. Norman lords who assisted in the Conquest were granted large tracts of favoured land, upon which mighty castles such as Roches-ter and Arundel were built. William fostered closer ties with Rome, and Norman churches, with their stout, solid towers, sprang up in nearly every village.

At that time, the South and South-East of England was a dense wooded country. From the Weald of Kent across to Hampshire, small towns and agricultural lands were interspersed by large tracts of deciduous forest. Deer still roam in the New Forest, but the Weald of Kent, though densely wooded in many parts, is today mainly a region of open countryside. The familiar conical outlines of neat, white-capped oasts and tall poles for training hops pierce the horizon, and fields of orchards and pastures link villages such as Biddenden, Tenterden and Benenden (the 'den'

Hampshire watercress is grown in stone beds fed by artesian springs beside the Test River.

Whitstable oysters and other local shellfish can be eaten or taken away from this famous oyster bar.

Carr Taylor Vineyard, near Battle: English vineyards located throughout the South of England have become an established feature of the countryside.

suffix indicated, originally, a clearing in the woods). Such villages, with their tile-hung timber-framed houses, expansive village cricket greens and solid parish churches seem eminently self-satisfied, timeless.

Hampshire, East and West Sussex, and Kent make up a vast chunk of the country, rich in every way: soaked in history; economically prosperous; scenically splendid; and a horn of plenty, a provider of some of the very best of solid yeoman food and drink. Game is plentiful; in addition to venison from the New and other forests, partridge, woodcock, pigeon, rabbit and hare are all hunted. Mutton from the South Downs of Sussex is a famous delicacy, while spring lamb from the salty pastures of Romney Marsh in Kent is equally renowned.

Both along the coast and inland, this area is rich in native produce: oysters from Whitstable, sole from Dover and Rye Bay, Arundel mullet, Selsey cockles and shrimps, lobsters and crabs from Chichester, eel, whiting, sea bass, gurnet are all superb. Trout and tench come from the Test, Itchen and Avon rivers. Native English vegetables abound, such as watercress in Hampshire, while home gardens supply many with sprouts, potatoes, runner and broad beans, lettuces and other vegetables. Cherries (both sweet and sour) from Kent, Cox's Orange Pippin apples, strawberries from Hampshire, gooseberries, plums, pears are all among the finest in the land.

The heavy oak tables in many a country house here are always well-laden. Prosperous and in proximity to the nation's capital, the South of England has never had to develop a diet to make a little feel like a lot, as was the case in the hard-working North and the Midlands. As such, the region's attitude to food epitomizes good English cooking at its best, for it takes an abundance of the finest ingredients and presents them simply and without fuss or frills. Whole saddles and legs of succulent Romney Marsh or Southdown lamb are simply roasted. Pigs, which grow fat on windfalls from orchards and acorns in the forests, provide a diet of good sweet pork, roasted until the skin is crisp and crackling. Roast duck is served with a rich, sticky sauce made with dark, tart, locally-grown morello cherries. The comfortable doughy aroma of steamed suet puddings pervades the country kitchen, and basins are turned out filled with creamy chicken and extravagant mixtures of partridge and rump steak. Heavy satisfying puddings round off long meals: steamed Sussex pond pudding, plum duff, plum heavies, cherry batter pudding, and much else.

As is the case elsewhere in Britain, one encounters intense, but charming local rivalries. Who says the British aren't proud of the quality of their natural produce? Dover sole might be one of the best known fish in Britain, but people from further around the coast swear that the similar

96

fish caught in Rye Bay is even better (they call it, naturally, Rye Bay sole). Whitstable oysters, we have been sternly lectured, are far better than those from Colchester, while cockles from the Medway are likewise superior to bivalves gathered by 'those bounders from Essex' (even though the fishermen from Leigh-on-Sea probably work the same or adjacent grounds).

The South can be proud, too, of its contribution to British drink. Cider was first made in the South by the Normans, thirsting for their national drink. At Battle Abbey, the first major Norman settlement, built on the site of their famous victory, cider making developed both for the monks' own use, and to sell to neighbouring villages. Good strong ciders are still produced in the South-East, primarily from table fruit, not cider apples. Beer, the national drink of England, also owes a debt to the region, for it would not be what it is without the famous Kentish hops. The conical oast for drying hops is a feature of the countryside here, and there are a number of fine traditional breweries throughout the South. The revival of English wine came about here, too, for it was at Hambledon, in Hampshire, that Sir Guy Salisbury-Jones planted the first modern commercial English vineyard in 1952; today there are over seventy members of the English Vineyards Association in the South, many producing superb wines. Luscious fruits, too – raspberries, strawberries, sloes, cherries and pears – are fermented into sweet or dry country wines: innocuously innocent, one thinks, but surprisingly potent and effective.

Numerous cultural and international festivals take place in the South: the theatre festival at Chichester, music and arts happenings at Arundel and Brighton, and the Glyndebourne Festival Opera. During the latter's lengthy interval, women in long evening dresses and men in formal dress relax in the grounds of the estate, with buckets of champagne, caviar or lobster, strawberries and cream. This quintessentially English activity contrasts with a more homely, rural atmosphere found generally in Hampshire, Sussex and Kent, in thatched country pubs, seaside tea shops or ample farm kitchens. Yet both are celebrations of the very best of life in the English countryside.

Hampshire Watercress

Watercress is one of the great salad vegetables of England: strong and peppery, rich in iron, vitamins and flavour. One of the most important centres for its production is the Test River Valley of Hampshire, around centres such as Alresford and Whitchurch. Watercress is not actually cultivated in the river itself nor is it allowed to be grown in river water. Rather, watercress is grown commercially alongside the river in stone beds, some of which have been used for generations. The water that flows continuously over this green crop comes from artesian springs which spurt up from the catchment area of the North Downs.

Now available throughout the year, watercress is a fresh English salad vegetable with a distinctive character and flavour that can be enjoyed even in winter. A watercress grower in Alresford tells us that his grandfather liked it best with a dash of vinegar and sugar; he himself prefers watercress with just a little salt. A bunch of watercress served with sliced oranges and a vinegar and oil dressing makes an excellent salad. It is delicious in omelettes and flans, or simply placed between two slices of buttered bread. One of our favourites is this creamy watercress soup, served chilled in summer, hot in winter.

Hampshire Watercress Soup

(Serves 6)

2 large bunches of watercress	600 ml/1 pt/2½ cups milk
	Salt
25 g/1 oz/¼ stick butter	Freshly-ground black
1 onion, finely chopped	pepper
450 g/1 lb potatoes, peeled and diced	150 ml/¼ pt/⅔ cup single cream
600 ml/1 pt/2½ cups chicken stock	

Wash the watercress well and set aside about a third of it. Cut off the stalks and coarsely chop the leaves and stems. Melt the butter in a large saucepan and gently sauté the chopped onions. Add the diced potatoes, chopped watercress, stock and milk. Bring to the boil, season with salt and pepper, and simmer for about an hour. Purée and, if serving cold, chill in a refrigerator. Coarsely chop the remaining watercress. Before serving, stir into the soup, and swirl in the cream.

Recipes from the South

Beachy Head Prawns   (Serves 8)

Beachy Head is a towering promontory below East-bourne which marks the beginning of the South Downs, a chalky ridge that once connected England and the Continent. Prawns are gathered all along the south coast, not just here, though this delicious first course comes from Drusilla's Thatched Barn Restaurant at nearby Alfriston.

450 g/1 lb diced cooked chicken	$\frac{1}{2}$ green or red pepper, diced
450 g/1 lb shelled prawns	1 cucumber, peeled and diced
300 ml/$\frac{1}{2}$ pt/1$\frac{1}{4}$ cups mayonnaise	Handful of fresh parsley, finely chopped
2 tsp tomato paste	Vinegar and oil
2 tsp chutney	Salt
3–4 dried apricots, chopped	Freshly-ground black pepper
1 tbsp curry powder	
2 eating apples, peeled, cored and diced	Scallop shells, cleaned
25 g/$\frac{1}{2}$ lb cooked and chilled rice	Whole prawns, lemon wedges and toasted almonds to garnish

In a bowl mix the diced chicken and prawns. Liquidize the mayonnaise, tomato paste, chutney, chopped dried apricots and curry powder. Add to the chicken and prawn mixture, and mix well. Add the chopped apples. Season to taste.

Mix the diced pepper, cucumber and parsley with the cooked rice. Dress with oil and vinegar, and season to taste. Make a ring of rice in each scallop shell or in individual dishes. Add the chicken and prawn mixture to the middle. Garnish each with a whole prawn, lemon wedge and toasted almonds.

Whitstable Dredgerman's Breakfast   (Serves 1)

Whitstable in Kent, together with Colchester in Essex and Helford in Cornwall, is one of the main oyster centres in Britain. The original Wheeler's Oyster Bar was founded here, and continues to serve as well as to sell both native oysters (only in months with an 'r' in them) and Pacific oysters (available all year round), in addition to cockles, whelks, jellied eels, prawns, shrimp, lobster, crab and crayfish. Native oysters have a more intense, full-bodied flavour than Pacific oysters. Today, oysters are usually served on the half-shell, raw with just a squeeze of lemon, or (for those who like such unnecessary additions) with a little cayenne, horseradish or tabasco. However, in the past, the dredgermen themselves would pocket a few shelled oysters in their oilskin aprons, and then, on returning home, would cook this simple meal for breakfast or tea. It is a good way to serve oysters for those who are a little squeamish about eating them raw.

About a dozen shelled oysters per person	Streaky bacon

Fry the streaky bacon in a pan until the fat runs. Place the shelled oysters over the rashers. Cook for about 3–4 minutes. Serve with thick slices of bread or toast and mugs of strong tea.

Dover Sole   (Serves 2)

Dover sole is not exclusive to either Dover or the South-East, although it was probably so named because Dover was an important port where it was landed in quantity, and from where it could be quickly transported to Billingsgate. The same fish, from further around the coast, however, is called Rye Bay sole, while in Ireland, where it is also plentiful, it is known as black sole. Whatever it is called, it is one of the finest and most highly prized fish in Britain and Ireland, far superior in flavour and texture to other flat fish such as plaice, lemon sole or dabs. The Dover sole is distinctive in appearance, longer, less round than any of the others, with a rather tough brown skin which is easy to remove. This fish, we feel, is best simply grilled.

2 Dover sole, cleaned	Parsley and lemon wedges to garnish
Melted butter	
Sea salt	
Freshly-ground black pepper	

Pre-heat the grill. Wash and pat dry the cleaned fish. Skin the fish, if desired (it pulls off fairly easily). Brush the fish with melted butter and season well with black pepper and sea salt. Cook under the hot grill for about 4–5 minutes per side (depending on the thickness of the fish), until the flesh is firm and surface is slightly browned. Serve at once, garnished with parsley and lemon wedges.

The cliffs at Dover.

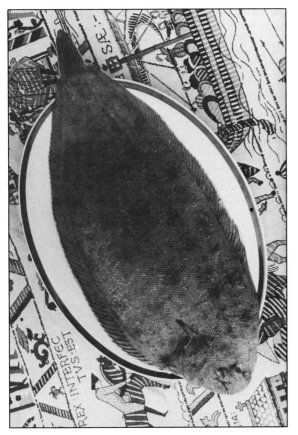

The distinctive Dover sole, though not exclusive to this region, is the finest of all flat fish.

Hampshire Haslet (Serves 6)

Hampshire, like many other parts of Britain, has a tradition of pork cookery, since pig farming is a traditional activity. This pork loaf is a simple, favourite country dish.

Half a loaf of bread
300 ml/½ pt/1¼ cups milk
1.25 kg/2½ lb shoulder of
   pork, coarsely minced
1 onion, finely chopped

Salt
Freshly-ground black
   pepper
Fresh sage, finely chopped

Remove the crusts from the bread, and cut into cubes. Soak the bread in the milk, and wring out. Mix the moist bread with the minced pork and chopped onion. Season well with salt and pepper, and mix in the freshly chopped sage. Pile the mixture into a greased loaf tin. Place in a pre-heated moderately hot oven (190°C/375°F/Gas Mark 5) for about 1–1½ hours. Haslet is generally served cold.

Buttered Hops

Hop shoots have been considered a delicacy since Roman times. They are generally gathered during early May, and are best simply boiled quickly then dipped in melted butter. A hop sauce can be made by cooking chopped hops in melted butter, and served with chicken or fish.

New Forest Venison

Some 900 years ago, the battle-worn Norman duke, William I, established a New Forest in the woods and heathland between Southampton Water, the Solent and the Avon River. This area was created specifically for the preservation of royal deer, and strict laws were laid down regarding the hunting of them. For generations afterwards, the hunting of venison and other game remained a sport for nobility and gentlefolk.

Venison today is available to all, though in the New Forest crown lands and elsewhere, strict laws and regulations still remain for the hunting and killing of roe, fallow, sika and red deer. The animals can only be hunted at certain times of the year which vary, depending on the variety and sex, as well as from region to region. Commercial deer farming has greatly increased the availability of venison throughout the year.

Venison is an extremely lean meat. Its distinctive flavour, like that of most other game, is improved greatly by hanging for two or even three weeks. While hanging, the venison can be rubbed with crushed black peppercorns, ground ginger, or juniper berries. Since it can be rather tough, it is often advisable to marinade it for at least a day or two before cooking. Care must also be taken while cooking: either cover the meat with strips of bacon or fat, or enclose it in a flour paste, or lard it by inserting strips of fat into the lean meat.

Roast Saddle of Venison

(Serves 6–8)

1½–2 kg/3–4 lb saddle of venison	2 bay leaves
450 ml/¾ pt/2 cups red wine	1 onion, chopped
450 ml/¾ pt/2 cups red wine vinegar	6 juniper berries, crushed
150 ml/¼ pt/⅔ cup olive oil	12 black peppercorns
1 clove of garlic	8 thick rashers of fat bacon
Sprig of fresh thyme	Salt
	Freshly-ground black pepper

Place the saddle of venison in a large bowl and cover with all the marinade ingredients (everything except the bacon). Cover and set aside in a cool place for at least 48 hours, turning occasionally. Remove the venison from the marinade and pat dry. Tie it into a neat shape, and cover with the bacon rashers. Season well with salt and pepper. Wrap loosely in foil and place in a roasting tin. Cook in a pre-heated moderate oven (180° C/350° F/ Gas Mark 4) for 30 minutes to the pound. Half an hour before the meat is cooked, remove the foil to brown. Serve with home-made quince jelly or with redcurrant jelly.

New Forest venison displayed at a butcher's in Lyndhurst.

Venison Stew (Serves 4–6)

900 g/2 lb shoulder of venison, diced	Freshly-ground black pepper
Half a bottle of red wine	2 sticks celery, finely chopped
6 juniper berries, crushed	
2 bay leaves	3 carrots, sliced
4 whole cloves	2 onions, sliced
$\frac{1}{2}$ tsp freshly-grated nutmeg	Sprig of fresh thyme
	25 g/1 oz/$\frac{1}{4}$ stick butter
Generous pinch of cinnamon	2 tbsp vegetable oil
	2 rashers bacon, chopped
Salt	Seasoned flour

Place the trimmed, diced venison in a large bowl, and pour on the wine. Add the spices, seasoning and chopped vegetables. Cover and set aside in a cool place for 2–3 days, turning occasionally. Remove the meat from the marinade and pat dry. Heat the butter and oil in a large casserole and fry the chopped bacon. Dust the venison in seasoned flour and add to the casserole. Brown on all sides, add the marinade and the vegetables, and place in a moderate oven (180°C/350°F/Gas Mark 4) for 2–3 hours or until tender. Adjust the seasoning, and serve with quince jelly.

Quince Jelly

(Makes about 1.8–2.25 kg/4–5 lb)

Quinces have been grown in the South of England since Roman times. Although they have a very sweet smell, their flavour is surprisingly tart.

1.8 kg/4 lb quinces	Juice of 1 lemon
Sugar	

Wash the fruit and roughly chop. Place in a large pan and cover with water. Bring to the boil, cover, and simmer until soft. Strain through a muslin-lined sieve without squeezing, as this would make the jelly cloudy. Measure the strained juice and weigh out 450 g/1 lb of sugar for every 600 ml/1 pt/2$\frac{1}{2}$ cups of juice. Gently warm the sugar in a pre-heated slow oven (140°C/275°F/Gas Mark 1). Return the juice to the rinsed pan and heat. Add lemon juice and the warmed sugar. Stir until dissolved. Bring the jelly to the boil and continue to boil until jelly reaches setting point. Put in sterilized bottles and seal.

Roast Saddle of Lamb (Serves 6–8)

In the South-East, spring lamb from sheep that graze on both the chalky South Downs and the salty grasslands of Romney Marsh vie with one another for supremacy; in truth, both are superb, and it is therefore always worth the trouble to seek meat from real local sources. A whole saddle of lamb, the piece between the ribs and the legs, is a splendid, extravagant joint, not an everyday one, and it requires an experienced and caring butcher to prepare it properly.

1 whole saddle of spring lamb (about 4.275 kg/9$\frac{1}{2}$ lb)	Freshly-ground black pepper
	Fresh sprigs of rosemary
Salt	Stock

A saddle of lamb, even from an experienced butcher, needs to be prepared before roasting. Turn the saddle on its back, remove the kidneys if not already done and set aside. Trim away the excess fat and sinews from the underside, and also trim fat off the back. Fold in the skirt on either side of the saddle, and tie around with string. Rub the joint with salt and plenty of freshly-ground black pepper, and insert sprigs of rosemary into slits cut in the meat. Place in a meat tin, and roast in a pre-heated moderately hot oven (190°C/375°F/Gas Mark 5) for 2–2$\frac{1}{2}$ hours or until the juices just run pink (cook for longer if desired). About 1 hour before cooking is finished, place the whole kidneys, cleaned and trimmed of their fat, in the meat tin and roast alongside the lamb. When done, remove the saddle and kidneys, and make a gravy by scraping the pan juices with the stock. Present the lamb on a large garnished platter, with the kidneys speared on top.

Savoury and Sweet Suet Puddings

'Kent will make a pudding out of anything,' it is said, and indeed, any number of things are popped into basins lined with moist suet pastry here in the Garden Counties, including joints of chicken and rabbit; partridge and pigeon; mixtures of pork, onion and apple; and shellfish such as mussels or scallops. In addition to such savouries, suet puddings are also made with a variety of sweet ingredients. Traditional Christmas pudding is of course eaten throughout the country, as is steamed treacle, jam or ginger pudding and spotted dick, so named because the suet is spotted with raisins, currants and sultanas. One speciality from Sussex, however, is unique to this region: Sussex pond pudding, containing a whole unpeeled lemon, bathed in a sugary, buttery sauce which forms a rich brown lake around the base of the pudding when it is turned out of its basin.

Pudding basins lined with suet pastry can be filled with any number of ingredients, sweet or savoury.

Suet Pastry

(To line and cover a 1.8 litre/3 pint pudding basin)

225 g/½ lb plain flour
Pinch of salt
2 tsp baking powder
100 g/4 oz/½ cup shredded suet
150 ml/¼ pt/⅔ cup water

Sieve the flour, salt and baking powder into a large mixing bowl. Mix in the shredded suet, and make a well in the centre of the mixture. Gradually add sufficient water to make a soft dough. Turn the pastry out on to a floured board and roll out into a large circle. With a sharp knife cut out a third of the circle and set aside as the lid for the pudding. Use the remaining pastry to line a well-greased pudding basin.

Ashdown Partridge Pudding

(Serves 4)

225 g/½ lb suet pastry
Boned meat from a brace of partridges
450 g/1 lb rump steak, diced
100 g/4 oz mushrooms, cleaned
Salt
Freshly-ground black pepper
Bouquet of fresh herbs
Freshly-chopped parsley
150 ml/¼ pt/⅔ cup red wine
150 ml/¼ pt/⅔ cup beef or game stock

Line a well-greased 1.8 litre/3 pint pudding basin with two-thirds of the suet pastry. Place the boned partridge (or partridge joints, if preferred) in the basin, together with the diced rump steak and whole mushrooms. Season well with salt and pepper. Add the bouquet of fresh herbs and chopped parsley. Pour the wine and stock into the basin, and place the remaining suet pastry over the top of the basin to make a lid, sealing well. Cover with foil pleated in the centre to allow for expansion, and tie to the basin with string, making a handle for easy retrieval. Stand the basin in a saucepan of simmering water, and steam for about 3 hours, adding more boiling water to keep the level halfway up the basin. When cooked, remove the foil, wipe the basin dry, and serve at the table.

Kentish Chicken Pudding

(Serves 4–6)

225 g/½ lb suet pastry
1 chicken
225 g/½ lb salted belly pork, diced
1 onion, chopped
Salt
Freshly-ground black pepper
300 ml/½ pt/1¼ cups cider

For the parsley sauce

1 tbsp butter	Salt
1 tbsp flour	Freshly-ground black
600 ml/1 pt/2½ cups hot milk	pepper
A handful of finely-chopped parsley	

Line a well-greased 1.8 litre/3 pint pudding basin with two-thirds of the suet pastry. Joint the chicken into ten pieces. Fill the pudding basin with the chicken, diced belly pork and chopped onion. Season with salt and pepper. Add the cider and top with the remaining suet pastry. Cover the basin with foil, pleated in the centre, tie down, and place in a saucepan of simmering water. Steam for about 3 hours, adding more boiling water to keep the level half-way up the basin.

To make the parsley sauce, melt the butter in a saucepan, and add the flour. Stir to make a thick paste. Add the hot milk a ladleful at a time, and stir until smooth. Continue to cook gently over a low heat until the sauce thickens, about 5–10 minutes. Add the chopped parsley, and season to taste.

When the pudding is cooked, remove the foil and wipe the basin dry. Serve the pudding from its basin at the table, together with the parsley sauce.

Sussex Pond Pudding   (Serves 4)

175 g/6 oz suet pastry	100 g/4 oz/½ cup Demerara
100 g/4 oz/½ stick butter, cut into small pieces	sugar
	1 large or 2 medium lemons

Line a well-greased 1.2 litre/2 pint pudding basin with two-thirds of the suet pastry. Seal the cut sides together well. Press half the butter and half the sugar into this suet lining. Prick the lemon or lemons all over with a skewer and place in the lined basin. Add the remaining butter and sugar. Place the remaining pastry on the top to make a lid, pressing the edges together well to seal them. Cover with foil pleated in the middle, tie to the basin with a string, making a handle over the top. Place in a saucepan of simmering water half-way up the basin. Cover and steam for 3 hours, adding more boiling water when necessary to keep up the level. Turn out on to a hot serving dish, and serve at the table, with home-made custard.

Cherry Batter Pudding   (Serves 6)

The orchards of Kent are a mass of pink cherry blossom in springtime, and many dishes have been invented to make use of this most English fruit.

225 g/½ lb plain flour	450 g/1 lb sweet black
Pinch of salt	cherries, stoned
2 eggs	50 g/2 oz/⅓ cup sugar
300 ml/½ pt/1¼ cups milk	

Sieve the flour and salt into a large mixing bowl. Make a well in the centre and add the eggs, beating vigorously. Gradually add the milk until the batter is smooth and frothy. Place the cherries in a well-buttered 1.5 litre/2½ pint pudding basin and sprinkle with half the sugar. Pour the batter over the cherries. Cover the basin with foil pleated in the middle and tie under the rim with string, making a handle over the top. Place in a saucepan with boiling water half-way up the basin. Cover and steam for an hour, topping up with more boiling water when necessary. Turn out on to a warmed serving dish and sprinkle with the remaining sugar. Serve with home-made custard.

Kentish Huffkins   (Makes 6)

These oval doughnut-shaped buns were once made specially to be eaten at the hoppers' feast at the end of the picking season.

450 g/1 lb plain flour	10 g/⅓ oz dried yeast
½ tsp salt	2 tsp sugar
50 g/2 oz/¼ cup lard	300 ml/½ pt/1¼ cups milk

Sieve the flour and salt into a large mixing bowl and rub in the lard. Gently heat the milk and add the sugar. Allow the milk to cool until lukewarm and sprinkle on the dried yeast. Set aside for 15 minutes until frothy. Pour into the flour mixture and mix well. Knead to make a smooth dough. Cover and set aside in a warm place until doubled in size. Knock back, knead and divide into six flat oval cakes about 1.3 cm/½ in thick. Make a hole in the middle of each. Place them on a greased baking sheet and set aside in a warm place until well-risen. Bake in a moderately hot oven (200°C/400°F/Gas Mark 6) for 15–20 minutes. Remove from the oven and wrap them in a warm clean cloth until cool (this keeps the crust soft). Serve with butter and jam for tea.

Oast Cakes (Makes 6–8)

Oast cakes are another tea-time favourite in the South.

225 g/$\frac{1}{2}$ lb plain flour
$\frac{1}{2}$ tsp salt
1 tsp baking powder
50 g/2 oz/$\frac{1}{4}$ cup lard

1 tbsp castor sugar
75 g/3 oz/$\frac{1}{2}$ cup currants
A little lemon juice
Fat or oil for frying

Sieve the flour, salt and baking powder into a large mixing bowl. Rub in the lard until the mixture resembles fine breadcrumbs. Stir in the sugar and currants. Add lemon juice and a little water to make a moist dough. Divide into small pieces and roll into circles on a floured board (they should be about 1.3 cm/$\frac{1}{2}$ in thick). Fry in hot fat or oil until golden brown, turning once. Drain on kitchen paper, and serve hot.

Sticky Black Gingerbread

Michelham Priory, an Augustinian priory near Hailsham, East Sussex, founded in the thirteenth century, is open to the public, and serves this sticky treat at tea-time.

2 tbsp black treacle
2 tbsp golden syrup
100 g/4 oz/1 stick butter
50 g/2 oz/$\frac{1}{4}$ cup light brown sugar
50 g/2 oz/$\frac{1}{4}$ cup dark brown sugar
1 egg

150 ml/$\frac{1}{4}$ pt/$\frac{2}{3}$ cup milk
175 g/6 oz/$1\frac{1}{3}$ cups plain flour
Pinch of salt
1 tbsp ground ginger
1 tsp cinnamon
1 tsp bicarbonate of soda dissolved in 1 tbsp milk

Heat the black treacle, golden syrup, butter and brown sugars in a saucepan until melted. Set aside to cool. Meanwhile, beat the egg and milk together. In a large mixing bowl sieve the flour and other dry ingredients. Add the melted treacle mixture to the flour, then add the egg and milk. Beat with a whisk until smooth. Add the dissolved bicarbonate of soda and stir in well. Immediately pour the mixture into a greased square 18 cm/7 in baking tin. Place in a pre-heated slow oven (150°C/300°F/Gas Mark 2) for 1 hour until springy to the touch. Cool, cut into slices, and serve for tea.

A Kentish oast house.

Drink in the South

The South is a great source of traditional English drink. Not only are there a number of fine breweries producing distinctive ales throughout the region, but additionally, the South-East in particular provides a large proportion of that essential brewing ingredient, hops, to breweries throughout the country. The South can claim to be the birthplace both of cider, and of the modern English vineyard. The abundance of fine fruits in the 'Garden of England' also results, not surprisingly, in the production of country fruit wines on both a small private scale as well as commercially.
Hours: see p. 30.

Traditional Beer

The South has a number of fine independent breweries. Shepherd Neame of Kent produce distinctive hoppy bitter beers; Harvey's of Lewes, Sussex are popular in that county, as are the Sussex beers brewed by King & Barnes at Horsham; further west, Gale's Brewery in Hampshire also produce a good range of traditional beers. As is the case throughout the country, the national brewing concerns maintain a strong presence in the region. Whitbread's Fremlins Brewery at Faversham provides good cask ales to their many pubs, while Charrington supplies the South-East with Charrington IPA and Draught Bass. Friary Meux pubs are part of the national Allied Breweries group, and supply the South and South-East with cask-conditioned ale brewed in Essex. To contrast with the large national breweries and their vast tied estates, an increasing number of mini-breweries are also trading in the region.

Kent

Shepherd Neame Ltd, Faversham Brewery, Faversham, Kent. Shepherd Neame is a highly regarded regional brewery, unusual in that it is able to supply all required hops for brewing from its own Queen Court hop farm in Ospringe. Not surprisingly, considering the brewery's location in the heart of the hop country, Shepherd Neame Bitter and Best Bitter are characterized by an intense hoppy

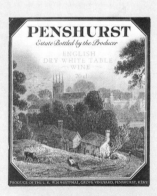

Assorted mats and labels of the region.

Hops

The hop is a vine-like plant cultivated in most major beer-making regions of the world, and in Britain primarily in the south-east counties of Kent and Sussex, as well as in Hereford and Worcester. Trained on a system of tall poles and complex wires, this unusual plant, ordered into hop alleys, its heavy, hanging cones oozing oils and resins, remains one of the classic sights of the English countryside.

In the spring, in many areas, hops are still strung by men working on stilts. The harvest, however, no longer depends on the cheap labour of Londoners in search of an inexpensive working holiday; today a special tractor roams the hop alleys, and a labourer on a platform slashes the vines which fall into a trailer below: not half as picturesque, but considerably more efficient. At least the rounded oast houses with their characteristic hardwood cowls still remain, though many of these picturesque kilns where the hops were once dried over slow charcoal fires have been converted into highly-desirable residences. Nevertheless, in spite of the fact that the size of the English hop garden has declined in recent years, the South-East still remains a leading area in world hop production, and it is also a most important centre for the research and development of this important crop.

Before the hop was established in Britain, the English drank unhopped ale, presumably a sweetish, malty brew, which probably was none too clear. 'Bere' or 'biere' – that is, ale flavoured with hops – was introduced to England from the Low Countries, probably in the fifteenth century, but it was resisted for some time; indeed, the use of hops in brewing was actually forbidden by law in many towns. However, by the seventeenth century, hop gardens were established in Britain, and beer gradually replaced ale in popularity. Today, the two terms are virtually interchangeable.

Hops originally were added to beer as a preservative, and to help clarification. They still serve both these purposes, but the main reason for their continued importance to the beer drinker is the unique flavour and aroma which they impart. Goldings and Fuggles, the two best-known English hops, are still grown in the South-East, though Fuggles, a somewhat coarser hop than Goldings, was struck severely by a fungal disease known as Verticillium wilt. Today new varieties have been developed which both have a higher bittering capacity, and which are also wilt resistant. These include Target, Northern Brewer, Challenger and Northdown, among others.

In the brewing process, hops are added to the copper, and boiled vigorously with the wort, thus extracting the bitter resins and oils. Afterwards, the wort is filtered through a bed of spent whole hops in a vessel known as a hop back (those breweries which use hop pellets, that is, whole hop cones ground into powder and compressed – experts claim that there is no loss of quality – extract the remaining hop residue in a whirlpool). But hops serve two purposes in brewing. In addition to adding bitterness, they also give traditional beer its pronounced aroma. This can be intensified by adding a handful of dry hops (hops that have not been boiled) to a cask of beer before it is despatched. As the beer conditions in the cellar, it acquires a wonderful, fresh, stinging scent that is difficult if not impossible to duplicate in brewery-conditioned beers.

Shepherd Neame's Queen Court hop farm is able to supply this well-known Kentish brewery with all its own hops required for brewing traditional ales.

Goldings hops, trained on a system of wires.

Casks and Coopers

'Traditional draught beers from the wood': nothing sounds more inviting to the beer drinker. In the not so distant past, all draught beer in Britain was sold from wooden casks, and the brewing industry kept thousands of skilled coopers employed. These bulging vessels, which have probably been in use to carry dry and wet ingredients in Britain since the first century AD, are still produced and repaired by hand with ancient, well-worn tools. Splayed oak staves are shaped or matched, then formed, bent and held in place with iron hoops; heads are formed and finished and shives or bungs tapped into place to form a liquid-tight seal.

The use of wooden casks, however, has declined considerably in recent years. Though the aluminium alloy casks that have replaced them may lack the romance of a bygone age, nevertheless they do present advantages to drinkers as well as brewers.

Aluminium alloy casks, it must be stressed, are different from the aluminium kegs which hold pressurized, bright, brewery-conditioned beer. Unlike in kegs, beer continues to develop and mature in the cask, and so it demands care and respect in its treatment from the public house landlord. Casks cannot be tapped too soon, for they must first be allowed to settle in the publican's cellar. A hard spile or plug is hammered into the wooden shive hole to regulate natural pressure. The cask, once tapped, should ideally be emptied within a few days. For this reason, conscientious breweries attempt to match the cask size with each pub's turnover, to ensure that stale beer does not linger. There are five different cask sizes, though the smallest and the largest are not generally in circulation: pin ($4\frac{1}{2}$ gallons), firkin (9 gallons), kilderkin (18 gallons), barrel (36 gallons) and hogshead (54 gallons).

Wooden casks made and repaired by hand: a skilled trade from a bygone age.

aroma and palate. Traditional dark mild is available in about one-third of the brewery's outlets. Founded in 1698, Shepherd Neame is the only surviving established independent brewery in Kent; its area of distribution is almost entirely in the South-East, with a large proportion of its beers sold through the free trade.

Master Brew Mild o.g. 1031
Master Brew Bitter o.g. 1036
Master Brew Best Bitter o.g. 1039
Stock Ale (winter only) o.g. 1040

Whitbread Fremlins, Faversham, Kent. Whitbread Fremlins brews beer primarily for the South-East and London (see p. 152). Fremlins Brewery was originally located in Maidstone, while George Beer and Rigden Ltd, was located in Faversham. As is the case with breweries throughout the country, both were absorbed into Whitbread's national group. Today two cask-conditioned ales are brewed in Faversham, as well as a brewery-conditioned beer, Fremlins AK, particularly for the Medway towns.

Fremlins Bitter o.g. 1034–37
Fremlins Tusker o.g. 1043 +

Ashford Brewing Company, Ashford, Kent. Established in 1983, this small brewing company produces one cask-conditioned ale, Challenger, named after the Challenger hop variety that was developed nearby.

Challenger Bitter o.g. 1038–39

Sussex

Harvey & Sons Ltd and Beard & Co., Lewes, East Sussex. Harvey's and Beard's are two small traditional Sussex breweries, independent of one another but closely linked by mutual agreement. All the brewing is done for Beard at Harvey's Brewery, and the range of well-liked Sussex ales are available in both Harvey's and Beard's houses, as well as in a number of free outlets, mainly in this county.

IPA o.g. 1030–34
XX Mild o.g. 1030–34
Sussex Best Bitter o.g. 1036–40
XXXX 'Old' (winter only)
o.g. 1040–43

King & Barnes, Horsham, West Sussex. This independent family brewing company produces only cask-conditioned and bottled beers, available primarily in West Sussex and Surrey. Like other breweries in the South-East, King & Barnes produce strong well-hopped bitter beers to suit the regional taste, such as the excellent Draught Festive. A sweet, dark mild is also produced as well as a strong mild for winter months only.

Sussex Mild o.g. 1034
Sussex Bitter o.g. 1034
Draught Festive Bitter o.g. 1050
Old Ale (winter only) o.g. 1046

Hampshire

George Gale & Co., Horndean, Portsmouth, Hampshire. This well-liked Hampshire company dates back to the time when almost all public houses brewed their own beers, for Gale & Co. originated at the Ship & Bell pub in Horndean some 250 years ago. As trade increased, a brewery was built in what is still the present brewery transport yard. The majority of Gale's public houses are located in East Hampshire, though the company trades as far north as Reading, as well as in neighbouring Sussex. Gale's produces a full range of traditional cask-conditioned ales, as well as a fine bottle-conditioned barley wine, Prize Old Ale, sold in half pints sealed with a cork.

Cask-conditioned ales:

BBB (Best Bitter) o.g. 1036
HSB (Horndean Special Bitter) o.g. 1050
XXXL (Light Mild) o.g. 1030
XXXD (Dark Mild) o.g. 1031
XXXXX (winter only) o.g. 1044

Bottle-conditioned ale:

Prize Old Ale o.g. 1093

Ballard's Brewery Ltd, Rogate, Petersfield, Hampshire. This small farm brewery started in a cow-shed near the Hampshire–Sussex border in 1980, and now supplies over thirty pubs with two distinctive beers, Ballard's Best Bitter and Wassail. Both are brewed with malt and hops only; no additional sugar is used in their manufacture. The beers are available direct to the public from the brewery.

Ballard's Best Bitter o.g. 1042
Wassail o.g. 1060

Ringwood Brewery, Ringwood, Hampshire. Ringwood, a town once famous for its strong ales but without its own brewery for over fifty years, had this situation rectified in 1978 when the small Ringwood Brewery began production.

Best Bitter o.g. 1040
Old Thumper o.g. 1060

New Forest Brewery, Cadnam, Hampshire. This small company has been brewing only since 1980. Both cask- and brewery-conditioned beers are produced, and supplied almost exclusively to clubs in an area bounded by Poole, Salisbury, Winchester and Portsmouth.

New Forest Real Ale o.g. 1036
Old Evel o.g. 1048

Bourne Valley Brewery, Andover, Hampshire. The Bourne Valley Brewery was begun by a former national chairman of CAMRA, the consumer movement which has done so much to safeguard Britain's traditional beers. Supplying the free trade within a twenty-mile radius of the brewery, the company now administers two of its own public houses.

Weaver's Bitter o.g. 1037
Andover Ale o.g. 1040
Henchard Bitter o.g. 1045
Wallop (Christmas only) o.g. 1056

English Wine in the South of England

Kent, Sussex and Hampshire have on average longer, warmer summers, and are considered by many to be the most suitable areas in Britain for growing grapes. There is a concentration of vineyards located in the South of England, and there are two important regional associations here for vine growers: the Central Southern Growers' Association, and the Weald and Downland Vineyards Association. Because there are a number of vineyards in relative proximity to one another, it is possible in summer to visit several vineyards which are open to the public, offering unaccompanied tours through the vineyard with informative pamphlets, or guided tours of the vineyard and winery by arrangement. An English Wine Route has been devised by the

English Vineyards Association whereby visitors are able to make arrangements to visit two vineyards in a day, including wine tastings and lunch. Help in co-ordinating vineyard tours and information about English wine in general is available from the English Wine Centre, which both makes its own English wine, Cuckmere, and keeps a large variety of English wines for sale. The English Wine Centre holds an annual English Wine Festival every September.

The English Wine Centre
Drusilla's Corner
Alfriston
East Sussex

Lamberhurst Priory Vineyard
Ridge Farm
Lamberhurst
Tunbridge Wells
Kent

The Lamberhurst Priory Vineyard has an historical link with vine growing in the past, since the monks of the Priory cultivated a vineyard at nearby Leeds Castle in the sixteenth century. Today thirty-two acres are cultivated with a number of grape varieties, including Müller-Thurgau, Seyval Blanc, Reichensteiner, Schönburger, Riesling, Gutedal, Pinot Noir and Seibel. The wines are made in a modern and efficient winery.

Visitors welcome (an informative Vineyard Trail is open all year, while guided tours of the vineyard and winery are by appointment only).

Tenterden Vineyard
Spots Farm
Small Hythe
Kent

This ten-acre vineyard was planted in 1977 on the site of an old orchard, and gnarled apple trees still stand on the fringes, making the scene a particularly pleasant English one. The vineyard, however, like so many in this area, is run on professional and dedicated lines, and the wines are made in the Spots Farm Winery, a building previously used for drying and pressing hops. Principal grape varieties planted include Müller-Thurgau, Gutenborner, Reichensteiner and Seyval Blanc. An apple wine, from Cox's and Bramleys grown on the farm, is also made here.

Visitors welcome.

Staple Vineyard
Church Farm
Staple
Canterbury
Kent

Staple Vineyard consists of seven acres located in the heart of traditional hop- and fruit-growing country, planted over a deep underlying layer of chalk. The main variety cultivated is Müller-Thurgau, together with Huxelrebe and Reichensteiner.

Visitors welcome.

Penshurst Vineyard
The Grove
Penshurst
Kent

Penshurst, a twelve-acre vineyard and modern well-equipped winery, is located just outside this lovely Kentish village. Grape varieties planted include Müller-Thurgau, Reichensteiner, Seyval Blanc and Ehrenfelser, and apple wine from apples grown in the Penshurst orchards is also made.

Vineyard tours arranged by appointment.

Biddenden Vineyards
Little Whatmans
Biddenden
Kent

A mile and a half from the village of the same name, Biddenden consists of eighteen acres planted with Müller-Thurgau, Ortega, Reichensteiner and Huxelrebe. Medium-dry wines are produced in the estate winery where traditional still cider, stronger mature apple wine, and apple juice are also made.

Visitors welcome; guided tours by arrangement.

Carr Taylor Vineyard
Westfield
Hastings
Sussex

In the heart of historic Sussex, on the beautiful slopes of the South Downs, David Carr Taylor has planted some twenty-one acres of vines on a high wire trellis system (see p. 72). A large range of wines is produced in the new winery, and they have gained recognition here and abroad. Grape varieties cultivated include Reichensteiner, Gutenborner, Kerner, Huxelrebe, Schönburger and others. A strong, wine-like Sussex

cider, Senlac, is also made.

Visitors welcome (tours and tastings by arrangement).

Rock Lodge Vineyard
Rock Lodge
Scaynes Hill
Sussex

Locals refer to the Rock Lodge Vineyard as the 'oven field' due to its excellent exposure. About three acres are planted primarily with Müller-Thurgau, and a single dry wine which needs ageing to mature is produced in the estate winery.

Visitors welcome by arrangement.

Chilsdown Vineyard
The Old Station House
Singleton
Chichester
Sussex

This thirteen-acre vineyard was planted in the Sussex Downs in 1972, primarily with Müller-Thurgau and, subsequently, Reichensteiner, Chardonnay (which did not fare well) and Seyval Blanc. A crisp dry wine is made in a winery which is housed in the disused booking hall and waiting-rooms of the old Singleton railway station.

Visitors welcome.

Hambledon Vineyards Ltd
Hambledon
Portsmouth
Hampshire

Within sight of Broadhalfpenny Down, the cradle of that most English game, cricket, a seven-acre vineyard now stands, planted mainly with Chardonnay, Pinot Noir and Pinot Meunier, the classic grapes of Champagne, as well as with Seyval Blanc. The vines thrive in a

The Biddenden twins.

English Wine

Most people do not think of Britain as a wine-producing country. Our national drink is beer, the homely English pub the universal hostelry of good cheer. Our images of the countryside include fields of waving golden barley and the conical outline of Kentish oasts, not the well-ordered slopes of vineyards, the low-lying silhouette of wineries, where the grapey aroma of fast-running juice, the gentle bubble and gurgle of fermentation, infuse the atmosphere with a primitive Bacchic joy. The British certainly have a history of wine drinking and, indeed, claret, port and sherry all have long historical associations with this island. But as for wine produced from grapes grown in British vineyards, there is a sad lack of awareness, indeed, even a rather ungenerous suspicion that it really does not exist.

Yet wine grapes have been grown successfully in Britain for nearly 2000 years. Currently there are some 230 commercial vineyards in England, Wales and the Channel Islands with a total of 1000 acres of vines under cultivation. Quality English wines produced from grapes grown in Britain (as opposed to 'British wine' produced from imported bulk grape concentrate: the distinction between the two is essential) are becoming more and more readily available, and they are winning awards and gaining recognition both at home and abroad.

Like other parts of Europe which they conquered, the Roman legions, when they came to Britain, brought the vine with them, both to make wine to satisfy their troops' legendary thirst, as well as to serve as a mark of civilization. By the time they left some 300 years later, vineyards were established throughout the country. The art of viticulture survived the Dark Ages, and when the wine- and cider-loving Normans came to Britain, William's Domesday Survey recorded forty-five extant vineyards in fourteen counties. Religious orders both kept alive wine-making traditions,

and also made advances in viticultural methods and techniques, but viticulture did not wholly cease with Henry VIII's Dissolution of the Monasteries. Indeed English wine continued to be made in country estates right up to the start of this century. However, cheaper, stronger and more richly-flavoured wines from France, Portugal, Spain and elsewhere were imported in increasing quantity, and this kept domestic wine production from ever developing on any commercial scale.

Today there has been a great revival in English viticulture. While there are many amateurs who are growing grapes in Britain (and indeed keen amateur interest has contributed greatly to viticultural knowledge), there is also a growing number of dedicated professionals who are cultivating vineyards and making wines using advanced viticultural and oenological skills, with the realistic aim of producing wines that can compete both in price and quality with those from the Continent. To this new breed of professionals, the activity of growing grapes and making wine is a serious commercial pursuit, indeed an all-encompassing way of life, as visitors to such vineyards may see for themselves (many English vineyards are very pleased to welcome visitors; vineyards and cellars are shown, wine-making techniques described, lunch together with wine tastings can be arranged, and wines can be purchased direct).

There are four major wine-growing areas in England which have their own regional associations (Weald and Downland Vineyards Association, Central Southern Growers, East Anglian Wine Growers' Association and South West Vinegrowers' Association), in addition to isolated growers located elsewhere. It is not yet possible to classify English wine into regional types, however, or to differentiate in general style between, say, a South-West and a Downlands wine. A

large variety of grapes is being grown throughout the regions, and vine growers continue to experiment to discover what particular varieties suit their soils and microclimates; thus the wines produced remain individual and distinct, not yet conforming to regional styles. The types of vines most commonly cultivated include Müller-Thurgau, Seyval Blanc, Reichensteiner and Schönburger, though many others are planted as well, including classics such as Chardonnay, and less well known varieties such as Zweigeltrebe and Gutenborner.

English wine, at its best, is characterized by a clean, crisp fragrance, a delicate fruitiness, and an underlying backbone of acidity. While many distinct and individual wines are produced, there are, broadly speaking, two main styles of English wine. Many wine makers follow the Germans practice of adding 'sweet reserve' to their wine, that is, a measure of pure unfermented grape juice to mellow the

acidity and make the wines more immediately attractive. This results in easy-to-drink medium-dry wines that resemble hocks or moselles. Other wine makers, however, feel that English wine must develop its own unique identity. The distinctive character of wine made from grapes grown in Britain, they argue, comes from a pronounced fruity acidity; thus they produce bone-dry wines that are initially aggressive and less forthcoming, and which take some time to mellow and mature – at least two or three years or longer in the bottle. Most English wine is white; some vineyards produce both dry and medium-dry styles; in addition, small amounts of red, rosé and sparkling wines are also being made. In some cases quite successfully. There is a remarkable range and variety of English wines currently being produced.

Some might ask, Why buy English wine? It is not cheap compared with many imports from abroad (inequitable taxation contributes in part to

this: 'British wine' made from imported concentrate attracts less duty than the indigenous product). Yet English wine is unique, a carefully nurtured quality product made from grapes grown on this island, and with a distinct character of its own.

ENGLISH VINEYARDS ASSOCIATION SEAL OF QUALITY

The English Vineyards Association Seal of Quality is awarded only to English wines that have undergone stringent laboratory tests, and which have been approved by a tasting panel of experts. It is a guarantee of quality.

Apple trees and vines grow side by side at Spots Farm, Tenterden.

similar deep chalky sub-soil, and from this first modern English vineyard planted in 1951, a dry white English wine is produced.

Open Days for the general public during summer months; parties can visit the vineyard by arrangement.

Aldermoor Vineyards
Poulner Hill
Ringwood
Hampshire

This five-acre vineyard is planted mainly with Müller-Thurgau, and some Reichensteiner; and two wines, medium dry and medium, are produced.

Guided vineyard tours by arrangement (minimum 12/maximum 30).

Cranmore Vineyard
Yarmouth
Isle of Wight

Wine, dessert and dual-purpose grape varieties are grown on this ten-acre site on the Isle of Wight, and a full range of vines are available for sale ('vine enquiries will be dealt with on receipt of a stamped addressed envelope'). The vineyard produces a medium-dry wine mainly from the Müller-Thurgau, blended with Gutenborner, Würzer and Pinot Blanc.

Open to parties of 10 or more by appointment only.

Barton Manor Vineyard
Whippingham
East Cowes
Isle of Wight

Barton Manor was mentioned in the Domesday Survey of 1086. Queen Victoria bought the estate in 1846, and the gardens were laid out by Prince Albert, though the Manor returned to private ownership in 1922. The present owners planted their five-acre vineyard in 1977, primarily with Müller-Thurgau, as well as with smaller quantities of Seyval Blanc, Huxelrebe, Reichensteiner, Schönburger and Zweigeltrebe (a red grape variety producing a light rosé wine). Apple wine is also produced in the estate winery.

Visitors welcome.

Adgestone Vineyard
Sandown
Isle of Wight

The second largest commercial vineyard in Britain comprises about twenty-seven acres planted with Reichensteiner, Seyval Blanc, Müller-Thurgau and Kerner, in addition to three acres planted with red grape varieties. All wines produced at Adgestone are estate-bottled, and the winery's production of about 60,000 bottles annually (conditions permitting) are marketed through the London wine shippers, Deinhard & Co.

In addition to the above, the following vine growers are members of the English Vineyards Association. Many sell wine direct.

Kent
Five Acres, Downe
Ightham, Ivy Hatch
Underriver, Sevenoaks
Littlefield, West Peckham
Knowle Hill, Ulcombe
Cherry Hill, Wateringbury
Parsonage Field, Newnham
Garden House, Saltwood
Devil's Cauldron, High Halden
The Harbourne Vineyard, High Halden
Pleasance, Ashford
The Beult, Pluckley
Bardingley, Staplehurst
Dingleden, Benenden
Conghurst Oast, Hawkhurst
Harefield, Hawkhurst
Leeds Castle, Leeds

Sussex
Houghton Green, Playden
Saxonhill, Battle
Pine Ridge, Staplecross
Stocklands, Staplecross
Little Pook Hill, Etchingham
Combe House, Heathfield
Beltane, Cross-in-Hand
Whiteoaks, Hailsham
Friston Forest, Westdean
Breaky Bottom, Lewes
Castlehouse, Lewes
Ditchling, Ditchling
Flexerne, Newick
Five Chimneys, Hadlow Down
Barnsgate, Uckfield
St Alfreds, Uckfield
Lyndhurst, Warninglid
Bookers, Bolney
Downers, Henfield
Thakeham, Thakeham
Nash, Steyning
Arundel, Arundel
Gipsy Glade, East Marden
Hooksway, North Marden

Hampshire
The Hook, Hook
Frensham Manor, Wheatley
Amery Farm, Alton
Harcombe Manor, Bishops Sutton
Ent House, Ropley
St Heliers, Ropley
Braishfield Manor, Romsey
Hill Grove, Southampton
Kiln Copse, Soberton
Beaulieu, Beaulieu
Efford, Lymington
Hillside, Ringwood
Poulner, Ringwood

Cider
Cider is certainly one of the great national drinks of Britain (see pp. 130–132), but it is most likely that it was only first introduced with the Normans sometime after the Conquest in 1066. The monks at Battle Abbey were both making and selling cider by 1265, and it has been produced commercially in the area since then. Indeed, for some time cider was mainly confined to Kent and Sussex, only spreading to the West much later.

The South-East is considered the 'garden of England', and the dessert and culinary fruit from apple orchards here is considered by many to be the finest in the world. The Cox's Orange Pippin, with its balance of sweetness, scent and fruity acidity, is possibly the finest flavoured of all eating apples, while the Bramley's Seedling is the country's most popular cooking apple. Other well-loved English varieties include the Spartan, Egremont Russet and Laxton's Superb. While such apples are cultivated primarily for the table, they are also used for the production of cider. Indeed, herein lies the principal difference between cider from the South-East and that from the West Country: in the South-East it is made only from such dessert and culinary fruit, not from bittersharp and bittersweet apples which are cultivated for cider throughout the West. The best Sussex and Kentish ciders thus have a correspondingly less harsh, less acid flavour; fermented dry, they are wine-like in character, with the delicate scent of the Cox apple predominating. West Country cider drinkers might find such ciders rather bland, missing that characteristic mouthpuckering bite, which is, after all, a certain acquired taste. On the other hand, others will prefer a smoother, milder character inherent in ciders produced only with dessert and culinary fruit.

While cider making here, and elsewhere in the country, was and to a certain extent remains a farm activity, one company in the heart of the Sussex countryside has grown to become the fourth largest commercial producer of cider in the UK. It is interesting to note that the Merrydown Wine Company was first started by two amateur wine makers, who, in a garage at Rotherfield, East Sussex, experimented to produce an extraordinarily potent cider, as well as some home-made redcurrant wine from locally grown fruit. Merrydown 'vintage ciders' (although made with apples from one year only, the ciders are blended to ensure uniformity from year to year) remain among the most potent – and palatable – on the market, still made almost entirely with local Cox and Bramley apples, pressed, then fermented in huge outdoor oak vats. And as in the past, the company still makes traditional country wines from fresh gooseberries, redcurrants, damsons, elderflowers and elderberries.

If the founders of Merrydown were enthusiastic amateurs of wine making and were particularly committed to the revival of English wines, it is interesting to note that several vine growers and wine makers are now also returning to their traditional country roots: in their modern sophisticated wineries, they too are making excellent wine-like ciders from locally grown fruit.

Merrydown Wine plc
Horam Manor
Horam
Heathfield
East Sussex
  Visitors welcome.

Sloe Gin and Cherry Brandy
The fine fruits of the South and South-East are used to make country wines, both commercially such as at Merrydown, as well as domestically. In addition to pressing and fermenting such fruit it is also macerated in spirits to make traditional drinks such as sloe gin and cherry brandy. Sloe gin is no more

Afternoon tea in the Garden Counties: (clockwise) sticky black gingerbread, oast cakes, Kentish huffkins, a selection of English sandwiches, scones and jam.

than sloes, the small bluish-black fruit of the blackthorn, pricked with a fork, then added to a jar of gin, together with sufficient sugar to sweeten the astringency of the sloes, about half a pound to a bottle of gin. The result is left to steep for six months to a year, the sloes are removed, then the concoction is rebottled. Cherry brandy, which is produced commercially, is similar: ripe, sour Morello cherries steeped in brandy.

Some Useful Addresses

South East England Tourist Board
(includes Kent, Surrey, East and
West Sussex)
Cheviot House
4–6 Monson Road
Tunbridge Wells
Kent

Southern Tourist Board
(includes Hampshire, Isle of Wight
and part of Dorset)
The Old Town Hall

Leigh Road
Eastleigh
Hampshire

John Strange of Lyndhurst
High Street
Lyndhurst
Hampshire
Venison and game specialist.

Avon River Fisheries
Bickton Mill
Fordingbridge
Hampshire
Home-produced fresh trout,
smoked trout, smoked poultry,
mackerel and other products
available in the shop, which is
situated in the old mill.

Weald and Downland Open
Museum
Singleton
near West Dean
Sussex
Open: April 1–October 31, daily,
11.00–17.00. November 1–March
31, Wednesday, Sunday and Bank
Holidays, 11.00–16.00.

Wheelers of Whitstable
Whitstable
Kent
This small oyster bar is the original
of the now famous chain begun in
1856. Native oysters and other
shellfish and fish, to eat on the
premises or take away.

Drusilla's
Alfriston
East Sussex
In addition to the English Wine
Centre, the complex at Drusilla's
includes a restaurant serving Sussex
and English foods, English wines,
real ales and ciders, as well as a
traditional bakery selling home-
made regional baked products.

THE WEST COUNTRY

To many, the West Country recalls endless childhood summers at Treyarnon Bay and Padstow, Ilfracombe, Salcombe, Exmouth and Lyme Regis; equally endless traffic jams at the Exeter bypass; glorious Devon cream teas and Kelly's Cornish ice-cream; and a first (and unforgettable) taste of alcohol in the shape of 'scrumpy' together with an enormous home-made pasty down at the Farmer's Arms. Those from the industrial Midlands or the North of England who descend on this colour-saturated landscape each July and August can be forgiven for thinking that the West Country, jutting into the Gulf-warm waters of the Atlantic, with its rich red earth, whitewashed thatched cottages, pastel apple orchards and motley fishing villages, is little short of paradise.

Much of this is lush, moist land, enjoying the mildest climate in England (every year, early daffodils from Cornwall and the Scilly Isles tease of coming spring, while the rest of the country remains locked in winter). The luscious hills of Devon, corseted by hedgerows and narrow lanes into a decorous patchwork of striped red and brown, green and waving yellow, appear almost too fertile. Indeed, the dairy cattle that graze here – black and white Friesians, fawn Guernseys, and (especially) large-eyed Jerseys – produce milk so rich in butterfat that it needs only to be left on a low heat overnight to form a thick, yellow crust of scalded cream which is then skimmed off by hand. Packed in little tubs or cartons, this clotted cream is sent off as souvenirs throughout the country, a happy memento of wicked, fattening cream teas, themselves a symbol of Britain's most popular holiday area.

The beaches of Dorset, Devon and Cornwall are possibly the finest in the country; certainly in summer they are the best attended. The sea, too, provides a livelihood for many West Countrymen, not just those in the tourist industry. Newlyn and Brixham are two important harbours for prolific catches of mackerel, pilchards (though not as plentiful as they once were – in the past, Cornishwomen would hang them up to dry on a line with clothes pegs), white fish such as cod, hake and whiting, and crabs and lobsters, all of which make their way by road or rail to the new Billingsgate Market in London, to be despatched up-country and abroad. Much, however, stays at home, and though such regional curiosities as star gazey pie (traditionally made with pilchards, whose heads poke from the crust, gazing philosophically starwards) are still made for special occasions, regular West Country favourites include mackerel with gooseberry sauce, Cornish crab soup, plaice or Torbay sole simply grilled with butter and lemon, and cod baked in milk. Change comes slow in this westernmost part of England, and anything too different (such as john dory, skate, monkfish or red gurnard, all caught in these waters) is viewed as suspiciously 'furrin'.

Elsewhere in the region, particularly in the country around and beyond Cheddar Gorge, the plentiful milk of Somerset is used to make traditional farmhouse Cheddar cheese. Though cheddar-type cheese is made throughout Britain and indeed the world, true traditional Cheddar comes only from a pocketful of farms here and in the neighbouring counties of Avon, Dorset and Devon. To those who have never tasted the real thing, it is a revelation, for true Cheddar is without doubt one of the great cheeses of the world. With such fine cheese, nothing can beat the West Countryman's lunch: no more than a good wedge of farmhouse Cheddar, a chunk of crusty bread, some pickled onions or walnuts, farm fresh butter and home-made chutney, and a foaming pint of real ale, or potent farmhouse 'scrumpy'.

Farmhouse cider is the true drink of this rural region, epitomizing a bygone way of life. Made from the juice of milled and pressed cider and

Summer afternoon at Exmouth.

eating apples which ferment into alcohol simply through the action of natural yeasts, this was – and to a certain degree remains – the everyday beverage of farmer and farm labourer alike (indeed, most labourers were entitled to a hefty ration of a gallon a day). On Saturdays, friends, villagers and farmhands would gather in old cider barns, to sit on upturned barrels or perch on huge wooden presses, just drinking cider and having a 'good old natter'. Throughout the apple season, the same men would come to the farm and help with the cider making to repay all they'd drunk. Such traditions continue today.

Cider, as well as being the popular drink of the land, finds its way into the cooking pot, too. Pork stewed in cider and rich cream is a Somerset favourite, chicken in cider is prepared on many a Devon farm, and mackerel, fresh from Cornish trawlers, is quickly gutted and simply simmered in this inexpensive elixir.

But the West Country is not just a land of strawberries and clotted cream, 'zider' in stone jars, or donkey rides by the seaside. Bristol has long been the leading port of the west, with a tradition of trading in (among many other things) wine since Norman times. Bath, one of the most elegant and stylish cities in Britain, is of course famous for its therapeutic mineral waters, best taken (so it is said) with the plainly baked Bath Oliver biscuit. The Victorians who came to this fashionable spa were often recovering from over-eating, but while here, they probably did not fare at all badly. Bath buns, topped with crunchy lump sugar, can still be enjoyed to the strains of Mozart in the Pump Room, while Sally Lunn cakes – rich, sweet and yeasty – will make you no thinner today than they did a hundred years ago. Bath chaps, the pickled, smoked snouts of long-nosed pigs, may seem to you rather indelicate fare for this genteel city, but the gentlefolk of the past had no such squeamishness. Nor should you: muster up a pint of Courage (brewed in

Smoked Mackerel

Mackerel has long been one of the traditional mainstays of West Country fishermen, landed in seeming thousands, the green-blue bodies shimmering like quicksilver in the morning sun at Newlyn, Brixham and other harbours round the coast. The flavour of this firm, round fish is superb, particularly when extremely fresh; moreover, due to the great numbers that are landed, it remains relatively inexpensive. No doubt once the catch declines, this now 'common' fish will be declared a 'delicacy'.

Smoked mackerel is a particular West Country favourite which is gaining popularity throughout the country. Mackerel for smoking must be in prime condition, with a high oil content to assist the process. Most smoked mackerel available is hot smoked, that is, it is smoked in an oven which cooks it at the same time; this means that it can be eaten as it is, with no further preparation. Cold-smoked mackerel, less readily available but superb, is smoked (like salmon) for a longer period, but in a cool atmosphere, and thus the flesh is cured but remains uncooked, to be eaten cut across the grain into very thin slices. Hot-smoked mackerel is generally available whole or in fillets. We find that whole smoked mackerel has a more subtle, finer flavour because the actual surface upon which the smoke has been deposited is not eaten.

Topsham Smoked Mackerel Paste
(Serves 4)

2 whole smoked mackerel, or 4 smoked mackerel fillets	Salt
	Freshly-ground black pepper
100 g/4 oz/1 stick butter	6 tbsp sour cream
$\frac{1}{2}$ small onion, very finely chopped	Freshly-chopped parsley
	Lemon wedges

Remove skin and any bones from the mackerel and mash thoroughly. Melt the butter in a saucepan and sauté the onion until soft and golden. Add this to the mackerel, season well, and beat in the sour cream. Chill, garnish with chopped parsley and lemon wedges, and serve with hot toast.

nearby Bristol), and enjoy this excellent pub food, rolled in breadcrumbs and already cooked, to be eaten cold with pickles or mustard.

Dorchester, to the south, remains an important provincial county centre, as it was when Thomas Hardy used it as a model for his Casterbridge, set in a fictional Wessex very much like the Dorset of today. Towns such as Cerne Abbas, Sturminster Newton, Milton Abbas (Hardy called them the Giant's Hill, Stourcastle, Middleton Abbey) today remain introverted, indeed rather secretive, as if, perhaps, there are black stories still lurking in the shadows of their past, stories which no stranger has any business knowing about. When it comes to secretiveness, what, too, about the elusive Blue Vinny? So much has been said about the hunt for this legendary cheese, made blue, supposedly, by dipping a mouldy old piece of leather in the milk, yet today it still remains virtually impossible to find (one farm only, in Winterbourne Abbas, has recently revived production of this ancient cheese). Formerly, cheese experts scoured the county from Sherborne to Abbotsbury, Bere Regis to Blandford Forum; there were tales of Blue Vinny reaching customers via tortuous routes to protect the identity of the maker, and accusations of a rampant 'black market' trade in sub-standard Stilton which is passed off as Blue Vinny. And yet, by all accounts, and according to an expert cheese researcher in Shropshire, it was a thin cheese to begin with, made from buttermilk, with a stinging, mean acidity.

North of Dorset, a vast plain extends from Salisbury to Devizes, while the Marlborough Downs lead up to Swindon. This is the fat, pork-fed county of Wiltshire with a strategic central position astride all the main roads to the West: the old A4 to Bath, the M4 motorway from Wales to London via Bristol, the A303 and A30, both old routes from London to Exeter. In the past droves of pigs were herded east to London, and in towns such as Chippenham, Calne and Swindon, trade in commercial pork butchering and curing was

Cornish smoked mackerel.

Morris dancers entertain regulars at the Ring of Bells, North Bovey.

established. In the past, home-curing was an annual ritual for many a smallholding or farm, the flitches of bacon, hams, joints of shoulder or collar, all carefully dry-salted and sometimes smoked, then hung to dry in attic rafters, providing meat throughout the winter. The famous Wiltshire cure, which has replaced much traditional dry-salting, consists of treating the meat in concentrated brine baths for much shorter periods. The resulting gammon or bacon may not be able to stand up to the rigours of a winter's hanging (after all, curing meat was originally a means of preserving it in the days before freezers and refrigerators), but nowadays that is no longer the main purpose.

Like the rest of the West, Wiltshire is countryman's country, and you would not be looked at amiss if you entered the public bar of many a roadside inn or tavern in your Wellington boots. Prepared pig products, such as faggots, black and white puddings, cooked gammon and brawn, satisfy appetites sharpened by honest work outside, while pints of Arkell's Best Bitter, Wadsworth's 6X, or the potent Bishop's Tipple brewed by Gibbs Mew in Salisbury quench long thirsts during extended hours on market days.

The entire region is good country for drinking. In addition to draught ciders available in Devon, Somerset and Cornwall, there are a number of large and small independent breweries, most offering a good range of cask-conditioned beers served by traditional hand pump. Furthermore, many pubs in the West Country are free houses, and thus offer a heartening selection of beers brewed not only in this region, but much further afield, too. Thatched pubs on tiny Devon lanes, busy city 'boozers' in Dorchester, Plymouth or Bristol, lonely establishments on windswept Dartmoor, corner 'locals' serving mainly residents of just one or two streets only, or brash seaside inns with playrooms for children and tables outside: they all reflect the varied character (and characters) of the West Country.

Recipes from the West Country

Cornish Crab Soup (Serves 4–6)

West Country crab fishermen from Dartmouth, Brixham, Padstow and elsewhere sail out daily in small boats to check their pots. The crabs they bring home, unrivalled in size and succulence, are almost always sold already freshly boiled. They are superb in this rich, creamy soup.

The daily fish auction at Newlyn Harbour, Cornwall.

1 large boiled crab	Salt
50 g/2 oz/$\frac{1}{3}$ cup rice	Freshly-ground black
600 ml/1 pt/2$\frac{1}{2}$ cups chicken	pepper
stock	150 ml/$\frac{1}{4}$ pt/$\frac{2}{3}$ cup double
600 ml/1 pt/2$\frac{1}{2}$ cups milk	cream
Freshly-grated nutmeg	

Prise open the crab, discard the stomach bag and feathery gills or 'dead man's fingers'. Remove all flesh from the crab body and pound the white meat with the dark. Set the claw meat aside. Rinse the rice, and put in a large saucepan with the chicken stock. Stir, bring gently to the boil, and simmer for 10 minutes. Add the milk, nutmeg, salt and plenty of black pepper, bring back to the boil, and simmer until the rice is soft. Mix the white and brown crab meat into the soup, and liquidize. Return to the rinsed out saucepan, and add the claw meat, cut into pieces. Adjust seasoning, and allow to simmer for a further 10 minutes. Before serving, stir in cream, and heat gently but do not boil.

Baked Red Mullet   (Serves 4)

Red mullet was once plentiful in Weymouth and Portland, and it is still landed in Devon and Cornwall at certain times of the year. It is an excellent fish, with a characteristic 'gamy' flavour which comes from leaving its liver intact.

4 red mullet	Knob of butter
2 bay leaves	4 tbsp white wine
Freshly-chopped parsley	1 tbsp lemon juice
Freshly-chopped fennel	Salt
$\frac{1}{2}$ small onion, sliced	Pinch of cayenne pepper

Scale, clean, wash and pat the fish dry. Remove the gills and fins, but keep the liver intact, as this is a delicacy. Lay the fish in an ovenproof dish and cover with all the remaining ingredients. Cover the dish with foil, and bake in a moderate oven (180°C/350°F/Gas Mark 4) for 30–40 minutes, or until just tender (depending on the size of the fish). Serve immediately.

Mackerel with Gooseberry Sauce   (Serves 4)

Plentiful West Country mackerel is delicious served in this traditional manner, for the rich oiliness of the fish is balanced by the tartness of fresh gooseberries.

4 mackerel, filleted	Salt
8 bay leaves	3 tbsp dry cider
24 black peppercorns	Knob of butter

Seine Fishing on the Exe

In 1141, Baldwin de Redvers, Earl of Devon, granted half the tithe from salmon fishing in Topsham, a village just a few miles down-river from Exeter, to the newly built St James's Priory. Even up until the beginning of this century, the salmon fishery in this small Devon village kept over a hundred men employed.

Today, only a handful of commercial salmon fishermen continue to fish the Exe (as well as other Devon estuaries such as the Taw and the Dart). They follow the tide as it ebbs, in small wooden craft. In teams of two or three, the fishermen work morning or night, laying their orange seine nets, then painstakingly drawing them in by hand. These long nylon nets have weights on the bottom and cork floats on top. One man stays on the bank holding a shore line attached to the seine, while another rows across the river channel, feeding the net behind. He makes a large loop in the river, then returns to the bank, and the men slowly haul in the net. With luck, their efforts are rewarded with an Exe salmon. But sadly for all, the days when this king of fish was as plentiful as mackerel are long gone.

For the gooseberry sauce

225 g/$\frac{1}{2}$ lb gooseberries,	25 g/1 oz/$\frac{1}{4}$ stick butter
topped and tailed	A little sugar to taste
150 ml/$\frac{1}{4}$ pt/$\frac{2}{3}$ cup water	

Place a bay leaf and 3 peppercorns on each mackerel fillet, season with salt, and roll up. Secure each with a cocktail stick. Lay in an ovenproof dish, pour over the cider, and dot with butter. Cover with foil and bake in a moderate oven (180°C/350°F/Gas Mark 4) for about 30 minutes.

Meanwhile, put the gooseberries, water and butter in a saucepan over a low heat. Cover and cook until soft, about 15 minutes. Liquidize and press the soft fruit through a sieve. Return this purée to the saucepan, add a little sugar to taste (it should be tart, not sweet), and re-heat. Serve the sauce separately, hot, with the mackerel.

Star Gazey Pie   (Serves 4–6)

Pilchards were once so plentiful in Cornwall that they were hung on lines to dry. They were also pickled in vinegar and spices, or eaten fresh, fried and served with potatoes. Star gazey pie, however, was a fun dish, made for special occasions, or to amuse the children. Indeed, it is striking to see the heads and tails of the fish poking through the crust to gaze starwards. However, there is a practical reason for this: the heads of pilchards contain a rich oil which runs back into the pie to moisten it.

6 pilchards, or herring or
   small mackerel
3 rashers bacon, chopped
2 hard-boiled eggs,
   chopped
1 small onion, chopped
Salt
Freshly-ground black
   pepper

A handful of chopped
   parsley
2 eggs, beaten
3 tbsp cream
225 g/$\frac{1}{2}$ lb shortcrust or puff
   pastry (see pp. 25 and 66)

Clean the fish, and bone by running the flat blade of a knife along the backbone while pressing down firmly, then working the bone free. Snip off the tails with scissors and set aside. Season with salt and pepper. Grease a 23 cm/9 in pie dish. Lay the chopped hard-boiled eggs, onion, and bacon in the bottom of the dish. Lay the cleaned and boned fish on top. Mix the parsley, beaten eggs and cream together, and pour over the fish. Roll out the pastry, dampen the edges, and use to cover the pie. Make slits in the pastry and push the fish heads through. Insert the fish tails in the pastry. Bake in a hot oven (200°C/400°F/Gas Mark 6) for about 40–45 minutes.

Above right: Star gazey pie.

Right: Home-made chutneys and jams in a well-stocked West Country larder.

Opposite above: The ploughman's lunch – farmhouse Cheddar, home-baked bread, chutney and pickled onions, together with a pint of farmhouse cider or beer drawn from the wood – tasty, simple fare after a morning's work tilling the red earth of Devon.

Opposite below: Chutney and jam-making are traditional British ways of preserving vegetables and fruits over winter.

Devonshire Squab Pie (Serves 6)

There are no squabs in this pie, but it is typical West Country fare: a deep dish of meat, tart cooking apples and farm cider, topped with pastry – homely, delicious, pub fare, easy to make at home. If you happen to have a few squabs, then add them to the pot, too.

450 g/1 lb cooking apples, peeled, cored and sliced	Pinch of allspice
2 onions, sliced	1 tbsp sugar
675 g/1½ lb shoulder of lamb, diced	150 ml/¼ pt/⅔ cup farm cider
Salt	225 g/½ lb shortcrust pastry (see p. 25)
Freshly-ground black pepper	A little milk

Butter a deep pie dish and place a layer of apples at the bottom, followed by a layer of sliced onions. Add half the lamb, and season with salt, pepper and allspice. Add another layer of apples, onions and lamb, season, and finish with a layer of apples and onions. Sprinkle sugar on top, and pour the cider into the dish. Roll out the pastry, and make a cover to fit the pie dish. Press down the edges well, and brush with a little milk. Cover with foil and bake in a moderately hot oven (200°C/400°F/Gas Mark 6) for 15 minutes, then reduce heat (150°C/300°F/Gas Mark 2) and cook for a further hour, removing foil for the last 10 minutes.

Apple and Tomato Chutney

(Makes about 2.25 kg/5 lb)

Home-made chutneys, made from fruits and vegetables grown in gardens and on allotments, are essential accompaniments to simple English fare such as cold meats and cheeses. These favourite relishes and pickles were originally introduced from India, where they were served as condiments with curries and other Indian foods.

225 g/8 oz/1⅓ cups raisins	450 g/1 lb brown sugar
450 g/1 lb tomatoes, peeled and chopped	150 ml/¼ pt/⅔ cup cider vinegar
6 small onions, chopped	3 tsp salt
2 green peppers, chopped	1 tsp mixed spice
900 g/2 lb eating apples, peeled and chopped	

Soak the raisins in warm water for 30 minutes or so to plump them up. Place all the ingredients in a large heavy-based saucepan and simmer for 1½ hours, stirring occasionally. Ladle into sterilized pots or jars, seal, and leave to mature for at least one month.

West Country Cheeses

Farmhouse Cheddar Traditional farmhouse Cheddar is one of the great cheeses of the world: the classic hard-pressed cheese, made by hand, with a natural rind, a firm waxy texture, and a characteristic tangy, nutty flavour. The name comes from the small Somerset village famous also for its steep ravine and mysterious caves but it has been so overused and abused by cheese makers throughout the world producing cheeses bearing little if any resemblance to the original that many people are not even aware of what the real thing is like. Traditional farmhouse Cheddar is made only on a handful of West Country farms in Avon, Dorset, Somerset and Devon, from milk from that farm or from farms local to each cheese dairy.

As with all cheese making, the transformation of hundreds or thousands of gallons of milk into hundredweights or tons of solid cheese is a strenuous and laborious daily task. Early each morning, the milk from the previous day is soured (most farms also pasteurize the milk), then separated into curds and whey through the addition of rennet. The whitish, watery whey drains off to be saved, for it contains valuable butterfats and cream, leaving behind a shimmering tank of moist, pudding-like curds. These curds are cut with mechanical knives, releasing more whey, and then the laborious manual process of cheddaring begins.

Manual cheddaring is what really differentiates traditional farmhouse-made cheese from the factory product. It takes personal judgement and skill learned from years of experience on the part of the cheese maker, for each cheese develops differently, depending on the time of year, the temperature, the milk and a hundred other factors. The cheddaring process is fascinating to watch, for these white, elastic curds are cut and turned by hand, a process that releases more and more whey, and at the same time builds up acidity. The slabs of curd are lifted and slapped strenuously down, again and again, until the cheese maker is satisfied that the moisture and acid levels are correct.

Once these levels are reached, the slabs of curd are passed through a cheese mill, which spits out chips of new, fresh cheese. These mild-tasting, rather rubbery bits are salted by hand (this, again, is a critical task, for the salt both flavours and preserves the cheese, and also helps further whey drainage), before being packed into traditional sixty-pound moulds or into smaller 'truckles'. The metal moulds are placed in horizontal presses and left under pressure for a full three days. Then the cheeses are taken out of their moulds and given a traditional bandage of cheesecloth wrapped in molten lard. This helps the formation of the hard rind characteristic of traditional Cheddar cheese – an important factor, for the rind allows the cheese to breathe as it matures. A naturally-formed rind is the hallmark of traditional farmhouse Cheddar. It is difficult to see how cheese made in block form and wrapped in plastic can mature in the same way, yet confusingly for the consumer such block cheese made on farms can still be called 'farmhouse'.

The new cheeses are finally transferred to a store where they lie for several months. During this period they must be tended carefully, turned twice a week for the first four months of storage and once a week thereafter. Mild Cheddars are stored for five to seven months, while mature cheeses are left for seven months to a year or more. Traditional farmhouse Cheddar is as different from the prevalent products that masquerade under a similar name as Chablis is from the hundreds of imposters which have stolen its rightful *appellation*. That is not to say that all wines from regions other than the Yonne are undrinkable; or that 'cheddars' made in factories in England or Ireland, New Zealand or Vermont are not good. They are different products and should be judged as such. Quite simply: one is genuine, a classic; all the others ersatz.

Blue Vinny and Dorset Blue The elusive Blue Vinny is finally being made once more, on one farm only, in Winterbourne Abbas. For some time previously, this cheese was virtually unobtainable. It was, apparently, originally a sharp, acid cheese made from skimmed milk. The blue mould, or *vinew*, developed naturally and unevenly, assisted by country dairy remedies such as the dipping of an old boot or harness into the milk. Experts disagree as to why its production had lapsed, and whether or not the cheese called Dorset Blue is anything like old Blue Vinny. There are stories that Dorset Blue is not made in the county, but rather finds its way south through some complicated route from the Vale of Belvoir (Stilton country). This does not

Traditional farmhouse Cheddar, one of England's great cheeses.

seem the case to us, for the Dorset Blue that we have enjoyed in that county does have a distinctive sharp acidity which belies its rich creamy appearance. Both the new Blue Vinny and Dorset Blue are delicious with the almost equally elusive Dorset knobs, a knob-shaped crispy biscuit produced by the Moores of Morecombelake in winter only.

NEW ENGLISH CHEESES:

Lymeswold Launched with full publicity as the first really new, natural English cheese for centuries, Lymeswold is a full-fat soft blue cheese. Pale cream in colour, with a natural white velvety rind, Lymeswold ripens and develops a flavoursome tang and a runny, softer, spreadable texture.

Melbury Melbury is another new, soft, mould-ripened full-fat cheese. It is loaf-shaped and has both a firmer texture and a milder taste than many other soft cheeses.

Glazed Wiltshire Gammon

(Serves 4–6)

Wiltshire is famous for its bacon, ham and other pork products. In fact, the Wiltshire brine cure is today probably the most widespread commercial method of curing hams. Wiltshire bacon and gammon are available smoked or 'green' (unsmoked) and either can be used in this recipe.

900 g/2 lb piece of Wiltshire gammon	1 tbsp brown sugar
1½ tbsp prepared Urchfont mustard	2 tbsp cream
	Whole cloves

Soak the gammon if very salty, then boil for 1–1½ hours, or until tender. Meanwhile, make a paste with the mustard, brown sugar and cream. When the gammon is cooked, remove from the pot. Pat dry, score the skin into a diamond pattern and spread with the mustard mixture. Stud with whole cloves, and place in a pre-heated hot oven (220°C/425°F/Gas Mark 7) for about 30 minutes. Baste occasionally with the pan juices. The glaze should become brown and very crispy. When cooked, slice into thick slabs and serve at once, with Urchfont mustard and mugs of cider or beer.

Cheddar Cheese Straws

(Makes up to two dozen)

Real traditional farmhouse cheese has much more flavour than factory-made cheese, and it is very good for cooking, too. These straws are really cheesy, rich and buttery.

75 g/3 oz/¾ stick butter	Pinch of dry mustard
75 g/3 oz/1 cup mature farmhouse Cheddar, finely grated	Pinch of salt
	Pinch of paprika
100 g/4 oz/1 cup plain flour	1 egg, separated

Cream the butter and cheese together until soft, then add the sifted flour and seasonings. Mix well and add the beaten egg yolk. Make into a stiff dough, and chill in a refrigerator for an hour. Roll out on a lightly floured board to a thickness of 6 mm/¼ in. Cut into straws 7.5 cm/3 in long. Place on a greased baking sheet, brush with lightly beaten egg white, and bake in a moderately hot oven (190°C/375°F/Gas Mark 5) for 10–15 minutes. Serve warm from the oven.

Cornish pasty.

Somerset pork and apples in cider.

Cornish Pasty (Makes 4)

The Cornish pasty is one of those regional foods that has extended far beyond the boundary of the Tamar. Today it can be found throughout Britain, though with varying degrees of authenticity. Originally the pasty was a portable meal-in-one, made with a shortcrust paste that was tough enough to survive being shoved into the pocket of a tin-miner, who would then descend by man-engine into the damp, deep mines of Pendeen, Boscaswell, St Agnes and elsewhere. Though just about anything can be put in a pasty (the Cornish say that the devil won't cross the Tamar for fear of being chopped up and cooked), the classic Cornish pasty contains simply 'turmut, tates, and mate'.

450 g/1 lb shortcrust pastry (see p. 25)
1 small swede, diced into small, uneven pieces
2 medium potatoes, finely diced
450 g/1 lb chuck steak, chopped by hand, not minced (ground)

1 onion, finely chopped
Salt
Freshly-ground black pepper
Knob of butter
1 egg, beaten

Roll out the pastry and cut into four 23 cm/9 in circles. Lay each circle flat, and over half, place first some swede, then potato, then chopped meat, and finally chopped onion. Season well with salt and plenty of black pepper. Dot with butter. Dampen the edges with water, and fold over so that the seam is halfway between the top and the side edge. Pinch the edges together to seal. Prick the surface with a fork to allow air to escape. Brush with beaten egg and place on a greased baking sheet.

Bake in a pre-heated, moderately hot oven (200°C/ 400°F/Gas Mark 6) for about 15 minutes, then reduce heat (180°C/350°F/Gas Mark 4) and cook for a further 30–40 minutes. Pasties can be served cold but they are best hot from the oven, with a clay mug of West Country 'scrumpy' or a pint of St Austell's Best Bitter.

Bath buns in that city's elegant Pump Room.

Somerset Pork and Apples in Cider   (Serves 4–6)

Pork and apples simmered in cider and clotted cream is a classic West Country combination.

25 g/1 oz/$\frac{1}{4}$ stick butter
1 tbsp oil
1 onion, finely chopped
6 fresh sage leaves, chopped
900 g/2 lb diced pork
Salt
Freshly-ground black pepper

4 dessert apples, cored and sliced
300 ml/$\frac{1}{2}$ pt/1$\frac{1}{4}$ cups dry farm cider
3 tbsp clotted cream
Freshly-chopped parsley

Heat the butter and oil in a large casserole. Sauté the onion with the sage until soft and golden. Add the pork and brown. Season with salt and pepper. Add the sliced apples, and pour on the cider. Slowly bring to the boil, cover, and simmer for 1$\frac{1}{2}$–2 hours. Just before serving, take a couple of spoonfuls of the gravy and mix with the clotted cream to a smooth paste. Return to the casserole, stir in well, and heat gently for a few minutes. Serve garnished with parsley.

Devonshire Junket   (Serves 4)

Junkets have been popular since the Middle Ages all over England, and particularly in the West Country where there is no doubt often a glut of fresh farm milk with which to make this curd pudding.

600 ml/1 pt/2$\frac{1}{2}$ cups milk
$\frac{1}{2}$ tbsp sugar
1 tbsp brandy
1 tsp rennet

150 ml/$\frac{1}{4}$ pt/$\frac{2}{3}$ cup clotted cream
Freshly-grated nutmeg

Warm the milk gently to blood heat, remove from the heat and stir in the sugar and brandy. Pour into a glass bowl, and gently stir in the rennet. Allow to stand until set (not in a refrigerator). Serve topped with clotted cream, and dusted with nutmeg.

Bath Buns   (Makes 6)

Though their exact origin is unknown, Bath buns have been enjoyed in the Pump Room in the Roman Baths for a long while. They are a delicious indulgence to nibble there while listening to the refined strains of the Pump Room Trio. Groups of musicians have performed here regularly since the days of Beau Nash.

150 ml/$\frac{1}{4}$ pt/$\frac{2}{3}$ cup milk
1 tsp sugar
10 g/$\frac{1}{3}$ oz dried yeast
350 g/12 oz/3 cups plain flour
Pinch of salt
100 g/4 oz/1 stick butter

1$\frac{1}{2}$ tbsp castor sugar
2 eggs, beaten
3 tbsp currants
1 heaped tbsp chopped, candied lemon peel
About 10 sugar cubes, roughly crushed

Heat the milk until tepid, remove from the heat and dissolve the teaspoon of sugar. Sprinkle on the yeast and set aside in a warm place until frothy, about 15 minutes. Meanwhile, sieve the flour and salt into a large mixing bowl and rub in the butter, then mix in the castor sugar. Add the beaten eggs (reserving a little for glazing) and the yeast mixture. Knead to form a soft dough. Cover with a damp cloth and set aside in a warm place until doubled in size, about 1 hour.

Divide the risen dough into 6 pieces. Shape each into a small bun and place on a greased baking sheet. Brush with the beaten egg and sprinkle with the currants, lemon peel and crushed sugar. Leave again in a warm place to rise for 20 minutes, then bake in a pre-heated hot oven (220°C/425°F/Gas Mark 7) for 15–20 minutes or until golden brown and cooked through. Serve warm with butter.

125

Dorset Apple Cake

Apples from West Country orchards are made into fruit tarts, and also into this excellent apple cake from Dorset, which provides yet another excuse to serve clotted cream. Devon and Somerset also have their own similar apple cakes.

225 g/8 oz/1¾ cups plain flour
Pinch of salt
1½ tsp baking powder
100 g/4 oz/1 stick butter
225 g/8 oz cooking apples, peeled, cored and finely chopped

100 g/4 oz/½ cup sugar
3 tbsp currants
1 egg, beaten

Sieve the flour, salt and baking powder into a large mixing bowl. Rub in the butter. Stir in the apples, sugar and currants. Mix to a firm dough with the beaten egg. Turn into a greased 20 cm/8 in sandwich tin, and bake in a moderate oven (180°C/350°F/Gas Mark 4) for 45–60 minutes, until golden on top. Serve warm, cut into slices, with clotted cream.

Saffron Cake

Saffron was once cultivated and gathered extensively in Cornwall, and though today it is an expensive delicacy, the tradition of its use remains in this Celtic outpost, where orange-yellow saffron cakes are displayed in the windows of village bakers, to be consumed eagerly especially at Easter. Since it is so expensive, the bright colour often comes, no doubt, through the judicious use of a drop or two of food colouring.

Several threads of saffron
900 g/2 lb plain flour
Pinch of salt
1 tsp allspice
100 g/4 oz/½ cup sugar
175 g/6 oz/¾ cup butter
175 g/6 oz/¾ cup lard

300 ml/½ pt/1¼ cups milk
1 tsp sugar
20 g/⅔ oz dried yeast
450 g/1 lb/2¾ cups dried fruit
50 g/2 oz/½ cup chopped citrus peel

Place the saffron threads in half a cup of hot water and leave to infuse overnight. Sieve flour, salt, allspice and sugar into a large mixing bowl. Rub in the fat. Meanwhile gently heat the milk until tepid, and add 1 teaspoon of sugar. Sprinkle on the yeast, and set aside for 15 minutes until frothy. Make a well in the centre of the flour and pour in the yeast mixture. Pour the saffron and its liquid into the flour. Mix and knead gently to make a smooth dough. Cover with a damp cloth and set aside in a warm place until the dough has doubled in size. Work in the dried fruit and peel, and knead well. Turn into two well-greased loaf tins, and set aside again in a warm place for about 30 minutes. Bake in a moderate oven (180°C/350°F/Gas Mark 4) for about 45 minutes.

Cornish Fairings   (Makes up to two dozen)

Souvenirs of summers by the seaside: limpet and scallop shells, a heart-shaped pebble, a tiny tuft of thrift gathered from the cliff, and three pressed forget-me-nots, stored in a tall blue tin that once contained these crunchy ginger biscuits.

100 g/4 oz/⅘ cup plain flour
Pinch of salt
1 tsp baking powder
1 tsp bicarbonate of soda
1 tsp ground ginger
1 tsp allspice

1 tsp cinnamon
50 g/2 oz/½ stick butter
2 tbsp castor sugar
Grated rind of 3 lemons
3 tbsp golden syrup, warmed

Sieve the flour and dry ingredients into a large mixing bowl. Rub in the butter until the mixture resembles breadcrumbs. Stir in the sugar, lemon rind and warmed golden syrup. Shape into small balls the size of walnuts, and space well apart on a large well-greased baking tray. Bake in a moderately hot oven (190°C/375°F/Gas Mark 5) for 15–20 minutes or until golden.

Wiltshire Lardy Cake

These sticky fruity cakes are often seen on West Country market stalls, particularly in Wiltshire, kingdom of the pig. They are yet another example of the region's expertise at baking good, fattening things to eat at tea-time.

225 g/8 oz/1¾ cups plain flour
Pinch of salt
150 ml/¼ pt/⅔ cup milk
25 g/1 oz/¼ stick butter
1 tsp sugar
10 g/⅓ oz dried yeast

1 egg
50 g/2 oz/¼ cup lard
50 g/2 oz/¼ cup sugar
1 tsp mixed spice
50 g/2 oz/⅓ cup dried fruit
1 tbsp golden syrup

Sieve the flour and salt into a large mixing bowl. Gently heat the milk and butter until the butter has melted. Add the sugar and sprinkle on the yeast. Set aside for 15 minutes until frothy. Make a well in the flour and pour in the yeast mixture. Knead gently to make a smooth dough. Cover with a damp cloth and set aside in a warm place until the dough has doubled in size.

Turn out on to a floured board and roll into a rectangle about 6 mm/¼ in thick. Dot with knobs of about a third of the lard at intervals. Sprinkle with a third of the sugar and spice, and half the dried fruit. Fold in three, turn to the left, and roll out again. Repeat this process. Roll out once more to a rectangle about 2.5 cm/1 in thick, dot with the remaining lard, and sprinkle with sugar and spice. Put in a greased baking tin, and score the top with criss-crosses. Bake in a moderately hot oven (200°C/400°F/Gas Mark 6) for 30–40 minutes. Brush top with golden syrup and serve hot or cold with tea.

Beekeeping

When the Romans came to Britain, they found scores of dome-shaped straw skeps or hives dotted throughout the country, from which honey was gathered to make mead, the heady alcoholic drink of Celtic Britain. For centuries, until sugar was introduced, honey was an essential sweetener. Beeswax, too, was an important by-product, for candles were a main source of light. Thus the beekeeper, in eccentric veil and protective gauntlets, buzzing industriously about his ordered colonies, has always been a part of the English rural scene. William Cobbett, in his treatise *Cottage Economy* (1821) states with characteristic firmness: 'He must be a stupid countryman indeed who cannot make a beehive; and a lazy one if he *will* not.'

While today much beekeeping is undertaken by keen amateurs who keep just a few colonies as a fascinating hobby, Brother Adam, at Buckfast Abbey in South Devon, maintains over 300 colonies located throughout Devon and Cornwall, and gathers a rich harvest of honey which is sold in the Abbey shop. The colour, texture and flavour of honey comes from the flowers from which the bees have gathered their nectar. In June, for example, the honeybees visit flowering blackberry hedges in country lanes and fields; later in July, they forage out patches of sweet clover from the lush meadows of the South-West; but at the end of summer, Brother Adam transports his strongest colonies to nearby Dartmoor where they gather nectar from the moorland heather. The honey that results is a valuable prize, with a unique flavour that is rich yet not very sweet; it is dark in colour, and has a viscous, almost jelly-like consistency. Clover honey, on the other hand, is lighter in colour, more liquid, and considerably sweeter. Oil-seed rape produces light neutral honey, while buckwheat (the crop which Cobbett states is 'foremost') yields honey that is pungent, treacly, almost black in colour.

Beekeeping at Buckfast Abbey.

127

Cream Teas

To thousands who visit the West Country, the memory of wickedly indulgent cream teas remains vivid, enjoyed at tables outdoors among the daffodils and delphiniums, or in thatched inns, cosy country tea houses, or seaside cafés. The combination is exceedingly simple, unforgettably delicious: merely the very freshest scones, still warm from the oven, crumbly and light, or yeasty, rich Cornish splits, spread with a generous spoonful of clotted cream – quite simply the richest, the most fattening, the most delicious in the world – and topped with a dollop of home-made strawberry or other fruit jam.

Clotted cream is made from the rich milk of the West Country scalded slowly over steam. The cream rises to the top of the pan and as it cools, it forms a thick yellow crust which is then skimmed off and packed. It is as thick as butter, and delicious not only with scones and strawberry jam, but with other sweets and puddings, too; indeed here it is served with just about everything, and is even used in cooking. Because clotted cream has been heated, it has a relatively long life, and thus it is safe to take home or send by post.

Scones   (Makes 12)

225 g/$\frac{1}{2}$ lb/1$\frac{3}{5}$ cups plain
   flour
50 g/2 oz/$\frac{1}{2}$ stick butter
$\frac{1}{2}$ tsp bicarbonate of soda
1 tsp cream of tartar
1 tsp sugar
Pinch of salt
A little milk

Sieve the flour into a large mixing bowl and rub in the butter. Add the remaining ingredients and enough milk to make a soft dough. Roll out to 1.5 cm/$\frac{1}{2}$ in thickness, and cut into small rounds. Put on to a greased baking tray and bake in a hot oven (220°C/425°F/Gas Mark 7) for 7–10 minutes. Serve warm, with clotted cream and jam.

Cornish Splits   (Makes 12)

450 g/1 lb plain flour
Pinch of salt
300 ml/$\frac{1}{2}$ pt/1$\frac{1}{4}$ cups milk
25 g/1 oz/$\frac{1}{4}$ stick butter
1 tsp sugar
10 g/$\frac{1}{3}$ oz dried yeast

Sieve the flour and salt into a large mixing bowl. Gently heat the milk and butter until the butter has melted. Add the sugar and allow to cool until lukewarm. Sprinkle on the dried yeast and set aside for 15 minutes until frothy. Make a well in the flour and pour in the yeast mixture. Knead gently to make a smooth dough. Cover with a damp cloth and set aside in a warm place until the dough has doubled in size. Knead again, form into small round balls, and place on a lightly floured baking sheet. Bake in a hot oven (220°C/425°F/Gas Mark 7) for 15–20 minutes. Serve warm, split, and spread with clotted cream and jam, or with treacle and clotted cream ('thunder and lightning').

Clotted Cream

Clotted cream can be made at home, but only with the freshest milk, preferably straight from the cow. Strain the milk into a shallow pan, and allow to stand for 12 hours in summer and 24 hours in winter. Transfer the pan carefully to the stove and heat gently over a steam bath. Do not allow to boil. As the milk is heated, the yellow cream will rise to the top and form a crusty rim around the edge. Carefully remove the pan from the heat, so as not to disturb the cream, and set aside in a cool place for about 12 hours. Skim off the thick crust of clotted cream with a slotted spoon.

Cream tea at the Southern Cross, Newton Poppleford.

Drink in the West Country

The visitor to the West Country will find little shortage of choice when it comes to drink. This, of course, is the home of farmhouse 'scrumpy' as well as milder, factory-made ciders. Numerous fine traditional beers are brewed throughout the region; the beer drinker, moreover, has a larger choice here than in many areas due to the preponderance of free houses. English wine, made from grapes grown and ripened in the milder, gentler climate of the West, is pressed, vinified, and bottled in modern private wineries. Cornish mead, the Celtic drink of honeymooners (and tourists), remains popular, and the distinctive gin from Plymouth is still the traditional tipple of the Royal Navy (and available in most pubs in the region). Farmers' wives and others continue to make fruit and country wines from elderberry flowers and berries, and other fruit gathered in West Country hedgerows, while fine wines from the classic wine regions of the world are still shipped to Bristol.

Hours: see p 30.

West Country Farm Cider

No other drink is so associated with the West Country as farm cider. Tasted straight from the wood, then purchased at the farm where it is made, or drunk in cider pubs in Somerset, Devon or Cornwall (order a pint of beer in such places and you will be looked at oddly), it is so different to the milder bottled ciders available elsewhere as to be virtually unrecognizable: non-sparkling, mouth-puckering, rich in acid and tannin, and extraordinarily potent. It is one of the classic drinks of Britain, with a history dating back several centuries.

Farm cider, in the past, was never a drink made for profit. Rather, most farms in the West Country had an orchard planted with both cider apple trees and trees bearing dessert and culinary fruit. Cider was made each season for the farmer and his own family, as well as for farm labourers and friends. Indeed, the farm labourers' wages were paid in part in cider, a

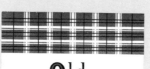

Assorted mats and labels of the region.

practice that was only abolished less than a hundred years ago. Even today, on some West Country farms an allowance of cider is still given, though the days when the ploughman could count on a gallon or more as his rightful daily ration are long gone.

Naturally, different areas have developed different tastes, in part from the varieties of apples available locally. Generally in the West Country the style of cider preferred is rich in acid and tannin. The 'bite' so necessary to good West Country cider comes from the use of cider apples known as bittersharps (high in acid and tannin) and bittersweets (lower in acid, but high in tannin). These apples, contrary to expectation, are wholly ripe (though if you bite one, the excessive tannin masks the sugar). In the South-East, on the other hand, cider is traditionally made only with culinary and dessert fruit.

The production of farm cider on a small scale remains beautifully simple, uncomplicated by modern machinery, engagingly unscientific. In the West Country, the cider orchards are timeless, large gnarled trees with branches high enough to allow cattle or sheep to graze below. While some harvesting is done by climbing the trees, more often than not the apples just fall off when sufficiently ripe. The apples are then simply milled to a pulp, made into a 'cheese' (that is, layered with straw or nylon mesh), and pressed. The juice is run off into barrels and allowed to ferment naturally, in many cases simply from the natural yeasts present on the fruit or carried over from previous years on equipment which never appears to be cleaned too strenuously. If the cider fails to ferment, country remedies are taken: a fistful of earth might be thrown in the barrels, or even slices of meat.

This is farm cider making at its most basic. It should perhaps be pointed out, however, that farms making cider in this fashion produce only a tiny fraction of the total amount drunk in Britain today; as in the past, farm cider remains primarily a drink consumed by family, friends and farm labourers. At the same time, there are other cider producers here who make this traditional drink on a much larger scale than the small farm producers, but on a relatively small

Top left: Cider is sold direct from farms in the West Country.

Top right: Bittersharp and bittersweet cider apples are milled into a pulp.

Middle left: A 'cheese' of milled apples is carefully built in layers then pressed to extract the juice.

Middle right: After fermentation in oak casks, the cider is racked into clean barrels; after a brief period of maturation, it is ready to drink.

Bottom: Wassailing Somerset's apple orchards at Monty's Court, Norton Fitzwarren.

Wassailing

Old apple tree
We wassail thee
And hoping thou wilt bear
Hat fulls, cap fulls,
Three bushel bag fulls,
And a little heap under the stairs.

Wassailing the apple orchards is an old West Country ritual which probably stems from the pagan belief that plants would grow and crop more fruitfully if the beneficial spirits were encouraged and the evil ones frightened away. In the dead of winter (traditionally the old Twelfth Night, 16 January, for how were the spirits to know that the calendar had been changed in 1752?) one Somerset cider firm still carries out this ancient ceremony in great style. The annual Wassail Queen is carried into the orchard on the shoulders of strong youths, and she and her attendants drink from the large two-handled Wassail Cup. She soaks pieces of toast in the mulled cider and places them in the branches of the oldest tree in the orchard (the cider-soaked toast is for the robins, who embody all good spirits). The young maiden then pours the remaining cider around the roots of the tree to encourage growth and fertility. Meanwhile all the guests bang sticks together and men fire shotguns into the tree's branches to frighten away laggard evil spirits. Everyone joins in singing the Wassail song, and afterwards more libations in honour of the coming crop are liberally downed until the small hours of the morning.

can be marvellous, consistency has never been their strongest asset, nor did it need to be. The drink, after all, was primarily for family and farm labourers. However, in recent years, tremendous strides have been made in cider technology, and the few large firms which dominate the industry are now able to make consistent, clean and good products which vary little from year to year. Moreover, a number of styles of cider are blended to result in a range to suit a variety of tastes. The mistaken impression about commercially-produced nationally available ciders is that they are all harmless fizzy drinks, a sort of apple 'pop'. This is as far from the truth as is the conception that farm cider, or scrumpy, is a drink fit only for madmen and lunatics! It is important to appreciate the variety of one of our most important national drinks.

Today, over ninety per cent of cider produced and drunk in Britain comes from three immense firms, two in the West Country and one in Hereford. Cider produced on such a large scale must necessarily eliminate those unpredictable elements which are present in farm cider production. The apples used by the Taunton Cider Company, for example, come primarily from orchards planted mainly with bittersweet cider apples under a scheme which both guarantees the company a supply of premium fruit, and the farmer a constant market for his produce. (Lately, with the cider market expanding, however, local fruit production has been insufficient to meet all needs, and so imported apple concentrate is being used.) Wild yeasts are removed and a controlled yeast culture is introduced to activate the fermentation. Once the ciders have been made, they are aged in oak vats, and then carefully blended by a master cider maker to result in consistent brands, including traditional draught ciders (available locally only); sweet, carbonated bottled ciders; strong, dry ciders available on draught in pubs throughout the country; and bottled ciders of almost wine-like character and strength.

commercial scale when compared with the giant companies which dominate the industry. Such small commercial companies adapt measures that are somewhat less hit-and-miss than the small farm producers, and the ciders they produce are excellent. Some might blend a tried and trusted proportion of different fruits that have been found to give the best result. Others even produce single apple variety ciders made from choice fruit such as the prized Kingston Black. Such 'premium' cider is certainly worth seeking and paying extra for.

When you are in the West Country, purchase farm cider direct, wherever you see a sign along the road. It comes in a range of styles, from bone dry to sweet (we suggest you purchase dry cider and do as the locals do: if too sharp, add a dash of lemonade to your glass). Always taste before you buy.

Some West Country Cider Makers:

R. J. Sheppy & Son
Three Bridges
Bradford on Tone
Taunton
Somerset

F. Hill & Son
Barkingdon Manor
Staverton
Totnes
Devon

Inch's Cider Co.
Western Barn
Winkleigh
North Devon

Countryman Cider
Felldownhead Farm
Milton Abbot
Tavistock
Devon

S. G. Bromell
Lower Uppacott Farm
Tedburn St Mary
Nr Exeter
Devon

Sherston Earl Vineyard & Orchards
The Vineyard
Sherston
Malmesbury
Wiltshire

Large-scale Cider Production

Farm cider making on a small scale, it is perhaps apparent, is a rather haphazard occupation. Though such rough ciders

Taunton Cider Co.
Norton Fitzwarren
Taunton
Somerset

Coates Gaymers Ltd
Shepton Mallet
Somerset

Traditional Beer

A wide range of traditional beers is on tap throughout the region. National breweries Courage, Bass and Whitbread have a strong presence, and their cask-conditioned ales like Courage Directors' (brewed in Bristol), Whitbread Flowers Original (Cheltenham) and Draught Bass (from Burton), although available elsewhere in the country too, all have their devotees here. Additionally, there are a number of independent family breweries which represent traditional regional brewing at its finest: Eldridge Pope of Dorchester, Wadsworth's of Devizes, Hall & Woodhouse, with its Badger beers brewed in Blandford Forum, Arkells, Gibbs Mew, and others. Finally, in this most idyllic part of Britain, there are a growing number of mini and pub breweries, providing individual cask ales to the free trade, or to their own pubs only. The most famous home-brew pub in the West Country is the Blue Anchor, Helston.

Dorset

Eldridge Pope & Co., Dorchester, Dorset. Dorchester is a centre of fine regional brewing, and this family brewery remains 'unashamedly traditional' in its production of an excellent range of Huntsman ales, using, for example, only whole cone hops, and a yeast which has been regenerated for 'as long as anyone can remember'. Eldridge Pope owns nearly 200 pubs, and its beers are available throughout the south coast and as far as London and Bristol. Additionally, Eldridge Pope pubs which have been awarded the 'Tuck Inn' designation serve food, often much above the general standard of 'pub grub'. The company is unique, too, in its production of a 'Dorset' whisky, Old Highland Blend, made from a high proportion of fine single malt whiskies matured in bond and blended at the brewery. The Dorchester Brewery, located near the town centre, is an outstanding example of Victorian architecture.

Dorchester Bitter o.g. 1030–34
Dorset Original IPA o.g. 1039–43
Royal Oak o.g. 1046–50

J. C. & R. H. Palmer Ltd, Bridport, Dorset. Before the upsurge in mini-breweries, Palmer's claimed the distinction of being the smallest commercial brewery in Britain. Two cask-conditioned ales are produced, available generally within a twenty-five mile radius of the brewery, though there are exceptions such as the Ferry Inn, Salcombe, South Devon. The brewery operates in part under a thatched roof.

BB (Bitter Beer) o.g. 1030.4
IPA o.g. 1039.5

Hall & Woodhouse, Blandford Forum, Dorset. Hall & Woodhouse, an independent family brewery for over two hundred years, is located in the heart of the county, and produces a range of traditional beers dispensed mostly by hand pump. The brewery's tied trade is mainly in Dorset, Wiltshire, and Somerset, though Badger beers are available in free houses in Devon and Avon, as well as further afield. Badger Inns are managed houses offering traditional food as well as drink.

Hector's Bitter o.g. 1032–36
Badger Best Bitter o.g. 1039–43
Tanglefoot o.g. 1045–49

Devenish Brewery, Weymouth, Dorset. Devenish is a true West Country brewing company, which, with its second brewery in Redruth, Cornwall, supplies its beers to some 400 tied houses located throughout the region, from Land's End to Bournemouth. The brewery in Weymouth was established in 1742, while brewing in Redruth has been carried on since 1934.

John Devenish Bitter o.g. 1032
Wessex Best Bitter o.g. 1042

Wiltshire

Wadsworth & Co., Devizes, Wiltshire. The redbrick Northgate brewery of Wadsworth's is a prominent feature in the market town of Devizes. Wadsworth's beers are much loved by traditional ale fans in Wiltshire, where most of the company's tied houses are located, as well as throughout the South-West, South, and further afield too. In Devizes itself, Wadsworth's horse-drawn drays still make regular deliveries of IPA, 6X and the strong winter warmer, Old Timer, to public houses near the brewery.

PA (Pale Ale) o.g. 1031
IPA (India Pale Ale) o.g. 1035
6X o.g. 1041
Old Timer o.g. 1053

Ushers Brewery Ltd, Trowbridge, Wiltshire. Ushers is a member of the national brewing group of Watney Mann & Truman, a subsidiary of Grand Metropolitan. The company produces a good range of traditional cask-conditioned beers available throughout the West Country. Ushers operates a tied estate of some 600 public houses.

Ushers PA o.g. 1030–34
Ushers Best Bitter o.g. 1036–40
Founders Ale o.g. 1042–48

Arkells, Swindon, Wiltshire. The Arkell family have been brewing near Swindon since 1843. In the Kingsdown Brewery at Upper Stratton, they produce traditional cask-conditioned beers available in some sixty tied or managed public houses and hotels, located primarily within a twenty-five mile radius of the brewery.

John Arkell Bitter o.g. 1031–35
BBB (Best Bitter Beer)
o.g. 1037–41
Kingsdown Ale (Strong Ale)
o.g. 1049–53

Gibbs Mew plc, Salisbury, Wiltshire. This family brewery owns some 100 public houses in the surrounding area, and has an extensive network of free trade throughout the South of England. Gibbs Mew produces three fine traditional beers; the most distinctive, The Bishop's Tipple (available in bottle as well as draught), is a potent old ale.

Wiltshire Traditional Bitter
o.g. 1036
Premium o.g. 1039
The Bishop's Tipple o.g. 1066

Archer's Ales Ltd, Swindon, Wiltshire. This relatively new brewery produces four cask-conditioned ales available in about seventy outlets in an area bounded by Bristol, Gloucester, Devizes and Reading. The brewery owns one pub, the Drillman's Arms at Stratton, Cirencester.

Village Bitter o.g. 1035
Best Bitter o.g. 1040
Golden Bitter o.g. 1048
Headbanger ('for idiots')
o.g. 1065

Thomas Hardy's Ale

Thomas Hardy was a native of Dorchester and lived in the area for much of his life, observing and writing about rural life in his beloved 'Wessex'. A friend of the Pope family, he was well acquainted with Dorchester beers, and wrote this description in *The Trumpet-Major*: 'It was of the most beautiful colour that the eye of an artist in beer could desire; full in body, yet brisk as a volcano; piquant, yet without a twang; luminous as an autumn sunset; free from streakiness of taste but finally, rather heady.' In 1968 Eldridge Pope decided to mark Hardy's centenary with a brew as close as possible to that lyrical description. Thomas Hardy's Ale is a remarkable bottle-conditioned beer which is one of the strongest in Britain (o.g. 1122–28), and which will continue to mature in the bottle, so Eldridge Pope claim, for up to twenty-five years.

Thomas Hardy's Ale: a potent ale brewed by Eldridge Pope to a lyrical description of Wessex beer in *The Trumpet-Major*.

Wootton Vineyard, Somerset.

Harvesting grapes in Somerset on a warm, late autumn day.

Tisbury Brewery Co. Ltd, Tisbury, Wiltshire. Tisbury is another new brewery, founded in 1980 in the premises of the old Styrings Brewery which had closed in 1922. Beers are served straight from the cask and by traditional hand pump in about seventy outlets in Wiltshire, Somerset, Avon, Dorset and Hampshire.

> Local Bitter o.g. 1037
> Local Heavy o.g. 1045
> Old Grumble (winter only)
> o.g. 1060

Mole's Brewery, Melksham, Wiltshire. Mole's Brewery was established in 1982 and brews one cask-conditioned bitter.

> Mole's Cask Bitter o.g. 1040

Avon
Courage (Western Ltd), Bristol, Avon. Though Courage is one of the major six national brewing combines, the com-pany still remains very much a tra-ditional brewery with strong West Country roots. In addition to its prin-cipal brewery in the West at Bath Street, Bristol, there is another brewery in Plymouth and a maltings at Oakhill in the Mendip Hills which dates back to 1767. Traditional Courage ales brewed in the West are distributed throughout the South of England. Directors' Bitter, originally brewed for the company's boardroom, is a classic full-bodied ale.

> Bitter Ale o.g. 1030
> Courage Best Bitter o.g. 1039
> Directors' Bitter o.g. 1046
> Festivale (a special ale brewed once only and different each year, produced for the Great Western Beer Festival)

Butcombe Brewery Ltd, Butcombe, Bristol, Avon. One of the largest of the new breed of 'mini-breweries', the But-combe brewery is located in an old farm building overlooking the Mendips. One beer only is produced, available in about 120 free outlets primarily within a thirty-mile radius of Bristol.

> Butcombe Bitter o.g. 1039

Smiles Brewing Co., Bristol, Avon. Founded in 1978 but already well-established, this city centre brewery supplies two cask-conditioned beers primarily to free trade outlets in Bristol and throughout Avon, Somerset, Gloucestershire, and surrounding counties. The brewery has now ac-quired its own pub, The Highbury Vaults in Bristol.

> Best Bitter o.g. 1040
> Exhibition o.g. 1051

Devon
Courage (South West) Ltd, Plymouth, Devon (see Courage above). The Ply-mouth brewery of this national com-pany produces a unique traditional dark mild, Heavy, available only in the South-West.

> Heavy o.g. 1032

Blackawton Brewery, Totnes, Devon. This one-man brewery was established in South Devon in 1977, and produces two popular beers made from malted barley grown in the fields of Devon. The brewery is located in an old farm barn.

> Blackawton Bitter o.g. 1037
> Headstrong o.g. 1048

Bate's Brewery, Bovey Tracey, Devon. One strong traditional beer, is produced by this new mini-brewery, available in several Devon pubs.

> Bate's Bitter o.g. 1045

Thompson's Brewery, Ashburton, Devon. Thompson's Ashburton Ales were originally brewed behind the London Inn, but the company has now ex-panded to larger premises, and trades in the Dartmoor and South Devon area.

> Mild o.g. 1034
> Bitter o.g. 1040
> IPA. o.g. 1045

Somerset
Golden Hill Brewery, Wiveliscombe, Somerset. Begun in 1980, the Golden Hill Brewery produces a popular, cask-conditioned beer available in Somerset, Avon, Dorset, Devon and Cornwall.

> Exmoor o.g. 1039

Cotleigh Brewery, Wiveliscombe, Somer-set. Another relatively new brewery, Cotleigh serves the free trade in Devon, Somerset. Avon and Cornwall with three cask-conditioned beers.

> Nutcracker o.g. 1036
> Tawny Bitter o.g. 1040
> Old Buzzard (winter only)
> o.g. 1048

Miners' Arms Brewery Ltd, Westbury-sub-Mendip, Somerset. Home-brewed beers were originally produced at the well-known Miners' Arms Restaurant in Priddy, but in 1981 a larger brewery was established in Westbury-sub-Mendip to produce a cask-conditioned ale available in a trading area within ten miles of Wells.

> Own Ale o.g. 1040

Cornwall
St Austell Brewery, St Austell, Cornwall. Founded over 130 years ago in the centre of Cornwall, originally to satisfy the thirsts of tin miners, fishermen and farmers, beers brewed by St Austell today find equal favour with tourists to this most popular West Country holiday county. The brewery owns a number of pubs throughout Cornwall, most of which serve cask-conditioned ales.

BB o.g. 1031
XXXX Mild o.g. 1032
Hicks' Special Draught o.g. 1050

Devenish Brewery, Redruth, Cornwall
(see Devenish above).

Cornish Best Bitter o.g. 1042

Pensans Brews, Penzance, Cornwall.
This small local brewery has been brewing since 1982 and hopes to expand its trading area in Penzance and the surrounding area. Charter Pensans or 'C.P.' was developed for the annual Penzance Heritage festival.

MSB o.g. 1050
Charter Pensans o.g. 1055

English Wine in the West Country

The West Country, with the mildest climate in Britain, is not surprisingly a centre of importance for English wine (see pp. 110–111). There are productive commercial vineyards in Avon, Somerset, Wiltshire, Devon and Cornwall, producing a variety of styles including dry and medium-dry white wine, sparkling wine produced by the *méthode champenoise*, and even some red wine. Some West Country vineyards have long historical associations, such as Pilton Manor in Somerset, which dates back to at least 1189 when it was recorded as part of the vineyards of Glastonbury Abbey, whose vineyards were mentioned in the Domesday Survey. Other new vineyards have been planted on land previously devoted to traditional West Country farming. As elsewhere, visitors are welcome at most vineyards, and wines can often be purchased direct. It is usually advisable, however, to telephone in advance. The following is a selection of some West Country vineyards.

Wootton Vineyard
North Wootton
Shepton Mallet
Somerset
This well-established six-acre vineyard is planted primarily with Müller-Thurgau, Schönburger and Seyval Blanc grape varieties. Wootton wines as well as wines for other neighbour growers are produced in the estate winery.
Visitors welcome.

Pilton Manor Vineyard
The Manor House
Pilton
Shepton Mallet
Somerset
Pilton Manor is a picturesque vineyard in the grounds of the Manor House, on the site of an historic vineyard that belonged to nearby Glastonbury Abbey. Main grape varieties planted include Müller-Thurgau and Seyval Blanc. Dry and medium-dry wines, and sparkling wine made by the traditional *méthode champenoise* (secondary fermentation in the bottle) are produced in the estate winery.
Visitors welcome.

Brympton d'Evercy Vineyard
Brympton d'Evercy
Yeovil
Somerset
This vineyard is planted in the grounds of a stately family home, primarily with Müller-Thurgau and Reichensteiner vines. The wine is made on the estate, and both the vineyard and the house can be visited.

Wraxall Vineyard
Vine Lodge
Wraxall
Shepton Mallet
Somerset

Wraxall is a six-acre vineyard planted with Seyval Blanc, Müller-Thurgau and Madeleine Angevine, using the Geneva Double Curtain high wire trellis system of training (see p. 72).

Yearlstone Vineyard
Bickleigh
Tiverton
Devon
Devon's first commercial vineyard is planted with Siegerrebe, Madeleine Angevine, Chardonnay and a selection of red grapes for the production of a unique red wine. All are made in the estate winery, and vintage cider and mead are also produced.
Visitors welcome (viticultural courses for vine growers are held at Yearlstone throughout the year).

Loddiswell Vineyard
Lilwell
Loddiswell
Kingsbridge
Devon
Planted in 1977 with 6000 vines, Loddiswell now has three acres of Müller-Thurgau, Reichensteiner and Huxelrebe in production. A section of the vineyard is devoted to experiments using polythene tunnels to improve quality. The wines are made on the estate.
Visitors welcome.

Bristol and the Wine Trade

Bristol, one of the most important ports in the West Country, has long associations with wine. As early as the twelfth century, wine was imported here in substantial quantity, mainly to satisfy the thirst of Norman barons who had sufficient money to indulge their taste for wines from their homeland. Once Henry II married Eleanor of Aquitaine in 1152, vine growing in Britain may have declined, but wine imports from Aquitaine increased greatly, and huge amounts were imported through Bristol; indeed in the fourteenth century this leading West Country port was second only to London as a centre for the wine trade.

When commerce with France declined, owing to continual wars, sack (sherry) from Spain, and later, port, became the national favourites. Sherry was imported in such quantity through Bristol that it was referred to as early as the seventeenth century simply as 'Bristol Milk'. The following century saw the rise of famous wine firms which remain cornerstones in the fine wine trade today: Howell's, Avery's, J. R. Phillips and John Harvey & Sons. The latter's popular Bristol Cream has made this West Country town synonymous with sherry the world over.

An annual World Wine Fair is now held each year in Bristol's waterfront. It is a colourful international event, and keeps alive this city's long associations with wine.

In addition to those opposite, the following West Country vine growers are members of the English Vineyards Association. Many sell wine direct.

Avon

Cambarn Vineyard, Dunkerton, Bath
Char Valley, Dundry
Thornbury Castle, Thornbury, Bristol

Cornwall

Wheal Sara, Camborne
Pollmassick, St Ewe

Devon

Clyston, Broadclyst, Exeter
Whitstone, Bovey Tracey

Dorset

Downwood, Blandford Forum
Waterloo, Sturminster Newton
King's Green, Bourton

Somerset

Caisson House, Coombe Haye
Valley Spring, Coombe Down
Axbridge, Axbridge
Cheddar Valley Vineyards, Axbridge
Batts Combe, Cheddar
Cufic, Cheddar
Castle Cary, Castle Cary
St Andrews, West Hatch

Wiltshire

Tytherley, West Tytherley
Chalkhill Vineyard, Bower Chalke
Jesses, Dinton
Fonthill, Tisbury
Corsley House, Warminster
Stert, Stert
Southcott, Pewsey
Stitchcombe, Marlborough
Bosmere, Chippenham
Sherston Earl, Sherston

Plymouth Gin

The Plymouth Gin Distillery is located in the picturesque waterfront quarter of Plymouth known as the Barbican, in the old Black Friars monastery. It has been producing Plymouth gin here since 1793. Plymouth gin differs in taste somewhat from London gin, and is available in pubs throughout the region. To make the naval officer's favourite, pink gin, add a dash of angostura bitters to a glass, swill around and remove, then add Plymouth gin.

Mead

Mead, an alcoholic drink of fermented honey, has been made in Britain for thousands of years. To the Celts and Saxons, it was celebratory libation for men. It was made long before the Roman's arrival, and during the Dark Ages, the arts of both beekeeping and mead making were kept alive in monastic houses. Because of its association with the Celts, it is still considered a West Country drink. Commercially-made mead remains more as a souvenir for tourists, or a drink to be served at mediaeval banquets. Mead making in the past, like home brewing, was more than likely done on a small private scale for each household's own use. Today this tradition continues. Brother Adam, at Buckfast Abbey, for example, makes a fine mead for the monks themselves, not for sale. To produce this, he mixes his finest Dartmoor heather honey with soft water from the moor, ferments it with a pure strain of wine yeast, then ages the resulting liquor for several years in wooden casks prior to bottling. It is a rich drink, in appearance like a cream sherry, but with the distinctive bouquet of heather honey, and a taste like pure nectar, which is, after all, what it is. Brother Adam also makes a lighter, dry mead which gains its sparkle from secondary fermentation in the bottle. It is, he tells us, very refreshing.

Some Useful Addresses

West Country Tourist Board
37 Southernhay East
Exeter

Cornish Smoked Fish Company
Duck Street
St Austell
Cornwall
Hot- and cold-smoked mackerel, salmon, sea trout and other fish and meats. Mail order service.

Marinpro Ltd
Ferry Road
Topsham
Devon
Locally smoked mackerel and other traditionally-cured fish available at the smokehouse shop.

Buckfast Abbey
Buckfastleigh
Devon
Heather honey and the famous Buckfast Tonic Wine available from the Abbey shop.

Cheese Dairy
Priory Farm
Chewton Mendip
Bath
Somerset
The entire process of making traditional farmhouse Cheddar can be viewed at the dairy, and the cheeses can be purchased in the farm shop.

Home Farm
Newton House
Newton St Cyres
near Exeter
Devon
Traditional farmhouse Cheddar, Double Gloucester, whey butter, ice-cream and clotted cream all produced on the premises can be purchased in the farm shop.

Dartington Cider Press Centre Farm Shop
Dartington
near Totnes
Devon
Traditional farmhouse cheeses, farm ciders, English wine, home-made jams and preserves, honey and other products for sale in the farm shop of this busy centre.

Wiltshire Tracklement Company
44 Church Street
Calne
Wiltshire
A full range of Urchfont mustards and other tracklements.

Hales Snails Ltd
25 Pages Walk
London SE1
Mendip snails stuffed with cheese and herbs.

Moores' Dorset Shop
Morecombelake
near Bridport
Dorset
Dorset knobs and other biscuits.

Stapleton Farm
Langtree
Torrington
North Devon
Clotted cream and other dairy products from Stapleton's mixed herd. Mail order service.

LONDON

London is cosmopolitan, the capital of the nation, political centre of the Commonwealth, and one of the world's leading centres for trade, banking and commerce. People from around the world, and particularly from former and existing Commonwealth nations and countries within the European Economic Community, have made the city their home; thousands from all over England, Scotland, Wales and Ireland continue to converge here in search of their proverbial fortunes; and of course an essential core of true Londoners remains – those cockneys born within the sound of Bow Bells, the chimes of the church of Mary-le-Bow, which called young Dick Whittington back to the City where he eventually prospered and rose to become Lord Mayor.

As befits such an important and international city, anything and everything can be found in London, particularly in regard to food and drink. There is certainly no shortage of foods from outside the country (indeed, one might almost be forgiven for believing that it is easier to hunt out a good Italian, Indian, French, Chinese or Greek restaurant than an English one). Londoners enjoy a staggering choice of foodstuffs to choose from. Stalls in the covered Leadenhall Market offer

Lisle Street.

138

exotic fruits and vegetables flown in from every corner of what was once the Empire. In Soho, shoppers take home neatly wrapped packets of fresh pasta, *prosciutto di Parma*, or French pastries, while the street-corner groceries in Islington, Kilburn or Lambeth as likely as not sell yams and mangoes, *phyllo* pastry, cardamom and fresh coriander alongside more mundane tins and packets. In warehouses along the river as well as in the hushed premises of traditional merchants in the centre of the city, wine drinkers can choose from what is undoubtedly the largest and most catholic selection in the world.

Within Britain, too, the very best produce from the provinces is sent to the capital. Fish from Cornwall or the west coast of Scotland, vegetables and fruit from market gardens in Evesham or Kent, spring lamb from Wales or prime beef from Aberdeen, oak-smoked kippers, Scotch salmon or traditionally-cured hams from Suffolk or Cumberland – all are often easier to come by here than in their own locality. London has always been the prime market for farmers and fishermen alike, and an efficient nationwide network exists which ensures that their produce and products are on display at such important central markets as Billingsgate or Smithfield, or the food halls of Harrods or Fortnum & Mason's within hours of being despatched.

It is this very diversity, this fusion of different people and cultures from within Britain as well as from without, that makes London such a colourful and exciting capital. Yet beneath the noise and bustle of the modern city lies an older, traditional world which in many ways has changed very little over the centuries.

Just around the corner from the bustle of Piccadilly Circus, for example, is the area known as St James's, surely one of London's most intimate and timeless parts. Here are shops such

Berwick Street Market.

as Paxton & Whitfield, famous for its selection of the finest English and continental cheeses; Fortnum & Mason, a luxury grocery (now also a department store) founded in 1707 by a footman to Queen Mary; wine merchants such as Berry Bros & Rudd, Justerini & Brooks and O. W. Loeb. The area was developed by Henry Jermyn in the seventeenth century, and after the Great Fire in 1666 became the favourite residential area of courtiers and gentlemen.

Today, in addition to bespoke tailors and shops selling handmade shoes, hats, pipes and other such manly necessities, St James's also has a concentration of uniquely British gentlemen's clubs, within convenient reach of the Court of St James's or, for that matter, Westminster and Buckingham Palace. Clubs such as Boodle's, the RAC, the Reform, Brooks', the Carlton, the United Services, the Athenaeum and others, are institutions of considerable age with exclusive roll-calls of distinguished members. The food served in the dining-rooms of such establishments is solid clubman's fare – roast meats and stews, mixed grills and the like – but these clubs have also contributed classics like Reform cutlets and Reform sauce, Boodle's orange fool and fruit cake, and that favourite decadent breakfast tipple, Buck's fizz.

A solid conservative dining tradition is apparent elsewhere in London, too. Establishments such as Ye Olde Cheshire Cheese, off Fleet Street, continue to serve fare similar to that which made this ancient and famous inn so popular with Dr Johnson, such as steak and kidney pudding, roast meats, platters of cold beef and game pies. Restaurants such as Simpson's-in-the-Strand excel at roasting meats to perfection. There the Master Cook oversees his vast subterranean kitchen, ensuring that sirloins of Scotch beef, saddles of Southdown lamb and fat legs of pork are all treated with due respect. Simpson's serves up to a thousand diners a day, and the sheer logistics of organizing the foodstuffs required daily is staggering. Hundreds of pounds of meat arrive at the kitchens early each morning. The beef for which Simpson's is so renowned must be trimmed of fat (losing a fifth of the total weight, but providing fresh beef suet for traditional English puddings), then hung at the correct temperature and humidity for thirteen days. It is often stated that traditional English cooking is simple, requiring only the finest ingredients, but this is not wholly true, for the art of roasting, basic though it may appear, is a delicate, intuitive one. At Simpson's, for example, thirty-pound sirloins are roasted in such a way that the thick

The kitchen at Simpson's-in-the-Strand.

end, placed in the hotter part of the oven, comes out well done, while the thin end is medium and the middle rare, so that the diner can enjoy his meat exactly as he wants it. The Master Cook can tell simply by picking up a joint to feel its weight and moisture content whether or not it is fully cooked. Such superbly roasted meats are finally taken up to the sedate dining-rooms where they are expertly carved at the table off silver trolleys. This is English cooking at its finest, on a grand scale to be had only in the nation's capital.

Not all of London's food traditions are grand and exclusive, by any means. Equally representative of the capital are those favourite (though diminishing in number) eel and pie shops where East Enders can still tuck into steaming plates of meat pie or eel served with mashed potatoes and green parsley 'liquor'. Jellied eels are another cockney favourite ('with 'ot vinegar,' a friend tells us, thumbs up in excitement), available from street stalls such as Tubby Isaac's at Aldgate. Boiled beef and carrots, another simple but delicious cockney staple, was immortalized in a popular music hall song, while bubble and squeak is the whimsical name of a dish which uses up left-over potatoes, brussel sprouts and (if there is any) meat. Green pea soup or London particular, thick and warming, gave its name to the fog which once enveloped London so intensely. In the past, oysters were a common food of the poor, but today they have become almost prohibitively expensive. Nevertheless, traditional oyster and shellfish bars such as Wheeler's and Sheekey's still serve them by the dozen, together with simple but perfectly fried or grilled fish such as sole, turbot, cod and halibut. Fresh fish is readily available in London, equally popular eaten at home or in pubs or restaurants.

Fried fish (without chips), after all, was the original English street food; today mobile fish and chip vans are often about after evening football matches at White Hart Lane and elsewhere, while there is hardly a part of London without its corner chip shop. Additionally, barrows selling dishes or pints of winkles, prawns, whelks and cockles, all sprinkled with malt vinegar, are a common sight in central London, as are those cheerful street vendors who roast chestnuts over coal braziers on bitter January

'Chestnuts, chestnuts. All hot from the pot!'

nights. (How pleasant, emerging from the Underground, to purchase a bagful to eat with the fingers, warming your hands in the process!)

If both her grandest and her simplest foods seem to recall another age, so do the scores of public houses still to be found throughout the city, with their steamy, etched windows, dark mahogany panelling and tall hand pumps for the dispense of traditionally-brewed ales. In such a warm atmosphere, having supped a pint or two of Young's or Fuller's, it is not difficult to imagine the London of Dickens, where rosy-cheeked saucy wenches and landlords with enormous bellies serve an honest pint; where travellers sit down to supper in chop houses and carveries serving huge joints of roast beef, haunches of venison and the like; where the flower girls and porters, in spite of their rough exteriors, always have a kind word and a heart of gold.

The Lamb Inn, Leadenhall Market.

Burlington Arcade, founded in 1819; beadles still ensure that shoppers neither 'whistle, sing, nor hurry'.

At Covent Garden, the refrains of flower girls may no longer pierce the midnight air, nor does the rhyming slang and good cheer of Billingsgate's porters now liven the riverside at Lower Thames Street in the early mornings (the market has since moved to premises in the West India Docks). But elsewhere, in the back streets of elegant Mayfair, or in the City (the historic square mile granted a charter by William I in 1067), traditional London endures.

Admittedly, London's rather stereotyped image, like the top-hatted beadle who patrols Burlington Arcade ensuring that the public neither 'whistle, sing, nor hurry', is jolly good for business, adored as it is by hordes of visiting tourists. But people in the City really do wear bowler hats and carry umbrellas. Ye Olde Cheshire Cheese may be frequented by American,

German and Japanese visitors these days as much as by City bankers and Fleet Street journalists, but that takes nothing away from the excellence of its steak and kidney pudding, which, we dare say, would still satisfy even as exacting a patron as Dr Johnson. And those remarkable gentlemen's clubs in St James's, anachronistic though they seem to most of us, are taken very seriously indeed by those who belong to them, many – though not all – of whom actually are MPs, OBEs, MBEs and, for that matter, OAPs.

London is a cosmopolitan capital, an international centre for banking and commerce. Yet in many ways, it remains an intimate town, a collection of so many unique villages and neighbourhoods, all with their own character. Herein lies its enduring charm.

Recipes from London

London Particular   (Serves 6–8)

'I asked him whether there was a great fire anywhere? For the streets were so full of dense brown smoke that scarcely anything was to be seen.

"O dear no, miss," he said. "This is a London particular."

I had never heard of such a thing.

"A fog, miss," said the young gentleman.

"O indeed!" said I.'

from Charles Dickens's *Bleak House*.

Dickens's name for London's famous 'pea soup' fog came to denote not only the fog but also the soup.

50 g/2 oz/½ stick butter
3 rashers smoked streaky bacon, chopped
1 large onion, sliced
450 g/1 lb split green peas, soaked overnight
2.4 l/4 pt/10 cups water
1 ham knuckle (soak if necessary)
Salt
Freshly-ground black pepper
About 2 tsp Worcestershire sauce

Melt the butter in a large heavy-based saucepan and cook the bacon gently. Add the onion and fry for a further 5 minutes. Add the drained soaked peas and stir well to coat in fat. Pour on the water, add the ham knuckle, season with pepper but not salt, and bring to the boil. Skim, cover and simmer for about 2 hours, or until the peas are soft and mushy. Remove ham knuckle and liquidize the soup. Take off and shred the meat from the bone and return with the liquidized soup to a clean saucepan. Re-heat and adjust the seasoning. Add Worcestershire sauce to taste and serve hot.

London particular.

Whitebait   (Serves 4)

Whitebait – the small fry of herring and sprats – used to be netted extensively in the Thames. In Greenwich, whitebait feasts at the Trafalgar Tavern and the Old Ship Tavern were popular events. Fresh whitebait is still caught in quantity at the mouth of the estuary at Southend, where a Whitebait Festival takes place annually, a celebration and blessing of the first catch.

450 g/1 lb whitebait	Salt
Seasoned flour for coating	Lemon wedges
Oil for frying	Freshly-chopped parsley

Wash and dry the fish and coat in seasoned flour. Heat the oil and put about a quarter of the fish in the frying basket. Shake out any loose flour. Deep fry until crisp, about 3–4 minutes. Remove the fish from the pan to a warmed serving dish and continue to cook the remaining whitebait. When all are done, return the fish to the basket and fry for a few seconds in very hot oil to crisp up. Drain well on a kitchen towel, sprinkle with salt, and garnish with lemon wedges and parsley. Serve with brown bread and butter, and, if desired, Tabasco or cayenne pepper.

Jellied Eels   (Serves 4–6)

Jellied eels are an old East End favourite where they are still sold from street stalls, to be eaten from china bowls sprinkled with hot chilli vinegar. Tubby Isaac has manned his corner stand at Aldgate for over fifty years now. While jellied eels are the sort of street food you wolf down while standing up, perhaps on the way home from the pub, they are surprisingly easy to make yourself, so long as you can get very fresh eel.

900 g/2 lb eel	12 black peppercorns
900 ml/1½ pt/3¾ cups water	Freshly-chopped parsley
6 tbsp malt vinegar	1 onion, thinly sliced
Salt	1 carrot, sliced

Skin and clean the eel. Cut into pieces about 2.5 cm/1 in long and rinse thoroughly under running cold water. Place the eel pieces in a large saucepan and pour on the water. Add all the other ingredients and bring to the boil. Cover and simmer for 15–20 minutes, skimming if necessary. Transfer the eel to a large china bowl, and pour over the strained stock. Allow to cool, then refrigerate. The liquid should jellify. Serve directly from the bowl, sprinkled with hot vinegar (whole dried chillies soaked in malt vinegar).

Jellied eels: a favourite East End street food.

Water Souchet   (Serves 4)

Water souchet, a fish soup utilizing the catch from the Thames, comes from the Dutch *waterzootje*. Perhaps it was introduced to London in the seventeenth century, when William III of Orange was on the throne. It was about this time, after all, that the Dutch-born king passed laws to encourage the English production of Dutch geneva, or gin, which soon became the favourite drink of the capital.

450 g/1 lb white fish bones, skin and heads for stock	Large bunch of parsley, chopped
600 ml/1 pt/2½ cups water	Bouquet of fresh herbs
150 ml/¼ pt/⅔ cup white wine	1 bay leaf
	450 g/1 lb fillets of whiting or plaice, cut into pieces
Salt	
12 black peppercorns	1 lemon

Place the fish trimmings in a large pan and add the water, wine and salt. Bring to the boil and skim. Add the peppercorns, most of the parsley, fresh herbs and bay leaf. Simmer for 40 minutes. Strain through a fine sieve and reserve the liquid. Place the fish fillets in a clean pan and add the strained stock. Bring to the boil and simmer for about 10–15 minutes. Serve some fish in each warmed soup bowl. Add the juice of half the lemon to the stock and adjust the seasoning. Pour over the fish and decorate each bowl with a slice of lemon and the remaining chopped parsley.

Bubble and Squeak   (Serves 4)

Joe Curley, Master Cook at Simpson's-in-the-Strand, loves the curious names of many English dishes such as this. Once, when he was demonstrating English cooking, a foreign assistant chef asked where he could purchase the 'bubbles' for this favourite dish. Another time, Joe was making Toad-in-the-Hole and a harassed French chef told him that since no fresh toads were available, he had to pick up some frog's legs instead and hoped they would do! Bubble and squeak, as every schoolboy knows, is the sound of Sunday's left-over meat and vegetables sizzling as it cooks in the pan on Monday.

Ye Olde Cheshire Cheese.

50 g/2 oz/¼ cup beef dripping	1 large onion, finely sliced
350 g/12 oz cold roast beef, cut into chunks	Salt
	Freshly-ground black pepper
450 g/1 lb cooked mashed potato	Dash of Worcestershire sauce
225 g/8 oz cooked green vegetables, such as cabbage or sprouts	

Heat the beef dripping in a large heavy-based frying pan and add the beef. Brown well, then add the mashed potato, cooked green vegetables and onion. Mix together well and fry until brown and crisp on both sides. Season well and add a dash of Worcestershire sauce to taste. Serve at once.

Toad-in-the-Hole (Serves 4)

Toad-in-the-hole – *without* the toad, but with lamb chops and kidneys instead of the more usual sausages – is splendid traditional fare, the type of food that once was served in London chop houses and dining clubs.

Yorkshire pudding batter (see p. 18)	4 lamb kidneys, skinned, cleaned and chopped
Knob of lamb or beef dripping	Salt
8 lamb chops	Freshly-ground black pepper

Make the batter according to the recipe, and leave to stand. Melt the dripping in a frying pan, and brown the seasoned chops and kidneys briefly. Transfer the chops, kidneys and dripping to a flat, ovenproof dish. Place in a pre-heated moderately hot oven (190°C/375°F/Gas Mark 5) for a minute or two to get the dripping really sizzling, then remove and pour on the batter. Return to the oven and cook for about 1 hour, without opening the door, until the batter has risen and the chops are cooked through. Serve immediately.

Steak and Kidney Pudding

(Serves 8)

Steak and kidney pudding is solid English fare, still enjoyed in London taverns. In Dr Johnson's time, such puddings were comparable in size and scope to his famous tome, for they contained not only beef-steak and kidneys, but also oysters by the dozen, whole birds such as lark and pigeon, mushrooms, port and much else.

450 g/1 lb suet crust pastry (see p. 102)	12 oysters (if available)
	Salt
900 g/2 lb stewing steak	Freshly-ground black pepper
225 g/8 oz ox kidney	
Seasoned flour	600 ml/1 pt/2½ cups water
1 onion, finely chopped	
225 g/8 oz button mushrooms	

Line a 2.4 l/4 pt greased pudding basin with the suet crust pastry, reserving one-third to make a lid. Trim the beef and cut into small cubes. Remove the skin and core from the kidney and dice. Pat the steak and kidney in seasoned flour, then layer it in the lined basin with the onions, mushrooms and oysters, if used. Season well with salt and pepper and pour on the water. Moisten the edges of the pastry with water, and top with the pastry lid, pressing the edges together well. Cover with a circle of foil pleated in the middle and tie securely with string. Place the basin in a large saucepan of simmering water which should come half-way up the sides. Steam for about 3–4 hours, adding more boiling water when necessary.

Serve the pudding from the basin, removing the foil first, and wrapping the basin with a clean cloth. Serve with sprouts, cabbage and mashed or boiled potatoes.

Omelette Arnold Bennett (Serves 1)

This dish was created at the Savoy Hotel for the writer and critic who used to dine here after an evening at the theatre. It is elaborate but delicious, like Bennett's rich Victorian prose.

75 g/3 oz Finnan haddock, cooked and flaked	3 eggs
1 tbsp freshly-grated Parmesan cheese	1 tbsp water
	1 tbsp butter
Salt	1 tbsp double cream
Freshly-ground black pepper	

Mix the flaked Finnan haddock with the cheese and season with salt and pepper. Lightly beat the eggs in a bowl with the water and salt and pepper. Melt the butter in an omelette pan and when the froth subsides, pour in the eggs. Place the fish and cheese on top of the eggs just when they are beginning to set. Pour on the cream while the eggs are still liquid, and transfer to a hot grill for a few minutes until the top is golden brown. Do not fold, but slide on to a hot plate and serve immediately.

Mixed Grill (Serves 4)

The old chop houses, taverns and grill rooms in the City and elsewhere in London earned their reputations by serving the Englishman's favourite meats — lamb chops, kidneys, sausages, steaks and gammon — quickly grilled over charcoal, and garnished with tomato, mushrooms and watercress.

4 lamb chops, trimmed	Salt
4 lamb kidneys, skinned, halved and cored	Freshly-ground black pepper
4 small steaks	4 tomatoes
4 small gammon steaks	Large mushrooms
4 pork sausages	Watercress
Butter	

Prepare a charcoal grill, or pre-heat a grill to its hottest. Brush the chops, kidney halves and steaks with melted butter and season with salt and pepper. Place the chops, kidneys, sausages and gammon on the grill, and cook for about 5–7 minutes each side. Add the steaks when desired, allowing about 3–5 minutes per side for rare to medium-rare, depending on thickness. Remove the meats to a very hot plate and keep warm. Brush the tomatoes and mushrooms with melted butter, and grill for about 5 minutes. Arrange on four very hot plates and garnish with watercress.

Reform Cutlets (Serves 4)

London clubs such as the Reform made a lasting contribution to the food of the capital. Reform cutlets and Reform sauce were invented by Alexis Soyer, gastronome, writer and club chef.

8 lamb cutlets	Handful of fresh parsley, very finely chopped
Salt	Fresh fine white breadcrumbs to coat
Freshly-ground black pepper	Oil and butter for frying
2 eggs, beaten	
50 g/2 oz cooked ham, very finely diced	

Trim the cutlets and scrape the bone to make a handle. Dip in beaten egg and season with salt and pepper. Meanwhile, mix the finely diced ham and chopped parsley with the breadcrumbs. Press the cutlets dipped in egg into this breadcrumb mixture to coat. Melt the oil and butter in a large frying pan until just smoking, and fry the chops for about 6 minutes a side, until golden brown and cooked through. Drain on paper and serve immediately with Reform sauce.

Reform Sauce

2 tbsp wine vinegar	1 small cooked beetroot, cut into very thin strips
1 tbsp castor sugar	2 gherkins, cut into very thin strips
About a dozen black peppercorns, crushed	
1 small onion, finely chopped	1 hard-boiled egg white, very finely chopped
300 ml/½ pt/1¼ cups brown stock	Salt
1 tbsp redcurrant jelly	Freshly-ground black pepper
50 g/2 oz ham or tongue, cut into very thin strips	

Place the vinegar, sugar, crushed black peppercorns and onion in a saucepan and cook over a high heat until the onions are soft. Stir in the stock and redcurrant jelly and simmer for about 20 minutes. Strain into a clean pan and add the ham or tongue, beetroot, gherkins and hard-boiled egg white. Stir well and bring to the boil. Adjust the seasoning and serve hot with Reform cutlets.

The Master Cook

Traditional British cooking has always placed the highest regard on the perfect roasting of meats. In mediaeval times, whole sides or barons of beef, wild boar, sheep, venison and other meats were cooked on a turning spit above the huge fire in the kitchen. The care of such meats was the prerogative of the Master Cook, for it was the most skilled and critical task of all. While tending the meats, however, his hat naturally collected a great deal of soot and debris from the chimney, and thus it evolved that the Master Cook always wore a short black cap rather than a white one. For the past century the profession has bestowed this traditional honour on a few Master Cooks only, and today only Joe Curley, Master Cook at Simpson's-in-the-Strand, wears this mark of professional expertise. To Britain's only Master Cook, however, his black cap does not just symbolize technical excellence; rather, he believes that this unique tradition looks back in its origins to the English wayside inns, noted for their hospitality. He would like to see the black cap bestowed on more English cooks who maintain not only the highest standards in the kitchen but also this essential philosophy of warmth towards the visitor.

The black cap: insignia of the Master Cook.

Boiled Beef and Carrots (Serves 6–8)

Boiled beef served with carrots, dumplings and pease pudding is an old cockney favourite.

1.35 kg/3 lb joint of silverside or brisket of beef
2 large onions
2 sticks of celery
2 leeks, cleaned
1 small turnip

Bouquet of fresh herbs
1 bay leaf
Salt
About a dozen black peppercorns
900 g/2 lb small whole carrots, peeled

For the dumplings

100 g/4 oz/$\frac{4}{5}$ cup plain flour
Pinch of salt
$\frac{1}{2}$ tsp baking powder
50 g/2 oz/$\frac{1}{4}$ cup suet, finely chopped

1 tbsp freshly-chopped herbs
About 5 tbsp water

Place the beef in a large saucepan and add enough cold water to cover. Bring to the boil and skim. Cover and simmer for about $1\frac{1}{2}$ hours. Add the onions, celery, leeks, turnip, herbs and seasonings. Simmer for a further hour. Add the carrots and cook for a further 30 minutes (about 3 hours cooking time in total).

To make the dumplings, sieve the flour, salt and baking powder into a mixing bowl. Stir in the suet and herbs and add sufficient water to make a stiff dough. Shape into small walnut-sized balls. When the beef is cooked remove it and the vegetables to a warmed serving dish and keep hot. Drop the dumplings into the cooking liquid and boil for about 10 minutes each. Drain and serve around the beef and vegetables with pease pudding, horseradish and English mustard.

London's Markets

From four in the morning, at Billingsgate's new premises on the Isle of Dogs, at New Covent Garden, at Smithfield and at Spitalfields, fish and shellfish, vegetables and fruit, and home-produced and imported meat to feed London and the nation, are on the move. Produce from throughout Britain and from abroad comes to the capital's great wholesale markets, where it is then redistributed to London's retailers – her butchers, fishmongers, greengrocers, general shops and restaurants – as well as to traders elsewhere in the country. Cheerful porters ensure that the massive task of shifting tons of produce from seller to buyer is carried out smoothly, and by eight or nine in the morning, stalls are hosed down and cleared, and there is a tired end-of-the-day feel as all relax in nearby public houses with specially-granted licensing hours (The Hope, located on the aptly named Cowcross Street at Smithfield Market, serves butchers and porters alike with bacon and eggs, steak and pints of ale from 6 am).

Elsewhere in London, retail markets liven the city with their particular colour, banter and atmosphere. From one-man vendors to whole streets devoted to selling, London's markets are unique. Stroll down the fruit and vegetable market in Berwick Street, in the heart of Soho, or visit the rather more subdued Leadenhall Market, a Victorian shopping arcade with permanent tiled stalls offering the best poultry and game, fish and shellfish, Scottish beef and English lamb, and exotic vegetables and fruit to a select City clientele. Petticoat Lane, with its monkeys on chains and candy floss vendors, offers not just fruit and vegetables but blankets and sheets, sets of silverware, bone china with 'exclusive' designs (repeated, predictably, at other stalls down the Lane), clothing, knitware and every kitchen or household gadget imaginable. The Portobello Road, Lambeth Walk, Leather Lane and Chapel Market, Islington, are just a few of London's many colourful markets. They are all worth seeking and frequenting: go there for the bicker and banter, the furious bargaining over a ha'penny, the sales pitch and the come on, or for the satisfaction of becoming a regular who gets an occasional extra apple or a few cherries thrown in as a treat.

A Billingsgate porter.

Portobello Road.

Smithfield Market.

An elegant butcher's shop in Mayfair.

Boodle's Orange Fool (Serves 6)

Boodle's Club, in St James's Street, is perhaps more famous for the fact that Beau Brummell used to gamble here than for this delightful orange fool. It is rich and delicious, nevertheless. This is Boodle's own recipe.

1.2 l/2 pt/5 cups double cream	6 Savoy fingers or sponge fingers
6 large oranges, zest and juice	6 orange shells, hollowed out
1 lemon, zest and juice	
Approximately 4 tbsp honey, to taste	

The fool must be made at the very last moment before serving, as it readily falls back. Partially whip the cream and add the juice and zest. Continue to whip vigorously, while adding the honey, until stiff.

Pile this mixture into the orange shells and serve with Savoy fingers or sponge fingers.

Chelsea Buns   (Makes about 12)

These sticky, spicy buns have been a great favourite since the seventeenth century when a 'Captain Bun' sold them by the thousands from the Old Chelsea Bun House. George III used to park his carriage outside the shop, and though no doubt this royal patronage accounted in part for the success of the business, the buns today are as delicious as ever.

150 ml/$\frac{1}{4}$ pt/$\frac{2}{3}$ cup milk
100 g/4 oz/$\frac{1}{2}$ cup castor sugar
10 g/$\frac{1}{3}$ oz dried yeast
450 g/1 lb plain flour

Pinch of salt
100 g/4 oz/1 stick butter
3 eggs, beaten
100 g/4 oz/$\frac{2}{3}$ cup currants
1 tsp mixed spice

Glaze
175 g/6 oz/1 cup sugar
   boiled with 6 tbsp water

Heat the milk until tepid, remove from the heat and dissolve 1 tsp of sugar in it. Sprinkle on the yeast, and set aside in a warm place until frothy, about 15 minutes. Meanwhile, sieve the flour and salt into a large mixing bowl. Rub in half the butter and stir in half the sugar. Add the beaten eggs and the yeast mixture. Mix well to form a dough. Knead until smooth. Cover and leave in a warm place for about 1 hour until doubled in size.

Soften the remaining butter. Turn the dough on to a floured board and knead gently. Roll into a rectangle about 1.3 cm/$\frac{1}{2}$ in thick and spread with the softened butter. Sprinkle with half the remaining sugar. Fold the dough in half and roll out again to a similar thickness. Sprinkle with the last of the sugar, the currants and the spice. Roll it up quite tightly and cut into slices about 2.5 cm/1 in thick. Place them on a baking tray about 1.3 cm/$\frac{1}{2}$ in apart with cut sides uppermost. Cover and set aside in a warm place for 30 minutes.

Bake in a moderately hot oven (200°C/400°F/Gas Mark 6) for about 25 minutes. As the buns rise they will spread together. When done, glaze with the syrup and allow to cool before separating.

Harrods.

St James's Park, a haven for office workers from Whitehall.

Drink in London

'Besides which there were bottles of stout, bottles of wine, bottles of ale, and divers other strong drinks, native and foreign.'
from Charles Dickens's
Martin Chuzzlewit.

Dickens's description might well apply to drink in London as a whole. For, as befits a thirsty capital, all manner of drinks are to be found here, both native and foreign. There are approximately 7000 pubs in the city serving traditional ales both brewed here, as well as 'imported' from breweries in surrounding areas and further afield. London gin is enjoyed around the world, though it is a far cry from the vile concoctions sold in the seventeenth and eighteenth centuries, when the catch-phrase 'Drunk for a penny; dead drunk 2d.', seen over the gin shop in Hogarth's famous etching, must have been common throughout the city. Today London dry gin is considered the finest of all, unrivalled in quality, purity and flavour; it is the perfect base for the Englishman's favourite drink, gin and tonic, as well as for other cocktails. London maintains its position today as the capital of the wine trade, a role it has enjoyed for several centuries at least. Fine wines are regularly auctioned and exclusive merchants specialize in the best clarets, burgundies and vintage ports. Less expensive, more accessible wines come to London, too, giving the London wine lover probably as great a choice as any drinker on earth. London is also the centre for another drink – tea – a commodity so important in the lives of the British.

Hours: Public houses in London are generally open Mondays–Saturdays, 11.00–15.00 and 17.30–23.00; Sundays, 12.00–14.00 and 19.00–22.30.

Traditional Beer

The brewing industry throughout Britain may be dominated by a handful of giant national companies, but in London such firms as Whitbread, Watney, Truman and Charrington remain

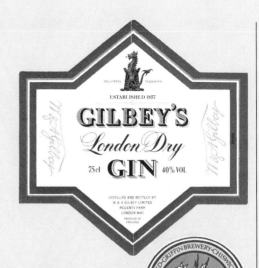

Assorted mats and labels of the region.

just the local brewers, with their roots firmly established in the capital. After 200 years of brewing in the capital, Taylor Walker's Barley Mow brewery in Limehouse ceased operating when the company merged with Ind Coope to form part of the Allied Breweries group, but this established old company maintains some 600 pubs in and around the Greater London area. Courage, another national brewing company, has a major brewery in nearby Reading and is also well represented in London.

Two much smaller, fiercely independent and traditional breweries continue to quench the thirst of their devoted customers: Young & Co. of Wandsworth and Fuller's of Chiswick, while many other breweries, particularly those in surrounding areas, see London as an important and expanding market. Beers from Shepherd Neame, Adnams, Greene King, Tolly Cobbold and many others are all available in certain outlets. Most London pubs, however, are tied or managed houses linked to breweries. An interesting, if necessarily small-scale development, though, is the rise of free houses which are brewing their own beer.

London in the past had its own unique style of beer, 'entire' or 'porter'. It was first brewed at the Bell Brewhouse in Shoreditch in 1727, and numerous breweries soon adapted to what became the new public taste. This dark beer was known as 'porter' possibly because of its popularity with the porters of Covent Garden and Billingsgate. Whitbread, Charrington and Watney all rose in prominence as brewers of porter, though today this style of beer has so declined that it has become almost non-existent. More recently, the drinking taste in London as well as elsewhere appears to be moving towards lighter lagers, though at the same time traditional cask-conditioned beers remain the mainstay of the serious beer drinker. However, as a footnote to the continuing saga, the wheel has now apparently swung full circle: Watney Combe Reid has recently introduced a 'new' beer, porter, to the capital once more.

Whitbread & Co., The Brewery, London E1. Whitbread & Co., today one of the national brewing giants, was originally a local London brewery, founded by Samuel Whitbread in 1742. At the time when this young man came to London from Cardington to seek his fortune, the new brew, porter, was finding popularity among both beer drinkers and brewers alike, for it replaced the former strong ales, small beers and tuppenny ales (a compromise between the former two, its name indicated the price per quart) which were often mixed by customers to taste. Though the popularity of porter only lasted for a hundred years, its success enabled Sam Whitbread's brewery to become the largest in London in less than forty years. Though Whitbread no longer brew at Chiswell Street, cask-conditioned ales from Wethered (Marlow), Fremlins (Faversham), and Flowers (Cheltenham) are available in the company's significant number of public houses in the capital.

Whitbread Bitter o.g. 1037
Wethered's Bitter o.g. 1034–37
SPA o.g. 1050
Winter Royal (winter only)
o.g. 1050 +
Fremlins Tusker o.g. 1043 +
Flowers Original o.g. 1043–47

Charrington, Anchor House, London E1. Though the company merged with Bass in 1967, Charrington maintains firm roots in the capital. John Charrington founded the company in 1739 and it grew to become the second biggest brewer in London by the early nineteenth century. Cask-conditioned Charrington IPA, though no longer produced in the capital, is a full-flavoured bitter brewed to satisfy London taste. Draught Bass from Burton and William Stones' bitter from Yorkshire are also available in many Charrington tied houses, together with the group's other products. The bottle-conditioned Worthington White Shield is a classic. Charrington is responsible for group trading not only in London but in the South-East in general. The company operates some 1700 tied public houses in this area.

Charrington IPA o.g. 1039
Draught Bass o.g. 1043
William Stones' Bitter o.g. 1038

Bottle-conditioned ale:

Worthington White Shield
o.g. 1051

Truman Ltd, The Brewery, London E1. Truman Ltd, founded in 1666, remains the last company brewing in central London. One of a number of autonomous companies within the Watney Mann & Truman brewing group, Truman's trade remains concentrated in London, north Kent and East Anglia. Truman's has nearly 900 tenanted and managed public houses, and supplies its beers to a further 4000 free outlets within this area.

Truman Prize Mild o.g. 1034
Truman Bitter o.g. 1036
Truman Best Bitter o.g. 1045

Watney, Combe, Reid & Co., Stag Brewery, London SW14. Watney, Combe, Reid & Co., like Truman's, forms part of the Watney Mann & Truman brewing group, itself a division of Grand Metropolitan. The company, however, has a long-established history of brewing in the capital. Indeed, beer had been brewed on the Stag site since 1636; 'Pimlico ale', brewed in this part of London, dates back well before even this, since the monks of Westminster apparently carried on this important activity with great vigour centuries earlier. Watney's cask-conditioned London and Stag bitters are available in the majority of the company's 1500 or so tied houses. Hammerton's Porter, based on a traditional London recipe, is brewed from roasted barley and is highly hopped.

Hammerton's Porter o.g. 1038
London Bitter o.g. 1036–40
Stag Bitter o.g. 1042–48

Ind Coope Taylor Walker, Muswell Hill, London N10. The Taylor Walker Brewery (as it subsequently came to be known) was established in East London in the suburb of Limehouse in 1730. Over the years the company prospered, and acquired a number of other breweries as it expanded (the amalgamation of breweries is not a recent phenomenon). Taylor Walker was finally taken over by Ind Coope, which itself subsequently joined forces with Ansell's and Tetley Walker to form the Allied Breweries group. Though the Taylor Walker brand name disappeared for some years, it was reintroduced as part of Allied's strategy of promoting distinct regional companies. Taylor Walker operates over 600 tied public houses in and around Greater London, including Benskins, Friary Meux and Ind Coope public houses, each of which has its own brand of cask-conditioned ale brewed at Romford and Burton.

> Taylor Walker Bitter o.g. 1037
> Taylor Walker Mainline
> o.g. 1041
> Benskins Bitter o.g. 1037
> Friary Meux Bitter o.g. 1037
> Ind Coope Bitter o.g. 1037
> Burton Ale o.g. 1047

Young & Co. Ltd, The Ram Brewery, Wandsworth SW18. Young & Co. remains an independent family brewery with a reputation firmly based on the excellence of its traditional cask-conditioned ales. Located in south-west London, the majority of its tied houses are also south of the river. Perhaps rather eccentrically, Young & Co. is equally well-known for its ram mascot, as well as for the brewery farmyard, open at weekends for city children who might not otherwise have the opportunity to see such farm animals. Young's still delivers by horse-drawn dray to pubs within three miles of the brewery.

> Young's Bitter o.g. 1036
> Young's Special o.g. 1046
> Young's Winter Warmer (winter only) o.g. 1055

Fuller, Smith & Turner plc, Griffin Brewery, Chiswick. Beer has been brewed on this Griffin site for over 320 years, and Fuller, Smith & Turner remains today an important independent brewery providing distinctive cask-conditioned ales to the capital. Fuller's Extra Special Bitter is one of the strongest regularly-brewed draught beers in the country.

> Chiswick Bitter o.g. 1035
> London Pride o.g. 1041
> Extra Special Bitter (ESB) o.g. 1056

Home-brew Pubs in London

In the distant past, all public houses brewed their own beer. While the trend in recent years has been for independent breweries to amalgamate with national concerns, a new and refreshing development at the other end of the scale is the re-emergence of both tiny mini-breweries and pub breweries. In

Young's, an independent company producing excellent cask-conditioned ales, still delivers by horse-drawn dray to public houses near its Wandsworth brewery.

London, a number of pub breweries are now operating. For example, Bruce's pub breweries all brew their own beers in addition to the original Dogbolter (o.g. 1058–60). Bruce's pub breweries in London are:

The Goose and Firkin
47–48 Borough Road
London SE1

The Fox and Firkin
316 Lewisham High Street
London SE13

The Frog and Firkin
41 Tavistock Crescent
London W11

The Pheasant and Firkin
166 Goswell Road
London EC1

The Traditional London Wine Merchant

Wine, though only recently once more a significant product of English soil, has always been important to the discerning Englishman. Because of its relative scarcity, wine in Britain has always enjoyed a certain exclusive aura. Beer, after all, was the drink of the people, while cheap Dutch and home-produced gin made the lives of London's poor miserable. Fine wine, particularly claret, Burgundy and vintage port, however, remained the prerogative of those gentlemen and the nobility who could afford to lay down such wines to maturity, and wine merchants were established to serve this exclusive trade. The firm of Berry Bros & Rudd, of No. 3, St James's Street, dates back to the seventeenth century. Before this, the firm was involved in the coffee trade, and indeed even today, in the venerable front room with its sloping floor and slanting desks, the old coffee mill and the beam scales for weighing sacks of coffee can still be seen. When Berry Bros & Rudd began dealing in wine, its customers wanted to enjoy the then novel pleasure of having their avoirdupois recorded for posterity in leather-bound volumes. The old weigh books remain, (along with the special bottles made for the Great Exhibition) bearing the names of kings and princes, ministers, actors and gamblers – good and discerning drinkers all.

Today, of course, wine is no longer exclusive, and supermarkets sell bottles from every corner of the wine-producing world. Yet established wine merchants like Berry Bros & Rudd remain, offering the unique personal service and advice upon which their reputation is based. Their lists, not surprisingly, are strong in those classic areas still important to British connoisseurs: classed-growth clarets, the great wines of Burgundy and Germany, vintage port and champagne. Such wine merchants can claim customers whose fathers and grandfathers were also their customers, and perhaps there is something to that. Besides, where else in the world can you purchase a bottle of wine and (if you are a very good customer) have yourself weighed on a seventeenth-century balance at the same time?

The Dickensian atmosphere of Berry Bros & Rudd.

The Ferret and Firkin in the Balloon up the Creek
114 Lots Road
London SW10

London Gin

Gin is a spirit distilled from grain and flavoured with juniper berries, coriander and other herbs and flavourings. Originally a rather coarse spirit from Holland, its rawness was disguised by the pungent, distinctive flavour of juniper (the Dutch name for this aromatic bush is *genever*, which the English shortened to gin). In the seventeenth century gin was imported to Britain in great quantity, and after William of Orange took the throne in 1688 and freed distillation from royal control, London distillers began to make a similar spirit themselves. Lack of control over the industry, however, led to a flood of cheap, poisonous spirit on the

Proof Spirit

Several centuries ago, when the distilling of spirits was a somewhat more haphazard and inexact science than it is today, the strength of a spirit was 'proved' by mixing it with gunpowder to see if it would ignite. Today, as in the past, HM Government is naturally concerned with this important matter, particularly in relation to the benefits to the Exchequer. Therefore the meaning of proof spirit is defined rather more exactly: proof spirit, that is spirit described as 100° proof, is that which contains 57.1 per cent alcohol by volume. In Britain, both gin and whisky are usually sold at 70° proof, that is, 30° under proof, or 40 per cent alcohol by volume. Confusingly, the British proof system differs significantly from the American. To Americans, 100° proof indicates spirit which contains 50 per cent alcohol by volume. 70° British proof, therefore, is the equivalent of 80° American proof; 75° British proof is 86° American proof. This situation can cause confusion among cavalier American drinkers in Britain who mistakenly misjudge the supposed weakness of British spirits.

market, sold in rough-and-ready gin-shops to the poorest and most miserable inhabitants of London.

Today, however, gin is probably the purest of all spirits. Dutch gin remains pungent and highly flavoured, while London dry gin – whether produced in the capital or not – denotes gin which is lightly flavoured and unsweetened. The finest, it is generally agreed, is still distilled in London, by companies whose histories extend back to the eighteenth and nineteenth centuries (such as James Burrough, Gordon & Co., Charles Tanqueray & Co., Booth's Distilleries Ltd and others). Each produces gin by its own methods, perfected over the centuries, using its own unique and secret formula of flavourings.

The production begins with colourless, neutral grain spirit which is further rectified by repeated distillation in continuous column stills to result in a very pure spirit. This potent spirit is run in batches into copper gin stills similar to the pot stills used by malt whisky distillers in Scotland. A charge of flavourings, including juniper berries and coriander seeds, as well, possibly, as angelica, liquorice, cardamom, citrus peel and other herbs and roots (each company has its own special formula), is added to the flavouring still and allowed to macerate. The still is then heated, either by steam coils or directly, and the spirit vapourizes and then condenses. At this stage, the skill and experience of the stillman is critical, for by nose and palate he must determine the purest and most desirable parts of each run, rejecting both the foreshots (the early part of the run) and the feints (the tail end) to be redistilled, and keeping just the middle cut. This pure gin is tested for quality, and finally blended for uniformity. It is reduced to drinking strength with the addition of pure water.

How best to drink gin? In Victorian times, it formed the base for punch and cordials. Gin toddies were popular, being a mixture of gin, sugar and boiling water, as were gin punch, gin twist, gin and bitters, and gin and hot beer. Gin was also very popular in the far outposts of the Empire, where it was particularly enjoyed mixed with quinine water. The latter was a treatment for malaria, and so the Englishman's favourite gin and

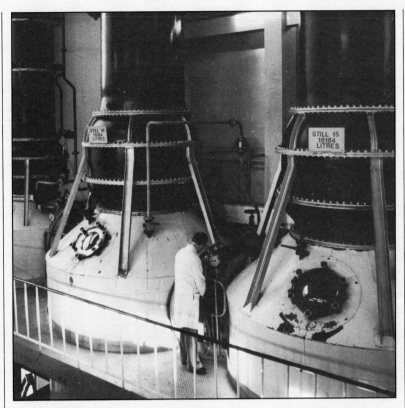

Column gin stills at James Burrough's Beefeater Distillery, Kennington.

tonic was an early example of that sensible English philosophy of 'a spoonful of sugar' helping the medicine go down. The naval officer's favourite, pink gin, is another classic combination (simply gin and angostura bitters), while at Raffles in Singapore, the Singapore Sling was invented, an exotic concoction to sip out of frosted glasses under slow-revolving fans. The Collins (John in Britain, Tom in America) and numerous other gin-based cocktails remain popular.

Pimm's

The production of this former colonial's favourite thirst-quencher began and remains today in the City of London. It was originally developed by James Pimm, a shellfish merchant, who served it in his oyster tavern in Poultry. Customers realized that this unique, flavourful cup could most suitably quench a large thirst worked up in the hot tropical colonies, and so the first case of Pimm's was sent to the Galle Face Hotel in Colombo, Ceylon. Pimm's sub-sequently travelled up the Nile and appeared at Khartoum. Army officers requested it for their own personal provisions stores, and planters enjoyed it in the shade of cool verandas.

While its exact composition remains a strictly guarded secret (the present Managing Director tells us that only six people know the formula), Pimm's No. 1 Cup has a gin base, flavoured with continental fruit liqueurs and herbs. When cocktails became popular, Pimm's at one time made six different cups, all with different bases, including whisky, brandy, rum, Canadian whisky and vodka. Today only the No. 1 Cup remains (although very limited amounts of a vodka-based Pimm's are still produced). To make a perfect Pimm's, mix one measure of Pimm's with two or three of lemonade. Add plenty of ice, a strip of cucumber peel, a slice of lemon, and – if desired – a sprig of mint, but, according to the manufacturers, no maraschino cherry or borage, although many people like to add such fresh fruit as strawberries and peaches.

The London Tea Trade

The Tea Trade Centre at Sir John Lyon House, on the banks of the Thames south of St Paul's Cathedral, is the hub of an industry of vital importance in the everyday lives of the British. Tea is undoubtedly the British national drink: every man, woman and child over ten years of age consumes an average of over four cups a day or some 1500 cups annually. It accounts for over half of everything drunk, including coffee and alcoholic beverages, but excluding water. Out of the world's exports of tea (2500 million pounds is manufactured each year, half of which is exported) some thirty per cent makes it way to London. The United Kingdom is by far the largest and most important importer of tea in the world. Samples from the hundreds of millions of pounds of tea brought in to slake a seemingly insatiable national thirst make their way to this unassuming building in the heart of the City where they are tasted by skilled professional tea brokers before coming under the hammer at each week's tea auction.

The British taste is for strong, sappy

London is the centre of the world tea trade.

tea, rich in tannin, taken usually with milk or with milk and sugar. The popular branded teas which account for some ninety per cent of the volume of tea sold are made up of a variety of as many as twenty to thirty different teas. These original teas come to London from their country of origin (today India, Sri Lanka, Kenya and Malawi are the most important sources of supply, though originally the East India Company's monopoly on China tea led to the popularization of this drink among the British). Shipped in their familiar paper- and foil-lined plywood chests, all the chests of a particular grade from an estate or tea garden are grouped together into 'breaks'. In addition to the details of its region of origin, each break contains information relevant to the prospective purchaser, including its grade of leaf (Orange Pekoe, Broken Pekoe or Souchong, for example), its season of manufacture, and its net weight.

Every Monday the tea auction takes place at Sir John Lyon House where buying brokers bid for breaks listed in the sellers' catalogues. Before the auction samples of tea from each break are distributed to both the selling and the buying brokers and tea companies. Each sample is tasted to determine its quality and value in relation to the current state of the tea market. Selling brokers must determine the price that they believe each tea should fetch at auction. Buyers must not only assess market value, but additionally determine whether each tea is needed for their particular company's blends.

It is fascinating to see the professional tea tasters at work. Over a hundred samples may be lined up on long tables. A portion of each is carefully weighed out and individually brewed to double strength with freshly-boiled water. The teas infuse for six minutes precisely, then they are poured into bowls, and the wet leaves are laid out on saucers for inspection. Teas are generally tasted with milk, since that is how the majority in Britain drink their tea. The tasters move down the line with surprising speed, tasting each lukewarm sample from a spoon then ejecting it into a copper spittoon. With their expert palates and experience, they are able to taste and assign a value to within a few pence per kilo of what each tea should fetch at the auction. Such skilled professional tasters may sample up to five hundred different teas in a day. At the end of it all, they put their feet up, and relax with – yes, what else? – a refreshing 'cuppa'.

Teas such as these which come under the hammer each week form the backbone of the blended brands of tea so popular with the British. Though relatively inexpensive, such blends are nevertheless of a very high standard. The best have a fresh malty aroma, a brisk pungency, a bright copper colour: in short, an overall roundness which is the result of the skilful combination of numerous teas from different sources and countries of origin.

The finest teas, like the finest wines, however, are the product of individual gardens, their quality dependent on soil, altitude, climate and microclimate, as well as care in manufacture. The finest, again like the finest wines, possess a host of delicate but distinctive flavours and scents reminiscent of herbs, flowers, fruit, spices, nuts. Some favourite teas for connoisseurs include:

Assam Rich full-flavoured tea from the Brahmaputra Valley of North India with a strong, pronounced malty flavour.

Darjeeling The 'champagne of teas', grown in the foothills of the Himalayas, with a delicate and stinging flavour and bouquet.

Oolong The world's most expensive tea, produced with meticulous care in mainland China and Taiwan, valued for its delicate peach flavour.

Professional tea tasters sample over a hundred different teas at a session.

Ceylon Teas from Sri Lanka (still known as Ceylon teas by the trade) have mellow nutty flavours and a good bright colour.

Kenya East Africa has become an ever more important tea-producing region; Kenyan tea, though not generally sold on its own, is valued by the blenders for its bright 'new penny' copper colour and its refreshing taste.

Keemun Pale, mellow China tea.

Lapsang Souchong Another China tea with a distinctive pungent smoky flavour.

Jasmine A scented China tea containing jasmine petals which give a delicate flavour and fragrance.

FAVOURITE ENGLISH BLENDS:

Earl Grey An English favourite of India or India and China teas flavoured with the distinctive oil of bergamot. Some say that this tea epitomizes the gentility of English afternoon tea.

English Breakfast Tea An established robust blend of Northern India and Ceylon teas noted for its full rich flavour.

Some Useful Addresses

English Tourist Board
4 Grosvenor Gardens
London SW1 0DU

London Tourist Board
26 Grosvenor Gardens
London SW1 0DU

The Pub Information Centre
93 Buckingham Palace Road
London SW1

Fortnum & Mason
Piccadilly
London W1A 1ER
Famous food hall and mail order service.

Harrods
Brompton Road
Knightsbridge
London SW1X 7XL
Harrods' Food Hall consists of seventeen departments in all. Mail order service.

Paxton & Whitfield
93 Jermyn Street
London SW1
Excellent selection of English cheeses. Mail order service.

Berry Bros & Rudd
3 St James's Street
London SW1
Traditional wine merchant. Mail order service.

Markets

Berwick Street and Rupert Street, W1
Busy fruit and vegetable market in the heart of Soho.
Open: Monday–Saturday, 9.00–18.00

Petticoat Lane, E1
Famous street market selling just about everything.
Open: Sunday, 9.00–14.00

Leadenhall Market, EC3
Victorian shopping arcade in the City. Quality shops sell cheese, meat, game, fish, fruit and vegetables.
Open: Monday–Friday, 9.00–17.00

Lambeth Walk, SE11
General street market.
Open: Friday & Saturday, 8.00–18.00

Portobello Road, W11
General street market.
Open: Monday–Saturday, 9.00–17.00 (Thursday, mornings only)

Wholesale Markets

(While members of the public cannot purchase produce at London's wholesale markets, the atmosphere in the surrounding areas is lively and well worth a visit.)

Billingsgate
North Quay,
West India Docks,
Isle of Dogs
The capital's principal fish market moved from historic Lower Thames Street premises to a new market on the Isle of Dogs, but the atmosphere here remains just as lively.
Open: Tuesday–Saturday, 5.30–10.00

Smithfield, EC1
London's wholesale meat market, with livestock connections since the fourteenth century.
Open: Monday–Thursday, 5.00–12.00; Friday 5.00–7.00

Spitalfields, E1
Fruit, vegetables and flowers in this East End market founded in 1682.
Open: Monday–Saturday, 4.30–10.00

New Covent Garden, Nine Elms, SW5
The old site of the Covent Garden market has been developed into a sophisticated city centre complex, but the flower girls and porters have moved across the river.
Open: Monday–Friday, 4.00–11.00; Saturday, 4.00–10.00 (summer only); Sunday, 4.00–10.00

IRELAND

An Irish farmhouse table is laid: at one end of the long trestle, the warm china plates are stacked, ready for serving. There is a platter of carved chicken (freshly killed, drawn, plucked and singed, then simply cooked in the solid fuel stove), and a steaming bowl of boiled potatoes beetled with boiled cabbage and butter; more boiled potatoes, too, still pink in their tight jackets; thick, dark gravy, and bread and onion stuffing. The tea cups and pot are also stacked at one end of the table, together with a platter of freshly-baked soda farls, a brown wheaten loaf and a blackberry tart, made with fruit gathered from the hedgerows only hours earlier. After the main meal is finished, the tea – strong, even stewed, and always drunk with milk and sugar – is poured into the waiting cups, and then it is time to start again, on soda bread, butter and jam, and warm slices of the tart, covered with lashings of thick, fresh cream.

The character of Ireland and the Irish remains essentially down-to-earth, and in the country especially, the basic foods of the land continue to satisfy. Every farm, even every cottage (or so it seems), has its own potato patch – not just a few rows, but enough to supply a mountain of spuds to last the whole year, until the next crop of early new potatoes appears in summer. Perhaps, after the Great Potato Famine of the last century when the country was so catastrophically devastated, a residual instinct remains, a feeling that so long as there are potatoes in the shed outside or down in the cellar, then things can somehow sort themselves out. Or as the Irish toast states simply: *Go mbeirimíd beo ar an am seo arís* – May we be alive at the same time next year.

Potatoes certainly remain the essential Irish staple, and there is nothing quite so good as Kerr Pinks, thin-skinned, almost fuchsia in colour, floury in texture, boiled in their skins, and served swimming in rich Irish butter. Colcannon is a mixture of boiled potatoes, cabbage, onions and butter, all mashed together, while champ, particularly favoured in Ulster, consists of potatoes mashed with butter and spring onions (called 'scallions' in Ireland). Potato bread along with soda bread is essential to an Ulster fry (a platter of grilled sausage and bacon, eggs, perhaps a chop or a bit of liver, mushrooms and tomatoes – a popular start to the day in the North). Potato cakes, potato soup, potato dumplings, potato pancakes are all popular indications of the importance of this staple in the national diet, while Irish stew and much else besides also feature the beloved 'murphy' as an essential ingredient.

It is just as well that the Irish love potatoes so much since in times past there was often precious little else to eat. For the common Irish people, living under a brutal system of tenancy whereby landlords (often absentee) were able to charge extortionate rents, existence was harsh and difficult. Persecuted under the harsh Penal Laws for their steadfast allegiance to Catholicism, they were treated virtually as second-class citizens in their own country. Even during the Great Famine, those who lived by the sea could not gather such free foods as mussels and cockles without the permission of the landlord. Milk, too, was delivered to the landlord, who skimmed off the cream and butterfat, returning only the meagre buttermilk. Is this, perhaps, one reason why Ireland, a rich dairy country, never developed any indigenous cheeses?

It is hardly surprising, under such conditions, that a native Irish cuisine did not exist. The word 'cuisine' implies a certain self-conscious attitude to food and drink. The people of the land most likely simply ate and drank what was available, depending on the season. A cast iron pot of mutton (in good times) and potatoes cooked over the turf fire would have been simply dinner, nothing so grand as 'Irish stew'. Yet Irish stew it has become, and very delicious it is.

The gentry, meanwhile, the privileged Norman-Irish and Anglo-Irish landowners and officeholders known collectively as the Ascendancy, looked to London, and many aspects of life and certainly food and drink were consequently anglicized. In the North, on the other hand, the Scottish planters, the Orangemen (loyalist and Protestant) who settled in Ulster, naturally maintained ties both with the mainland of Great Britain and with Scotland in particular. There is a relationship still between Ulster and Scottish foods, for example. Champ is similar to Scots stovies; colcannon is but a variation of kailkenny and rumbledethumps. Good porridge made with pinhead oatmeal is enjoyed on both sides of the Irish Sea. Fresh herring landed at the Co. Down harbours of Kilkeel or Ardglass is often fried in oatmeal, as in Scotland.

Northern Ireland (which consists of six of the nine counties that make up the ancient province of Ulster) is today part of the United Kingdom. Apart from historical links extending back to the days of the planters, there is also a well-established geographical link between Northern Ireland and the mainland of Great Britain. Drive along the fabulous Antrim coast on a clear day, and Scotland appears just a literal stone's throw away (the Giant's Causeway was in legend Finn MacCool's pathway to Scotland). Farmers, too, traditionally found the path to Scotland to market their produce. The shortest crossing between Ireland and Britain is Larne to Stranraer, and thus it was as quick – if not quicker – to get produce over to Glasgow as to Dublin. A strong cultural interchange developed over the centuries and remains today (the Ulster accent, for instance, seems closer to the Scots burr than to the soft Irish lilt of southern counties such as Kerry and Clare).

The Irish diet, both in the Republic and the North, remains essentially a simple one. While Irish lamb and beef are superb (many country butchers still raise, slaughter and butcher their own meat), pork is a staple, a carry-over, perhaps, from the old days when a pig was kept at the bottom of every garden, and fed with mashed

Off for a 'jar'.

159

potatoes and turnips to fatten before winter. Limerick, Cookstown and Belfast are famous for their hams, while boiled bacon and cabbage is a simple favourite throughout the country. Dublin coddle is no more than rashers of bacon, sausage, onions and potatoes (of course) simmered in water or milk – the sort of food that tastes fine with a 'jar' of Guinness and a hunk of soda bread.

Other such foods remain popular, though perhaps in some instances they are eaten today out of a certain nostalgia for the past, as much as for their good taste. Cruibíns, for example, are no more than pickled pigs' trotters, but at social events like the Galway Oyster Festival, people in evening dress and black tie like nothing more than digging into them with their fingers at the end of the long evening. Cruibíns are also sometimes served in pubs on Friday and Saturday nights – the sort of food which soaks up great quantities of stout. Another favourite is pickled spare-ribs (known colloquially in Cork as 'a bit o' bodice'), boiled and served with cabbage. Pickled (or corned) beef is eaten traditionally for Sunday lunch, while spiced beef remains a Christmas treat.

In the old covered market of Cork, stall-holders vie with one another for the sale of drisheen and tripe, two local favourites. Drisheen, a type of blood pudding, is missed powerfully by Corkmen when they have been too long away from home, for it is available nowhere else. It has a smooth texture and a rather strange grey appearance, sold in long coils. Would a Corkman eat drisheen for breakfast? 'Oh yes, indeed. Yes indeed. Particularly if he'd been savouring some of our Irish brew the night before,' we were told by a pretty colleen in the market. Tripe, boiled and served in a white sauce with potatoes and carrots, like spare-ribs and cabbage, is another typical hearty supper dish much loved by all.

When we see Dubliners in evening dress enjoying cruibíns, there is a sense, we feel, of looking back to the past. Does the same attitude apply to Irish affection for that unique national beverage: poitín? Poitín is both illegal, and, from our experience, pretty vile to say the least. And yet, ask any Irishman and chances are that he knows a friend of the brother-in-law of the fellow who has a still out there in the islands, or the woods, or some lonely place. Moreover, most people actually seem to have a bottle of the stuff in their house, 'only for cooking, mind' or 'to give a taste to good friends like yourself'. Perhaps this reflects an anti-authoritarian streak in the Irish, but one thing is certain: they have a total sympathy with the man out there in the woods. After all, why shouldn't a fellow be able to do what he likes with his own barley, or potatoes, or rice, or treacle, or . . .

If the Irish have a certain sentiment to the past (made up in large part, no doubt, by the hordes of visiting expatriates once or twice or thrice removed who return for free-spending pilgrimages to the homeland), they are also looking to the future. Previously, perhaps, the finest produce and products of the land were not accessible to the Irish themselves, but went across the Irish Sea, or else to the tables of the gentry in their grand country mansions. Today, such is not the case, and there is a great excitement and pride in homes and restaurants throughout the country, as a new awareness and a new style of Irish cooking develops.

In the past, for example, there was not a great tradition of fish eating, but today the daily Irish catch landed in Dingle, or Ballycotton or Kilkeel, and elsewhere, takes pride of place on the Irish table, and not just on Fridays. Plaice is cooked in cheese sauce or batter; black sole (the same fish known in England as Dover) is grilled simply on the bone; monkfish and ray are poached and served with simple butter sauces, while lobsters, crawfish, shrimps, mussels, oysters, and that most famous Irish crustacean, the Dublin Bay prawn, are all highly prized and enjoyed now by the Irish themselves. Salmon, king of fish, continues to be a much sought delicacy, as it has been since the days of Finn, son of Cool, head of the Fianna, who gained his wisdom through eating the salmon of knowledge. Trout is caught by sportsmen in Fermanagh, Kerry and Clare, while large quantities of eel are caught in Ulster's Lough Neagh. Smoked eel, like smoked Irish salmon, is a fine delicacy.

Irish beef and lamb are, or can be, top quality, and mutton, elsewhere in Britain virtually non-existent, is still available in many rural areas. Such fine produce is put to imaginative use both

'When the Scotch House closed they went round to Mulligan's. They went into the parlour at the back and O'Halloran ordered small hot specials all round. They were all beginning to feel mellow.'
from James Joyce's story 'Counterparts' in *Dubliners*.

in homes and by master chefs in restaurants and country houses throughout the island who are creating repertoires of exciting and individual dishes making use of the best local and national ingredients available. Stout, the national drink, for example, is finding its way into the cooking pot in a variety of dishes such as Shanagarry porter steak and Guinness stew, while new styles of lighter, fresher cooking based on *nouvelle cuisine* principles but using traditional Irish ingredients are also being developed.

Similarly, if Ireland did not historically have a tradition of indigenous cheese making, today a handful of enterprising individuals have begun producing unique new Irish farmhouse cheeses, primarily from unpasteurized milk from their own herds. Milleens, Gubbeen, St Killian, Gigginstown, Lough Caum are the names of but a few, all of which reflect a remarkable variety in style and type. Such cheeses are certainly worth trying when in Ireland; some are available outside the country, too.

Food in Ireland is developing in parallel with the development of the island, and to reflect the changing tastes of people who travel increasingly abroad. To those who visit Ireland, though, it is not a modern sophistication that one remembers. Rather, it is the simple warmth of a unique people, an almost tribal hospitality to strangers in what must be one of the most beautiful lands on earth. Simple, unrepeatable flavours and memories of the country are perhaps the most lasting: oysters fresh out of Galway Bay, served with home-baked brown soda bread and a creamy pint; bars that are also groceries, hardware shops or general stores; warm 'snugs' with thoughtful, discreet hatches to the bar; piping hot cruibíns, eaten with the fingers among like-minded friends; pink potatoes beetled with cabbage, onions and lashings of fresh butter. To finish, an Irish coffee, a tot of Old Bushmills or Power's 'Gold Label', or, on winter nights, a single, small, hot whiskey.

Doyle's Seafood Bar.

Recipes from Ireland

Dublin Bay Prawns with Herb Mayonnaise (Serves 4)

Ireland's most famous shellfish is neither confined to Dublin Bay, nor is it a member of the prawn family. Rather, the Norway lobster, as it is properly known, is fished in the deep cold waters of the north, as well as the west of Ireland. It was a popular street food in Dublin, sold by the Mollie Malones of another age, together with 'cockles and mussels, alive alive-O!'

12–15 Dublin Bay prawns, cooked, shelled, de-veined and cut into chunks (leave one whole prawn per serving as a garnish)

1 lettuce, chopped
Lemon wedges

Herb Mayonnaise

6 tbsp mayonnaise
1 tbsp thick cream
Juice of 1 lemon
1 tbsp mixed fresh herbs – dill, fennel, chives, parsley or thyme – finely chopped

1 spring onion, finely chopped
Pinch of dried mustard
A little tomato purée
Salt
Freshly-ground black pepper

Make a bed of chopped lettuce on each plate. Mix the ingredients together for the herb mayonnaise and toss the prawn meat in this dressing. Arrange on the lettuce, and garnish with prawns and lemon wedges.

Sweet Pickled Herrings   (Serves 6)

Fresh herring is landed throughout Ireland, in fishing ports such as Ardglass and Kilkeel in Co. Down, where the colourful fleet bobs up and down on the high tide, the smallest skiffs tied up at one end, the larger trawlers at the other. This method of preparing herring emphasizes the interchange between Northern Ireland and Scotland.

6 large fresh herrings, cleaned and filleted	1 onion, thinly sliced 12 bay leaves

For the marinade

300 ml/$\frac{1}{2}$ pt/$1\frac{1}{4}$ cups malt vinegar	$\frac{1}{4}$ tsp mixed spice Fresh thyme
2 tbsp brown sugar	12 black peppercorns
6 bay leaves	Salt
1 onion, finely chopped	

Combine the marinade ingredients in a small saucepan, and boil for 3 minutes. Set aside to cool. Pat the herring fillets dry and place the onion slices and a bay leaf on each. Roll up and secure. Place the herrings in a baking dish, pour over the marinade, and cover with foil. Bake in a moderate oven (180°C/350°F/Gas Mark 4) for 15 minutes. Serve chilled.

Fish Chowder   (Serves 4–6)

A good fish chowder makes use of ingredients plentiful throughout Ireland: freshly-landed whitefish, good creamy milk and potatoes. We wonder, did the popularity of chowder in New England come in part from the numerous Irish who settled in that part of America in the last century?

50 g/2 oz/$\frac{1}{2}$ stick butter	1 bay leaf
2 onions, chopped	Bunch of fresh thyme, tied together
3 stalks celery, chopped	
1 carrot, chopped	Salt
450 g/1 lb haddock, cod, whiting or hake, skinned and boned	Freshly-ground black pepper
600 ml/1 pt/$2\frac{1}{2}$ cups milk	450 g/1 lb potatoes, peeled and diced
600 ml/1 pt/$2\frac{1}{2}$ cups cold water	Freshly-chopped parsley

Melt the butter in a large soup pot and gently fry the onions, celery and carrot until soft. Add the fish and toss with the vegetables. Add the milk and cold water, herbs and seasoning. Bring gently to the boil, cover and simmer for 30 minutes. Add the potatoes and continue to cook until they are soft. Remove the bunch of thyme, adjust the seasoning and serve sprinkled with chopped parsley.

Ballycotton Fried Plaice   (Serves 1)

Plaice is one of the commonest and most popular fish in Ireland. It is landed in abundance not only in Ballycotton, a small harbour south of Cork, but throughout the country. As with all fish, its flavour and texture are best when freshly caught, and at such times, it needs only the simplest preparation.

1 fresh whole plaice, cleaned and gutted	1 tbsp vegetable oil 1 tbsp butter
1 tbsp seasoned flour	Finely-chopped parsley
Milk to moisten	Lemon wedge
Fresh breadcrumbs to coat	

Dip the washed and cleaned whole fish in seasoned flour and then in milk, and coat with breadcrumbs. Meanwhile, put the oil and butter in a frying pan and heat. Fry the fish for about 4 or 5 minutes a side over a medium heat. Garnish with finely-chopped parsley and lemon wedges.

Dulse and Yellow Man

Did you treat your Mary Ann
To dulse and yellow man
At the Oul' Lammas Fair
At Ballycastle-O?

Two specialities that will be encountered, particularly at country fairs such as Ulster's oldest and most famous at Ballycastle, are dulse and yellow man. Dulse is a reddish-brown seaweed gathered all around the coast, dried in the sun and sold in shops to be chewed or eaten straightaway (it can also be soaked and cooked). Yellow man is a honey-coloured toffee for which young lads save their pennies to buy as presents for their sweethearts.

Mutton Broth   (Serves 4–6)

A simple, warming broth, the sort that once would have been simmering constantly in an iron pot over a turf fire in cottages in the west of Ireland. Mutton is still available in some parts of the country, though unfortunately harder to come by elsewhere.

675 g/1½ lb neck of mutton	50 g/2 oz/½ cup medium
Water	oatmeal
25 g/1 oz/¼ cup pearl barley	Salt
1 carrot, chopped	Freshly-ground black
1 onion, chopped	pepper
2 stalks celery, chopped	Freshly-chopped parsley
2 leeks, chopped	

Put the meat in a large pot and cover with water. Bring to a gentle boil, and skim the grey scum that rises. Add the vegetables, barley, oatmeal and seasonings. Cover and simmer for 2 hours. Remove the meat from its bones and return to the pot. Adjust the seasoning, garnish with parsley, and serve with home-made wheaten bread.

Corned Beef and Cabbage   (Serves 6)

Corned beef and cabbage is simple food, as popular today in Dublin as in the country. In the past, many folk would have 'corned', or salted, the meat themselves, though nowadays it is generally bought already prepared.

900 g/2 lb corned beef	1 medium head of cabbage,
(silverside or brisket)	shredded
Bouquet of fresh herbs	Salt
Cold water	Freshly-ground black
3 carrots, sliced	pepper
2 onions, sliced	

Soak the corned beef in cold water for a couple of hours, if it is very salty (ask your butcher). Place in a large pot with fresh herbs, and cover with cold water. Bring to the boil and skim. Cover and simmer gently for 1½ hours. Add the vegetables and cook for a further 30 minutes. Season, and serve the beef sliced on a platter surrounded by the vegetables (reserve the cooking liquid for soup).

Galway Oyster Festival

At the end of September every year, people come from all over Ireland to take part in one of the liveliest communal parties of the year, the Galway Oyster Festival. The Festival was started some thirty years ago as an informal get-together for locals as well as for those who came to Galway from Dublin and elsewhere each year to consume oysters and stout, and enjoy the peace and loveliness of the west of Ireland. Now it's an altogether more grand international affair, extending over three days, with a world oyster-opening championship and a formal festival banquet which is renowned for its unique atmosphere of spontaneous singing, bottle clanking and dancing on the tables.

The star attraction, lest we forget, is of course the Galway oyster. The main centres for this celebrated shellfish are Clarenbridge and Kilcolgan, both at the east end of Galway Bay. The oysters are mainly located in beds between the Dunkellin and Clarenbridge rivers where fresh water mixes with sea. It is important for such famous oyster bars as Moran's and Paddie Burke's to get a good harvest in December to last throughout those months with an 'r' in them.

In Galway, oysters are always consumed in as simple a manner possible: raw, on the half-shell, with lemon and home-made brown soda bread. Take a dozen or so and a pint of creamy Guinness, and go and sit outside by the water to 'watch the sun go down on Galway Bay'.

Opposite: The Oyster Pearl.

Right: The Mayor of Galway samples the first oyster of the year.

Below: Galway oysters, home-made brown soda bread and Guinness: a classic combination at Moran's, Kilcolgan.

Potatoes

The Irishman's beloved 'murphy' or 'spud' remains a staple throughout the country. It is a poor house indeed that does not have its own patch. Kerr Pinks are stockpiled through the winter in huge mountains, enough to make a man's heart glad. They find their way into most stews and soups, and they feature in a number of dishes as the main ingredient: potato soup, potato bread, colcannon, champ, boxty and others. When potatoes are boiled, they are always cooked in their skins, a method of cooking which retains their flavour, as well as minerals and vitamins. Here are four traditional recipes:

Potato Soup   (Serves 6)

900 g/2 lb potatoes, peeled and sliced	Freshly-ground black pepper
2 onions, sliced	Bouquet of fresh herbs
1.8 l/3 pt/7½ cups of half milk, half water	150 ml/¼ pt/⅔ cup single cream
Salt	Freshly-chopped parsley

Put the potatoes and onions in a large pan and cover with the milk and water. Season and add the herbs. Cover and cook gently on top of the stove for 1½ hours. Remove the bouquet of herbs, and sieve or liquidize the soup. Add the cream and re-heat gently. Adjust the seasoning, and serve hot sprinkled with parsley.

Champ   (Serves 4–6)

Champ is an Ulster speciality.

6–8 potatoes, washed	Salt
8 spring onions, chopped	Freshly-ground black pepper
300 ml/½ pt/1¼ cups milk	
100 g/4 oz/1 stick butter	

Boil the potatoes until just tender, drain and skin. Cut roughly into pieces. Meanwhile, heat the milk in a saucepan, and cook the spring onions until soft. Add the milk and onions to the potatoes, and roughly mix. Add about half the butter and beat well, mashing the mixture, but still leaving rough chunks. Season to taste and turn on to a warmed serving dish. Serve on plates, make a well in each, and add the remaining butter. The champ should be eaten with a spoon, each mouthful dipped in the pool of melted butter.

Colcannon   (Serves 4–6)

8 potatoes, scrubbed	300 ml/½ pt/1¼ cups milk
1 medium head of cabbage, finely shredded	Salt
	Freshly-ground black pepper
1 onion, finely chopped	100 g/4 oz/1 stick butter

Boil the potatoes and cabbage separately and drain. Skin the potatoes. Meanwhile gently cook the onion in the milk. Mash the potatoes with the warm

Guinness Beef Stew   (Serves 6)

Stout, the Irish national drink, finds its way increasingly into the cooking pot, too. It is important, however, to balance its distinctive bitter flavour with some sweetness, such as, in this case, dried prunes.

900 g/2 lb stewing steak, cut into cubes	Handful of fresh parsley
	Salt
600 ml/1 pt/2½ cups Guinness	Freshly-ground black pepper
2 onions, sliced	450 g/1 lb dried prunes
6 carrots, sliced	25 g/1 oz cornflour, mixed to a smooth paste with a little cold water
1 tbsp brown sugar	
3 bay leaves	
2 sprigs thyme	

In a large casserole, marinate the beef with all the remaining ingredients (except the cornflour) for 1 or 2 days (the longer the better). Bring slowly to the boil on top of the stove, and skim frequently. Cover and place in a warm oven (160°C/325°F/Gas Mark 3) for 2 hours. Remove from the oven and add the cornflour mixture to thicken. Adjust the seasoning, cover and return to the oven for a further 15 minutes. Serve hot, with colcannon or champ, and, of course, Guinness.

milk and onion. Add the cabbage and butter, and mash well. Season and serve.

Boxty in the Pan

Boxty on the griddle, boxty in the pan,
The wee one in the middle is for Mary Ann.
Boxty on the griddle, boxty in the pan,
If you don't eat boxty, you'll never get a man.

Boxty on the griddle is a type of potato bread, while boxty in the pan is a potato pancake. Both, traditionally, are eaten on Hallowe'en.

225 g/½ lb raw grated potatoes
225 g/½ lb cooked mashed potatoes
225 g/½ lb/1⅔ cups plain flour
1 tsp baking powder
1 tsp salt
1 tsp sugar
100 g/4 oz/1 stick melted butter
About 300 ml/½ pt/1¼ cups milk

Squeeze out the raw grated potatoes to remove excess liquid. Mix with the mashed potatoes, flour, baking powder, salt and sugar. Add the melted butter and enough milk to make a batter of pancake consistency. Drop spoonfuls of the batter on to a hot greased pan, and cook on both sides until nicely brown. Serve at once with more butter and sugar.

A potato patch near Killarney.

Shanagarry Porter Steak   (Serves 2)

Shanagarry is a small village some twenty miles south-east of Cork, near the fishing harbour of Ballycotton. Ballymaloe House, a grand old country mansion, stands here amidst 400 acres of prime farmland, the produce of which finds its way on to the tables of its restaurant, celebrated for its superb Irish cuisine. The stout used to make the porter sauce should really be Beamish or Murphy in keeping with the Cork origins of this dish, but Guinness will do fine at a pinch.

50 g/2 oz/½ stick butter
2 175 g/6 oz rump steaks
Salt
Freshly-ground black pepper
1 medium onion, finely chopped
1 tsp sugar
Bouquet of fresh herbs
8 tbsp stout
4 tbsp home-made beef stock
Freshly-chopped parsley.

Pat dry the steaks, and season with black pepper and a little salt. Heat three-quarters of the butter in a frying pan. Fry the steaks for 1–2 minutes a side (depending on how steaks are preferred). Remove and set aside in a warmed serving dish. Add the remaining butter and fry the onions with the sugar until they have caramelized to a nice dark colour. Return the steaks to the pan, and add the herbs, stout and stock. Cover and cook for a further 2–3 minutes. Again remove the steaks to the serving dish, and boil down the remaining liquid to a thickish syrup. Adjust the seasoning and pour this sauce and onions over the steaks. Garnish with parsley.

167

Irish Farmhouse Cheese

Milleens The first of the new Irish farmhouse cheeses, Milleens is produced on the fertile Beara Peninsula in the south-west from the farm's own unpasteurized milk. Milleens is a soft, ripe cheese with a striking orange natural rind. As it ripens, it becomes softer and more runny, and its distinctive pungent flavour is intensified. Beara is also produced on the Milleens Farm in Eyeries.

St Killian St Killian is a rich full-fat soft cow's milk cheese recognizable by its distinctive hexagonal shape. It is produced from the unpasteurized milk of the Ballyshannon Farm herd, in Co. Wexford. St Abban, an octagonal brie-type cheese, is also made on the farm.

Gubbeen From the rich dairyland of Co. Cork comes this distinctive cheese, of which just twenty-five are made on a good day. Gubbeen is a round, firm cheese with an assertive flavour.

Gigginstown This unique farmhouse cheese from Co. Westmeath has a thick, natural Stilton-type crust, a firm yet fairly crumbly texture and a full-bodied flavour.

Bonane Bonane is a full-fat, hard-pressed cheese, with a traditional natural rind. It is made from the milk of cows which graze on the slopes of the Caha mountains in Co. Kerry. Sheep are also raised on the farm, and both hard and soft ewe's milk cheeses are produced.

Beara Produced by cheese makers in the Milleens area, this gouda-type cheese comes in a flat wheel, and has a mild character.

Lough Caum This hard goat's cheese comes from Inagh, Co. Clare.

Coisceam Hard goat's cheese from Co. Clare.

Lavistown Produced on a small scale in Kilkenny from the milk of Kerry, Jersey and Ayrshire cows, Lavistown is an open-textured round cheese with a mild flavour.

Scrivog This hard farmhouse cheese, like many other new varieties, was originally only made for private consumption, but surplus found its way into local shops and restaurants.

Opposite: An Irish farmhouse cheese board: (from l. to r., top to bottom) Lavistown, Scrivog, Bonane, Coisceam, Beara, Gigginstown, (brown soda bread), St Killian, Lough Caum.

Ulster fry: the hefty start to the day in the North.

Spiced Beef

Most families have a large joint of spiced beef on hand to eat cold during the Christmas festivities which continue over several days. In the English Market in Cork, many butchers specialize in this favourite, and they are extremely proud of their individual secret recipes and combinations of spices. While it is generally considered a holiday food, there is no reason why spiced beef should not be eaten all the year, as it is in Ireland's second city.

2.7 kg/6 lb joint of beef
450 g/1 lb coarse sea salt
1 tsp ground cloves
1 tsp ground mace
1 tsp cinnamon
1 tsp nutmeg
1 tsp allspice
1 tsp coarsely-crushed
   black peppercorns
1 tsp saltpetre
1 tbsp juniper berries,
   crushed
4 bay leaves, crushed
225 g/½ lb/1 cup brown
   sugar
450 g/1 lb carrots, sliced
3 onions, sliced
3 sticks celery, chopped
Bouquet of fresh herbs
Water

Unroll the beef joint, if necessary. Mix the salt and spices together. Rub thoroughly into the joint, and lay in a very clean shallow dish on a bed of more salt and spices. Keep in a cool place. Turn the meat daily, rubbing the salt and spices in thoroughly, for three–five days. When ready to cook, wash and roll up the joint and tie securely with string. In a large casserole, put in the chopped carrots, onions and celery, then place the beef on this bed of vegetables. Cover with cold water, add the fresh herbs, and slowly bring to the boil. Cover, and simmer gently until tender, for up to 4 or 5 hours, depending on the size of the joint. Remove from the liquid, and allow the meat to cool; stand in a flat dish with a weighted board on top. Serve cold.

Irish Stew (Serves 6–8)

This most famous Irish dish is really merely a humble one-pot affair, again the sort that would be left hanging over the slow-smouldering turf fire for hours, thus tenderizing as well as bringing out the flavour of tough old mutton. Lamb takes less time to cook, but it does not give this classic its true character.

1.35 kg/3 lb neck of mutton or lamb, trimmed and cut into pieces	Salt
	Freshly-ground black pepper
900 g/2 lb potatoes, peeled and sliced	1 tsp thyme
3 onions, sliced	Finely-chopped parsley
3 carrots, sliced	About 750 ml/1¼ pt/3 cups cold water

In a large casserole, arrange alternate layers of potatoes, meat, onion and carrots. Season each layer well with salt, black pepper and herbs. Finish with a thick layer of potatoes. Pour on the water, cover, and cook in a slow oven (140°C/275°F/Gas Mark 1) for about 2–2½ hours, or until the meat is tender. Serve the stew directly from the casserole.

Baked Chicken with Leeks

(Serves 4–6)

One of our best meals in Ireland was at a country farmhouse in Limavady, Co. Derry: freshly-killed chicken, quickly cleaned and baked in a solid fuel cooker on a bed of buttery leeks.

1–1.5 kg/2½–3 lb chicken (preferably free-range)	3 leeks, sliced
	2 tsp cornflour
Salt	150 ml/¼ pt/⅔ cup chicken stock
Freshly-ground black pepper	1 egg yolk
2 tbsp butter	3 tbsp double cream
1 tbsp oil	

Season the chicken and brown the breast in a little butter and oil in a large casserole. Remove the chicken and add the remaining butter. Cook the leeks for 2–3 minutes, then return the chicken to the pot. Cover and bake in a moderately hot oven (190°C/375°F/Gas Mark 5) for 40 minutes to 1 hour. When cooked, remove the chicken to a warmed serving platter and carve. Meanwhile, sprinkle the cornflour into casserole and stir well over a moderate heat. Add the stock, and continue to stir, while the sauce thickens. Remove from the heat. Beat the egg yolk with the cream, and add to the sauce. Return to a very low heat,

and stir for a minute or two but do not boil. Adjust the seasoning, and serve separately in a sauceboat with the carved chicken.

Cruibíns (Serves 6–8)

Cruibíns are a late Friday or Saturday night accompaniment to the 'one for the road'. They are eaten, we have been told, for their ability to soak up great quantities of liquor, but whether or not this is true, we suspect that many enjoy them simply for their superb taste.

8 pickled pigs' trotters	Salt
1 large onion, chopped	Freshly-ground black pepper
1 carrot, sliced	
1 bay leaf	Water
Bouquet of fresh herbs	

Wash the trotters and soak overnight, if necessary. Put into a large saucepan with the onion, carrot, bay leaf, herbs and seasoning. Cover with cold water, and slowly bring to the boil. Skim, cover and simmer for about 2½ hours, or until the meat comes easily away from the bones. Remove the trotters and reserve the liquid for soup. Serve hot from the pot, or cold, with mustard, soda bread and (of course) more stout.

Carrageen Moss Pudding

(Serves 4–6)

Carrageen, the famous Irish moss, is a small, reddish seaweed that grows abundantly around the coast of Ireland. It is gathered at low tide, and laid out to dry, then sold in little packs. It is available outside Ireland in some health shops and delicatessens. When soaked in water, carrageen swells and oozes jelly, and this makes it a natural setting agent for puddings.

7 g/¼ oz/½ cup carrageen	2 tbsp sugar
900 ml/1½ pt/3¾ cups milk	1 egg yolk, beaten
1 vanilla pod	1 egg white, whisked

For the topping

300 ml/½ pt/1¼ cups double cream	2 tbsp sugar
	2 tbsp Irish whiskey

Wash the carrageen, and pick out any pieces of grass or other extraneous seaweeds. Soak in tepid water for 10 minutes, and drain. Put in a saucepan with the milk and vanilla pod. Bring to the boil and simmer very gently for 20 minutes. Pour through a fine strainer, making sure to rub through all the jelly. Beat the sugar and egg yolk into the milk mixture, and fold in the egg white. Allow to set and chill.

Meanwhile, add the sugar and Irish whiskey to the double cream, and beat until stiff. Serve the carrageen moss pudding in glasses with this topping.

Guinness Cake

This and the following recipe are two more Irish classics, again making good use of the national drink. Make both well in advance to allow the flavours to mature.

- 225 g/8 oz/1 cup butter, softened
- 225 g/8 oz/1 cup soft brown sugar
- 4 eggs
- 300 g/10 oz/2 cups plain flour, sieved
- 2 tsp mixed spice
- Pinch of salt
- 225 g/8 oz/$1\frac{1}{2}$ cups seedless raisins
- 225 g/8 oz/$1\frac{1}{2}$ cups sultanas
- 100 g/4 oz/$\frac{2}{3}$ cup glacé cherries, chopped
- 100 g/4 oz/$\frac{2}{3}$ cup mixed peel, chopped
- 100 g/4 oz/1 cup walnuts, chopped
- Grated rind of 1 lemon and 1 orange
- 150 ml/$\frac{1}{4}$ pint/$\frac{2}{3}$ cup Guinness

Cream the butter and sugar together until smooth. Beat in the eggs one at a time. Fold in the flour and spice. Add the fruit, peel, nuts, rind and half the Guinness and mix well. Turn into a well-greased 18 cm/7 in round cake tin. Bake in a moderate oven (160°C/325°F/Gas Mark 3) for 1 hour. Reduce the oven to 150°C/300°F/Gas Mark 2 and bake for a further $1\frac{1}{2}$ hours.

Allow to cool, then turn out. Prick the cake several times and spoon over the remaining Guinness. Keep in an airtight container, preferably for at least a month, adding more Guinness when necessary to keep the cake moist.

Guinness Christmas Pudding (Makes 2 puddings)

- 225 g/8 oz/$1\frac{3}{5}$ cups flour
- 225 g/8 oz/$6\frac{1}{2}$ cups fresh breadcrumbs
- 225 g/8 oz/1 cup soft brown sugar
- 225 g/8 oz/$1\frac{1}{2}$ cups currants
- 225 g/8 oz/$1\frac{1}{2}$ cups raisins
- 175 g/6 oz/1 cup mixed candied peel, chopped
- 175 g/6 oz/1 cup sultanas
- 300 g/10 oz shredded suet
- $\frac{1}{2}$ tsp salt
- $\frac{1}{2}$ tsp ground nutmeg
- 1 tsp mixed spice
- Grated rind of 1 lemon
- 1 tbsp lemon juice
- 2 large eggs, beaten
- 150 ml/$\frac{1}{4}$ pt/$\frac{2}{3}$ cup milk
- 300 ml/$\frac{1}{2}$ pt/$1\frac{1}{4}$ cups Guinness

In a large bowl, mix all the dry ingredients together. Stir in the lemon juice, eggs, milk and Guinness. Mix well and turn into two 1.5 l/$2\frac{1}{2}$ pt greased pudding basins, leaving at least 2.5 cm/1 in headroom for the puddings to rise. Cover with greaseproof paper, then foil. Tie them around with string and loop more string over the top to make a handle. Set aside for 12 hours.

Steam for about 7 hours in a large pan of boiling water, checking occasionally to see that the water level is within an inch or two of the top. Use boiling water to top up. If not eating puddings immediately, then allow to cool, replace the covers with clean ones, and store in a cool place to mature. When required, steam for 2 or 3 hours before serving. Remove covers, invert and serve on a warm serving platter with a sprig of holly to decorate.

Barm Brack

Barm brack is a speckled yeast bread, similar to Welsh *bara brith*. Cut into wedges, and spread with good Kerry butter, it should be accompanied by strong tea, served with milk and sugar.

- 450 g/1 lb plain flour
- Pinch of salt
- $\frac{1}{2}$ tsp nutmeg
- $\frac{1}{2}$ tsp cinnamon
- 50 g/2 oz/$\frac{1}{2}$ stick butter
- 1 tsp dried yeast
- 3 tbsp sugar
- 300 ml/$\frac{1}{2}$ pt/$1\frac{1}{4}$ cups tepid milk
- 1 egg, beaten
- 225 g/8 oz/$1\frac{1}{2}$ cups currants
- 100 g/4 oz/$\frac{2}{3}$ cup mixed candied peel, chopped
- 1 egg yolk, beaten

Sieve the flour, salt and spices together, and rub in the butter. Put the yeast and 1 tablespoon of sugar into a jug with 3 tablespoons of tepid milk. Cream together and leave in a warm place until frothy. Meanwhile, add the remaining sugar to the flour mixture and mix well. Add the rest of the tepid milk and beaten egg to the yeast mixture and then combine with the flour mixture and beat well. Turn on to a floured board and knead. Return the dough to the bowl and cover with a damp cloth. Set aside in a warm place until it has doubled in size.

When risen, turn the dough out on to the floured board and gently knead in the fruit. Put into a well-greased 23 cm/9 in round tin and again cover with a damp cloth and leave to rise for a further 25 minutes. Brush the top with egg yolk and place in a moderately hot oven (200°C/400°F/Gas Mark 6) for about 50–60 minutes. Test with a skewer before removing from the oven. Turn on to a wire rack to cool, and serve cut into wedges, with butter.

Ulster Breads

Making bread at home remains a part of life throughout Ireland, but in Ulster especially the tradition is very much alive. Many if not most housewives bake at least a certain proportion of their bread daily, and for those who do not, there are numerous 'home bakeries' which produce a variety of traditional breads on the premises. Generally, breads and scones are raised with bicarbonate of soda mixed with fresh buttermilk, a method of baking which is both easy and quick to get good, simple results. Soda farls cooked on the griddle (a farl is a triangular quarter of bread), fruit soda loaf, wheaten, potato and treacle breads: all are popular, and every housewife and farmer's wife has her own recipe for each, generally engagingly imprecise ('take two fistfuls of flour . . .'). Here are some of our favourites:

Soda Farls (Makes 8)

225 g/8 oz/1⅗ cups plain white flour
1 tsp bicarbonate of soda
1 tsp baking powder
1 tsp sugar
1 tsp salt
Approximately
300 ml/½ pt/1¼ cups buttermilk

Mix together the dry ingredients. Add sufficient buttermilk to make a soft, fairly sticky dough. Roll out half the dough into a circle. Cut with a sharp knife or spatula into four farls (quarters). Place the four farls on a hot greased griddle or heavy-bottomed frying pan. Cook for 5–7 minutes on each side. The underside should brown nicely, but not burn. When the farls are done, they will make a hollow sound when tapped. Repeat with the remaining dough. Serve with butter and jam for tea.

Wheaten Bread

Called 'wheaten' in the North and simply 'brown bread' in the rest of Ireland, most bakers take greatest pride in this staple soda loaf.

100 g/4 oz/⅘ cup plain white flour
350 g/12 oz/2⅖ cups wholewheat flour
1 tsp bicarbonate of soda
1 tsp baking powder
1 tsp sugar
1 tsp salt

1 whole egg
Approximately
450 ml/¾ pt/2 cups buttermilk

Mix together the dry ingredients. Add enough buttermilk and the egg to make a very sticky dough. Turn into a buttered loaf tin. Invert a larger tin over this. Bake in a pre-heated hot oven (220°C/425°F/Gas Mark 7) for about 45 minutes.

Potato Bread

Fried potato bread is an essential ingredient to an Ulster fry, the start to the day in the province.

225 g/8 oz mashed potatoes
50 g/2 oz/⅖ cup flour
25 g/1 oz/¼ stick butter
Pinch of salt
¼ tsp baking powder
1 egg, beaten
Milk

Put the potatoes and sieved flour in a large bowl and rub in the butter. Add the salt, baking powder, egg and enough milk to make a pliable dough. Turn on to a floured board, and knead until smooth. Take half the dough, and roll out into a circle about 6 mm/¼ in thick. Divide into four farls. Bake on a hot greased griddle or heavy-bottomed frying pan until brown on both sides. Repeat with the remaining dough. Serve hot, or prepare in advance, and fry in bacon fat for Ulster fry.

Brown Soda Scones

(Makes approximately 12)

125 g/4 oz/⅘ cup wholewheat flour
125 g/4 oz/⅘ cup plain flour
Pinch of salt
¼ tsp bicarbonate of soda
50 g/2 oz/½ stick butter
Approximately
300 ml/½ pt/1¼ cups buttermilk

Sieve the brown and white flours together and mix with the salt and soda in a large bowl. Rub in the butter and add enough buttermilk to make a soft dough. Turn out on to a floured board and knead gently. Roll out and cut into round 5 cm/2 in scones. Place on a greased baking tray and bake in a hot oven (200°C/400°F/Gas Mark 6) for about 15–20 minutes, or until risen and golden.

Soda farls are made daily in many Irish homes: (from l. to r.) mix the flour, bicarbonate of soda, baking powder, sugar and salt; then add fresh buttermilk to make a moist dough; roll out and cut dough into farls, or quarters; cook them for 5–7 minutes on each side on a griddle or heavy-based frying pan (they should sound hollow when done).

Drink in Ireland

Drinking, it could be said, is the national pastime in Ireland. A pub or bar is never far away, and in dark mahogany-panelled Dublin 'snugs' or in country bars the draught Guinness flows as freely as the proverbial Irish wit. In the Republic there is a disproportionate number of licenses granted for the serving of alcoholic beverages, and, indeed, in many towns or villages, it is possible to enjoy your pint while purchasing a yard of material or a pair of shoes, or while making arrangements for Uncle Pat's funeral. The little village of Dingle, for example, with a population of only 1400, has, we have been told, over 50 licenses. In the North, there are fewer pubs, but a greater number of private clubs. While pubs remain, on the whole, non-sectarian, the clubs are often affiliated to one section of the community or another.

Hours: In Eire pubs and bars are generally open on weekdays, 10.30–23.00 and Sundays, 12.30–22.00. In Dublin and Cork, they close for an hour between 14.30 and 15.30. This daytime break is known as the 'Holy Hour'; while it is supposedly designed to keep people from propping up the bar all day long, cynics say it is so the priests can have a drink in peace. In Northern Ireland, public houses stay open Monday to Saturday all day, 11.00–23.00. However, public houses are closed all day Sunday. Hotels may serve drinks on Sundays with main meals. Clubs are permitted to serve drinks on weekdays for any twelve hours between 10.00 and 23.30, and on Sundays at limited hours.

Stout

In Joyce's short story *Counterparts*, Farrington sneaks over to O'Neill's shop for a quick g.p., that is, glass of plain porter, or simply a 'plain' as opposed to the more robust, stronger 'stout'. This was the everyday tipple of the Irish working man; it was dark and had a characteristic roasted colour and burnt aroma – a sort of lower-gravity, cheaper stout, a cloth-cap drink. Porter was once brewed throughout Britain, too, and

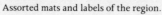

Assorted mats and labels of the region.

The Giant's Causeway, Co. Antrim.

Irish Crystal

Glass making is an Irish craft that extends back to the Bronze Age, practised over the centuries throughout the island, from Belfast to Galway, from Cork across to Waterford – the town which today remains one of the foremost cut-glass centres in Europe. Though the crystal objects themselves represent the height of refined elegance, the activity remains strangely primitive: it is a wonder, indeed a miracle, that such beautiful objects come from such humble raw materials, produced by the hot breath of young apprentices, and the sure hand and eye of qualified and master craftsmen under conditions that seem still almost mediaeval.

Lead crystal itself comes from silica sand, red lead oxide and potash. Lead gives crystal its intense silver-white brilliance and its satisfying weight (Waterford crystal consists of the maximum possible quantity of lead, $33\frac{1}{3}$ per cent). These basic ingredients are fed into monstrous, belching, oil-fuelled furnaces which are never extinguished (they would take a full two months to re-light); around these central furnaces, teams of four men – apprentices, qualified blower and master craftsman – cluster at work stations, labouring together as a unit. Using breath and the guidance of primitive wooden moulds, delicate stemware, jugs, decanters and the like are fashioned from blobs of red-hot molten crystal.

Teams also work together for the intricate tasks of cutting the crystal by hand. In the past, sweating apprentices worked the treadles of the heavy carborundum cutting wheels; today they are powered by electricity, but the task is no less demanding. Graceful curves flowing across the bodies of decanters are all done by hand and eye alone.

Irish crystal: transforming earth's raw materials into elegant forms.

was so named, apparently, due to its popularity among those in Covent Garden, Billingsgate, Smithfield and elsewhere. Porter is no more, but its successor, stout, remains the national drink in Ireland.

Traditionally, stout is brewed primarily from a grist of pale ale malt, with an added proportion of highly roasted unmalted barley. Roasted barley gives stout its characteristic black colour and its roasted palate. Considerable quantities of hops are added to the copper during its brewing, for despite its creamy, smooth appearance, Irish stout has a characteristic bitter astringency which to many is an acquired taste. Contrary to popular conception, however, stout is not a heavy beer. Nowadays, even in most parts of Ireland, it is served chilled on draught. A complicated mixture of nitrogen and carbon dioxide both in the brew, and in dispense, is responsible for the tight, slow-forming, creamy head so loved by pint drinkers. There are three major brewers of stout in Ireland today.

Arthur Guinness Son & Co., St James's Gate Brewery, Dublin To most people even in Ireland, stout is Guinness: there is no other (only Rebel Cork, home of both Beamish & Crawford and Murphy, has the audacity to disagree). In Dublin's fair city, the 200-year-old St James's Gate Brewery remains not so much a business as an institution, a way of life. Walk over O'Connell Bridge at five in the afternoon on a windy Dublin day, and the unmistakable brewery scent of hot, porridgy mash envelopes the city, as it wafts down-river, rising like steam from the Liffey. Guinness is everywhere. St Patrick's Cathedral was refurbished by the family. Major Irish events such as the Galway Oyster Festival, the Rose of Tralee, the Cork Jazz Festival and numerous other such happenings would not be what they are without both the generous patronage of 'Uncle Arthur' or the countless number of pints of his beloved black brew that are consumed seemingly non-stop. Guinness, moreover, has been around the Irish scene for so long that it seems almost to be a part of the countryside. Small, ancient enamelled signs over doorways from Donegal to Dingle preach to the converted: Guinness is Good for You; the familiar Irish harp on its background of black is as much a symbol of Eire as the green shamrock worn by every Irishman on St Patrick's Day.

Draught Guinness is undoubtedly the favourite drink. It is often said that it tastes better in Ireland than anywhere else, and why shouldn't it? The network of distribution throughout the country is so efficient and pervasive, the rate of consumption so high that it is not necessary to pasteurize this natural product, resulting in a pint that is inevitably fresher in taste, hoppier in aroma, creamier in appearance. While draught is far and away the most popular drink, there are those who

argue that bottled Extra Stout is even finer. Make no mistake: they are two different drinks altogether. Extra Stout, like draught in Ireland, is a natural, unpasteurized beer which conditions in the bottle through the action of living yeasts that continue to feed on the sugar present, resulting in a slow secondary fermentation. Extra Stout is more bitter in taste than draught, and has a natural gassy character which results in a coarser, less tight head. If draught is most popular throughout the country, there are pockets where the bottled version reigns supreme, principally in parts of the counties of Waterford, Monaghan, Cavan and Donegal.

Other bottled varieties of stout are also produced at the St James's Gate Brewery. Foreign Extra Stout, as the name implies, is only for the export market, a high gravity stout that is both sweeter, more bitter and acid than Extra Stout (a higher gravity beer, incidentally, generally retains a higher level of unfermented residual sugar; this, in turn, must be balanced by a higher hop level). Export Stout, available in Europe, is similar in strength to Foreign Extra Stout, but it is not so dry and astringent. A unique, new stout is also available, Bottled Draught Guinness, for the pint drinker who wants to quench his thirst at home or after hours. It sounds contradictory, but it tastes good.

Draught stout:

Draught Guinness o.g. 1040

Murphy Brewery Ireland Ltd, Lady's Well Brewery, Cork. Murphy's, an old traditional stout brewery founded over a hundred years ago below the holy pilgrimage site of Our Lady's Well, began in what was originally a home for foundlings. Today, within earshot of the 'bells of Shandon', stout continues to be brewed in virtually the same manner as it has been since the brewery was founded. Though a famous Dutch lager company, Heineken, recently took the company over, and extensive plans for modernization are under way, at present it is fascinating to see the antiquated brewery at work, for little has changed here in decades. The original copper mash tun, for example, is still in use. Once the largest in Great Britain or Ireland, the hot mash from its twice weekly brews is still emptied by hand.

Whereas Guinness, with its pronounced hoppy bitterness and distinctive roasted palate, is certainly an acquired taste, the character of Murphy's stout is altogether different, for it is considerably more mild in flavour (though not in alcohol). Roast barley, not pale ale malt, gives stout its dark colour and characteristic flavour. Murphy's roast their barley to a dark ruby red, but stop short of roasting it to a burnt astringency. Other factors, such as the degree of hopping, the yeast strain and the brewing liquor also contribute to the individual, smooth flavour of Murphy's.

Murphy's stout, like Beamish & Crawford's, for some unfathomable reason has never really been popular outside the Cork area. However, its new owners are determined to expand the appeal of Murphy's both in Ireland and abroad, and it will be interesting to see lager marketing expertise directed to this traditional product.

Draught stout:

Murphy's Stout o.g. 1040

Beamish & Crawford Ltd, South Main Street, Cork. Cork (and its surroundings) is virtually the only place in Ireland where bars and pubs give the drinker the choice of three brands of stout. Once the largest brewery in Ireland, Beamish & Crawford's South Main Street premises were known until recently as the Cork Porter Brewery, emphasizing this company's devotion to the national style of beer. Now owned by Carling O'Keefe, stout continues to be produced here, though an increase in lager production reflects current drinking trends. (Bass, an ale, is also brewed under license.) Beamish is a superb stout, with a distinctive nutty flavour and a refreshing astringency. Interestingly, though stout traditionally was top-fermented like other major styles of British and Irish ale, modern brewing techniques have blurred the former distinction between top- and bottom-fermenting styles of beer. Stout, and indeed other ales, can now be fermented, like lager, in conical vessels in which the yeast sinks to the bottom.

Draught stout:

Beamish Stout o.g. 1040

The Dingle peninsula.

Rebel Cork is about the only place in Ireland offering three different varieties of the national drink, stout.

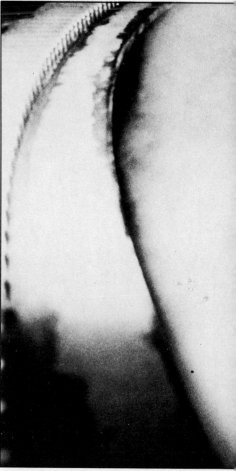

Irish Ales and Lagers

The Harbour Bar in Portrush, Co. Antrim, is unique. There is no sign outside even indicating that it's a bar, just the orange-red glow of lamps and the murmur of Ulstermen lined up on stools along the counter in the front room. There are more rooms in the back, with tables and benches facing each other, warmed by the glow of coal fires burning in ancient grates. The Harbour is perhaps a trifle shabby by lounge bar standards. But it is a marvellous bar. May it forever be saved the indignity of plush velvet seats! The pints of Guinness poured at the Harbour are as good as any to be had in Ulster. Of course, there are the ubiquitous keg ales on tap, such as Smithwick's and Bass. Harp and other lagers are available. Some regulars, on a cold night, might opt for a 'Hot Bush', that is, a hot

The mash tun at Murphy's Lady's Well Brewery was once the largest in Great Britain or Ireland, with a capacity of over a thousand barrels; today it is an antiquated relic, and must still be emptied by hand.

whiskey made with Old Bushmills, distilled just a few miles up the coast. At one end of the bar there are tall hand pumps. Are they just for decoration? No, they are real, for the Harbour is one of a small but growing number of pubs offering cask-conditioned ales from Northern Ireland's two new breweries: Hilden and Herald. A new real ale brewery, Dempsey's, has also recently begun trading in Dublin.

Apart from these few exceptional breweries, the beer drinker in Ireland is hardly inundated with choice. Northern Ireland's main supply of beers and lagers comes from Bass (brewery-conditioned Bass and Tennent's lager) and Scottish & Newcastle (cask-conditioned Younger's No. 3 is available in some outlets). Guinness supplies both the North and the South with Smithwick's ale (brewery-conditioned) and Harp lager, while other Irish ales such as Macardle's, Phoenix and Cherry's are available in certain areas only. In the South, Bass is brewed by Beamish & Crawford under license (but bears no relation to the cask-conditioned classic from Burton). Beamish & Crawford also brew Carling and Carlsberg lagers, while Murphy's, owned by Heineken, supply the island with that famous lager. Both lagers and beers, incidentally, are considerably stronger in alcohol in the south. They are also considerably more expensive.

Hilden Brewery, Lisburn, Co. Antrim. This small, independent brewery supplies about thirty pubs in the North with its distinctive cask-conditioned ales. Hilden ale is a fresh, strong bitter with a pronounced hoppy aroma. Hilden's second beer, Special, is darker in colour, sweeter and lower in alcohol. The brewery plans to introduce an unpasteurized lager in the near future, as well as a range of bottle-conditioned beers.

Hilden Ale o.g. 1040
Special o.g. 1035

Herald Brewery, Coleraine, Co. Derry. This new traditional ale brewery, begun in 1983, produces a dark, malty cask-conditioned ale, available primarily in the north-west of the province.

Herald Ale o.g. 1034–38

City Snugs and Country Bars

Walk into Doheny & Nesbitt's, Ryan's or any other central Dublin pub at dusk on a weekday afternoon, and you will find yourself pressed among a thirsty crowd, fresh from emptied offices. Shoulder to shoulder – tweed pressed against pin-stripe pressed against jumpers with bare elbows – arms are raised expertly, glasses emptied and replenished with just a nod or wink at the knowing barman. In the front, however, or in discreet corners, wood-panelled compartments open to reveal private, partitioned snugs – little sheltered dens with a convenient hatch to the bar: a perfect place for an amorous rendezvous, discreet conversation or political intrigue.

In the country, bars are somewhat different, for they often serve not only as dispensers of drink, but also as the post office, hardware and general store, grocery, filling station, butcher, shoe shop, undertaker and just about anything else. Order a drink in such a bar, and the pouring of your pint might be interrupted while the barman/shopkeeper ambles out to serve Mrs Robbie with her general provisions. Take a seat meanwhile on that wooden bench among the dangling rubber boots, brushes, brooms and rakes. Here no one raises an eyebrow if you want a pint or a quick 'hot' while purchasing some fertilizer, or this week's joint. And why should they?

The variety of 'watering holes' in Ireland.

Dempsey's Brewery, Jamestown Rd, Dublin. The first real ale brewery in the Irish Republic, and the first new brewery in Dublin in 200 years produces a cask-conditioned ale, Dempsey's, available primarily in Dublin (some pubs serving Dempsey's include Ryan's, O'Dwyer's and the Palace Bar).

Dempsey's o.g. 1038

Irish Whiskey

Don't let the Scots tell you otherwise: whiskey (note the 'e') was first distilled in Ireland. It is a drink as old as the hills, and indeed in times past it must have seemed to many a frustrated Revenue man that it was being produced over (or under) just about every bit of rising ground in the land. Of course, there was distilling long before there were Revenue men, since the sixth century AD at least, when the art was brought to the island by thoughtful missionaries. *Uisce beatha* ('water of life' in Irish) soon became popular throughout the island, as the Irish discovered that surplus grain, pure spring water and yeast alone could be transformed into this glorious, mellow drink. Indeed, in centuries gone by, home distilling was practised by many, a long-established tradition that contributes, no doubt, to the benign attitude that most Irish feel towards those honest folk out in the woods labouring over their butane fires.

Foreigners from across the Irish Sea and further afield, too, quickly took a liking to it, as well: *uisce* was enjoyed by Henry II's soldiers when they invaded the island, and was later praised by Elizabeth I, Sir Walter Raleigh and Peter the Great, who stated categorically: 'of all the wines, the Irish is the best.'

In 1608, Old Bushmills Distillery in Ulster took out a license to distill. By the eighteenth century there were an estimated 2000 distilleries in Ireland, but many remained no more than rough huts with copper kettles and other assorted paraphernalia, kept well out of view of prying eyes. In Dublin, the Bow Street Distillery of John Jameson was opened in 1780, and this famous name continues to be the most well-known Irish whiskey outside Ireland. Jameson's great rival on the opposite bank of the Liffey was James Power. Power's 'Gold Label' is today the favourite whiskey in its home country.

There was also a concentration of distilleries in the heart of the grain-growing belt which supplied thirsty Cork with whiskeys such as Paddy's, Murphy's, Dunphy's, Hewitt's and others, while another famous whiskey, Tullamore Dew ('give every man his Dew') was distilled in central Ireland.

The principle of distilling is basically a simple one. Alcohol vapourizes at a lower temperature than water; thus, by boiling an alcoholic drink in an enclosed kettle, the alcohol will rise into the neck and condense into spirit as it passed through the cooled, coiled worm. The alcohol and flavouring elements of the original liquid have been concentrated, distilled into an essence. Irish, like Scotch, is the distillation of a fermented beer-like liquid known as wash, made from a mash of malted barley and other cereals. Moreover, most Irish whiskey, like most Scotch, is a blend of both malt whiskey distilled in pot stills, and grain whiskey distilled in continuous column stills.

Unlike Scotch whiskey, however, Irish, though made from a mash of malted barley, does not have the characteristic smoky peat aroma of Scotch, for the malted barley used has not been dried over peat fires. Another important difference between the two is that Irish whiskey is triple distilled, while most Scotch malts are distilled only twice. Triple distillation is costly and time consuming, but the process gives the distiller more control over precisely the fractions of spirit and flavouring congenerics to keep. This process is essential to the mellow character of Irish whiskey.

The raw new spirit, however, is far from the mellow, golden amber liquid that we anticipate; rather, it is as clear as spring water and extremely potent. Before it is ready for drinking, it is reduced in strength with pure water, and must mature in oak casks. Most Irish used to be 'pure pot still', as the etched glass mirrors in many pubs testify. Today, the taste is for lighter whiskey, so pot still, or pure malt whiskeys are generally blended with lighter, more neutral grain whiskeys produced in tall vertical column stills. All the distilleries of Irish whiskey banded together to form the Irish Distillers Group in 1966. The Old Bushmills

Distillery is located in the North in Co. Antrim, while the rest are concentrated in the highly modern distilleries complex at Midleton, Co. Cork.

Irish whiskey is a gloriously mellow drink, as old as the hills and as much a part of the land. Here in Ireland it is generally drunk neat, or with just a drop of water. Because it is gentle and mellow in flavour, it also mixes well, though traditional whiskey drinkers would frown on this. Hot Irish is an old favourite, the sort of drink you crave if you've been out in the soft Irish mist too long; and of course, whiskey is the star ingredient in the country's newest classic, Irish coffee.

Hot Whiskey
(Makes 3 good whiskeys)

In bars or pubs, hot whiskey is made in the glass: a measure of whiskey, a teaspoon of sugar and a clove-studded lemon, over which boiling water is poured. We have been told on good authority, however, that the best 'hot' must be made in a pan.

3 slices of lemon, studded
    with three cloves each
A good pinch of cinnamon
2 glasses of water
1 glass of Irish whiskey
3 tsp sugar, or to taste

In a stainless steel pan, heat the water to boiling, and add the lemon and cinnamon. Boil for 3–4 minutes. Remove from the heat and add the whiskey. Return the pan to the fire and just bring up to the boil again. Take off the heat. Meanwhile, warm 3 stemmed glasses by pouring boiling water into them. Add sugar to each. Fill the glasses with hot whiskey.

Irish Coffee

Irish coffee, like Guinness, is a glorious combination of black liquid topped by light, foamy cream. Similarly, Irish coffee is meant to be sipped through the cream, as a stout drinker enjoys his pint by drinking through the head, leaving a ring of foam to mark each long swallow. To make Irish coffee, warm a stemmed glass. Add 1 or 2 teaspoons of brown sugar and a good measure of Irish whiskey. Fill the glass to within half an inch or so from the top with fresh,

Old Bushmills Distillery

It is perhaps fitting that the very first license to distill whiskey in 1608 was granted to Sir Thomas Phillips. Sir Thomas was King James's appointed deputy in Ulster. Presumably even this respected pillar of society must have been distilling on the premises prior to issuing himself the first license: the King's deputy, in short, was making poitín on the side. Perhaps it is for this reason that the Old Bushmills Distillery continues to qualify its claim: 'the oldest (licit) whiskey distillery in the world'.

Distillation on the site (illicit or otherwise) does indeed go back even further. There are references to the production of *uisce beatha* at Bushmills in 1276. Certainly the area has the main requisites: a plentiful supply of local barley and pure water from St Columb's Rill, a tributary of the Bush River. Moreover, located on the Antrim coast, it is on the old Celtic trade road between Tara, home of the High Kings of Ireland, and Dunseverick castle.

Old Bushmills whiskey has its own character, different from Scotch, but equally different from the other Irish whiskeys produced in the South. The water from St Columb's Rill rises through the same basalt that resulted in the nearby Giant's Causeway as well as through a layer of peaty topsoil. This naturally affects the character of the whiskey. Whereas, for example, most Irish whiskey has no peat character (the distinctive smoky flavour which is a hallmark of Scotch whisky), Old Bushmills is an exception, gaining a certain peatiness both from the water of the Rill, as well as from the malted barley, which is very slightly peated in the kilning process. While Old Bushmills is a blended whiskey, it is further unique as a blend of just one single malt whiskey (triple distilled), and one single grain whiskey (from a sister distillery at Coleraine, though in the future, grain whiskey from the Irish Distiller's main plant at Midleton, Co. Cork, may be used). Black Bush is a rare deluxe whiskey which has a considerably higher proportion of mature malt whiskey to grain.

Old Bushmills Distillery.

How to Pour Stout

Once you've ordered your pint of Guinness, Beamish or Murphy, relax, sit down and read the papers or have a chat with the fellow next to you. For a pint of stout is not to be rushed.

In the old days, the pre-aluminium-keg days, two wooden casks of stout were kept side by side. The barman first poured out the cream – the delicious, thick, close, tight head – from the high, or lively, barrel; then he gently floated this head up the glass by adding low, or flat, stout. Today, the same principle applies, for the taps to dispense stout have two positions. The barman thus first adds the cream, then adjusts the position of the tap to low, filling the glass perhaps three-quarters full. There is that lovely creamy surge, rising up to form the close-knit head, leaving behind and below the beloved black. It is this stage which takes the time.

Your barman, having poured out the pint and left it on the bar-top together with three or four others, is now probably serving someone else, having a bite to eat, continuing his natter with old Murph in the corner, perhaps even catching twenty winks. The pint, she's also resting. Finally, just when you think the barman's forgotten your very existence, he ambles back, tops up the glass with a mere flick of the wrist, thus adding more flat stout to float the creamy head right to the rim of the glass. In a perfect pint, there should not be a single bubble in the head, nor should it be levelled off with a knife. If there is, or he does, gaze at him disapprovingly, send it back if you must, for indifference has no place in the serious business of serving a pint of Irish stout.

strong black coffee. Stir well. Then carefully pour lightly whipped cream over the back of a spoon so that it floats on top of the coffee. Do not stir. Sip the hot whiskey-laced coffee through the cool cream. 'Sure, t'is grand.'

Poitín

On islands off Donegal or in the Glens of Antrim, in rugged Connemara, in counties Tyrone and Fermanagh or anywhere that is relatively remote, the dual arts of distillation and evasion of the law continue to this day. What is poitín? In Irish it means simply 'little pot', but it refers, generally, to the clear, strong spirit manufactured therein, a potent, colourless liquor that benefits those who make it and drink it, but not the Revenue men. While it can be made from grain (either malted barley, barley, wheat or corn), it is also made from potatoes, beets, sugar, treacle, molasses and just about anything else that will ferment (most things do).

This unique Irish drink, moreover, far from being a fringe curiosity only consumed by wild men in the woods, is actually drunk widely by people from all walks of life. We know wealthy businessmen from Belfast who always keep a bottle or two at their homes ('mind you, it's the good stuff, the stuff *they* [the poitín makers] drink themselves'). A representative from a tourist office, when she heard that we were enquiring about this unique product of local interest, promptly produced a small bottle 'to help us with our research'. Farmers in Tipperary and Kerry were surprisingly obliging and helpful when they heard of our interest. Even those who do not actually drink it seem to have no hard feelings whatsoever for those honest fellows out there just trying to make a decent living.

It perhaps comes as no surprise that poitín is popular throughout the land, costing as it does less than a quarter the price of legal whiskey. It is the duty, of course, that makes drink so extortionately expensive in the Republic, as well, for that matter, as in Northern Ireland where the situation is only just a little better.

Obviously, there is poitín and there is poitín. Due to the haphazard nature of the activity, some skilful folk may well make a drink which – so we are told, with great and convincing insistence –

is little short of ambrosia; but others no doubt certainly end up with a raw, fiery, throat-burning liquor at best. Moreover, poitín that has been badly distilled can contain harmful undesirables, so the unwary tourist should be warned. It may not make you go blind, but it can certainly give you a thick head the next morning. Nevertheless, poitín is undoubtedly part of the Irish experience and many who visit the Emerald Isle may well encounter the opportunity to try it.

Irish Cream Liqueurs

Ireland is a great dairy country, and the nation's vast amount of rich cream has resulted in new, but already exceedingly popular drinks made with fresh cream and Irish whiskey and other spirits. Bailey's Irish Cream liqueur is the best known and most widely available, while Emmet's Cream Liqueur is also popular. The latter, it is interesting to note, is produced by the Bailieboro Co-op Society, a farmers' co-operative in Co. Cavan, which ensures an ample and reliable supply of the freshest top quality cream.

Some Useful Addresses

Bord Fáilte
Irish Tourist Board
Baggot Street Bridge
Dublin 2
Eire
(UK Office: 150–51 New Bond Street, London W1)

Northern Ireland Tourist Board
River House
48 High Street
Belfast

Irish Export Board
Ireland House
150–51 New Bond Street
London W1

Dairyworld Marketing Ltd
Robinhood Industrial Estate
Clondalkin
Dublin
Eire
Information and supply of a full range of Irish farmhouse cheeses. Dairyworld also has a shop selling Irish farmhouse cheeses in Dublin's central Powerscourt Townhouse Centre.

Kenmare Trading Ltd
Kenmare
Co. Kerry
Eire
Irish smoked salmon, trout and terrines. UK distribution by Jubilee House Foods, 70 Cadogan Place, London SW1.

John Duffy (Meats) Ltd
Hacketstown
Co. Carlow
Eire
Irish whiskey salami. UK distribution by Kingdom Foods Ltd, 39 King Street, Luton.

Phillips & Dobbs
Ballyfree House Bakery
Wicklow
Co. Wicklow
Eire
Rich Irish fruit cake. International mail order service.

Bellarena Smokery
Limavady
Co. Derry
Northern Ireland
Traditional Irish smokehouse.

The Old Bushmills Distillery
Bushmills
Co. Antrim
Northern Ireland
The world's oldest (licit) distillery welcomes visitors. Tours can be booked in advance and begin at 10.30 and 15.00 every weekday except Friday afternoon. Other times can be scheduled by prior arrangement.

Braycot Foods
Bray
Co. Wicklow
Eire
Traditionally-made Irish biscuits. UK distribution by Scandinavian Suppliers (London) Ltd, 171 Alderton Road, London SE16.

The burning of turf has kept the Irish warm for centuries.

SCOTLAND

Way out on the western reaches of Skye the pungent reek of peat permeates the air, as smoke drifts out of the doors and windows of a crofter's cottage, a two-room dwelling made of granite, its low thatched roof weighed down with stones to keep it from being torn away by savage Atlantic gales. Beside the cottage is a mound of peat. The smallholding seems barely large enough to support a patch of vegetables, a row or two of oats or barley. Sheep, goats and shaggy Highland cattle, glowering under their long red fringes like angry Norse warriors, graze on nearby moorland and in the bare hills and mountains that sweep down to the deep sea lochs.

It is difficult to believe that this ancient way of life still prevails in parts of the Inner Hebrides, further west on Lewis and Harris, North and South Uist, in mainland outposts in Ross & Cromarty and Sutherland, on the Orkneys and Shetlands, and elsewhere. The crofting system is a harsh one, where tenants work small patches of land, keep some livestock, and supplement these activities with fishing and gathering shellfish and seaweed. Not surprisingly, the mainly self-sufficient diet in such communities is a simple, frugal one. Every house has its own *girnel*, the oatmeal barrel out of which are made the staple oatcakes and bannocks so loved by the Scots. Filling soups and porridges, mutton, salt fish, herring and mackerel, are supplemented with occasional delicacies from the sea, including prawns and salmon. Milk from goats, sheep or cows is made into butter and simple cheeses, such as crowdie, a soft-curd cheese produced domestically by draining the curds from the whey in muslin bags.

Whisky used to be produced illicitly throughout the Highlands and Islands, using primitive distilling equipment and craft to outwit the Revenue men. If the tell-tale wisp of smoke no longer rises from the glens, it is probable that in places such as Skye, Lewis and Harris, and other

remote outposts, shebeens are still a feature of local life: small thatched drinking huts secluded from the community, where men gather to drink informally, untroubled by either the elements or their womenfolk, to the vehement disapproval of the powerful religious sects which still dominate life here.

Only a tiny percentage of the population lives in these most remote parts of Britain, and even in the furthest, change has come. Fishing communities in the Shetlands have been altered by the arrival of North Sea oilmen, and their money; throughout the Highlands and Islands few people today cook over open fires, in iron cauldrons or on girdles. Yet come down from the Highlands: take single-lane roads down to Inverness, then across to Aberdeen and Dundee; or skirt alongside Loch Ness to Fort William, then down to the banks of the Clyde, across to elegant Edinburgh. Here in the Lowlands, or in the southern uplands and the lush rolling Border counties, one finds an unyielding pride – even a romance – in traditions firmly rooted in this harsh, majestic land.

The haggis, for example, is generally considered the national dish of Scotland (though the Scots readily agree that they did not invent it). It is nothing more than an overgrown sausage, variations of which are common to any whose diet is one of necessity, of whatever nationality, for it utilizes those parts of an animal which in better times might otherwise be discarded, including the stomach bag and pluck. It is a frugal feast, the sort of warming, spicy meal to satisfy the appetite of husky, bearded Highlanders who have spent a day or days out in the cold. Yet, immortalized by Robert Burns, it is loved and eaten by Scots from all areas and social backgrounds, and not just on Hogmanay or at Burns' suppers.

Other foods, too, reflect origins in a harsher, less accommodating world than today. If the haggis was originally a food of hard times, mealy

The peat fire: the source of warmth and a means of cooking in the Highlands and Islands.

pudding or skirlie are even more frugal, for both are simply beef suet, onions, oatmeal and seasonings – in short, haggis without even the offal (the former is stuffed into a casing, the latter fried in a pan). Scottish soups are filling hearty fare, the sort of one-pot meals that once were cooked in iron cauldrons over open turf fires: Scotch broth made with fatty mutton and pearl barley, cock-a-leekie made from an old boiling fowl, cullen skink (Finnan haddock and potato soup), simple kale brose, lentil brö, and many others. Similarly, a tradition of girdle baking remains, in homes and in village and town bakeries, where such favourites as drop scones, potato scones, oatmeal scones, fatty cutties, oatcakes and bannocks are prepared and often delivered by van, together with breads, cakes, tea cakes and shortbreads to more remote areas (indeed the baking van is as important here as the milk float).

Baking in Scotland is a tradition which has always been highly valued, and baked goods form an important part of meals. No Scottish breakfast is complete without its morning roll, a yeasted bap, preferably warm from the oven, soft

The Immortal Memory of Robert Burns

A Scottish Burns' Night celebration is a unique event: at once a feast, a serious literary evening and a time for Scots to gather together and celebrate Scotland and Scots' values and attitudes as immortalized by the nation's favourite poet. In Scotland, Burns' suppers take place in January and February (the poet was born on 25 January 1759), while throughout the world thousands of members of Burns Clubs and Caledonian Societies don the tartan and celebrate this special day in great style. The central event of the evening is an oration by a distinguished guest or Burns scholar entitled 'The Immortal Memory of Robert Burns'. It is, above all, an evening of good cheer, good food and drink, and thanksgiving at friends and countrymen being together once more. As Burns himself said:

Frien'ship mak's us a' mair happy,
Frien'ship gi'es us a' delight,
Frien'ship consecrates the drappie,
Frien'ship brings us here tonight.

'And then, O what a glorious sight,/Warm-reekin' rich.'

and doughy, dusted with a light cover of flour. At midday, many an appetite is satisfied with a simple Scottish lunch of 'pie and a pint', the pie being a hot water pastry case filled with mince and gravy, the pint most probably brewed by Scottish & Newcastle (80/-) or Younger (No. 3 or 70/-). Bridies, particularly from Forfar, are another lunchtime favourite, filling shortcrust pasties stuffed with steak, onions and gravy.

The Scots' love of baked goods, however, is most evident at tea-time, and particularly at that favourite meal, high tea. This is the main evening meal, eaten as early as five or six, and consisting of such savouries as fish and chips; sausage, egg and tomato; kippers, Finnan haddock, or smokies; cold meats such as the favourite 'beef ham'; pies or bridies. These are followed by an equally substantial array of Dundee cake, gingerbread, bannocks, Border and other tarts, cream cakes, marzipans, truffles, sponge cakes and that favourite Scottish speciality, shortbread, in all its many guises (petticoat tails, oatmeal shortbread,

Ayrshire shortbread, Balmoral shortbread, and many others). Bread, butter and jam is consumed throughout this meal, together with pots of strong tea, drunk with plenty of milk and sugar. (We should not forget, after all, that the favourite British institution, the tea room, was first established in Glasgow by a Miss Cranston at the turn of the century.)

Scottish foods, however, are not all simply heavy and filling (important though such bulk is to appetites whetted by hard labour in this most northern part of Britain). There are other, more sophisticated influences in the traditions of this rich and varied nation, too. The Scottish aristocracy, in their castles and mansions which once dominated the countryside, were long at odds with the English, even after the Act of Union (1707); thus rather than apeing the court in London, as the elite landed gentry in both Wales and Ireland tended to do, the proud Scots went their own way. The Auld Alliance with France against the English left its mark on the Scottish

The majesty of the Highlands, above Loch Shin on the road to Kinlochbervie.

kitchen: it is curious to find that here, for example, a leg of lamb is a gigot (pronounced *jigget*), a plate is an ashet (from *assiette*), and collops are *escalopes*.

Some of the greatest British dishes are Scottish specialities, particularly those made from produce native to these lands north of Hadrian's Wall. Scotland is famous for some of the finest shooting and fishing estates in the world, providing both sport for those who can afford it (or who can poach it), as well as good eating for those fortunate to come across such specialities either in shops or restaurants. Red grouse, the finest of all game birds, is most highly prized, and the 'Glorious Twelfth' (August 12, the start of the shooting season) is an exciting day for Scottish sportsmen and gastronomes alike. A grouse shoot is a formal affair, with paid beaters who startle the birds from their nests in the moorland heather. The bagging of red grouse, and other wild fowl such as ptarmigan, blackcock and capercaillie, may be an expensive and exclusive sport, but the birds themselves are delicacies worth all the fuss, especially when prepared in the Scottish manner, stuffed with native rowanberries or cranberries, then simply roasted. Partridge, wild duck, pheasant and snipe are all shot in Scotland during their respective seasons, and enjoyed either roasted or braised.

Deer continue to roam wild in the forests of the Highlands (they are also being farmed commercially). Venison, not surprisingly, is an old Scottish favourite, particularly on Highland estates such as Blair Castle, home of the Duke of Atholl, and on other aristocratic estates. The tradition of the hunt here is well-established: Mary Queen of Scots, for example, was 'entertained' to a hunt in the Atholl forest in 1564. Prime cuts such as the haunch or saddle of venison are most often roasted, while less tender cuts of this rich, deep-red lean meat are devilled, stewed or braised.

Even the pluck of venison is highly prized: it is used to make an extra-special venison haggis.

To sportsmen, Scotland's salmon and trout rivers are equally highly-esteemed. The Tay, the Dee in Aberdeenshire, the Spey, the Tweed, and many others are all well-stocked with salmon, sea trout and brown trout, and throughout Scotland it is common to see anglers in their waders and oil-skins deftly whipping their flexible rods and wet and dry flies with pin-point accuracy into deep pools and fast-running eddies. Salmon fishing, however, is not mere sport for anglers: it is an important commercial livelihood for fishermen on both the east and west coasts.

Both wild and (increasingly) farmed salmon are smoked to produce another famous Scottish delicacy valued around the world. As in everything, there is smoked salmon and there is smoked salmon. In the Summer Isles, salmon is first cured in a spicy, aromatic brine flavoured with juniper berries, molasses and rum, followed by gentle smoking over shavings from whisky casks and juniper wood for eight to twelve hours.

Such craftsmanship in the preservation of fish and meats by smoking and pickling is not uncommon, for the skills are important ones long valued by the Scots. Mutton hams were once popular and are still available, while the Scots maintain a keen taste for 'beef hams'. Regional fish curing and smoking has resulted in Loch Fyne kippers, Finnan haddock and Eyemouth pales (both are similar lightly-cured, undyed haddock fillets that have been cold smoked), and the Arbroath smokie.

Fishing remains an important Scottish industry. Great catches of herring, haddock, mackerel, halibut, sole, cod, plaice and other fish continue to be landed at busy Aberdeen, and elsewhere, and fish remains an essential staple here, even more so perhaps than in other parts of Britain. Herring in oatmeal is a national favourite (this same method is an equally effective way of preparing mackerel and other oily fish), while haddock, whiting and cod are poached, baked, made into fish pies, and eaten in any number of ways. Never ones to waste anything, the Scots even make use of the heads of large fish such as cod, cleaned and stuffed with fish liver and oatmeal (this dish is known, rather dubiously we feel, as crappit heads).

Scottish Highland games work up giant-size appetites for participants and spectators alike.

To a Haggis

Fair fa' your honest, sonsie face,
Great chieftain o' the puddin'-race!
Aboon them a' ye tak your place,
    Painch, tripe, or thairm:
Weel are ye wordy o' a grace
    As lang's my arm.

Robert Burns

The haggis was probably developed centuries ago as a way of utilizing offal by mixing it with oats and seasonings, then stuffing it all in the stomach bag. It more than likely wasn't even Scots in origin, yet Robert Burns immortalized this simple, humble food, today proudly recognized as the national dish of Scotland. On Hogmanay (December 31), Burns' Night (January 25, the birthdate of the poet), and St Andrew's Day (November 30), tremendous amounts of haggis are consumed at home, south of the border, and in Scots communities around the world (in Scotland, moreover, it is enjoyed throughout the year).

There is, the Scots are the first to admit, considerable ritual attached to the eating of this simple food. Whether at Burns' suppers or Scottish evenings, the Ceremony of the Piping of the Haggis is a great and stylish event: the shrill skirl of the bagpipes announces the arrival of the haggis, carried in, generally by the chef, on a silver platter. The host, or an honoured guest then gives a spirited rendition of Burns' *Address to a Haggis* (all eight verses), during which the haggis is slashed joyously open with a *skein dhu* (the little dagger worn in the knee-length sock): '. . . Trenching your gushing entrails bright,/Like onie ditch;/And then, O what a glorious sight,/Warm-reekin, rich'. Host, piper and chef take the opportunity to down a wee dram – indeed, most guests, too, empty a measure of Scotland's finest. The haggis is solemnly piped back to the kitchen, where it is dished out, together with the traditional accompaniments of 'bashed neeps n' champit tatties'. Some people like to season their haggis with yet another dram of whisky.

Scottish beef and lamb, like her salmon and wild fowl, have gained fame throughout the world, but similarly, in days past such fine produce was sent down south to Smithfield and other markets, rather than eaten regularly as part of the native diet. This, however, is no longer true today. In private homes, as well as in country houses, restaurants and hotels, the finest produce and products of Scotland take pride of place. The foods of the past might reflect hard and unyielding origins but today the basic produce of Scotland is being used to create new but inarguably Scottish dishes that are excellent and refined. Thus, Aberdeen-Angus steaks are served in sauces made from rare malt whiskies, while native shellfish such as lobsters, Dublin Bay prawns, crab and scallops are turned into rich, elegant creations by inventive Scottish chefs. Such foods, born in a more affluent and modern world which sees greater numbers of both Scottish and 'foreign' visitors touring the country every year, contrast strikingly with crappit heads, skirlie or even haggis.

Scotland is a large and varied country, and contrasts are encountered throughout. The lush affluent meadowlands of the Borders are opposite in character to the high, bare hills of the Grampians; the seaside cries from bustling holiday towns such as St Andrews echo against the silent isolation of towns in the Speyside whisky region, with their drab grey-stone houses and occasional general stores and bars, all overlooked by brooding copper-green pagoda roofs. The scarcely intelligible (to outsiders) La'land speech of Ayrshire and Glasgow contrasts sharply with the gentle, rolling burr of the Highlands. There could scarcely be two more different cities than Glasgow and Edinburgh. Yet striking though the contrasts are, throughout Scotland one senses a common national pride, an awareness and value of natural riches and resources, and a fierce determination to celebrate a majestic heritage, come what may.

A selection of warming Scottish soups: (from l. to r.) Highland game soup, Cullen skink, lentil brö, Scotch broth, cock-a-leekie.

Recipes from Scotland

Highland Game Soup   (Serves 6–8)

Game from Scotland is among the best in the world; this rich soup is made with left-over trimmings and carcases of wild fowl such as grouse, pheasant or partridge, or, if available, with left-over rabbit, hare or venison.

25 g/1 oz/¼ stick butter
2 rashers lean bacon, chopped
900 g/2 lb game bones (approximately)
1 large onion, chopped
2–3 carrots, sliced
2 sticks celery, chopped
2 leeks, chopped
1 small parsnip, chopped

2.4 l/4 pt/10 cups game or chicken stock
Bouquet of fresh herbs
Salt
About a dozen black peppercorns
4 cloves
450 g/1 lb left-over meat, shredded
A dash of port

Melt the butter in a large saucepan, and fry the bacon. Add the bones and fry gently. Add the onion, carrots, celery, leeks and parsnip and stir and shake the pot until the vegetables and bones are well browned. Pour on the stock and add the herbs and seasonings. Bring to the boil, and simmer for 2 hours. Skim whenever necessary. Strain the soup and remove any pieces of meat from the bones. Skim off the fat and adjust the seasoning. Add left-over meat to the strained soup, and simmer for a further ½ hour, adding a generous dash of port in the last 5 minutes. Serve immediately.

Lentil Brö   (Serves 6)

The Shetlands' proximity to Scandinavia is evident in its traditional celebration Up-Helly-A, during which the inhabitants, dressed as Vikings, carry a long-boat through the streets of Lerwick and later set it on fire. Norse influence is also evident in the food traditions of the Shetlanders.

25 g/1 oz/$\frac{1}{4}$ stick butter	Salt
225 g/8 oz/1$\frac{1}{4}$ cups lentils	Freshly-ground black
1 carrot, diced	pepper
1 large onion, finely	1.5 l/2$\frac{1}{2}$ pt/6$\frac{1}{4}$ cups ham or
chopped	other stock
2 sticks celery, chopped	Freshly-chopped parsley
$\frac{1}{2}$ small turnip, diced	

Melt the butter in a large pot and sauté the lentils and all the vegetables. Season with salt and black pepper and add the ham stock. Bring to the boil and simmer for two hours. Adjust the seasoning to taste, and serve garnished with parsley.

Scotch Broth (Serves 6–8)

This is the Scottish version of the classic one-pot meal. The broth is often served separately from the meat and vegetables, though served together, with Dunlop cheese and oatcakes, it makes a full meal.

900 g/2 lb neck of lamb or	2 sticks celery, chopped
lean stewing beef	1 small turnip, finely diced
3 l/5 pt/12$\frac{1}{2}$ cups water	Salt
50 g/2 oz/$\frac{1}{3}$ cup pearl barley	Freshly-ground black
100 g/4 oz/$\frac{1}{2}$ cup dried peas,	pepper
soaked overnight	Half a small cabbage,
2 leeks, chopped	shredded
3 carrots, diced	Freshly-chopped parsley

Trim the meat, put into a large saucepan and cover with the water. Add the pearl barley and dried peas, bring to the boil, and skim off the rising scum. Add all the vegetables except the cabbage and season with salt and pepper. Bring to the boil, cover, and simmer for about 2$\frac{1}{2}$ hours. Add the shredded cabbage and cook uncovered for 20 minutes. Adjust the seasoning and serve in bowls, garnished with parsley; alternatively, strain the soup, and serve the broth first, then the meat and vegetables moistened with a little liquid.

Cock-a-Leekie (Serves 6)

This traditional soup comes originally from Edinburgh; today it is enjoyed all over Britain. On Hogmanay, or at Burns' suppers or Scottish evenings, it is often served before the haggis and neeps.

1 boiling fowl	Freshly-ground black
Water	pepper
Bouquet of fresh herbs	6 leeks, chopped
Salt	100 g/4 oz soaked prunes

Place the bird in a large pot, and just cover with cold water. Bring to the boil and remove any scum. Add the herbs and seasoning. Add the chopped white of the leeks and bring to the boil again. Cover and simmer for about 3 hours, or until tender. Remove the bird and take the meat off the bones. Shred and return to the soup. Skim off any excess fat, and adjust the seasoning. Add the remaining leeks and soaked prunes. Simmer for a further 15 minutes and serve immediately.

Cullen Skink (Serves 4)

This typical fisherman's soup must be made with true Finnan haddock, which is undyed, lightly smoked, and has a delicate straw-brown colour. Use the whole fish, for the skin and bones add flavour.

1 large Finnan haddock	600 ml/1 pt/2$\frac{1}{2}$ cups milk
1 onion, chopped	25 g/1 oz/$\frac{1}{4}$ stick butter, cut
300 ml/$\frac{1}{2}$ pt/1$\frac{1}{4}$ cups water	into small pieces
Salt	225 g/$\frac{1}{2}$ lb mashed potato
Freshly-ground black	4 tbsp cream
pepper	Freshly-chopped parsley

Place the haddock in a saucepan with the onion, and cover with the water. Bring to the boil and simmer for about 15 minutes. Remove the fish and separate the flesh from the skin and bones. Set the flesh aside. Return the skin and bones to the pan, season and cook for a further hour. Strain this fish stock, discarding the skin and bones, and add the flaked fish. Return to the heat, add the milk, butter and mashed potato. Bring to the boil and simmer for a few minutes. Adjust seasoning and stir a spoonful of cream into each bowl before serving. Garnish with chopped parsley.

Highland Brose (Serves 1)

This makes a hefty, rousing breakfast for those spending the day out of doors working or shooting (it is also recommended nourishment for those contemplating tossing the caber).

40 g/1$\frac{1}{2}$ oz/$\frac{1}{2}$ cup medium	2 tbsp double cream
oatmeal	1 tbsp honey
Boiling water	Generous shot of whisky
$\frac{1}{2}$ tsp salt	

Put the oatmeal in a dish and pour on enough boiling water to make a soupy porridge. Add a pinch of salt. Make a well in the centre, and pour on the cream, honey and whisky. To eat, take first a spoon of porridge, then a spoon of the cream mixture.

Herring in Oatmeal   (Serves 4)

Herring is an important Scottish staple, particularly to the western Highlanders. Though supplies have been less plentiful in past years, traditional Scottish fishing grounds have been reopened. Frying fish coated in oatmeal is a typical Scots method, superb with herring or mackerel, both of which are high in natural oil.

4 large herring	100 g/4 oz/$\frac{3}{4}$ cup medium
Salt	oatmeal
Freshly-ground black	100 g/4 oz/$\frac{1}{2}$ cup dripping
pepper	Lemon to garnish
A bowl of milk	

Clean and scale the herring, then split, run a knife blade down the backbone, pressing firmly, and lift out the bones. Score the skin with a sharp knife. Season well on both sides and dip in milk. Coat the fish in oatmeal, pressing it in well. Heat the dripping in a large frying pan, and fry the fish for about 3–5 minutes each side, until brown and crisp. Drain well, and garnish with lemon wedges. Serve with oatcakes.

Tweed Kettle   (Serves 6)

The Tweed is just one of the great salmon rivers of Scotland. This method of preparing salmon comes from Edinburgh, where it is served with 'bashed neeps' or 'tatties'.

900 g/2 lb fresh salmon	150 ml/$\frac{1}{4}$ pt/$\frac{2}{3}$ cup dry white
Water	wine
Salt	25 g/1 oz/$\frac{1}{4}$ stick butter
Freshly-ground black	100 g/4 oz mushrooms,
pepper	chopped
2 shallots, chopped	Freshly-chopped parsley
Pinch of mace	

Place the fish in a large pan or fish kettle, and barely cover with water. Slowly bring to the boil, and simmer very gently for about 3 minutes. Remove the salmon from the pan, skin, and take out all the bones. Cut the fish into small cubes and set aside. Return the skin and bones to the cooking liquid, bring to the boil, and simmer for 15 minutes. Strain and pour off 150 ml/$\frac{1}{4}$ pt/$\frac{2}{3}$ cup into a clean pan. Add the fish, seasoning, shallots, mace and white wine. Cover and simmer gently for 10 minutes. Meanwhile, melt the butter in a saucepan and gently sauté the chopped mushrooms. Drain and add to the salmon and continue to cook for 5 minutes. Garnish with parsley and serve with mashed swede or potatoes.

Roast Grouse   (Serves 2–4)

The grouse family includes – in addition to red grouse – capercaillie, blackcock and ptarmigan, all of which are native to Northern Europe. Red grouse, undoubtedly, is the most highly prized, and August 12 marks the start of the brief shooting season which lasts only until December 10. Young birds are best roasted, while older birds can be braised or casseroled most successfully. Grouse wants to be hung for at least a week prior to eating, depending on the weather. While it remains a relatively scarce delicacy, this same recipe is also good for roasting young pheasant or partridge (adjust cooking times depending on the size of the birds).

2 young grouse, plucked	100 g/4 oz cranberries,
and drawn	redcurrants or
50 g/2 oz/$\frac{1}{2}$ stick butter,	rowanberries
softened	4 rashers of fat bacon
Salt	Livers from the grouse
Freshly-ground black	2 slices of toast
pepper	Watercress to garnish
Juice of 1 lemon	

Wipe the insides of the birds. Mix most of the softened butter with the salt, pepper, lemon juice and berries. Divide in two and stuff into the cavities of each bird. Season birds with salt and pepper, lay two strips of bacon on the breasts of each and cover with foil. Roast in a moderately hot oven (200°C/400°F/Gas Mark 6) for about 30 minutes. Meanwhile, in a separate pan, boil the grouse livers in water or stock for 2–3 minutes, remove (reserving the liquid) and mash with the remaining butter and salt and pepper. Spread the liver paste on the toast. Take the grouse from the oven, remove the foil from the breast, and place the birds on the rounds of toast. Return to the oven, and roast for a further 10–15 minutes, basting with the pan juices.

Remove the grouse to a warmed serving platter, pour off any fat from the roasting tin, and add the reserved liver stock. Bring to the boil, simmer and season. Garnish the birds with watercress, and serve with the gravy, and with other traditional accompaniments, such as bread sauce, game chips and rowanberry or redcurrant jelly.

Scottish Salmon

It is often stated that salmon was once so plentiful that apprentices, servants and schoolboys protested against the 'monotonous' diet of this cheapest fish. The Scottish salmon fishermen whom we have spoken to, however, say that this fishy myth is a load of cod's wallop: salmon has been highly prized here for at least two or three hundred years, and the industry is a well-established one. In those days, though, the fish was generally pickled in brine or dry-salted on the site, and then sent down to London or exported to the Continent. The East India Company witnessed the use of ice in China to preserve fish and other foods and thus by the early nineteenth century numerous ice-houses were built around and into the Scottish coast. When the railway came to Inverness in the latter half of the nineteenth century, fresh Scottish salmon, packed in ice, could be transported quickly down to Billingsgate, reaching the market in prime condition. Such extremely fresh fish led to the famous Billingsgate cry of 'stiff alive!', indicating salmon so fresh that it is still in a state of rigor mortis.

Scotland's fast-flowing rivers may be rated by game fishermen as among Britain's best for catching this exciting fish on the end of a rod; commercial salmon fishermen, however, believe that their method of fishing with bag or trap nets results in salmon of even higher quality. Up and down the east and west coasts, there are fishing sites that have been established for at least 150 years. Just as salmon caught in the sea differs from river salmon,

An ice house over a hundred years old, still in use today at Achiltibuie, opposite the Summer Isles.

so does it differ from salmon reared in hatcheries. The latter has certainly helped to bring down the price of this luxury fish, but most connoisseurs agree that it does not have the same quality of flavour or texture.

We doubt that salmon was ever scorned – even by apprentices or schoolboys – for it is a magnificent food. Its flesh is very dense and compact, full of flavour and at once rich and nourishing; even a small portion of salmon is quite filling.

Braised Haunch of Venison

(Serves 8)

Venison is often served in the dining-room of Blair Castle, home of the 10th Duke of Atholl, as deer still roam extensively in the hills surrounding the estate. This is one favourite method of preparation.

2 onions, chopped
2 carrots, sliced
4 sticks celery, chopped
2 bay leaves
Sprig of fresh thyme
Handful of fresh parsley
Pinch of mace
4 cloves, crushed
Pinch of cayenne pepper
Salt
Freshly-ground black pepper
1.8 kg/4 lb haunch of venison
900 ml/1½ pt/3¾ cups stock
150 ml/¼ pt/⅔ cup red wine

Place all the vegetables in a large, deep casserole. Add the herbs, spices and seasonings. Place the venison on the bed of vegetables, and pour on the stock. Bring to the boil, simmer and transfer to a moderate oven (180°C/350°F/Gas Mark 4) for 3 hours or until the meat is tender. Remove the meat, skim off any fat, and add the wine. Reduce this cooking liquid rapidly, adjust seasoning, and serve with the venison.

Smoked salmon, a great Scottish delicacy.

Fresh salmon is best prepared simply in the Scottish manner: poached in brine.

Smoked and Preserved Fish

Prehistoric man devised ways of preserving food to tide himself over lean winter periods. Fish caught during summer months could be hung up to dry in the wind. It is probable that in an early age this drying process was assisted by hanging the fish near a fire of wood or peat, a process which not only greatly improved preservation but also added new, distinctive flavours. The Scots, as befits a hardy race which has long had to make do with foods gathered from the sea or moor, have long continued to develop such age-old methods of preservation. Even today, when fresh or fresh-frozen fish is readily available, such smoked foods continue to form an essential part of the diet.

Arbroath Smokies The origins of this favourite smoked fish of the north-east are obscure, though it is fairly certain that it was brought to the fishing community of Arbroath when the fisherfolk moved here from the nearby community of Auchmithie. An Arbroath smokie is a fresh haddock, de-headed, cleaned, dry-salted for about two hours, then tied in pairs and hot-smoked over oak or beech logs for half an hour to forty minutes. Numerous small family firms in the town still have their own 'smoke barrel' (the smoke pit is so named because the fishwives used to smoke the fish in half-barrels sunk into the ground); it is a rare treat to sample this copper-brown delicacy as soon as it has finished smoking, while still warm and juicy.

Finnan Haddock North of Arbroath, the little town of Findon has contributed its name to this well-known haddock cure. A Finnan haddock, unlike an Arbroath smokie, is cleaned and split up the belly, leaving the backbone intact, on either the right or left side. The fish is then lightly brined, and cold-smoked over slow smouldering oak dust (not logs) for up to six hours. Unlike the garish, dyed 'golden fillets' often seen on fishmongers' slabs, neither true Finnan haddock nor Arbroath smokies have colouring added to them; the former is a pale, straw-brown colour. Since it is cold-smoked, Finnan haddock needs to be cooked before eating: the best way is to poach it in a little milk and butter. The Eyemouth pale is a similarly cured haddock from the area around that Border fishing town.

Loch Fyne Kippers Herring was once a staple throughout Britain, and particularly in the west of Scotland, where 'herrin' 'n tatties' was often all there was to eat. The fish are still caught in vast quantities here, salted and pickled in vinegar, as well as kippered. The method of kippering herring, it is generally acknowledged, developed in Craster, Northumberland (see p. 16), but kippers from Loch Fyne are considered among the very best.

Smoked Salmon If salmon is the king, smoked salmon is the lord of cured and preserved fish. Regional and individual cures vary in different parts of Scotland, from smokehouse to smoke-house. Basically, the fish is first filletted into sides, then either cured in dry salt or in an aromatic brine. Choice of ingredients in the brine is highly individual, and can add considerably to the flavour of the finished product. After this session of either dry salting or soaking in brine, the fish is dried, then smoked over a slow, smouldering fire of oak and other wood chips and dust (again, choice of wood affects flavour: some smokehouses claim that impregnated whisky casks are essential, others use such added aromatics as juniper berries, herbs and other flavourings). Though salmon is always cold-smoked, it does not need to be cooked before eating: indeed, this raw, cured delicacy, sliced razor thin, and eaten with home-made brown bread is one of Scotland's greatest foods.

In addition to the above, mackerel, trout, eel and other fish are smoked in Scotland, while meats such as mutton, venison and beef are also traditionally cured and smoked.

A small smokehouse in Arbroath: the haddock are tied in pairs by their tails and hot-smoked for forty minutes to emerge a rich copper-brown colour, fully-cooked and ready to eat.

Scotch Beef and Lamb

Scottish expertise in animal husbandry dates back over three hundred years, and indeed, today Scotch quality beef and lamb are recognized as among the finest in the world. Traditional beef breeds include the famous Aberdeen-Angus, the Galloway and the Highland. The Aberdeen-Angus breed was developed in the north-east of the country, an area regarded today as one of the main beef-producing areas in Britain. Though the mainly black, short-legged Angus appears relatively small, its bulk is deceptive, for it yields a superior-quality carcase with a high proportion of the more expensive cuts. Its meat, moreover, is marbled with fine veins of fat, ensuring tenderness, juiciness and flavour. Scottish cattle are generally bred on hill and upland farms, then fed and finished on the lush pastures of the Lowlands.

Scotch lamb is equally highly-regarded. Blackface lambs, which graze mainly on the higher Scottish hills and mountains, subsist on a diet of heather which gives their meat a sweet, delicious flavour. Cheviots are bred in the Border hills as well as in lower ground in the north. The Shetland breed, known for its hardiness, leanness and small size, feeds on a diet of grass, heather and seaweed; small, whole lambs weighing only fifteen to twenty-five pounds are famous for their distinctive, slightly gamy flavour.

Throughout Britain, regional names for similar cuts of meat differ widely; in Scotland, not only the names of the cuts but also the methods of butchering vary considerably from the English. Generally speaking, the Scots prefer more cuts of both beef and lamb sold boned and rolled. Chops are also very popular, while the legs of small spring lamb, so highly valued in England, are not so important here. In fact, the favourite Scots method of dealing with legs of lamb is to slice them into gigot chops, a cut of lamb virtually unobtainable south of the border. Hough (shin), flank, and runner (top rib) are cuts of beef popular for the Scots' favourite long-simmering stews, soups and hotpots. Heuk is the name here for rump, while fleshy end (softside in Glasgow) is the thick flank or top rump.

Highland Beef Balls

(Makes 6 small balls)

Spices are used frequently in Scottish cooking. While degree of seasoning is always a matter of taste, these beef balls should be highly flavoured.

450 g/1 lb beef, minced	$\frac{1}{2}$ tsp ginger
50 g/2 oz/$\frac{1}{4}$ cup suet, finely chopped	$\frac{1}{2}$ tsp mace
Salt	$\frac{1}{2}$ tsp ground coriander
Freshly-ground black pepper	$\frac{1}{2}$ tsp dark brown sugar
	1 egg, beaten
$\frac{1}{4}$ tsp ground cloves	Medium oatmeal to coat

Mix all the ingredients together thoroughly, and shape into 6 balls. Roll in oatmeal, and fry in deep fat for about 5–7 minutes, depending on size, until they are a deep brown colour, and cooked through.

Aberdeen-Angus Fillet Steak with Whisky Sauce   (Serves 2)

Although not an old or traditional dish, this combination of superb beef cooked with whisky reflects how Scottish cooks are developing new dishes making use of their finest and most proud products.

50 g/2 oz/$\frac{1}{2}$ stick butter	Freshly-ground black pepper
$\frac{1}{2}$ onion, finely chopped	Generous shot of whisky
2 175 g/6 oz Aberdeen-Angus fillet steaks	150 ml/$\frac{1}{4}$ pt/$\frac{2}{3}$ cup stock
Salt	4 tbsp cream

Melt the butter in a frying pan and gently sauté the onion. When soft, increase the heat and add the steaks. Cook for 3–5 minutes each side, depending on thickness of the steaks and how preferred. Remove to a hot dish and keep warm. Skim off the excess fat from the frying pan and add the whisky. Stir the juices and scrape the bottom of the pan with a wooden spoon. Add the stock and reduce to a thick syrup. Add the cream and heat through gently. Adjust the seasoning and pour over the steaks. Serve immediately.

Howtowdie   (Serves 6)

This method of cooking chicken is typically Scottish, though the name is thought to come from the Old French *hutaudeau*, meaning a young chicken. It can be served on its own or, more elegantly, on a bed of spinach topped with poached ('drappit') eggs.

1 roasting chicken, about 1.5 kg/3½ lb	Freshly-ground black pepper
50 g/2 oz/½ stick butter	600 ml/1 pt/2½ cups giblet stock
8 baby onions	1 chicken liver, finely chopped
2 whole cloves	
Pinch of grated nutmeg	
Salt	

Stuff the chicken with skirlie (see below) and secure. Melt the butter in a heavy-based casserole. Add the whole baby onions and allow to soften. Add the chicken, and brown. Add the spices and the seasoning. Pour over the stock, cover, and cook in a preheated moderate oven (180°C/350°F/Gas Mark 4) for about 1½ hours. Remove the chicken from the casserole and keep warm. Strain the stock into a saucepan, add the chopped chicken liver, and bring to the boil. Reduce the stock and adjust the seasoning. Carve the chicken, and serve with the skirlie and the chicken gravy.

Skirlie   (Serves 4–6)

Skirlie is typical frugal Scots food, originally a complete meal in itself when there was little else to eat, now often served as a side dish, or used as a stuffing for chicken. The name suggests the noise which the suet makes as it sizzles in the pan, reminiscent of the bagpipe, with a little imagination.

50 g/2 oz/¼ cup beef suet, finely chopped	Freshly-ground black pepper
2 medium onions, finely chopped	½ tsp coarsely-ground coriander
100 g/4 oz/1 cup medium oatmeal	½ tsp mace
Salt	Freshly-grated nutmeg to taste

Heat the suet in a frying pan, add the onions and brown well. Add the oatmeal, seasoning (skirlie, like haggis, should be well seasoned, so don't stint on the black pepper), and spices. Fry until the oatmeal is brown and crunchy. Serve as a side dish, or use as a stuffing.

Rumbledethumps   (Serves 6)

Similar to Irish combinations of potatoes and other vegetables mashed together, rumbledethumps makes a good supper or high tea dish, or it can be served as an accompaniment to stews or roasts.

450 g/1 lb potatoes	Freshly-ground black pepper
450 g/1 lb cabbage, shredded	50 g/2 oz/⅔ cup grated Dunlop or Cheddar cheese
50 g/2 oz/½ stick butter	
1 large onion, sliced	
Salt	

Cook the potatoes in salted boiling water and mash them. Boil the cabbage until tender. Melt the butter in a pan and fry the onion gently. Add the mashed potato and cooked cabbage, and mix well. Season and turn into a greased baking dish. Cover with grated cheese and bake in a moderately hot oven (190°C/375°F/Gas Mark 5) for about 20 minutes or until the top is brown. Serve hot.

Stovies   (Serves 6)

Stovies are often made with left-over meat, poultry or game, chopped and added to the potatoes. They are stewed in a pot on the cooker, not baked in an oven – in other words, stoved.

2 tbsp meat dripping	150 ml/¼ pt/⅔ cup water (approximately)
1 large onion, chopped	225 g/½ lb left-over meat or poultry (optional)
900 g/2 lb potatoes, peeled and cut into thick slices	
Salt	
Freshly-ground black pepper	

Melt the dripping in a large, heavy saucepan, and fry the onion lightly. Add the potatoes, season well with salt and pepper, and pour on the water (there should be enough to come half-way up the potatoes). Bring to the boil, cover with a tight-fitting lid, and simmer gently for about 1 hour. Shake occasionally to prevent the potatoes from sticking, but do not remove the lid. Add the left-over meat or poultry if using, cook for a further 10 minutes and serve at once.

Scottish Cheeses

The old Highland method of making cheese was to sour the milk naturally by leaving it in the sun. The cream was skimmed off for butter, then the thickened milk was 'scrambled' on the stove, causing the whey to drain. The resulting curds were wrapped in muslin and hung up on the bough of a tree to drain further. As soon as the cheese had stopped dripping, it was mixed with salt (and, perhaps, a bit of cream) and eaten on oatcakes. This is crowdie, a simple cheese made and eaten in the Highlands and Islands since the days of the Picts.

Crowdie Made with unpasteurized skimmed milk, crowdie is a low-fat cheese with a distinctive lemony, citric taste which results from the long, slow souring process (no rennet is used). The name 'crowdie' comes from the Lowland Scots 'cruds' or curds; in Gaelic, crowdie is called *gruth*, as in *gruth dhu*.

Caboc Caboc, originally, was a cheese of chieftains; today it is produced from a fifteenth-century family recipe from Skye. Extremely rich yet delicate in flavour, it is made with pure double cream, a soft full-fat cheese rolled in toasted pinhead oatmeal.

Gruth Dhu The name means 'black crowdie': crowdie rolled in crushed peppercorns and oatmeal.

Hramsa In the past, when crowdie was made, cream as well as wild herbs and oatmeal might be stirred into the cheese. Hramsa is crowdie mixed with wild garlic, a herb highly treasured in the Highlands, as well as with pepper and cream. Galic is similar, but rolled in mixed nuts.

Highland Soft This full-fat soft cheese, originally popular in Ayrshire, is used primarily for cooking.

Ayrshire, a Lowlands county in the south-west, is rich dairy country, and has given its name to the breed of cattle developed here, second in milk yield and popularity throughout Britain only to the Friesian. Ayrshire milk is high in butterfat, and is thus ideally suited for cheese manufacture. Dunlop is a distinctive hard cheddar-type cheese made in this part of the country, as well as on the Orkneys, Arran and Islay. Celtic expertise at smoking has led to the traditional production of peat-smoked cheeses in the Lowlands and the Orkneys. Scottish Cheddar is produced in creameries in the Scottish uplands and elsewhere, while new cheeses such as Pentland and Lothian (both soft cheeses similar to French camembert and brie respectively) are also produced.

Highland cheeses: (from l. to r.) Caboc, Crowdie, Galic – delicious with oatcakes.

A range of traditional Scottish baked goods: (from l. to r.) potato scones, morning rolls, oatcakes, Forfar bridie, wholemeal scones, (centre) meat pie.

Forfar Bridies   (Serves 4)

These oval, meat-filled pasties are a favourite Scottish 'convenience' food, similar to the Cornish version, although bridies only contain onion, suet and steak.

450 g/1 lb shortcrust pastry (see p. 25)	50 g/2 oz/$\frac{1}{4}$ cup beef suet, finely chopped
450 g/1 lb rump steak	2 medium onions, finely chopped
Salt	
Freshly-ground black pepper	1 egg, beaten

Divide the pastry into four equal parts and roll each out into an oval. Pound the steak, then cut into thin strips. Place in a mixing bowl, season with salt and plenty of black pepper, and mix in the finely-chopped suet and onions. Divide equally, and place on each oval of pastry. Dampen the edges of the pastry, fold over and seal. Cut out a small hole in the top of each and brush with the beaten egg. Bake in a pre-heated hot oven (220°C/425°F/Gas Mark 7) for 15 minutes, then reduce heat to 180°C/350°F/Gas Mark 4 for a further 30–45 minutes. Serve hot.

Caboc, a rich double cream cheese, draining in muslin bags in a Highland dairy.

Oatcakes

Oats, according to Dr Johnson, are given to horses in England, fed to people in Scotland. Because oats are able to flourish in a poor soil with a minimum amount of sunshine, they have been a Celtic staple for centuries. Oatcakes are quite difficult to make (rolling them out thinly is the problem), but do persevere: served warm just off the girdle, they are delicious!

100 g/4 oz/1¼ cups medium oatmeal	1 tsp salt
	2 tsp melted bacon fat
Pinch of bicarbonate of soda	4 tbsp hot water
	Fine oatmeal for kneading

Mix oatmeal with bicarbonate of soda and salt. Make a well in the centre and pour in the warm fat. Stir in well and add enough hot water to make a stiff dough. Turn out on to a board dusted with oatmeal and roll out as thinly as possible. Dust with oatmeal to prevent sticking. Cut the rolled paste into quarters (farls). Lightly grease a girdle or heavy-bottomed frying pan and heat well. Cook the oatcakes for about 5–10 minutes on the hot surface until brown, then turn, and cook the other side. Serve warm, or cool and then store in an airtight tin.

Shortbread

There are almost as many versions of shortbread in Scotland as there are bakers. In Ayrshire the shortbread is a rich variety made with cream. Pitcaithly bannock is a festive shortbread made in a large round decorated with almonds and crystallized fruit. Oatmeal shortbread is popular in Cupar, while petticoat tails (round shortbreads shaped to look like petticoat hoops worn in the nineteenth century) came originally from Edinburgh. These and many others are all variations on a theme, but all good shortbread must be made with the best butter and high quality flour.

350 g/12 oz/3 sticks butter	100 g/4 oz/⅘ cup rice flour
100 g/4 oz/½ cup castor sugar	Pinch of salt
300 g/10 oz/2 cups plain flour	

Cream the butter and sugar together well. Sift in the flours and salt and work in lightly with the fingertips until the mixture resembles fine breadcrumbs. Press it together into two balls and turn out on to a board sprinkled with rice flour. Roll into round flat cakes about 1.3 cm/½ in thick. Pinch the edges all the way round with finger and thumb, mark into slices with a knife, and prick lightly all over with a fork. Place on a baking sheet lined with greaseproof paper and bake in a pre-heated slow oven (150°C/300°F/Gas Mark 2) for about an hour. Leave to cool on the tin before transferring to a wire rack. Dust with castor sugar and divide into slices while still warm.

Pitcaithly Bannock

225 g/8 oz/2 sticks butter	100 g/4 oz/⅘ cup rice flour
50 g/2 oz/⅓ cup castor sugar	50 g/2 oz/¾ cup flaked almonds
50 g/2 oz/⅓ cup icing sugar	
225 g/8 oz/1⅗ cups plain flour	50 g/2 oz/½ cup citrus peel

Cream butter and sugars together, add both flours, and mix well. Add almost all the flaked almonds, work them in and roll out into 1 large round or 2 smaller ones. Press in the remaining almonds and citrus peel and decorate the edge by pinching with the finger and thumb. Mark into slices and prick the top all over lightly with a fork. Place on a baking tray lined with greaseproof paper. Bake in a slow oven (150°C/300°F/Gas Mark 2) for an hour, or until just golden brown. Dust with castor sugar and divide into slices while still warm.

Dundee Cake

This rich fruit cake, patterned with almonds on top, though originally from Dundee, is made all over Scotland, and is famous throughout the world.

175 g/6 oz/1½ sticks butter	50 g/2 oz/½ cup mixed peel, chopped
175 g/6 oz/1 cup soft brown sugar	50 g/2 oz/½ cup glacé cherries, chopped
4 eggs	Juice and grated rind of half a lemon
225 g/8 oz/1⅗ cups plain flour	Juice and grated rind of half an orange
Pinch of salt	2 tbsp whisky
1 tsp baking powder	About 2 dozen blanched split almonds
2 tbsp ground almonds	
175 g/6 oz/1 cup sultanas	
175 g/6 oz/1 cup currants	
100 g/4 oz/⅔ cup raisins	

In a large mixing bowl, cream the butter and sugar together. Beat in the eggs, one at a time. Sieve the flour, salt and baking powder and fold in. Stir in the ground almonds, sultanas, currants, raisins, mixed peel, cherries, lemon and orange juice and rind, and whisky. Grease and line a 20 cm/8 in cake tin and turn in the cake mixture. Make a small hollow in the centre and arrange the blanched split almonds on top. Cover with buttered greaseproof paper and bake in a moderate oven (160°C/325°F/Gas Mark 3) for about 2 hours. Half-way through cooking, remove the grease-proof paper. Test with a skewer before removing from the oven. Allow to cool in the tin, then remove the lining paper and wrap in foil. Store in an airtight container.

Dundee Marmalade

(Makes about 4.5 kg/10 lb)

Marmalade, a British breakfast favourite whether in Edinburgh or London, Bristol or Cardiff, was origin-ally made first in the Scottish town of Dundee. A grocer named James Keiller purchased a bargain load of Seville oranges, but was unable to sell them because of their sharp, bitter taste. His wife, not wanting to waste the fruit, chopped the oranges up – including the rind – and preserved them. She called her new product 'marmalade' and its fame spread: the firm of James Keiller still makes one of the very best marmalades.

1.35 kg/3 lb Seville oranges	3.6 l/6 pt/15 cups water
3 lemons	2.7 kg/6 lb sugar

Wash the oranges and lemons and put them whole into a large heavy-based pan. Pour on the water, cover and bring to the boil. Simmer for $1\frac{1}{2}$–2 hours, or until the fruit is soft. Remove the fruit with a slotted spoon, allow to cool, and cut into chunks. Remove the pips and add them to the liquid in the pan. Boil this rapidly for 10 minutes, then strain. Put the strained juice, cut fruit and sugar back into the pan. Stir well until the sugar has dissolved. Bring to a rapid boil, and boil until setting point is reached, about 30 minutes. Remove any scum, allow to cool slightly, stir well to distribute the fruit, and pour into sterilized jars, cover, seal and label.

Cranachan or Cream Crowdie

(Serves 4)

There are many variations of the simple crowdie combination of oatmeal and water, a frugal staple in Scotland in times past. Cranachan or cream crowdie, made with rich double cream, is an excellent Scottish finish to a meal. The raspberries can be omitted if not available, but they do lighten this rather rich dessert. At Hallowe'en, charms are stirred into cranachan rather like the English custom of placing sixpenny pieces in Christmas puddings.

50 g/2 oz/$\frac{1}{2}$ cup pinhead oatmeal	2 or 3 tbsp heather honey
300 ml/$\frac{1}{2}$ pt/$1\frac{1}{4}$ cups double cream	100 g/4 oz fresh raspberries or other soft fruit
Generous shot of malt whisky	

Toast the oatmeal in the oven until lightly browned and crisp. Whip the cream until fairly stiff and fold in the whisky, honey, raspberries and most of the toasted oatmeal. Spoon into individual glasses and sprinkle the top of each with the remaining oatmeal.

Edinburgh Fog (Serves 6)

Edinburgh, like London, was once plagued by thick mists and fogs, and thus earned itself the nickname 'Auld Reekie'. This dessert is thicker than the mists that envelop the city today, but like Edinburgh itself, it is deliciously rich and elegant.

600 ml/1 pt/$2\frac{1}{2}$ cups double cream	6 tbsp whisky
2 tbsp castor sugar	100 g/4 oz/$\frac{2}{3}$ cup blanched almonds, chopped
A few drops vanilla essence	16–24 small ratafia biscuits

Whip the cream until stiff and stir in the sugar, vanilla essence and whisky to taste. Mix in the almonds and biscuits and chill well before serving.

Drink in Scotland

Amber-coloured whisky, as warming as a peat fire, as fragrant as the heather hills, does indeed seem the perfect drink for this majestic northern country. As elsewhere in Britain, beer is also a main drink in Scotland (indeed, often the two are drunk together, for a 'half and half' here signifies a dram of whisky together with a beer chaser). Country wines continue to be made both domestically and commercially in Scotland, while a touch of the romance and magic of a rugged landscape finds its way into a liqueur drunk throughout the world, Drambuie, the secret recipe for which, so the legend goes, was given personally to a captain on Skye by no less a Scots hero than Charles Edward Stuart.

The Scots themselves are the first to admit their national fondness for a wee drink now and again. This carousing, fun-loving attitude to life in general, however, is tempered by the influence of the Church of Scotland as well as by other, sterner Presbyterian sects. In the north-west Highlands and Islands where the power of the Free Kirk remains undiminished, the Sabbath is indeed held sacrosanct. Not only public houses, but restaurants, garages, even, in some instances, ferry services are all closed on Sundays. Generally, though, Scotland is more liberal than England concerning licensing laws. The pub, in Scotland, it should perhaps be added, is not quite the same family social gathering place as it is in England, for it was traditionally a male preserve; even today, hotel bars are often more welcoming and, additionally, they are generally open on Sundays in those parts of the country where everything else is shut.

Hours: In Scotland, public house opening hours officially are 11.00–14.30 and 17.00–23.00 Monday to Saturday, and, in those parts of the country allowed to open on Sundays, 12.30–14.30 and 18.30–23.00. In reality, though, continuous afternoon opening is permitted by 'regular extension' licenses in many public houses and hotel bars in Edinburgh and Glasgow, as well as in

Assorted mats and labels of the region.

other parts of the country; thus, in effect, in much of Scotland, it is possible to have a drink from 11.00 to 23.00.

Scotch Whisky

For centuries, in the wildest and most desolate hills of the Highlands and on islands such as Skye, Islay and the Orkneys, the skill of the Scots has turned such simple abundant raw ingredients as barley, pure spring water and peat into a beverage of rare flavour, potency and, above all, fragrance. In remote bothies far from the prying eyes of the Kings' Revenue men, crafty, ingenious distillers used the most primitive equipment to produce a spirit that warmed the heart and soul of a nation, its very name, in Gaelic, signifying its importance: *uisge beatha* – water of life. Today, in areas of Scotland where the modern world has hardly penetrated, as well as in more populated parts of the Lowlands, whisky continues to be produced from these same basic ingredients, twice-distilled in magnificent copper pot stills by traditional, time-honoured methods, producing a liquor which, with its warmth and peaty fragrance, is the essence of Scotland itself.

In total, there are some 116 malt whisky distilleries in Scotland. The whiskies produced are classified as Highland malts (by far the majority), Lowland malts, Campbeltown malts and Islay malts. Highland malts, particularly from Speyside, an eastern area south of the Moray Firth, incorporating the Glenlivet concentration of distilleries (there are twenty-three located near or around the Livet Valley), as well as such important distilling towns as Dufftown and Grantown-on-Spey, are prized for their fineness and complex, subtle fragrances. Such whiskies are generally lighter than the heavy, distinctive, pungent whiskies from Islay, an island whose dense, heavy peat adds unmistakable flavour and character to whiskies such as Laphroaig, Bowmore, Bruichladdich and others. Campbeltown, once an important whisky centre, today has but two remaining distilleries, while there are only some ten malt distilleries in the Lowlands. Each, however, is important, producing a totally unique whisky, either to be drunk on its own as a single malt, or, as is the destiny of the lion's share, to contribute its character to the popular brands of

blended whisky known and drunk not only in Scotland, but around the world.

For, though malts from single distilleries are most highly regarded by whisky connoisseurs as a drink in their own right – some might say the only drink – in fact, some ninety-eight per cent of all whisky sold is blended whisky. It was only after the practice of blending whiskies was pioneered in the 1860s that this potent liquor from the rugged Highland glens became first widely acceptable in England, then popular throughout the world. This position was achieved mainly through the development of a new, lighter and cheaper whisky, produced by methods considerably different to those used for the distillation of malt whisky in pot stills.

The development of a rapid, less expensive method of producing grain whisky from a mash of both malted and unmalted cereals came about in the early nineteenth century when a distiller, Robert Stein, invented the patent, or continuous column still. Distillation in the column still, unlike the pot still, is continuous, and thus spirit is produced both more quickly and more cheaply.

The bare, remote countryside of the Speyside whisky region, where smugglers once evaded the King's Revenue men.

The resulting grain whisky is a lighter, more highly-rectified spirit than malt whisky, whose character comes in great measure from beneficial oils, ethers and aromatics which are not lost during its lengthier distillation in pot stills. But the lighter, milder grain whisky needs less time to mature before it is ready for use. Grain whisky is not generally considered a drink in its own right (only one single grain whisky is bottled and sold as such: John Haig & Company's Choice Old Cameron Brig), but its more neutral character enabled it to revolutionize the whisky industry, for grain whisky provides an ideal base on which to blend any number of whiskies of varying characters and ages.

Malt whisky snobs may well turn their noses up at the blends, yet the craft of the blender at producing consistent whiskies year after year is an uncanny, intuitive one. The blender, by the skill of *his* nose alone, must decide what proportion of each single whisky in his stocks, what age and what colour must be combined to result in a product absolutely consistent in flavour, aroma and colour with the established brand that he is blending. When this formula is achieved, the casks of single whiskies are run into a large blending vat, mixed and allowed to marry for perhaps another six months (Scotch whisky must be legally at least three years old; many blends contain whiskies whose average age is considerably more than this minimum).

The resulting blends – and there are over 2000 – vary considerably in style, quality and character, ranging from inexpensive light whiskies to de luxe blends made with rare malts twenty years of age and older. There is no exact proportion of either malts or malt and grain whiskies; naturally, the finest blends contain high proportions of the finest malt whiskies. If there is an age label on a bottle of whisky, that age must refer to the youngest whisky – malt and grain – in the blend.

The Whisky Trail

The best way to learn about whisky, its history and production, is to visit distilleries and whisky blenders. Many of Scotland's distilleries do accept visitors, generally by prior appointment, while a seventy-mile-long sign-posted Whisky Trail leads through the heart of the famous Speyside whisky region, where five distilleries keep 'open house' for visitors without appointments.

Glenfiddich Distillery
Dufftown
Banffshire
Open to visitors, 10.00–12.00, 14.00–16.30, Monday–Friday all year. 10 am–12 noon, July–August only.

The Glenlivet Distillery
Glenlivet
Banffshire
Open to visitors, 10.00–16.30, Monday–Friday, Easter to end of October.
(Limited winter opening: by appointment).

Glenfarclas
Marypark
Ballindalloch
Banffshire
Open to visitors, 9.00–16.30, Monday–Friday all year.

Tamdhu Distillery
Knockando
Morayshire
Open to visitors, 10.00–16.00, Monday–Friday, May–September inclusive.
Otherwise by prior arrangement.

Strathisla-Glenlivet Distillery
Keith
Banffshire
Open to visitors, 9.00–16.00, Monday–Friday, mid-June–August.

To gain a further understanding of Scotch whisky, it is both informative and most interesting to visit a whisky blender. The following accept visitors, by appointment.

John Dewar & Sons Ltd
Inveralmond
Perth PH1 3EG
Write to the Visits Organizer for an appointment.

John Walker & Sons Ltd
Kilmarnock
Ayrshire KA3 14D
Write to the Visits Organizer for an appointment.

Wm Sanderson & Son
South Queensferry
West Lothian EH30 9SD
Parties up to 40 by previous appointment (large parties should book well in advance).

Het Pint and Atholl Brose

Both the het pint and Atholl brose are consumed in great quantity in Scotland over Christmas and Hogmanay. They are celebratory libations which no visitor should ever refuse.

Het Pint

1.2 l/2 pt/5 cups Scotch ale
Generous pinch of freshly-grated nutmeg
50 g/2 oz/$\frac{1}{3}$ cup castor sugar
2 eggs
300 ml/$\frac{1}{2}$ pt/1$\frac{1}{4}$ cups whisky

The old illicit methods of producing whisky were primitive but effective.

Traquair House Ale

Domestic brewing was once a regular activity in grand and humble houses alike. At Traquair House – the oldest inhabited house in Scotland, dating back to the twelfth century when it was a hunting lodge for Scottish kings – beer has been brewed for centuries. There was probably a brewhouse here in 1566 when Mary Queen of Scots stayed at Traquair. The workmen who erected the Bear Gates in 1737–8 received, in addition to payment, four gallons of ale. And was it after drinking Traquair ale with his guest Charles Edward Stuart that the 5th Earl vowed never to re-open Traquair's Bear Gates until a Stuart was restored to the throne? The Bear Gates remain chained shut, the approach to the house a broad, grassy avenue that is never used.

It was a desire to maintain links with the vivid past that led the 20th Laird of Traquair to restore the two-hundred-year-old brewhouse. Thus in 1965, Peter Maxwell Stuart, fired up the old brewing equipment (the copper – still in use – had been purchased in 1739 for £8), and stirred the mash of malt grist and hot liquor by hand with the original wooden paddles. The brew that resulted and which remains in production today is a potent Scotch ale, dark in colour, rich in flavour and alcohol (o.g. 1075–80). In addition to Traquair House Ale, a draught beer, Bear Ale (o.g. 1050) is now being produced. Traquair House is open to the public, Easter–October.

Traquair House.

Pour the ale into a saucepan, add the freshly-grated nutmeg, and bring to a simmer. Remove from the heat and add the sugar. Stir until dissolved. Beat the eggs, and add to the mixture. Return to the heat, but do not allow to boil or eggs will scramble. Add the whisky and mix well by pouring from one pan to another to work up a good froth. Drink immediately.

Atholl Brose

175 g/6 oz/1½ cups medium
 oatmeal
150 ml/¼ pt/⅔ cup water
5 tbsp honey
900 ml/1½ pt/3¾ cups whisky

Put the oatmeal in a bowl and mix it with the water to make a thick paste. Allow to stand for an hour, then put it through a fine sieve making sure that all the liquid is pushed through. Discard the oatmeal and blend the liquid with the honey. Pour into a bottle and add the whisky. Always shake well before drinking.

Scottish Ales and Lagers

Scottish ales are often designated by a price in shillings (in the past, this price was related to the cost of an entire cask). Today, in fact, such designations correspond roughly to English designations such as best, ordinary and light bitters: 80/- indicates a special, or high gravity ale; 70/- is a normal strength brew; 60/- indicates a lighter 'session' beer to be drunk over the course of an evening. Confusingly, the Scottish terms 'heavy' and 'light' have a different significance, too. Their closest English equivalents are bitter (heavy) and mild (light), so a light can be, and often is, darker in colour but not necessarily in weight or body than a heavy. The Scottish taste is generally for ales that are softer and somewhat sweeter than, for example, well-hopped Burton ales, though there are exceptions (such as Maclay's 70/- Heavy and Belhaven's 80/- Export). A 'wee heavy' is a small bottle of strong ale.

Cask-conditioned ales are available in Scotland, from the giant Scottish & Newcastle Breweries and Drybrough & Co., as well as from smaller independent breweries, but most of the beer drunk north of the border is still brewery-conditioned, pressurized keg ale and lager served in pubs, clubs and hotel bars. The Scots are huge consumers of lager (this pale drink, brewed in Glasgow for a hundred years, accounts for fifty per cent of the Scottish beer market). Canned lagers and beers satisfy the thirst of the significant Scottish take-home trade. A unique method of dispense for traditional beer is used in Scotland – the attractive tall pillar fount which involves the use of air pressure (not carbon dioxide) to raise the beer from the cellar.

Central Scotland

Scottish & Newcastle Breweries plc, Abbey Brewery, Edinburgh. Scottish & Newcastle Breweries is one of the six largest national brewing groups in the United Kingdom, and the only one with headquarters in Scotland. Indeed, Edinburgh has traditionally been one of the most important brewing centres in Britain. The company's origins date back to 1749 when a brewer named William Younger established a brewery which soon moved to Holyrood Abbey, near the present headquarters of the company (the Abbey's pure well water had been used by the former monks for brewing their own ales). In 1856 another famous Edinburgh brewery was founded by William McEwan in the nearby village of Fountainbridge. These two companies merged in 1931 to form Scottish Brewers Ltd; Scottish Brewers Ltd subsequently merged with Newcastle Breweries Ltd in 1960. Scottish & Newcastle products are available nationwide, but all Scottish ales are brewed in Edinburgh (the group also brews in Newcastle and Manchester). The company's best-selling Scottish ales and lagers include McEwan's Export – draught (keg) as well as in the familiar tartan can – Younger's Tartan, and McEwan's lager.

McEwan's 70/- o.g. 1034–38
McEwan's 80/- o.g. 1040–46
Younger's XXPS o.g. 1034–38
Younger's IPA o.g. 1040–46
Younger's No. 3 o.g. 1040–46

Drybrough & Co., Craigmillar, Edinburgh. This well-established Edinburgh brewery is now part of the Watney Mann & Truman brewing group though the company has been brewing in Edinburgh since 1750. Pentland, a dry, creamy cask-conditioned bitter is available mainly in Scotland and north-east England.

Pentland o.g. 1036
EIGHTY Shillings o.g. 1042

Tennent Caledonian Breweries Ltd, Glasgow & Edinburgh. The Tennent family were involved in brewing in Glasgow as long ago as 1556; Tennent's established the first successful lager brewing operation a hundred years ago in 1885 when Hugh Tennent brought over a team of German brewers. Tennent's lager continues to be the company's most important product, accounting for half of the Scottish lager market. Tennent's Export ale is a brewery-conditioned 80/- ale, while Tennent's 60/- Light is a lower-gravity dark ale. The company also produces a brewery-conditioned Bass Special (no relation to Draught Bass from Burton) and a strong bottled ale, Fowler's Wee Heavy, in addition to an extensive range of other canned and bottled products (Tennent's were one of the first breweries in Europe to introduce the use of cone-top cans). A cask-conditioned real ale has recently been introduced, Heriot Brewery Traditional 80/-, produced at the Heriot Brewery in Edinburgh. Tennent Caledonian Breweries are part of the Bass group.

Heriot Brewery Traditional 80/-
o.g. 1042

Lorimer & Clark, Caledonian Brewery, Edinburgh. Lorimer & Clark is part of the Vaux Breweries group based in Sunderland. The company's cask-conditioned ales are available not only in Scotland but in the north-east of England trading area of its parent company.

70/- o.g. 1036
80/- o.g. 1043

The Leith Brewing Co., Leith, Edinburgh. This young Edinburgh brewery was begun by real ale enthusiasts in 1982, and produces a fine traditionally-brewed, cask-conditioned Scotch ale, Leith Heavy, as well as a strong bottled dark heavy, Auld Admirality.

Leith Heavy o.g. 1039

Belhaven Brewery, Dunbar, East Lothian. The monks who settled at Belhaven in the fifteenth century soon discovered that the extremely hard water there was ideal for the brewing of beer; this same liquor, rich in natural mineral salts, continues to be used to produce a range of traditional beers that are among the most highly-regarded in Scotland. Unlike most other Scottish breweries, Belhaven's beers are available almost exclusively from free outlets rather than from brewery-controlled tied houses.

60/- Light o.g. 1031
70/- Heavy o.g. 1036
80/- Export o.g. 1042
90/- Strong Ale o.g. 1070

Maclay & Co., Thistle Brewery, Alloa. Alloa has long been a major Scottish brewing centre; the small Clackmannanshire town once had eight separate breweries in production. Maclay's, founded in 1830, remains one of the few long-standing independent breweries left in Scotland. The company produces cask-conditioned ales available in the brewery's tied houses mainly in central Scotland, as well as in numerous free outlets.

60/- Light o.g. 1030
70/- Heavy o.g. 1035
80/- Export o.g. 1040

Broughton Brewery Ltd, Broughton, Lanarkshire. Founded in 1979, Broughton supplies some 150 outlets in central and southern Scotland with its distinctive Greenmantle Ale.

Greenmantle Ale o.g. 1038

Borders
Traquair House, Innerleithen, Peebleshire (see p. 209)

Highlands
Aberdeen Ale Ltd, Devanha Brewery, Alford. This company was originally formed by real ale enthusiasts to provide north-east Scotland with a wide range of cask-conditioned ales from other breweries such as Jenning's, Marston's, Maclay's, Theakston's, Lorimer & Clark and others. An ambition was realized when it began brewing its own beers in 1982. Devanha ales are available in the Grampian and Tayside regions.

Devanha XB o.g. 1036
Devanha Triple X o.g. 1043

Alice Brewery, Inverness. The first local brewery in Inverness for fifty years was established in 1983, and produces Alice Ale, available in Aberdeen, Inverness, Fort William, and other parts of the Highlands.

Alice Ale o.g. 1040

Country Wines
As in other rural parts of Britain, domestic wine making using local fruits, wildflowers, saps and berries is a long-established tradition. At Moniack Castle, seat of the Clan Fraser, located in the rugged Highlands above Loch Ness, traditional Scottish country wines are being produced on a small commercial scale, to old clan recipes. Wines made from sap gathered from the silver birch (a favourite wine of Prince Albert's when he was at Balmoral), elderflower, rowanberry and meadow sweet are all being produced in this idyllic spot; visitors are welcome to visit the winery daily except Sundays, and there is a castle shop where the wines can be sampled as well as purchased.

Highland Wineries
Moniack Castle
near Inverness

Drambuie
Drambuie is as Scottish as the bagpipe, a whisky-based liqueur steeped in the legend and romance of the Highlands. After Charles Edward Stuart's crushing defeat at Culloden Moor in 1746, he sought refuge on Skye, with Mackinnon of Strathaird, a clansman who had fought alongside him. Bonnie Prince Charlie eventually lived out his life in exile, first in France then in Italy, but before escaping from Skye, he gave the Mackinnon family one of his few remaining treasures, the secret recipe for his personal liqueur. Today Drambuie is still made by the Mackinnon family to this well-guarded secret recipe. The exact combination of the drink, a mixture of rare whiskies flavoured with a secret Drambuie essence, is known by only one Mackinnon in each generation. The name, incidentally, is contracted from the Gaelic *dram buidheach* meaning 'the drink that satisfies'.

Some Useful Addresses
Scottish Tourist Board
23 Ravelston Terrace
Edinburgh

Charles Macsween & Son
130 Bruntsfield Place
Edinburgh
This traditional family butcher supplies haggis ranging in size from 1 lb to 18 lb ('Chieftain Haggis' hand-sewn in the paunch). Mail order service.

Summer Isles Foods
The Smokehouse
Achiltibuie
near Ullapool
Western Ross
Traditional smoked specialities, including smoked salmon, beer-cured ham, smoked mutton and smoked venison. Mail order service.

Highland Fine Cheeses
Tain
Ross and Cromarty
Crowdie, caboc and other Highland cheeses made on a small-scale by this family firm.

Highland Wineries
Moniack Castle
near Inverness
Scottish country wines. Mail order service.

Scottish Gourmet
The Bell Tower
New Lanark
Lanark
Scottish foods and specialities. Mail order service.

R. R. Spink & Sons
35 Seagate
Arbroath
Angus
Arbroath smokies and Finnan haddock available by post.

Cairngorm Whisky Centre & Museum
Inverdruie
Aviemore
Inverness-shire
Whisky audio-visual, tasting room with over seventy malt whiskies, and shop.

The Old Shop
Baxters of Speyside
Fochabers
Morayshire
Though Baxters' products are widely available, the company's reconstructed Old Shop in Fochabers is worth visiting if in the area.

Malt Whisky

Malt whisky is produced from a mash of malted barley only, fermented into a beery liquid known as wash, and twice-distilled in pot stills. As in the production of beer, barley must first be malted in order to enable its starches to be converted into fermentable sugar. This is achieved by steeping the barley in water to encourage germination, then (in a traditional floor maltings) spreading it out on the floor where the grains of barley sprout and soften. When the germination is complete, the green malt is dried in malt kilns (easily recognized by their pagoda roofs; most distilleries today, however, no longer have their own maltings, so the roofs have become purely decorative). Such kilns in the past were fired completely by peat, but now this fuel is only added to give a distinctive character to the malt. Each distillery has its own peat specification for its whiskies, ranging from very light, to the dense, pungent iodine-rich peatiness of the Islay whiskies. After the malt has been kilned, it is dressed and ground into grist.

The grist is mixed with hot water in a mash tun to draw off the soluble sugars, resulting in a sweet, syrupy liquid called wort, or worts. The characteristics of the water are very important, and distilleries are inevitably proud of their treasured source, tapped from an underground spring that has filtered through layers of peat or granite. The wort is passed into large fermenting vessels, into which the yeast is pitched, resulting in a vigorous fermentation that lasts for a few days. The beer-like alcoholic liquid that results from this brewing process is called wash. It is cloudy, watery and virtually undrinkable; yet through the magic of distillation, it is transformed into a fragrant, smooth and potent essence, malt whisky.

The process of distillation in pot stills requires two operations which turn successive liquids into vapours that are subsequently condensed and collected. First the wash is added to a squat, copper wash still (the shape of stills are unique to each distillery, their very dents and time-worn idiosyncracies essential to the final result). The still can be heated either directly by coal or gas fire, or indirectly by internal steam coils, and again either will effect the character of the whisky that results. As the wash vapourizes, it rises up into the tall neck of the still then condenses in the coiled worm into liquid. But the distillation that results is oily and impure, known as low wines (the residue of yeast and other matter left in the still, the pot ale, is sold for cattle feed).

The pungent low wines are next sent, via the low wines charger, to another copper vessel, the spirit still, and the process of distillation by vapourization is repeated once again. Now, however, the keen judgement of the stillman comes into play. For the vapour which first rises, the foreshots, contains undesirable impurities. It must therefore be directed back to the spirit still to be redistilled. Similarly, the tail end of each run, the feints, also contains elements which are unacceptable, and it must also be redirected for further distillation. The stillman, by viewing – never tasting – the emerging liquids in the spirit safe, is able to determine precisely what parts of each run make up the foreshots, the middle cut and the feints. Only the middle cut – pure, colourless malt whisky – is directed into the spirit receiver to be collected.

The final element necessary for the production of malt whisky is time. The complex flavouring elements of this marvellous spirit only emerge after patient ageing in oak casks, for a legal minimum of three, and up to twenty years and longer. Some distilleries age their finest whisky in sherry casks for it imparts a natural golden hue and perhaps a little smoothness, too; others use charred bourbon casks brought over from America. The majority of malt whiskies, of course, are never bottled as such. The public taste, say the whisky companies, is for lighter, less highly-flavoured spirits, and this has led to the popularity of blended Scotch whisky. True, some single malt whiskies have an assertive aroma and distinctive palate which is undoubtedly an acquired taste. Yet other malts are considerably lighter, positively elegant and aristocratic compared to the oily pungency of even some of the finer blends. Each to his or her own taste. What is inarguable is that pure single malt whisky is one of the greatest drinks in the world.

Peat is an essential part of the kilning process, for it is added to the fire to give flavour and aroma, the characteristic 'peat reek' so loved by malt whisky connoisseurs.

The wash and spirit stills at the Glenfiddich Distillery.

A variety of single malt whiskies in a blender's warehouse.

Opposite: Green malt in the loft at Balvenie Distillery's traditional floor maltings.

WALES

The food of Wales recalls its ancient, Celtic traditions. In the mining valleys of the south and in villages in the north perched below mountains of slate shards, in quiet coastal fishing harbours, through a rolling rural landscape of sheep-dotted hills and chuckling salmon rivers, to the rugged upland farms of Prescelly, it is one which has developed to satisfy the needs of hardworking men and women: the appetites of farm labourers and coal miners, of quarrymen and fishermen.

Many English culinary traditions developed from the top, that is from the amply stocked larders and groaning sideboards of aristocratic country mansions, but the true tastes of Wales, the 'old foods' that people still speak of and relish with such fondness, come from a harsh Celtic land which yielded not a lot, but enough to satisfy. The bleak uplands of the Principality could support few cereal crops other than oats, and thus, in common with other Celtic countries, they form part of the staple diet, used as a cereal in soups or porridge, or shaped into thin cakes and cooked on the *planc* or bakestone.

While today we regard sweet mountain lamb as the Welsh national speciality, that full-flavoured meat was almost certainly reserved for holidays or special occasions only; it was the lowly pig that formed the mainstay of the diet. In rural areas certainly, and even in semi-urban parts of the mining valleys, the *twlc*, or pig-sty at the bottom of every garden, was an enduring feature, the annual pig slaughter, performed by an itinerant butcher, an exciting ritual.

Bacon remains today an essential and favourite food. Together with root vegetables such as leeks and cabbage (the only two vegetables cultivated in Wales, according to the tenth-century Laws of Hywel Dda), it forms the basis for what is virtually the national dish of Wales: *cawl*. There is no exact translation for *cawl*; the word in Welsh signifies 'broth' or 'soup', but it is much more than that, a classic one-pot meal, originally cooked in an iron pot over an open fire, containing all the goodness of the land: fat home-cured bacon, scraps of sweet Welsh lamb to flavour the stock, cabbage and orange-tinted swedes, tiny marble-sized new potatoes, and slender, thin leeks, added to the pot only at the very end so that they are still raw and crunchy and peppery. Recipes for *cawl* vary from region to region, house to house, and from season to season, depending on what vegetables and produce are available. While *cawl* can be eaten all together, that is meat and broth served in a bowl, in many houses the broth is served first, and the meat and vegetables follow afterwards.

Another simple favourite that warms the heart of many a Welshman also indicates the importance of bacon and root vegetables in the daily diet of the past: *tatws rhost*, no more than fat rashers of bacon placed over slices of potato, sprinkled with green onions and a little water, and cooked over the open fire. A simple, filling food of the land, certainly, but today still enjoyed equally by businessmen and professionals in Cardiff or Swansea, as well as by farm-hands in Meirionnydd and coal miners in the Valleys.

Until the development of the coal mines in the south and the slate quarries in the north, Wales remained essentially an agricultural country, made up of numerous small-holdings and tenant farms. Along the coast, of course, fishing was and to a certain extent remains an important industry. Great shoals of herring and mackerel were caught off the west coast and these plentiful fish were simply fried in bacon fat, roasted on a toasting fork, salted or preserved.

Along the Gower, the lovely, magical peninsula that extends between Swansea and industrial Llanelli, oysters were once caught in great quantities at Port Einon. Indeed, throughout Britain, oysters used to be prolific, though here, as elsewhere, they have since become scarce, and thus an expensive luxury. Even in

The rugged countryside of North Wales.

the past they tended to be an item sold for cash rather than eaten locally. However, one shellfish that continues to provide a source of inexpensive protein to a coastal people is the cockle. Across the Gower, in Penclawdd and other tiny villages, the cocklemen and cocklewomen continue to gather this humble shellfish as they have for centuries. The Gower peninsula used to be the centre for another indigenous food industry, for indeed it is only in Wales, and parts of Scotland and Ireland, that an edible seaweed known as laver is gathered and processed commercially. Available already cooked and prepared in numerous markets throughout Wales, *bara lawr* (laverbread) is usually eaten sprinkled with fine Welsh oatmeal, then warmed in hot bacon fat and served with bacon for breakfast or supper. The seaweed itself can be found in some parts of the west coast, clinging to the rocks at low tide. But

its location is fickle, for it seems to shift and relocate at different times of the year. Perhaps it is there, but just covered in sand.

Wales is an ancient land, indeed, still in many ways very much a separate country, as visitors to the Welsh-speaking west and north soon realize. The lovely sing-song of the language, heard in pubs and shops and markets, is wonderfully, incomprehensibly strange to those of us not familiar with it. The fisherman who knocks at the back door of the pub with a string of trout, or maybe a salmon or *sewin* (the Welsh name for sea trout) speaks Welsh because it is his native language, the language he speaks at home, and which his children learn in school. It is a language as ageless as the pitch-covered coracle from which he plies his trade. The design of this tiny, almost circular boat has altered little since neolithic days. It is hardly more than a wicker frame

Welsh cakes, fresh off the bakestone.

St David's Day.

covered no longer with hide but with calico that has been sealed with boiling pitch. Coracles are remarkably manoeuvrable, and on rivers such as the Teifi, Tywi, Taf and Cleddau, remarkably efficient, too, a factor which has led to their unfortunate decline in use, due to overfishing.

Specialities such as salmon, *sewin* or other seasonal delicacies such as wild mushrooms might appear on the table not as a main meal, but at supper, just as a small taste to be savoured. Supper, as opposed to the main midday meal, is generally a light snack at eight or nine in the evening. However, mealtimes in Wales tend to revolve around the main householder's occupation. In the north, there is a meal known as the *swper chwarel* or quarry supper, at five in the afternoon, when the men return to the light once more from the subterranean depths of slate caves in Blaenau Ffestiniog and elsewhere. Coal miners

work shifts, and this obviously affects when meals are taken. Likewise, farmers' and farm labourers' mealtimes vary according to the time of year and the jobs at hand.

Today, certainly, many more people work regular hours, but one meal which remains loved by all, even if no longer indulged in daily, is the traditional Welsh tea. In the past, as elsewhere, baking was done just once a week, and in addition to breads such as wholemeal, rye, barley or maslin (made with a mixture of flours), such favourites as *bara brith* (the famous 'speckled bread' of Wales) would be put in the wall oven alongside the week's loaves. In many parts of Wales, however, more often than not Welsh breads and cakes were baked over or in front of an open fire in improvised pot and Dutch ovens. *Teisen lap* is one such traditional Welsh cake, no more than a moist, shallow fruit cake, while

Cawl.

others, delicious in their surprisingly extensive use of spices, include *teisen carawe* (caraway seed cake), *teisen sinamon* (cinnamon cake), and *teisen mêl* (honey cake). Such cakes are still made today throughout Wales, though the recipes of the past have been updated for cooking in modern ovens. Did they taste better when made the old way?

Alongside such cakes and breads, a wide selection of griddle cakes is also offered at teatime. The griddle or bakestone is a traditional flat iron, slate or stone plate that rests over an open fire, and cooking on this primitive utensil has been developed in Wales to a fine art. A variety of scones, pancakes, cakes, breads, turnovers and oatcakes are all cooked on the well-greased bakestone. There are few homes in Wales that do not have an ever-present tin of Welsh cakes on hand to offer to family and visiting friends. Welsh cakes are delicious when fresh off the bakestone: spicy and moist and sprinkled with sugar. Additionally, bread is cooked on the bakestone, *bara planc*, perhaps rather heavy for modern tastes, but unique in taste, and a reminder of the days when ovens were a luxury not in every or even in most homes. Fruit tarts such as gooseberry or rhubarb are also cooked on the bakestone: large pasty-sized turnovers, flipped with a flat wooden slice or spatula. Furthermore, the bakestone could be adapted to an oven by inverting an iron pot over the hot, flat surface.

The Welsh are extremely fond of their *crempog* (pancakes) stacked into layers, and oozing with good salty Welsh butter. *Bara pyglyd* (pikelets) are another favourite, the spongy holes unequalled in their ability to absorb butter. Welsh butter, incidentally, is generally very highly salted, perhaps to some an acquired taste, though much missed by Welshmen when far from home.

Welshmen, once away from Wales, have a sentimental longing for the tastes of their past. But the visitor to the Principality, curiously, will not find the Welsh over-enthusiastic about their food traditions. Perhaps this is because the true foods of Wales, the 'old foods' remembered with such gusto, are also reminders of another, less prosperous, less fortunate age. Surely such country foods as *cawl*, home-made faggots, or *tatws rhost* are delicious to us, though they might not be quite so appealing if that was all there was to

The Coracle

The coracle is one of the most ancient craft in Britain, a tiny one-man river boat whose design has changed little since neolithic days. Today, though diminishing, they are still to be found on rivers in Wales such as the Teifi, Taf, Tywi and Cleddau, fishing in pairs for salmon and *sewin*.

Though the individual design of the craft varies somewhat from river to river to take account of local water conditions, a coracle is made from a frame of hazel twigs and pieces of flat willow covered with calico and coated with boiling pitch to make it watertight. There is a wooden seat roughly in the middle of this almost circular craft. The fishermen carry their coracles over their heads to the river, hooking the ash paddle behind the seat to provide leverage and serve as a handle.

eat, day in, day out, supplemented by a dreary diet of *sucan* (a sort of gruel made from milled oats) and things like sheep's head broth. Social implications impede, too, for the diet of the past was a diet which had to make a little feel like a lot, albeit sometimes quite successfully and deliciously.

The rich in Wales, on the other hand, did not eat the foods of the country, but, living in their comfortable *plas* (such mansions are to be found throughout the country, topping the finest positions overlooking valleys and villages), tended to ape the English, to deny the Welshness of Wales. This social divide was apparent in many other aspects of life: the landed gentry were (mainly) Church of England, Conservative in politics, and, of course, non-Welsh speaking. The *gwern*, on the other hand (the word translates roughly as 'peasantry', though its meaning is much richer), were non-conformist, devout chapel-goers, Liberal or Whig in politics, and were concerned with safeguarding the culture and language of Wales. The foods of Wales are just as much a part of this nation's culture and history, and likewise should be safeguarded, not as an historical relic from times past, but simply because they can be so delicious.

A century ago there were some 300 licenses for coracle fishing on the River Teifi, but today only a handful remain. Coracle fishing is extremely efficient and stocks in the rivers have become depleted over the years. When fishing, a twenty-foot net is stretched between two coracles. The salmon or *sewin* enter the net through large holes, and when the fishermen sense this, they draw a horsehair rope tight, so closing the net. Then they paddle towards each other, the boats approaching one another with a strange shuffling dance. If there is a *sewin*, they empty their net of its precious catch, then part to begin fishing once more. Afterwards the fishermen, the coracles slung over their backs, may waddle down to the local pub or restaurant, where a grateful landlord relieves them of their fish in exchange for cash and, no doubt, a pint or two of well-earned Felinfoel or Buckley's bitter.

A Teifi coracle.

Recipes from Wales

Swper Scadan (Welsh Herring Supper)   (Serves 4)

Herring was once landed in great quantities in Wales, particularly at the western harbour of Aberystwyth. As elsewhere in Britain, it formed a staple diet for many.

6–8 herring, cleaned, scaled and filleted	900 g/2 lb potatoes, peeled and thinly sliced
1 tbsp prepared mustard	1 large onion, sliced
Salt	2 cooking apples, peeled, cored and sliced
Freshly-ground black pepper	Freshly-chopped sage
25 g/1 oz/¼ stick butter	

Clean the fish and pat dry. Spread the inside of each with mustard, season with salt and pepper, and roll up. Grease an ovenproof dish and layer with half the potato slices. Then layer with onions, then apples. Lay the rolled herring on top, and season with more salt and pepper and sprinkle with the sage. Cover with the remaining potatoes. Pour on enough boiling water to come half-way up the dish. Dot with butter, cover with foil and bake in a moderate oven (180°C/350°F/Gas Mark 4) for 45 minutes. Remove the foil and cook for a further 30 minutes.

Poached *Sewin* Cutlets with Cucumber Sauce   (Serves 4)

Sewin (sea trout) is a glorious fish, more prized in Wales even than salmon. It is delicate in flavour, and thus needs gentle treatment.

4 thick *sewin* cutlets	2 carrots, sliced
1 tsp sea salt	1 bay leaf
12 black peppercorns	1 tbsp vinegar
1 large onion, sliced	

Cucumber sauce

100 g/4 oz/1 stick butter	Salt
1 small onion, chopped	Freshly-ground black pepper
1 lettuce, shredded	
1 small cucumber, peeled and very finely diced	

Place the cutlets in a large saucepan and cover with cold water. Add the salt, black peppercorns, onion, carrots, bay leaf and vinegar. Poach, covered, on top of the stove for 10–15 minutes, or until just tender. When cooked, remove the fish from the liquid (reserve this) and skin, removing the centre bone if desired. Serve hot with the cucumber sauce.

To make the sauce, melt the butter in a saucepan, and gently fry the onion until soft but not brown. Add the lettuce and cucumber, and a spoonful of the reserved cooking liquid. Simmer for a few minutes, season to taste, and serve over the *sewin*.

219

Laverbread

Laver is a fine edible seaweed. In the south of the Principality, along the Gower coast and elsewhere, it used to be present in sufficient quantity to make it commercially viable for those who gathered and processed this indigenous sea vegetable. Its movement, though, is fickle, but it still lingers around the coastline of the country, clinging to the rocks at places such as Llangrangog. Come at low tide, when the thin, fine leaves have been left dry and revealed. As you pluck it from the rocks, it makes a plaintive sound, as if you were gently tugging the hair of a sleeping mermaid.

Bara lawr, or laverbread, is laver which has been collected and processed by slow cooking for upwards of six hours. It remains a popular Welsh favourite, found in markets throughout South Wales, and is still eaten regularly by many. It is not, of course, a bread at all; it looks like a shimmering mass of spinach-green jelly, when spooned out of large plastic tubs by Welshwomen in the Swansea market. It comes either 'with' or 'without' – fine Welsh oatmeal, that is. The oatmeal, claim some, makes the laverbread stay together better while it cooks. Laverbread when purchased, in fact, is already cooked, so it needs

Stuffed Trout with Bacon (Serves 4)

Fresh river trout, a fisherman's favourite, are quickly gutted, wrapped in bacon, then cooked on a hot bakestone, preferably beside the riverbank. The lemon and parsley stuffing included here is probably an English adaptation, gleaned from a mother or grandmother who worked in the kitchen of the *plas*, the mansion. Today it is easier to bake the trout, rather than to cook it on the bakestone.

Stuffed trout with bacon.

4 fresh, cleaned trout
8 slices of bacon, preferably thick-cut, home-cured

Parsley and lemon wedges to garnish

Stuffing

75 g/3 oz/1 cup dry brown breadcrumbs
Grated rind of 1 lemon
Pinch of marjoram or thyme
2 tbsp chopped parsley
Salt

Freshly-ground black pepper
2 tbsp melted butter
Splash of lemon juice to moisten

220

little more than to be warmed up. Though it is good as a side dish with roast lamb, or made into a sauce with the addition of fresh orange juice (serve this with cold Welsh salt duck), every Welshman or woman that we have spoken to eats it only one way: fried in bacon fat, and served with bacon, toast or bread, for breakfast or tea.

Laverbread with Bacon (Serves 2)

4 rashers back bacon
2–3 tbsp fine oatmeal
225 g/$\frac{1}{2}$ lb laverbread

Buttered toast or home-made bread

Fry the bacon in a pan until done. Remove and drain it on paper towels. Mix the oatmeal with the laverbread. Lower the heat, and add the laverbread to the hot bacon fat. Cook for about 5–10 minutes, or until heated thoroughly (but do not burn, or it will be very bitter). Serve immediately, with the bacon and toast or bread and butter.

Opposite: Laverbread and bacon: a favourite Welsh breakfast.

Leeks, the national emblem of Wales.

Take the heads and tails off the trout. Remove the backbone from the fish (do this by running the flat blade of a large knife along the back, pressing down firmly to loosen the bone; then turn the fish over, and work the backbone free with the fingers or a small knife).

To make the stuffing, mix the breadcrumbs with the lemon rind, herbs and seasonings, and moisten with melted butter and lemon juice. Stuff this mixture into the cavities of the boned trout. Wrap each fish in a couple of slices of bacon.

Place the fish in an ovenproof dish, and bake in a pre-heated moderately hot oven (190°C/375°F/Gas Mark 5) for 15–20 minutes. To serve, garnish with parsley and lemon slices.

Leek Soup (Serves 4)

The leek is the national emblem of Wales, pinned on to patriotic Welshmen's lapels at international rugby fixtures at Cardiff Arms Park and on St David's Day in March. Leeks were one of the few root vegetables indigenous to Wales, and remain an essential ingredient in many dishes.

25 g/1 oz/$\frac{1}{4}$ stick butter
4 rashers of bacon, chopped
4 large leeks, chopped
450 g/1 lb potatoes, peeled and quartered
600 ml/1 pt/2$\frac{1}{2}$ cups stock

Salt
Freshly-ground black pepper
150 ml/$\frac{1}{4}$ pt/$\frac{2}{3}$ cup milk
Freshly-chopped parsley

Melt the butter in a large saucepan, and sauté the bacon. Add the leeks and fry gently for 5 minutes, then add the potatoes. Pour on the stock, and season with salt and pepper. Bring to the boil and simmer for 30–40 minutes. Liquidize, add the milk and re-heat. Sprinkle with parsley and serve with a lump of Caerphilly on the side.

Cawl (Serves 4–6)

Cawl is virtually the national dish of the Welsh.
Everyone has their own recipe which inevitably
varies according to what is in season and available; it
is generally agreed that *cawl* gets better and better for
being re-heated, with new ingredients added to the
pot the following day. The meat used is bacon, lamb or
beef, or a mixture of all three. Any fresh winter
vegetables that are available, such as leeks, turnips,
potatoes, cabbage, swedes and carrots, complete the
mixture. Crunchy, raw young leeks are chopped and
added to each bowl before serving. Like famous one-
pot meals from other lands, the broth can be eaten
first, and the meat removed and served as the main
course. We feel, though, that it is even better eaten all
together in one bowl. Traditionally, *cawl* is eaten with
hand-made wooden *cawl*-spoons, which keep too-
eager mouths from burning. A piece of cheese is
generally nibbled while eating *cawl*.

1 tbsp lard or bacon fat
2 onions, coarsely chopped
2 parsnips, roughly
  chopped
4 carrots, coarsely sliced
1 swede, coarsely chopped
450 g/1 lb piece of brisket of
  beef or neck of lamb
675–900 g/1½–2 lb piece of
  smoked bacon (use collar
  or shoulder), soaked if
  necessary

12 black peppercorns
1 clove
1 bay leaf
Sprig of fresh thyme
Water or lamb stock
450 g/1 lb potatoes
  (preferably tiny and
  new)
4 leeks (slender, thin ones,
  if possible)

Heat the lard or bacon fat in a large soup pot, and
brown the onions, carrots, parsnips and swede.
Remove with a slotted spoon, and brown the meat in
the fat. Return the vegetables to the pot with the meat,
and add the bacon and herbs. Cover with water. Bring
to the boil, skim and simmer for 2–3 hours. If the
potatoes are not new, cut into pieces; add the potatoes
20 minutes before the end of cooking. Meanwhile,
finely chop the slender leeks, and reserve.

To serve, put a piece of meat in each bowl, together
with broth and vegetables. Garnish with lots of finely
chopped raw leeks. Serve together with a hunk of
cheese and bread, preferably home-made.

Welsh Salt Duck (Serves 4)

Salting duck as a means of preservation (like salt beef
or salt pork) is a traditional Welsh method which
changes this usually roasted bird into a different
animal altogether. Lady Llanover, who published her

Hand-making wooden *cawl* spoons.

Good Cookery in 1867, was a champion of this and
other indigenous Welsh cooking methods and dishes;
she preferred to cook her salt duck in a 'double', that
is, in a water-bath or *bain-marie*. Though it is superb
simply boiled and served hot or cold, our friend in
Llangoedmor who introduced us to this and other
Welsh foods confirms that cooking in a 'double' makes
this unique delicacy even more succulent and smooth.

1 good-sized duck
Water for boiling

225 g/½ lb sea salt

Wipe the duck and place in a deep dish. Rub all over
with sea salt and set aside covered in a cool place for 3
days. Turn the duck daily, and rub the salt well into
the skin. Before cooking, rinse off the salt, and place in
a large pot (or a 'double', if using). Cover with water,
and bring to the boil, then reduce the heat to a very
gentle simmer. Cook for about 2 hours or until tender.

Salt duck can be served hot (Lady Llanover suggests
serving it with a white onion sauce), or cold. To serve
cold, allow the duck to cool in its cooking liquid.
Remove (reserve the liquid for soup), skin, and cut the
flesh into strips. Lay on a platter lined with lettuce
leaves. Serve with a sauce made of laver warmed with
a little butter and fresh orange juice and zest.

Roast Welsh Lamb with Honey and Rosemary (Serves 8)

Sweet Welsh mountain lamb is as succulent and full of flavour as any in the land. Welsh clover honey and rosemary combine extravagantly with this meat, though in poorer times, precious honey would never have been 'wasted' on a meat which already has so much flavour.

1.35–1.8 kg/3–4 lb leg of lamb	Salt
8 tbsp Welsh clover honey	Freshly-ground black pepper
Sprig of fresh rosemary	300 ml/½ pt/1¼ cups dry cider or stock
Freshly-chopped mint	

Place the leg of lamb in a roasting tin. Heat 6 tbsp of the honey to thin it, and brush over the lamb. Season with salt and pepper, and sprinkle with chopped rosemary and mint. Pour on half of the cider or stock, and roast in a hot oven (220°C/425°F/Gas Mark 7) for 15 minutes, then lower the heat to moderate (180°C/350°F/Gas Mark 4) for a further 1–1¼ hours, or until the juices run just pink when the meat is pierced with a skewer (depending on the size of the leg of lamb; cook for longer if well-done lamb is preferred). Baste with the juices during cooking.

Remove the lamb from the oven, and transfer to a warmed serving dish. Keep warm and allow to rest before carving. Skim off the excess fat from the roasting tin, and add the remaining 2 tbsp of honey while stirring over a low heat. Add the remaining cider or stock, stir continuously and scrape the meat juices from the tin. Adjust seasoning, and serve this honey sauce separately in a gravy boat with the carved lamb.

Glamorgan Sausages (Makes about 10)

Glamorgan sausages contain no meat; they are a cheesy Welsh savoury, popular at tea-time.

100 g/4 oz/1⅓ cups mature Cheddar, grated	Pinch of thyme
100 g/4 oz/1⅓ cups fresh white breadcrumbs	Salt
1 small onion, finely chopped	Freshly-ground black pepper
1 tsp dry mustard	2 eggs
1 tbsp freshly-chopped parsley	Dry breadcrumbs to coat
	Oil or bacon fat for frying

Mix together the grated cheese, breadcrumbs and onion. Beat the remaining dry ingredients and seasonings into 1 whole egg and 1 egg yolk. Bind the cheese and breadcrumbs with this egg mixture. Form into about ten small 'sausages'. Dip in the beaten egg white and roll in the dry breadcrumbs. Fry in hot oil or bacon fat until crisp and golden. Drain on kitchen towel, and serve hot.

Caws Pobi (Welsh Rarebit) (Serves 4)

The Welsh have a particular partiality to 'toasted cheese'; this recipe, however, has since become a favourite throughout Britain.

225 g/8 oz/2½ cups grated cheese	Freshly-ground black pepper
25 g/1 oz/¼ stick butter	1 tbsp dry mustard
4 tbsp beer	4 slices hot buttered toast
Salt	

Put the grated cheese, butter and beer in a saucepan and melt gently over a low heat, stirring in one direction only. Add salt, pepper and mustard and mix well. Spoon over the toast, and brown under a hot grill. Serve at once.

Tatws Rhost (Roast Potatoes and Bacon) (Serves 6)

This simple dish would, in the past, have been cooked in a *ffwrn fach*, the little pot oven which once stood over every open fire.

900 g/2 lb potatoes, peeled and sliced	Salt
1 bunch of spring onions, sliced	Freshly-ground black pepper
6 rashers of bacon, preferably thick-cut, home-cured	

In a greased ovenproof casserole place the sliced potatoes and cover with the sliced spring onions. Lay the thick bacon rashers over the potatoes, and season with salt and plenty of black pepper. Add a little water, cover with foil, and cook in a moderately hot oven (190°C/375°F/Gas Mark 5) for 45 minutes.

Welsh Tea

Tea-time hardly ever passes unnoticed in the Welsh countryside. Every afternoon at about four o'clock the kettle is filled and placed on top of the glowing solid-fuel cooker. Chores are forgotten for the moment, and men come in from the outside. If a special friend from a neighbouring farm is visiting, then the best flowered bone china cups are carefully taken down from their cup hooks on the polished Welsh dresser. The *bara brith* is sliced and spread with good salty butter, and a plate is piled high with Welsh cakes, fresh off the bakestone. If you're offered a cup of tea, it never means just that: moist *teisen lap*, *teisen sinamon*, and *cacen gneifio* are laid out together with a substantial spread of home-made breads, scones and jam, pikelets and piles of pancakes oozing with butter, and much else. 'No, no, it's no trouble at all,' the farmer's wife smiles with a twinkle in her eye, as she thrusts yet another Welsh cake or slice of raisin-speckled bread towards you. How can you refuse?

A Welsh tea: (clockwise) *teisen sinamon*, Pembrokeshire buns, *teisen carawe*, *cacen Iago* (St James's cakes), *bara brith*, *ffroes*, apple cake, Welsh cakes.

Anglesey Eggs (Serves 4–6)

Anglesey, separated from North Wales by the Menai Strait, is a large island extending into the Irish Sea. Anglesey eggs, a simple, tasty way of using up left-over potatoes and heels of cheese, have been enjoyed for tea or supper by many Welsh and English holiday-makers here.

6 small leeks, chopped	1 tbsp flour
450 g/1 lb hot mashed potato	300 ml/½ pt/1¼ cups hot milk
75 g/3 oz/¾ stick butter	Pinch of grated nutmeg
Salt	75 g/3 oz/1 cup grated cheese
Freshly-ground black pepper	8 hard-boiled eggs

Boil the leeks for 5–10 minutes, strain and combine with the mashed potato. Season well, and beat in half the butter until the mixture is fluffy. Arrange in a greased ovenproof dish.

To make the cheese sauce, melt 25 g/1 oz/¼ stick of butter in a saucepan and stir in the flour. Cook for a couple of minutes, stirring constantly. Remove from the heat and gradually add the hot milk, mixing vigorously. When smooth, return to the heat and bring to the boil, stirring all the while. Allow to simmer gently until thick. Add nutmeg, most of the grated cheese, and season to taste.

Halve the hard-boiled eggs and arrange on the bed of leek and potatoes. Cover with the cheese sauce, sprinkle with the remaining grated cheese and dot with remaining butter. Bake in a moderately hot oven (200°C/400°F/Gas Mark 6) until brown.

Farm-fresh eggs for sale alongside the road in North Wales.

Welsh Cheese

Caerphilly is the only nationally known Welsh cheese. Cheese making was carried out in the past, particularly in the fertile, low-lying dairy lands. In the rugged and sparse uplands, however, the poor ground often could barely support sheep or goats. It is probable that ewes' milk cheeses were once made on such farms, and today there is a revival in soft, creamy goats' milk cheeses. Such cheeses, though, are most often for local consumption only, but if there is a surplus, then it is usually sold through local shops.

Caerphilly This mild, crumbly white cheese originated in South Wales, where it quickly became popular with the growing population in the industrialized Valleys. Today farmhouse Caerphilly, made in traditional rounds with natural rinds, is made only in Somerset, not in Wales, though mild, crumbly block cheese is made in creameries in the Principality as well as elsewhere.

Llangloffan Llangloffan is a hard, traditional cheese with a creamy texture, made on one farm only at Castle Morris, Pembrokeshire.

Ffroes (Pancakes)

Small pancakes, piled into a stack, and spread with lots of salty butter are another Welsh tea-time favourite.

225 g/½ lb plain flour	25 g/1 oz/¼ stick butter, melted
Pinch of salt	
2 eggs	
300 ml/½ pt/1¼ cups milk and water mixed	

Sieve the flour and salt into a large mixing bowl and make a well in the centre. Break in the eggs and gradually incorporate into the flour. As the mixture becomes thick, slowly add the milk and water, beating all the time. When the batter is smooth, add the melted butter and beat again thoroughly. Drop ladlefuls of batter on a hot, well-greased bakestone or heavy frying pan. Cook the pancakes until browned, then flip and cook the undersides. Transfer to a hot plate and spread with butter. Repeat, as above, layering the cooked pancakes on top of each other. Cut into wedges (like cake) and serve hot.

Welsh Cakes

These small griddle cakes are popular throughout the Principality; indeed, there are few houses that do not have an ever-present tinful on hand for guests and family alike.

450 g/1 lb plain flour
1 tsp baking powder
Pinch of allspice
Pinch of salt
100 g/4 oz/1 stick butter
100 g/4 oz/$\frac{1}{2}$ cup vegetable
   shortening

200 g/7 oz/1 cup sugar
100 g/4 oz/$\frac{3}{4}$ cup seedless
   raisins
2 eggs, beaten
Milk to mix
A little sugar to sprinkle

Sieve the flour, baking powder, allspice and salt together in a large mixing bowl, and rub in the butter and shortening. Add the sugar and raisins. Bind with the beaten eggs and a little milk to make a fairly stiff dough. Roll out and form into rounds, using a circular pastry-cutter with a serrated edge, or a glass.

Cook on a well-greased bakestone, or in a heavy iron frying pan for about three minutes a side. The cakes should just turn golden brown, and must be cooked through to the middle, but they should not be too dried out. Sprinkle with sugar, and serve while still warm.

Teisen Lap (Moist Cake)

This moist cake is a particular favourite of many a Welshman. Every recipe is different, but mother's is always the best.

Welsh cakes and breads, baked on the premises, at Nancy Morgan's, Swansea.

225 g/½ lb plain flour
Pinch of salt
1 tsp baking powder
Pinch of freshly-grated nutmeg

100 g/4 oz/1 stick butter
50 g/2 oz/¼ cup castor sugar
100 g/4 oz/⅔ cup currants
2 eggs, well beaten
150 ml/¼ pt/⅔ cup milk

Sieve the flour, salt, baking powder and nutmeg into a large mixing bowl. Rub in the butter. Add the sugar and currants and mix well. Beat in the eggs and slowly add the milk. The mixture should be soft and fairly moist. Turn into a round shallow baking tin, and place in a moderately hot oven (200°C/400°F/Gas Mark 6) for about 30–40 minutes.

Bara Brith

The famous 'speckled bread' of Wales was originally a variation of the weekly loaf, sweetened with sugar, and with raisins and currants pressed into the dough. Though some recipes now use baking powder as the raising agent, the best *bara brith* is still made with yeast.

150 ml/¼ pt/⅔ cup milk
50 g/2 oz/⅓ cup brown sugar
10 g/⅓ oz dried yeast
450 g/1 lb wheatmeal flour
1 tsp salt
1 tsp mixed spice

75 g/3 oz/¾ stick butter
75 g/3 oz/½ cup raisins
75 g/3 oz/½ cup currants
25 g/1 oz/⅙ cup chopped candied peel

Heat the milk until tepid, dissolve the sugar and sprinkle on the yeast. Set aside in a warm place until frothy, about 15 minutes. Meanwhile, mix the flour, salt and spices together, and rub in the butter. Make a well in the middle of the flour and add the yeast mixture. Mix well. Cover with a clean, damp cloth, and set aside to rise in a warm place until doubled in bulk (about 1½ hours). Knock back and knead, then work in the fruit and peel. Turn into a warmed and buttered loaf tin. Cover, set aside in a warm place, and leave to rise again for a further 1–2 hours.

Bake in a hot oven (220°C/425°F/Gas Mark 7) for 20–30 minutes. Cover the top of the loaf with foil for the last 10 minutes. Allow to cool, and serve cut into slices, buttered and arranged on a plate.

Cacen Gneifio (Shearing Cake)

In the old days, the first cakes were probably made with left-over bread dough into which light ingredients such as seeds were pressed. This shearing cake, with its distinctive flavouring of caraway, is a traditional harvest cake.

450 g/1 lb plain flour
225 g/8 oz/2 sticks butter
Pinch of salt
2 tsp baking powder
350 g/12 oz/1¾ cups castor sugar

Grated rind of 1 lemon
4 tsp caraway seeds
Pinch of freshly-grated nutmeg
300 ml/½ pt/1¼ cups milk
2 eggs, beaten

Sieve the flour into a large mixing bowl, and rub in the butter. Add all other dry ingredients. Stir in the milk and beaten eggs and mix well. Turn into a greased and lined cake tin and bake in a moderate oven (160°C/325°F/Gas Mark 3) for 30 minutes, then reduce to a slow oven (150°C/300°F/Gas Mark 2) for a further 2 hours.

Teisen Sinamon (Cinnamon Cake)

This cake is splendid both in appearance and in flavour, with its topping of meringue, and its moist, crumbly texture.

225 g/½ lb plain flour
Pinch of salt
½ tsp baking powder
100 g/4 oz/1 stick butter
100 g/4 oz/½ cup castor sugar

1 tsp cinnamon
3 eggs, separated
1 tbsp sugar
About 6 tbsp milk
Raspberry jam

Sieve the flour, salt and baking powder into a large mixing bowl. Rub in the butter. Add sugar, cinnamon, and 3 beaten egg yolks, and mix well to form a stiff paste. Add the milk to moisten, although the dough should be quite firm. Turn into a shallow baking tin and place in a moderately hot oven (200°C/400°F/Gas Mark 6) for about 25 minutes or until cooked. Allow to cool. Spread top with raspberry jam. Make a meringue by beating the 3 egg whites until stiff with 1 tbsp of sugar. Spread this meringue on top of the cake, and return to a slow oven (150°C/300°F/Gas Mark 2) until set and pale gold, about 20 minutes. This cake should ideally be eaten immediately, before the jam makes it go soggy.

The Village Mill

In the past, every village or rural area had its own mill, providing the community with stone-ground wholegrain flours for home-baking, and with essential feed for livestock. Ducks paddled in the mill-pond, and the noise of revolving gears, wheels and pulleys provided a constant background hum to life in the village. The mill, if not a focal point of rural life, was certainly an essential feature of it. Then progress came, and high-speed commercial roller mills eventually replaced the water-powered ones. But the flour that they provide us with is not of the same quality as that of old.

And so today the old mills are being revived. Mill-ponds that have lain stagnant and disused for decades are being cleared of rubble and rubbish, and old mill-wheels are restored to working order, the broken paddles replaced with newly-fashioned pieces of oak and beech. Water is diverted into mill-streams again, and the ducks have returned. In Dyfed two such old mills have been restored to working order: Felin Geri, at Cwm Cou near Newcastle Emlyn, and Y Felin, at St Dogmaels, above Cardigan. While we shall never return to the days when each locality had its own mill, nevertheless stone-ground flours from these and other mills throughout the country are now readily available.

Left: The mill-wheel at Y Felin, St Dogmaels, near Cardigan.

Opposite: A selection of Welsh breads: (from l. to r.) wheatmeal, maslin, dolly loaves (baked in earthenware marmalade pots), and wholewheat buns.

Welsh Breads

The diet in Wales in the past consisted mainly of root vegetables, bacon and grains. Breads, like almost everything else, were cooked on the bakestone or in the *ffwrn fach*, methods which no doubt took considerable skill to achieve acceptable results. Coarse, heavy breads were made from barley and rye flours, while wholewheat brown loaves were a staple, not the white loaves made from bleached flour, which were once the prerogative only of the gentry. *Bara planc*, simple bakestone bread, is a traditional loaf, rather heavy and chewy in texture, still popular in some areas.

Bara Planc (Bakestone Bread)

450 g/1 lb strong white flour	1 tsp bicarbonate of soda
Pinch of salt	About 300 ml/½ pt/1¼ cups buttermilk

Cooking on a bakestone (a flat griddle or heavy frying pan can also be used) is a basic but not simple method of cooking. An expert baker from Swansea advises, 'when you are cooking on a bakestone, you are only drying out the moisture from the dough, and giving the bread or cake colour. The heat is therefore very critical, as is the consistency of the dough. The heat must not be too great otherwise the outside will burn before the middle is cooked through. Likewise, if the dough is too wet, it will not cook completely through without burning the outside. How can you tell when the bread is done? It feels lighter and sounds hollow when knocked. Cooking on a bakestone is all a matter of trial and error.'

Sieve the flour, salt and bicarbonate of soda into a large mixing bowl. Gradually add the buttermilk to form a soft – but not too moist – dough. Knead and turn out on to a floured board. Shape into a round and cook on a slow, well-greased bakestone or heavy frying pan, about 10–12 minutes per side (if the bread browns too quickly, then reduce the heat). This basic bakestone bread, incidentally, is also good with raisins or sultanas added.

Wholewheat Bread   (Makes 4 loaves)

Wholewheat flour is 100 per cent of the grain; wheatmeal flour, on the other hand, retains the essential wheat germ, but not all of the bran and fibre. Mixing the two flours results in a somewhat lighter loaf than that made solely from wholewheat.

900 g/2 lb wholewheat flour	2 tsp sea salt
450 g/1 lb wheatmeal flour	25 g/1 oz/¼ stick butter
20 g/¾ oz dried yeast	900 ml/1½ pt/3¾ cups warm water
2 tsp brown sugar	

Mix the wholewheat and wheatmeal flours together in a large mixing bowl and set aside in a warm place. In a cup, dissolve the yeast and sugar in a little of the warm water. Set aside in a warm place until it becomes frothy. Dissolve the salt in the remaining warm water and add the butter. Make a well in the flour, pour in the yeast and add the rest of the liquid. Mix well, then knead until strong and elastic. Return the dough to the bowl, cover with a damp cloth, and leave in a warm place until doubled in size.

Remove the dough from the bowl, knock back and knead again. Divide in four, and shape each into a warm, well-greased loaf tin. Again, set aside in a warm place until the dough has reached the tops of the tins. Dust the tops with flour, and put in a pre-heated hot oven (220°C/425°F/Gas Mark 7) for 20 minutes. Reduce the heat to moderately hot (200°C/400°F/Gas Mark 6) for a further 20 minutes. Remove the bread from the tins and tap underneath to see if done. If not hollow-sounding, return to the cooling oven for a further 5–10 minutes.

Cockles

Cockle gathering in South Wales has been carried on for centuries (since Roman times at least), for these small shellfish, together with mussels, limpets, winkles and whelks have always been the staple food for a coastal people. Even today, in view of the belching chimneys of industrial Llanelli, timeless scenes take place regularly, as cockle gatherers from Penclawdd, Llanmorlais, Crofty and other Gower villages follow the receding tide out into Burry Inlet and Carmarthen Bay. As the tide ebbs, they take their small, tough, mangy workhorses up to four miles out, over a bizarre, revealed landscape of hidden gulleys, fast-flowing streams and treacherous, shifting patches of sand. The cocklers – young bearded men and well-wrapped, weathered women – proceed either solitarily, or in small convoys, their rubber-wheeled carts bobbing up and then down, as they tug and coax their horses over the windswept salt marshes where sheep and wild horses graze, across, finally, to the cockle beds of Llanrhidian sands.

It is backbreaking work: digging the cockles by hand with a sickle-shaped *scrap*; raking them into heaps; sieving them back and forth to discard the under-sized cockles; loading the shellfish into sacks; then packing the horse-cart for the long, dangerous return journey to the village. Once on land, the cockles are boiled in tin sheds along the road, washed and shelled (mountains of discarded cockle shells attest to this activity over the ages). They are now ready to be taken either door to door to regular customers, or to markets like Swansea, where they are sold by the mugful. A regular 'cockle train' from Penclawdd to Swansea used to carry the cockle wives to market every Saturday; nowadays, however, a family member – a mother, mother-in-law or daughter – takes care of the daily market stall, selling *bara lawr* as well as cockles, while the others are out gathering the next day's batch.

What is the best way to consume these small, brown or yellow bivalves? A cockle gatherer tells us with conviction: 'Simply boiled, with salt and pepper. A whole plateful, man.' Hardly very original or innovative, perhaps, but an honest meal after a day in the cold.

The cockle gatherers of Penclawdd.

Drink in Wales

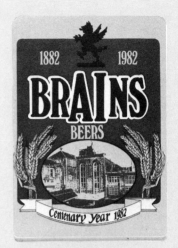

There has always been an ambivalent attitude to drinking alcohol in the Principality. The Methodist Chapel, so strong an influence in every aspect of life in Welsh villages, naturally frowned on drunkenness and the Temperance Movement of the last century had a strong hold here. Such severe attitudes die hard in the country; even today, in many parts of the west, licensed premises are not allowed to sell drink on Sundays, a condition which resulted from the Welsh Sunday Closing Act, introduced in 1881. Every seven years, Wales holds a public referendum on this matter; the last was in 1982, and it indicated that the majority of those people who live in such 'dry' areas still prefer it so. The chapel, after all, was the traditional focal point of community life, not the public house, and so it remains in many places today.

Nevertheless, beer is the national drink of Wales, and the visitor here will encounter little difficulty in finding pubs serving traditional ales. One important result of the Welsh Sunday Closing Act, incidentally, was the formation of large numbers of working men's clubs which were licensed to sell drink on Sundays. Today, such clubs still form the basis of the free trade in Wales.

As in many parts of Britain, Wales has a long tradition of brewing and wine making for private consumption. Domestic brewing was once a widespread activity on farms throughout the Principality, the resulting 'home-brews' essential beverages for the household and farm labourers alike. Special strong brews were made for once-a-year occasions such as Christmas and New Year, and many a farm wife always had a row of gallon bottles filled with nettle, elderflower and dandelion wines, gurgling and working away. Mead, fermented from Welsh clover honey, is another traditional drink, though perhaps more popular now as a novelty to serve at the numerous mediaeval banquets which take place in Welsh castles and stately mansions than as a true drink of the people. *Metheglin*, a sort of spiced mead

Assorted mats and labels of the region.

flavoured with thyme, rosemary, sweet briar and other ingredients, was another traditional drink dating back centuries; perhaps it is still made privately on some upland farms today.

Hours: Licensing hours in Wales are basically similar to those in England but with the important differences relating to Sunday trading. Though most of the Principality has voted to be 'wet', 'dry' areas remain, primarily in the south-west and parts of the north. In such areas, though, alcoholic drinks are served in licensed residential establishments to residents, as well as in registered clubs to affiliated members.

Traditional Beer

When people left rural areas to settle in the industrial Valleys and elsewhere, commercial brewing developed to satisfy the thirst of coal miners, quarrymen, and other labourers. Today, the two principal brewing centres of Wales are Cardiff (Brain's and Welsh Brewers) and Llanelli (Buckley's and Felinfoel). Cask-conditioned ales served by traditional hand pumps are available throughout the Principality. The Welsh preference is for dark, creamy milds, and full-flavoured, high-gravity 'special' bitters (though after rugby matches, more than a few pints of low-gravity Welsh ales have been known to be consumed on many a joyous occasion).

South Wales

Welsh Brewers Ltd, Crawshay St, Cardiff. Welsh Brewers in Cardiff is part of the national Bass brewing group, providing tied public houses as well as free outlets throughout the Principality with a range of brewery- and cask-conditioned ales. The company's keg bitter, Allbright, claims to be the largest selling beer in Wales.

> Hancock's PA o.g. 1033
> Worthington Dark o.g. 1034
> Worthington Best Bitter (BB)
> o.g. 1037
> Hancock's HB o.g. 1037

S. A. Brain & Co. Ltd, St Mary St, Cardiff. The Old Brewery in St Mary Street was established in 1713, and is one of the oldest buildings in Cardiff, though it was only bought by the Brain

Methodist chapel.

family just over a hundred years ago. The brewery recently underwent extensive modernization and redevelopment, but the emphasis is still on traditional draught beers. Red Dragon, the famous 'Cardiff dark', is a rich, creamy mild. Brain's beers are available mainly in the surrounding Cardiff area.

> Bitter o.g. 1033–37
> SA Bitter o.g. 1040–44
> Red Dragon Dark o.g. 1033–37

Home Brewing and Wine Making

In Wales, certainly, and throughout Great Britain, domestic brewing and wine making were once cottage pursuits as common as home baking. Indeed, brewing, like baking, was in many homes a weekly chore. The tin-lined copper mash tun and wooden fermenting vessels were always kept scrupulously scrubbed and ready at hand. At the beginning of the last century, only half the beer consumed in Britain was brewed commercially; even today, it is estimated that one in every fifty pints in Britain is brewed at home. Although at various times in history, successive governments have tried to restrict the brewing of beer at home, most people in Britain still regard it as a given right for men and women to be able to brew or ferment what they like for their own private consumption. In 1963 the Chancellor of the Exchequer acknowledged this fact when he abolished excise duty on beer brewed at home, provided that it was for private consumption only. Home wine making has never been subject to excise duty.

Home-brewed beer can be excellent: strong, rich in colour, flavour and alcohol. Like commercial cask-conditioned ales, it is a natural product, a real ale which continues to condition and mature in the cask or bottle. Furthermore, compared to the cost of a pint in a pub, it is ridiculously inexpensive, no doubt the main incentive – today as in the past – for brewing at home. Most home-brew is produced from kits containing already-hopped malt extract (this is a concentrated wort, the sugar-rich liquid extracted in the mash tun by boiling liquor with a grist of malt). To make up a kit, it is only necessary to add sugar and water, pitch the yeast, allow fermentation to take place and rack the beer into a clean barrel or bottles. It is more fun, however, and gives better results, to use a combination of malt extract, additional malt or other cereals and whole cone hops.

The tradition of home wine making remains equally established in Britain. Mead is the original country wine, after all, and wine from grapes grown in England and Wales is being produced, in many cases simply to provide the vine growers with a sufficient quantity to last themselves through the year. Additionally, throughout the land, hedges are scoured for fermentable fruits. Elder shrubs are stripped of first their delicate flowers then their purple-black berries. Fruit wines are made from blackberries, raspberries, cherries, redcurrants, damsons, plums and strawberries. Nettles, dandelions and birch sap are fermented, as are tea leaves, potatoes, parsnips and turnips. Such country wines can be very good – and they can be very, very bad! As in most things, it depends not only on the skill of the wine maker, but on his or her priorities (many, for example, measure the success of either home-brewed beer or home-made wine by its ability to fell an ox). Nevertheless, country wines are an important traditional drink of the land, well worth attempting to make or at least to drink.

In both home brewing and wine making, cleanliness is the most important factor; it is therefore essential to ensure that all instruments, vessels and bottles are sterilized. Here are two basic recipes.

Home Brew Bitter

(Makes 25 1/5 Imperial gallons)

1.8 kg/4 lb malt extract
900 g/2 lb white sugar
100 g/4 oz whole Goldings
    hops
Packet of dried brewers'
    yeast

Vigorously boil the malt extract, sugar and most of the hops together with about a gallon of water for 1 hour. Add the reserved hops 15 minutes before the end. Allow to cool a little, then strain through a cloth into a sterilized fermenting bin. Top up the bin with cold water to bring it up to 25 1/5 gallons, and allow to cool to room temperature. Sprinkle on the dried yeast, cover the bin and allow to ferment in a warm place for 5–7 days. Skim off the thick scum that forms initially. Ensure that fermentation is complete by testing with a hydrometer. Siphon into sterilized bottles, and prime with $\frac{1}{2}$ tsp of sugar per pint. Cap with crown corks and leave in a warm room for two days to encourage secondary fermentation, then stand in a cool larder for at least 1 month before drinking.

Elderflower Wine

(Makes about 4.8 l/1 Imperial gallon)

600 ml/1 pt/2$\frac{1}{2}$ cups
    elderflowers, cleaned
    and freed from stems
4.8 l/8 pt/10 pt (US)
    boiling water
1.575 kg/3$\frac{1}{2}$ lb sugar
Juice and rind of 1 large
    lemon
15 g/$\frac{1}{2}$ oz wine yeast

Place the elderflowers in a large bowl, add the boiling water, cover and leave to steep for one or two days. Strain the liquid into a large saucepan, add the sugar and lemon juice and rind, and heat to dissolve the sugar. Remove and allow to cool. When lukewarm, strain through a fine sieve into a sterilized fermentation jar. Sprinkle on the wine yeast, fit an airlock, and leave in a warm place until the fermentation is complete. Rack (siphon, leaving the sediment behind) into clean, sterilized bottles, cork and store for six months before drinking.

West Wales

The Felinfoel Brewery Co. Ltd, Llanelli, Dyfed. Llanelli, famous for its tin plate industry and its rugby football eminence, is also an important Welsh brewing centre. The Felinfoel Brewery produces three cask-conditioned beers, available in about eighty inns, hotels and public houses under control of the brewery, primarily located in South and West Wales. They are recognized by a distinctive emblem: the red Welsh dragon on a green background, marked, in many areas, with the slogan *'Cwrw Felinfoel'* (Felinfoel Ales).

> Mild (XXXX) o.g. 1031
> Bitter o.g. 1034
> Double Dragon o.g. 1041

Buckley's Brewery plc, Llanelli, Dyfed. That the Methodist Movement had a profound influence on drinking habits in Wales is accepted; Buckley's, however, must be one of the only breweries to claim their existence is due to this same movement. The Reverend James Buckley, a Methodist minister, married the daughter of the brewery's founder, and eventually took over as head of the company. (Reverend James was fortunate, apparently, to be able to manage his ministerial appointments so that he was never too far from the brewery.) Buckley's today has over 150 hotels, inns and public houses located in South and West Wales, most of which serve traditional beers.

> Bitter o.g. 1030–34
> Mild o.g. 1030–34
> Best Bitter o.g. 1034–38
> Gold o.g. 1039–44

North Wales

Border Breweries plc, Wrexham, Clwyd. Border Breweries, a long established company in North Wales, has been the subject of much recent take-over interest; whatever the outcome, Border's beer drinkers will no doubt hope that the company's fine range of low-gravity Welsh ales will continue to be produced.

> Mild o.g. 1032
> Exhibition Mild o.g. 1034
> Bitter o.g. 1035
> 4 X Mild o.g. 1035
> Old Master o.g. 1038

Welsh Wine

Commercial vineyards producing table wines from grapes grown in Wales are located in Dyfed and Mid Glamorgan.

Dyfed

Llanrhystud Vineyard, Llanrhystud
Wern Dêg, Llanarth

Mid Glamorgan

Croffta Vineyard, Pontyclun

Some Useful Addresses

Wales Tourist Board
Brunel House
2 Fitzalan Road
Cardiff

The Welsh Folk Museum
St Fagans
Cardiff

The Welsh Cookery Centre
Llangoedmor
Cardigan
Dyfed
A variety of courses in Welsh cooking are available throughout the year.

Nancy Morgan's Welsh Cakes
84 Bryn-y-Mor Road
Swansea
West Glamorgan
Home-baking of Welsh breads, cakes and other specialities on the premises. Nancy Morgan also has a stall in Swansea Market.

Llangloffan Farm
Castle Morris
near Mathry
Pembrokeshire
Llangloffan farmhouse cheese direct from the farm shop or by mail order. The cheese-making process can be viewed, and there is accommodation available in the farm guest house.

Y Felin
St Dogmaels
Cardigan
Dyfed
Stone-ground flours.

Felin Geri
Cwm Cou
Newcastle Emlyn
Dyfed
Stone-ground flours.

Blaenau Ffestiniog.

BIBLIOGRAPHY

Brother Adam. *Bee-keeping at Buckfast Abbey*. British Bee Publications, 1975.

Allen, Myrtle. *The Ballymaloe Cookbook*. Agri Books, 1977.

Ayrton, Elisabeth. *The Cookery of England*. Penguin, 1977.

———. *English Provincial Cooking*. Mitchell Beazley, 1980.

Bailey, Adrian, and the Editors of Time-Life Books. *The Cooking of the British Isles*. Time-Life Books, 1969.

Bedford, John R. *Discovering English Vineyards*. Shire Publications, 1982.

Brown, Catherine. *Scottish Regional Recipes*. Penguin, 1983.

Campbell, Susan, (ed.). *Guide to Good Food Shops*. Macmillan, 1979.

Cobbett, William. *Cottage Economy*. 1822; reprinted Harris Edwards, 1978.

Cooper, Derek. *The Whisky Roads of Scotland*. Jill Norman, 1981.

Daiches, David. *Scotch Whisky*. André Deutsch, 1969.

David, Elizabeth. *English Bread and Yeast Cookery*. Penguin, 1979.

Davidson, Alan. *North Atlantic Seafood*. Penguin, 1980.

Ellis, Audrey. *Traditional British Cooking*. Hamlyn, 1983.

English Food & Drink. English Tourist Board, 1983.

Farmhouse Cookery. Reader's Digest Association, 1980.

FitzGibbon, Theodora. *A Taste of the West Country*. Pan, 1975.

———. *A Taste of London*. Pan, 1976.

———. *A Taste of Ireland*. Pan, 1968.

———. *Traditional Scottish Cookery*. Fontana, 1980.

Freeman, Bobby. *First Catch Your Peacock*. Image Imprint, 1980.

———. *Welsh Breads*. Image Imprint, 1981.

———. *Is Welsh Cooking Really There?* National & Regional Styles of Cookery, Oxford Symposium 1981, (ed.) Alan Davidson, Prospect Books, 1981.

Good Beer Guide. CAMRA, annual.

Grigson, Jane. *English Food*. Penguin, 1977.

Hartley, Dorothy. *Food in England*. Macdonald, 1954.

Household, Joanna, (ed.) *Debrett's Guide to Britain*. Webb & Bower, 1983.

Jackson, Michael, (ed.) *The World Guide to Beer*. Mitchell Beazley, 1977.

———. *The Pocket Guide to Beer*. Quarto Marketing, 1982.

Kinsella, Mary. *An Irish Farmhouse Cookbook*. Appletree Press, 1983.

Lord Kinross. *The Kindred Spirit: A History of Gin and of the House of Booth*. Newman Neame, 1959.

Lovett, Maurice. *Brewing and Breweries*. Shire Publications, 1981.

McGuffin, John. *In Praise of Poteen*. Appletree Press, 1978.

Mabey, David, and Mabey, Richard. *In Search of Food*. Macdonald and Jane's, 1978.

Pike, Mary Ann. *Town & Country Fare & Fable*. David & Charles, 1978.

Quinion, Michael B. *Cidermaking*. Shire Publications, 1982.

———. *A Drink for its Time: Farm Cider Making in the Western Counties*. Museum of Cider, 1979.

Rance, Patrick. *The Great British Cheese Book*. Macmillan, 1982.

Read, Jan, and Manjón, Maite. *The Great British Breakfast*. Michael Joseph, 1981.

A Taste of Scotland. Scottish Tourist Board, 1983.

Smith, Joanna. *The New English Vineyard*. Sidgwick & Jackson, 1979.

Tibbott, S. Minwel. *Welsh Fare*. Welsh Folk Museum, 1976.

Wilson, C. Anne. *Food and Drink in Britain*. Constable, 1973.

Wilson, Ross. *Scotch, Its History and Romance*. David & Charles, 1973.

ACKNOWLEDGEMENTS

In the course of gathering the information and pictures for this book, we met and received assistance from hundreds of people. It is not possible to mention everybody, but we would particularly like to thank the following organizations, individuals, friends and family who have made this book possible.

Brother Adam, Buckfast Abbey; The Adelphi, Leeds; Adnams & Co. Ltd; Myrtle and Ivan Allen, Ballymaloe House; Apple & Pear Development Council; Aspall Cyder House; Robert Blair; Bass plc; Beamish & Crawford Ltd; The Bell, Aston Clinton; Berry Bros & Rudd Ltd; Betty's Café Tea Rooms; A. W. Biggs Jnr & L. C. Biggs, Whitchurch; Brewers' Society; Bromell's Farm Cider; Bruisyard St Peter Vineyard; The Burns Club of London; James Burrough plc; Mrs J. M. Butler; Butley Orford Oysterage, Mr and Mrs R. Pinney; Fiona Campbell; David Carr Taylor; Kathleen Chapman; Cliff Hotel, Penzance, Mary Rodda; H. H. Collins of Broadway; Colman's of Norwich; Cornish Smoked Fish Co.; Emma Craig, Limavady; Joe Curley, Master Cook at Simpson's-on-the-Strand; Anne Curry; Ray and Jean Daniels, Waungron Farm Hotel; Daisy and Ann Dawson; Ronald Davies, Cenarth; John Dewar & Sons Ltd; Dickinson & Morris Ltd; Doyle's Seafood Bar; Drusilla's, Alfriston; Paul Dunsby.

Eldridge Pope & Co. Ltd, Martin Cree; Elsenham Quality Foods Ltd; English Tourist Board, Dick Millard; English Vineyards Association, Christopher Ann; Y Felin, St Dogmaels; Fisher and Donaldson, Cupar; Food from Britain Organization; Clare Fynn; Colin Gillespie, Wootton Vineyard; Glenfiddich Distillery; Glenfarclas-Glenlivet Distillery; The Glenlivet Distillery; Aneurin George, Llangolman; Arthur Guinness Son & Co. Ltd; the Trustees of the Thomas Hardy Memorial Collection in the Dorset County Museum, Dorchester, Dorset; Highland Fine Cheeses; Hilden Brewery; Mrs Hutchinson Smith, Hinton Bank Farm; Irish Distillers Ltd; Irish Tourist Board; Ireland West, Ann Melia, Brian and Patricia Flynn; Irish Export Board; Tubby Isaac; A. Wynne Jones, Gwesty Plas Maenan; W. Jordan (Cereals) Ltd; Kirby Malzeard Dairy; Doreen Leitch; The Lindisfarne Liqueur Co.; Lion Salt Works; Long Clawson Dairy Ltd, Melton Mowbray; Maurice Lovett.

John Macsween, Edinburgh; Maldon Crystal Salt Co.; The Marlborough, Ipswich, David Brooks; James Mason; Tony Meddle, Leigh-on-Sea; Merrydown Wine plc, Richard Purdey; Michelham Priory, Hailsham; Milk Marketing Board; Edward Milne, Arbroath; Morrell's Brewery Ltd, Charles Eld; Jack Morris; Murphy Brewery Ireland Ltd; J. E. Neave & Son, Debenham; Bronwen Nixon, The Rothay Manor, Ambleside; The North British Hotel, Edinburgh; Northern Ireland Tourist Board; Northern Ireland Farm & Country Holidays Association; The 'Old Bushmills' Distillery Co. Ltd; The Old Original Bakewell Pudding Shop; The Old Swan, Netherton; Michael Paske Farms Ltd; Clive Pattinson, Calthwaite Dairy; Vicki and Alex Peel; Pimm's Ltd; J. G. Quicke & Sons; Rackhams of Birmingham; Harry Ramsden's, Guiseley; Patrick Rance; Frederic Robinson Ltd; L. Robson & Sons Ltd; The Royal, Ross-on-Wye; Scotch Whisky Association; Scotch Quality Beef and Lamb Association Ltd; Shepherd Neame Ltd; The Southern Cross, Newton Poppleford; John Strange of Lyndhurst; Peter Maxwell Stuart, Traquair House; Summer Isles Foods, Achiltibuie; Doreen Swain; Le Talbooth Restaurant, Dedham; The Taunton Cider Co.; The Tea Council; Joshua Tetley & Son Ltd; T. & R. Theakston Ltd; Bernard Theobald, Westbury Vineyard; Dorothy Tucker; Wales Tourist Board; Waterford Glass Ltd; The Welsh Cookery Centre; White Hart Hotel, Exeter; Janet Whitehouse, Nancy Morgan's Welsh Cakes; Wiltshire Tracklements; Bar Woodall, Waberthwaite; Young & Co's Brewery Ltd, Wandsworth.

The quotation from James Joyce's story 'Counterparts' from *The Dubliners* first published in 1914 is reproduced with kind permission of the Executors of the James Joyce Estate, Jonathan Cape Ltd, Viking Penguin Inc., and the Society of Authors, literary representative of the James Joyce Estate.

We would particularly like to thank Royal Doulton Tableware Ltd for lending us bone china; and Josiah Wedgwood and Sons Ltd for lending us bone china and oven-to-tableware for use in studio photography.

We would also particularly like to thank Bobby Freeman for her help and encouragement; Jean, Ann, Jill and Bev Jordan, Sheila Brodie and Dorothea Hales for assistance with testing recipes; and our editor Joanna Household.

INDEX